CLASSIC AND CONTEMPORARY READINGS IN SOCIAL PSYCHOLOGY

SECOND EDITION

Erik J. Coats
Vassar College

Robert S. Feldman
University of Massachusetts at Amherst

Prentice Hall, Upper Saddle River, NJ 07458

Library of Congress Cataloging-in-Publication Data

Classic and contemporary readings in social psychology / [edited by]
    Erik J. Coats, Robert S. Feldman. — 2nd ed.
        p.   cm.
    Includes bibliographical references.
    ISBN 0-13-743907-5
    1. Social psychology. I. Coats, Erik J., 1968– . II. Feldman,
Robert S. (Robert Stephen), 1947– .
HM251.C597   1998
302—dc21   97-15166
                                                      CIP

Editor-in-Chief: Nancy Roberts
Acquisitions Editor: Bill Webber
Director of Production and Manufacturing: Barbara Kittle
Senior Managing Editor: Bonnie Biller
Production Editor: Randy Pettit
Manufacturing Manager: Nick Sklitsis
Prepress and Manufacturing Buyer: Lynn Pearlman
Marketing Director: Gina Sluss
Cover Designer: Bruce Kenselaar
Cover Art: Diana Ong/Superstock

This book was set in 10/12.5 Berkeley OS
and printed and bound by Courier/Westford
The cover was printed by Phoenix Color Corp.

© 1998 by Prentice-Hall Inc.
Simon & Schuster/A Viacom Company
Upper Saddle River, New Jersey 07458

For permission to use copyrighted material, grateful
acknowledgment is made to the copyright holders listed
on pages 291–2, which is considered an extension of this
copyright page.

Printed in the United States of America
10   9   8   7   6   5   4   3   2   1

0-13-743907-5

Prentice-Hall International (UK) Limited, *London*
Prentice-Hall of Australia Pty. Limited, *Sydney*
Prentice-Hall Canada Inc., *Toronto*
Prentice-Hall Hispanoamerica, S.A., *Mexico*
Prentice-Hall of India Private Limited, *New Delhi*
Prentice-Hall of Japan, Inc., *Tokyo*
Simon & Schuster Asia Pte. Ltd., *Singapore*
Editora Prentice-Hall do Brasil, Ltda., *Rio de Janeiro*

✣ CONTENTS ✣

❖ PREFACE ❖

Classic and Contemporary Readings in Social Psychology is a unique set of 30 paired selections from articles and books encompassing the breadth of the field of social psychology. Each reading represents either a classic, seminal article or a contemporary work that addresses a topic relevant to social psychology.

The classic articles are written by a "who's who" in the field, including such figures as Kurt Lewin, Stanley Milgram, and Edward Jones. In addition, we have included more recent articles that have risen to classic status because of their impact on the field and the frequency with which they are cited.

The contemporary articles are written by a variety of individuals, most of whom are active scholars in the field of social psychology. Each is a recent and provocative report on some fundamental social psychological topic or issue. By pairing classic and contemporary articles, readers can plainly see the contrast between the old and the new, illustrating the progress and advances of the discipline.

In choosing these readings, we have cast our net widely. In addition to traditional journal articles, we examined book chapters, magazine articles, and even presentations at meetings and conventions. Our goal was not just to find articles that were technically sound or ones that revolutionized the field. Rather, we also sought to identify articles that helped to provide a picture of the development of the field, the concerns of its practitioners at a given moment in history, and a sense of the dynamic qualities of a constantly evolving discipline.

In editing the articles, we tried to provide sufficient detail to convey the depth, subtleties, and importance of the work being described. Furthermore, we tried to keep intact the original voice of the researcher who wrote the piece.* At the same time, we avoid including so much technical material that the readers would get mired in detail and miss the forest for the trees.

To meet these editing requirements, we were careful to choose sources that were accessible to students. In some articles, for purposes of clarity, we abridged and condensed the original text. In such cases, we have made clear where material has been dropped by inserting ellipses.

Each article begins with an introduction that provides a broad conceptual orientation to the piece. When appropriate, we have included a historical framework, discussing the import of the article and giving a sense of what social psychology was like at the time the article was written. These introductions not only show how the field has progressed and changed but also point out how the various parts of the field form a cohesive whole.

Each article is followed by a series of questions designed to promote recall of the information that is presented and to consolidate the material. These questions are also meant to raise intriguing issues and challenge assumptions that readers may have developed. Most important, they are designed to make readers think critically about the articles' content.

---

*As a result, the reader may occasionally come across attitudes or language in a classic article that is no longer considered appropriate or acceptable (e.g., regarding racial or sexual matters). Yet, after careful consideration, we have elected to leave unedited the offending text, not because we approve of the sentiments being expressed—we don't— but simply in the interests of historical accuracy.

READING ABOUT EXPERIMENTS IN SOCIAL PSYCHOLOGY

Each year researchers conduct thousands of empirical studies on topics related to social psychology. One of the challenges that face students who are just beginning to learn about the field is how to locate articles, chapters, and other reports of studies that are relevant to their interests. The goal of this section is to introduce you to the many outlets that social psychologists use to present their research findings. We begin by briefly describing five sources of psychological information and then focus on the most important source: the empirical article.

Five Sources of Information

As a consumer of psychological information, you can find ideas about psychology from five general sources: textbooks, professional conferences, empirical articles, academic books and review articles, and the popular press. Each type has its advantages and disadvantages.

Undergraduate textbooks. You are probably reading or have read one or two undergraduate textbooks about psychology. Such texts present a large amount of information in a relatively small amount of space. They are ideal for people who are first learning about psychology or one of its many subareas. However, as a secondary source, texts are somewhat limited. One limitation is that they represent the author(s)'s interpretation of other people's work. Although textbook authors strive to be accurate, occasionally their own biases creep into their work. Additionally, because new discoveries are made every day, you have to read primary sources to stay on top of the field.

Professional conferences. Perhaps the best way to learn about the most current research in psychology is to attend professional conferences. New findings are often presented at professional conferences before they appear anywhere else. If you are unable to attend a conference, you may be able to read a report of the talks that were given. Most psychologists will, upon request, send a paper version of their talk to people who were unable to hear them in person. Additionally, some organizations routinely publish all of the talks presented at their conferences. Reading 25 in this volume comes from such a published conference proceeding.

Empirical articles. Although data are often presented first at a professional conferences, the most important medium for communicating new findings is the empirical article. The empirical article is especially important because it is the only place where research projects are described in complete detail. This makes journals invaluable as primary sources. It is impossible to evaluate a research project fairly without reading the empirical articles that describe the work.

Empirical journal articles are an important source of information for another reason. Before a journal will agree to publish an article, the research report must pass a rigorous review process. Articles submitted for possible publication are sent to an action editor who is knowledgeable in the field that the article discusses. Action editors read the article themselves and then send it out to two or more experts on the issues raised in the article. Only after the reviewers and action editor are satisfied that an article is methodologically sound and will make an important contribution to the field will they agree to publish it. Many of the top journals reject 80 to 90 percent of the articles that researchers submit for publication. Because of this thorough review process, articles that journals agree to publish are likely to be largely fair and sound.

Unfortunately, empirical articles are somewhat difficult to read if you are not a psychologist yourself. In the next section we outline the typically empirical article. Knowing how empirical articles are organized will help get the most out of reading them. And you will soon get a chance to practice your new skills: Readings 7, 9, 15, and 17 in this volume come from top journals in social psychology.

Academic books and review articles. After a researcher has published several empirical articles on the same general topic, he or she may decide to write a paper that summarizes the most important or interesting of his or her findings. There are two outlets for such reviews: review articles and academic books. Many academic books are collections of edited chapters, with each chapter being written by a different researcher. Some authors of book chapters and review articles focus primarily on one person's research (usually their own). Reading 18 is an example of an article that primarily reviews the author's own work. In contrast, some authors of book chapters and review articles focus less on their own work and instead attempt to give a complete picture of all the latest research in a particular area. Reading 11 is an example of this type of review.

The popular press. Researchers whose work catches the attention of editors of journals and of edited books will also likely catch the attention of journalists writing for the popular press. It may surprise you to know that many of the magazines and newspapers you read each day are extremely interested in following the major developments in psychology. However, not all magazines are careful when selecting what research to report. Like research in any field, not all psychological studies are as valid as others. Some newspapers and magazines ensure that the research they report is of the highest quality; some others are less careful in their choices. The popular magazine articles that are represented in this book, such as those from *The Atlantic Monthly* (Reading 6), *Scientific American* (Reading 8), and *Newsweek* (Reading 12), are among those that are usually, although not invariably, trustworthy. Leading newspapers such as the *New York Times, Washington Post,* and *Los Angeles Times* are also respectable sources of information about the field of psychology.

Reading Empirical Articles

As discussed earlier, the empirical article is the most important medium for communicating new information to the larger psychological community. Unfortunately, because their intended audience is other psychologists, empirical articles can be somewhat confusing to budding psychologists such as yourself. In order to aid you when you begin to read the empirical articles included in this volume, we discuss their main features.

Empirical articles have five main sections: Abstract, Introduction, Method, Results, and Discussion. The goal of the Abstract is to give the reader a very brief review of the entire article. The Abstract lets us know what topic the article addresses, what specific hypotheses were tested and how, and whether the hypotheses were supported by the data. Because of strict word limits placed on Abstracts, they can be overly terse. Consequently, you should read Abstracts carefully (and possibly more than once) in order to understand fully what the article is setting out to do.

The Introduction is the beginning of the article proper. The Introduction is typically not explicitly identified by a heading. We know we are reading the Introduction because it comes first; we know the Introduction is over when the Method section begins. (All further sections of the article are identified by headings.) The goal of the Introduction is to introduce the readers to the general problem being studied, to review relevant prior research, and to interest readers in the area being addressed. For example, in the Introduction to Reading 7, the authors tell us that they are interested in how people know when they are experiencing an emotion. After reviewing previous research in this area, the authors explain that the goal of their research is to find support for a new theory of emotion identification. If at this point we find ourselves interested in emotion identification, then one of the goals of the Introduction has been accomplished.

In the Method section, the authors explain in detail how the research was conducted. The goal of the Method section is to give readers sufficient detail so that they could repeat, or *replicate,* the study themselves. Replication is an important part of the scientific process, so the Method section must be complete and exact. If the experimenters used only women as participants in their study, we, the readers, need to know this. If participants' attitudes were surveyed, we need to know the exact wording of the questions. If several types of attitudes were measured, we need to know in what order this was done.

In order to help organize all of this information, the Method section is itself divided into subsections. All articles include what is called a Participant (or what was previously called a Subject) subsection. (The American Psychological Association, which determines the linguistic style for psychological research articles, now recommends that people who participate in experiments be called "participants" rather than the previously employed "subjects." You'll see that both terms are used in the readings in this volume, reflecting when the article was written.)

In the Participant section, the authors describe the people who took part in the study. This typically includes stating how many people participated, as well as their age and gender. If a study made use of a complicated apparatus (e.g., the reel-racing device described in Reading 27), this will be described in an Apparatus subsection. If the study employed a newly developed questionnaire that would not be available to the average reader, selected questions may be reprinted in a Material subsection.

The final, and most important, Method subsection is Procedure. The Procedure subsection explains how the experiment was conducted in a step-by-step fashion, beginning with the moment the participants arrived for the study. After reading the Procedure subsection, the reader should know what it was like to have been a participant in the study. More important, the reader should be able to replicate the study in exact detail. The Method section also explains what data were collected from participants in the study.

After the data are analyzed, the results of the study are summarized in the next section— Results. The goal of the Results section is to explain the experimenter's findings in two ways: first in English, second in statistics. Reporting statistics is important because it allows readers to decide for themselves whether the author(s) performed the most appropriate analyzes. For now, assume that the journal editors have done their jobs and weeded out articles containing statistical flaws. Concentrate, instead, on the conclusions the author has drawn about the tests that have been carried out. As you become more knowledgeable about statistics, you will probably focus more on the statistics themselves, drawing your own conclusions instead of automatically accepting the authors' interpretations.

After reporting the study's findings in the Results section, the authors will next explain the practical significance of their findings in the Discussion section. The goal of the Discussion section is twofold: to remind the reader of the issues being considered and to explain how the current study has extended our knowledge of these issues. For example, in Reading 9, the authors compared participants' physical health after participating in the study. Reading the Results section we learn that some participants were healthier after being in the study. Yet after spending perhaps 15 to 30 minutes examining and considering the exact methods and findings of the study, readers may have forgotten why this is theoretically interesting. In the Discussion section, the authors remind us that their findings are important because they contribute to our understanding of the Freudian notion of catharsis.

Although empirical articles are written in something like a story format—with a beginning (Introduction), middle (Method and Results), and end (Discussion)—it is not essential that you read them in that order. Some people find it easier to read the Discussion immediately after the Introduction and before the Results. Some even skip the Introduction altogether and begin with the Method. However, we suggest that you first try reading articles as they were intended—first Abstract, then Introduction, then Method, then Results, and then Discussion. Later you might want to experiment with different strategies.

USING THESE READINGS

These readings can be used in several ways. Some professors may wish their students to focus on classic selections, whereas others may choose to focus on the contemporary readings. Some may wish to assign the questions at the end of each reading. These readings can be used to supplement any social psychology text, but they specifically reflect the 15 chapters of *Social Psychology,* the introduction to social psychology written by Robert S. Feldman.

In sum, *Classic and Contemporary Readings in Social Psychology* provides a worthwhile supplement for students being introduced to the field of social psychology. We welcome any feedback that readers are willing to provide and encourage you to write to us. Erik Coats is at the Department of Psychology, Vassar College, Poughkeepsie, NY 12601, email: ercoats@vassar.edu. Robert Feldman is at the Department of Psychology, University of Massachusetts, Amherst, MA 01003, email: feldman@psych.umass.edu.

ACKNOWLEDGMENTS

This second edition owes a great deal to the editors and production staff at Prentice Hall, and especially to Randy Pettit and Ilene Kalish. Their many suggestions have improved the quality of this book in countless ways. We would also like to thank our students at Vassar College and at the University of Massachusetts. Their comments—and those of the three reviewers Marilyn Mendolia, University of Mississippi; Michael Nielsen, Georgia Southern University; and Richard Ryckman, University of Maine—guided many of our decisions in updating this reader.

—*Erik J. Coats, Robert S. Feldman*

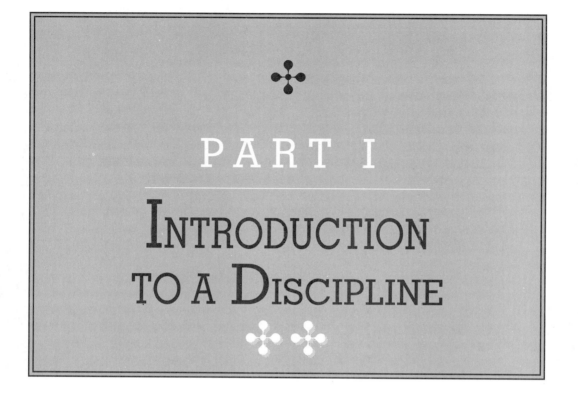

PART I

INTRODUCTION TO A DISCIPLINE

✤ CHAPTER 1 ✤

AN INTRODUCTION TO SOCIAL PSYCHOLOGY

Reading 1: Classic

Field Theory in Social Science

Kurt Lewin

Although social psychology emerged as a distinct discipline at the turn of the 20th century, it was not until the 1940s that it began to mature into the strong and diverse field it is today. At that time, several innovative thinkers saw the enormous potential of the psychological study of social phenomena and shaped the field with their vision. Among these early pioneers, no one was more influential than Kurt Lewin.

Born in Germany, Lewin immigrated to the United States during the rise of the Nazi regime and became an active voice in moving social psychology away from the excessive theorizing that plagued clinical psychology at that time. Psychology, he believed, must concern itself with the observable. However, blind empiricism was not the answer either. Instead, Lewin envisioned a psychology in which theory and empirical data slowly grew together.

In this first reading, Lewin explains his vision of a "Galilean" period in psychology. Citing examples from his own research, he points psychologists toward their proper goal, to understand and improve the human condition. But more importantly, he gives us the tools for fulfilling this goal.

✤

In recent years there has been a very marked change in the attitude of American psychology. During the 1920's and early 1930's psychologists were, on the whole, rather adverse to theory. Governed by a naive metaphysical belief, they were apt to consider "fact finding" the only task of "scientific" psychology, and were particularly skeptical of the idea of psychological laws in the fields of needs, will, and emotion, that is, in fields other than perception and memory.

Today, a definite interest in psychological theory has emerged, due partly to the efforts of a few psychologists (particularly Tolman and Hull in animal psychology). The need for a closer fusion of the various branches of psychology demands tools which permit better integration. The practical tasks of mental hygiene and education demand conceptual tools which permit prediction. Neither demand can be met without theory.

Now, however, it seems necessary to point to certain dangers of theorizing. Enthusiasm for Theory? Yes! Psychology can use much of it. However, we will produce but an empty

Source: Lewin, K. (1951). *Field theory in social science.* New York: Harper.

formalism, if we forget that mathematization and formalization should be done only to the degree that the maturity of the material under investigation permits at a given time.

Philosophically, there seems to exist only an "either-or": if scientific "facts" and particularly all so-called dynamic facts are not merely "given data," but inseparably interwoven with theoretical assumptions, there seems to be no choice other than to base every statement in psychology on theoretical assumptions.

For the psychologist, as an empirical scientist, the situation looks rather different. He finds himself in the midst of a rich and vast land full of strange happenings: there are men killing themselves; a child playing; a child forming his lips trying to say his first word; a person who having fallen in love and being caught in an unhappy situation is not willing or not able to find a way out; there is the mystical state called hypnosis, where the will of one person seems to govern another person; there is the reaching out for higher, and more difficult goals; loyalty to a group; dreaming; planning; exploring the world; and so on without end. It is an immense continent full of fascination and power and full of stretches of land where no one ever has set foot.

Psychology is out to conquer this continent, to find out where its treasures are hidden, to investigate its danger spots, to master its vast forces, and to utilize its energies.

How can one reach this goal? At first, in what might be called the "speculative epoch," the attempt was made to dig down deep into the ground. A peculiar something was reported to lie underground as the hidden source of energy. One gave it the name "association." New investigators drove their shafts down at somewhat different places. They found something different which they called "instinct." A third group of explorers reported a different entity, "libido," and all claimed to have found *the* foundation on which the land rested. By this time, psychologists had become rather tired of the various claims. It had become clear that the continent was much larger than was suspected at first. Perhaps there was more than one source of energy. The whole depth-sounding process had become rather open to suspicion, particularly since no explorer seemed able to bring his material up to the surface for inspection in broad daylight. How was one ever to prove a real connection between the entities supposedly existing underground and what was going on at the surface? There, open to all eyes, and unquestionable, interesting phenomena presented themselves. The psychologist now turned to extensive traveling over the surface of the continent, eager to find new phenomena, to describe them exactly, to count and to measure them, to register their growth.

This procedure, however, did not prove altogether satisfactory either. After all, what the psychologist observed were human beings. Children needed help and education; delinquent people needed guidance; people in distress wanted cure. Counting, measuring, and classifying their sorrows did not help matters much. Obviously one had to go to the facts "behind," "below the surface." How to accomplish this without the fallacies of the speculative epoch? That is the dominant methodological question of psychology today, at the beginning of its "Galilean period."

The answer is something like this: to make oneself master of the forces of this vast scientific continent, one has to fulfill a rather peculiar task. The ultimate goal is to establish a network of highways and superhighways, so that any important point may be linked easily with any other. This network of highways will have to be adapted to the natural topography of the country and will thus itself be a mirror of its structure and of the position of its resources.

The construction of the highway system will have to be based partly upon assumptions which cannot be expected to be fully correct. The test drilling in exploring the deposits will not always lead to reliable results. Besides, there is a peculiar paradox in the conquering of a new continent, and even more so in that of a new scientific field. To make the proper tests, some machinery has to be transported, and such transportation presupposes more or less the same road, the construction of which is contingent upon the outcome of the test. In other words, to find out what one would like to know one should, in some way or other, already know it.

What should science do to resolve this paradox? If it is wise, it follows the same procedure used in a systematic exploration of the resources of a new land: small paths are pushed out through the unknown; with simple and primitive instruments, measurements are made; much is left to assumption and to lucky intuition. Slowly certain paths are widened; guess and luck are gradually replaced by experience and systematic exploration with more elaborate instruments. Finally highways are built over which the streamlined vehicles of a highly mechanized logic, fast and efficient, can reach every important point on fixed tracks.

By and large, the actual development of a science seems to follow this general pattern. Yet frequently somebody, thinking he knows where an important treasure lies, tries to build a superhighway straight to this point without regard for the natural structure of the country. Much enthusiasm and work are put into such road building, but after some time it becomes apparent that this superhighway is a dead end leading nowhere.

Formalization and mathematization in psychology, if prematurely done, may lead us to the building of such logical superhighways. Formalization will have to be achieved if psychology is to become an acceptable science, and psychology can and must take definite steps in that direction now. However, the promising beginning and the growing interest for such an undertaking will soon turn into disappointment if certain dangers, arising partly from recent trends in philosophy and logic, are not frankly discussed and avoided.

I feel somewhat obliged to take this matter up, because two of my books[1] deal mainly with the conceptual tools of psychology. Some of the critics, who did not realize that these conceptual tools have been used for several years in a great number of investigations in a variety of fields, seem to have concluded that my main interest in psychology is formalization or mathematization. Nothing can be more erroneous. As psychologists we are interested in finding new knowledge about, and deeper insight into, psychological processes. That is, and always has been, the guiding principle. Theory, mathematization, and formalization are tools for this purpose. Their value for psychology exists only insofar as they serve as a means to fruitful progress in its subject matter, and they should be applied, as complex tools always should, only when and where they help and do not hinder progress.

Some psychologists interested in "strict logical derivations: have criticized our experimental work for not being written in the form: (a) definition, (b) assumption, (c) conclusion. On the other hand, French[2] writes:

[1]*Principles of Topological Psychology* (New York: McGraw-Hill Book Co., 1936); The conceptual representation and the measurement of psychological forces, *Contr. psychol. theor., 1938, 1,* No. 4, Duke University Press.

[2]Thomas M. French: A review of *A Dynamic Theory of Personality* and *The Principles of Topological Psychology,* by Kurt Lewin. In *Psychoanalytic Quarterly,* 1937, *6,* 122–128.

> In the course of fifty years [psychoanalysis] has developed an extensive system of scientific concepts, but the concepts have grown step by step as a necessary and inevitable product of Freud's attempt to orient himself in a bewildering chaos of psychological facts that no one previously had been able to understand. Due to close contact of these new concepts with the facts, one set of concepts was devised to explain one set of facts and a new problem would give rise to an entirely new set of concepts. . . . Topological psychology on the other hand starts with a self-consistent mathematical discipline and then goes to look for facts to fit it. [P. 127.]

As an answer I may be permitted to survey the actual historical development. My work in psychology began with experiments on association and the *determinierende Tendenz*.[3] The intention was not to criticize associationism but rather to refine the measurement of the "strength of the will" as developed by Ach. His work at that time, I believe, was the most precise theoretically in the field of will and association. After three years of experimentation with hundreds of series of nonsense syllables, and after thousands of measurements of reaction times (at that time one had to measure in 1/1000 seconds), I became convinced that there was no point in trying to improve the exactness of this measurement. The attempts were all based on the assumption of the classical law of association as stated, e.g., by G. E. Müller. The experiments however seemed to prove conclusively, contrary to my expectation, that this assumption had to be abandoned or decidedly modified. It was necessary to distinguish two rather different types of habits (associations): "need habits" (like alcoholism) and "execution habits" (like pulling a lever up rather than down). The first type represents a "tension" (source of energy), a need such as hunger, which demands satisfaction either directly or through substitution. The execution habit, on the other hand, is in itself no source of action. It is equivalent to a pattern of restraining forces determining a certain path. Without a need or quasi-need the execution habit does not lead to action.

After an interruption due to the first World War, a systematic attempt was made to test the positive assumption growing out of this criticism of the law of association. The first step was an attempt to achieve a more precise conceptual analysis. Dynamically, an "association" is something like a link in a chain, i.e., a pattern of restraining forces without intrinsic tendency to create a change. On the other hand, the tendency to bring about action is basic to a need. This property of a need or quasi-need can be represented by coordinating it to a "system in tension." By taking this construct seriously and using certain operational definitions, particularly by correlating the "release of tension" to a "satisfaction of the need" (or the "reaching of the goal") and the "setting up of tension" to an "intention" or to a "need in a state of hunger," a great number of testable conclusions were made possible.

After these basic conclusions had been proved valid, mainly through the experiments of Zeigarnik[4] and Ovsiankina,[5] the theory was expanded to include problems like psychological satiation, substitution on the reality and irreality level and in play situations, the measurement of substitute value, the level of aspiration, its shift after success and failure, the effect of dis-

[3]Kurt Lewin. Die psychische Tätigket bei der Hemmung von Willensorgängen und das Grundgesetz der Assoziation, *Ztschr. F. Psychol.*, 1917, *77*, 212–247.

[4]B. Zeigarnik: Über das behalten von erledigten und unerledigten Handlungen, *Psychol. Forsch.*, 1927, *9*, 1–85.

[5]M. Oviankina: Die Wiederaufnahme von unterbrochenen Handlungen, *Psychol. Forsch.*, 1928, *11*, 302–389.

tance from the goal upon the strength of psychological forces; in short, the pattern of goals and needs, their interrelation, and the ways of satisfying them were studied. Today, a multitude of problems including personality and personality development, cognitive structure, social and cultural relations are being attacked with a set of related concepts.

If one looks through our publications in the order that they have been published one will, I think, agree that the various theoretical assumptions and constructs have been developed rather slowly step by step. The assumptions were made rather tentatively at first and with a fair amount of hesitation. Only to the degree that more and more empirical facts could be brought together experimentally, the theory gained in firmness and more specific statements emerged.

This gradual elaboration based on empirical facts and a great variety of experiments holds true particularly for the mathematical aspects of the theory. The application of topological and vector concepts was first made in a way which left it open whether we had to deal merely with a pedagogical device or rather with a real scientific representation. Only to the extent that these conceptual tools proved to be valuable in formulating problems, and permitting derivations which could be tested experimentally, did they become essential parts of the theory and of its dynamic constructs.

French's criticisms of the *Principles of Topological Psychology* overlook the fact that this first attempt at a systematic survey of the conceptual tools used in our research was not made till after many years of empirical work with them. What French says about the gradual growth of psychoanalytic concepts out of psychological facts can as well be said in regard to the use of topological and vector concepts in field theory. As a matter of fact, the feeling for the necessity of rather slow and careful theorization was the main reason which restrained us from using strict, so-called formalistic derivations in those early experimental studies. That does not mean that I considered those derivations to be not fully stringent or that I did not esteem the value of a mathematical logical language which I had found very helpful when treating problems of comparative theory of science.[6] However, it would have been premature to present certain ideas "*more geometrico*," i.e., by setting forth so-called formal definitions, assumptions, and deductions without being able to do so in well-defined mathematical symbols, in the form of equations or similar representations of functional dependence. If one uses terms of everyday language such as "frustration," "need," "learning" without being able to coordinate mathematical entities to them, one might as well use the normal form of reasoning. To present statements employing amathematical constructs "*more geometrico*" suggests a degree of exactness of derivation which, I am afraid, cannot generally be reached with those types of constructs. This holds true even when these conceptually rather vague constructs are operationally well defined. We will come back to this point later.

One can go even one step further. The dynamic constructs used for example in the study of Zeigarnik may be said to be already of that type which readily lends itself to a strict mathematical representation. However, we felt that it would be wiser to wait with the formalistic representation until these constructs had proved more thoroughly to be empirically fruitful. A too high degree of formalization is likely to endanger this plasticity.

[6]Kurt Lewin: *Der Begriff der Genese in Physik, Biologie, und Entwicklungsgeschichte* (Berlin: Springer, 1922).

Psychology cannot try to explain everything with a single construct, such as association, instinct, or gestalt. A variety of construct has to be used. These should be interrelated, however, in a logically precise manner. Moreover, every theoretical statement brought forth to explain certain empirical data should be carefully examined not only in the light of these data but in the light of the totality of empirical data and theoretical statements of psychology. In other words *ad hoc* theories should be avoided. Bringing together the total field of psychology and doing that in a logically consistent manner might well be viewed as one of the basic purposes of our approach. The demand for a new level of precision in regard to the conceptual properties of the constructs, with a view to an ultimately strictly mathematical representation, is but a means to this end. On the other hand, it has been realized that without such mathematization the development of a consistent scientific psychology is impossible in the long run.

QUESTIONS

1. According to Lewin, what is the difficulty of "speculative" approaches in psychology? Why did psychology turn away from such approaches.

2. How does Lewin characterize the second phase of research in psychology? Why did psychologists turn sour on this approach?

3. Describe the "Galilean" period that Lewin believed psychology was entering. Why did he believe this period was superior to the previous two?

4. How does Lewin distinguish need habits from execution habits? Did the way in which he reached this conclusion fit the Galilean approach?

5. What role does Lewin believe mathematical representations and formalization should play in psychology? Are they the goal of psychology?

Reading 2:   Contemporary

A Glance Back at a Quarter Century of Social Psychology

Ellen Berscheid

If social psychology was born at the turn of the century and reached adulthood in the 1940s, its first midlife crisis came in the 1960s. At this time, social psychology was experiencing several crises: a crisis of growth caused by a boom of new Ph.D.s in the field, a crisis of faith as those outside (and inside) the field began to question its ability to discover anything other than temporary social fads, and a crisis of identity as social psychologists struggled to distinguish themselves from other branches of psychology and from other social sciences such as sociology. It was a critical time for the field, and social psychologists were not always sure what new paths the field was taking.

This was the atmosphere when Ellen Berscheid earned her Ph.D. in social psychology in 1965. In the 3 decades since, she argues, social psychology has matured into a much stronger, more robust field. In this article, Berscheid takes a personal look back at this period of growth and maturity. Noticing the improved lot of social psychologists today, she suggests a few reasons for how the uncertainty of the 1960s was overcome. Among the reasons are the acceptance and encouragement of women in the field; the guidance of important thinkers such as Kurt Lewin; expansion into new areas of research; and, surprisingly, the inadequacy of federal financial support.

❖

Twenty-five years ago, social psychology was experiencing growing pains. Hollander (1968) related that the size of APA's Division 8, now the Society of Personality and Social Psychology, had become so large that the convention program had reached "intimidating dimensions" and that "personal contact and communication [had become] unwieldy." Hence, the establishment of the Society of Experimental Social Psychology (SESP) in 1965, which the organizers envisioned as including "a relatively small number of social psychologists whose interests were primarily research-oriented," believing that "the common focus and smaller size of such a group [beginning with about 50 members and growing slowly to a limit of 100] would allow more flexible organization and would permit the group to engage in more intimate and informal dialogue than is possible at the conventions of the larger associations" (p. 280). Those who have attended an SESP conference recently and have had to shoehorn themselves into one of the meeting rooms (the "intimate and informal dialogue," where all attendees sat in one room and talked about a common problem of interest, having disappeared years ago) will conclude that the original vision for the society failed miserably in the execution. In retrospect,

Source: Berscheid, E. (1992). A glance back at a quarter century of social psychology. *Journal of Personality and Social Psychology, 63*, 525–533.

however, it is clear that, rather than creating a cozy atmosphere in which social psychologists could interact, it was the idea of bringing together social psychologists with a "common focus," specifically, a *research* focus, that was to play an important role in transforming social psychology from a gangly adolescent afflicted with growing pains and facing an uncertain future to the robust and mature discipline it is today. But I am getting ahead of myself.

The remarkable evolution social psychology has undergone over the past quarter century encompasses so many changes in the field's form and content, in the number and nature of its contributors, as well as in the context in which it is embedded, both in psychology and in society, that which of these changes can be singled out for notice in a brief, informal retrospective is necessarily a very personal and impressionistic matter. The comments that follow, which highlight only three of the many changes the field has undergone in the past few decades, meet none of the historian's claims. I hope only to give the flavor of social psychology's evolution over the past 25 years, a period which is clearly demarcated for me, for it was in 1965 that I received my doctorate in social psychology from the University of Minnesota, where I have remained ever since.

What happened to me after I received my degree at Minnesota, and what likely would happen to me today, illustrates with a single brushstroke many of the changes to which social psychologists in my age cohort have been witness. Like many female graduate students of the day, I had expected to retire from academic life after receiving my degree; women were rarely admitted into the academy and none of the three institutions at which I had received my undergraduate and graduate training (including the University of Nevada where I earned a master's degree with Paul Secord) had one female professor on their psychology faculty, although there were a few women "adjunct" professors. The Minnesota psychology department, I was told, once had a woman faculty member but relation of that fact was often followed by a somber pause and then, in sotto voce, the phrase "but it just didn't work out." Unexpectedly, however, my retirement plans were shelved when I was offered a temporary but open-ended, non-tenure track assistant professorship in the Department of Marketing of Minnesota's business school. There, I quickly became known as "the lady professor" (as in "Good morning, lady professor!"), being the only female professor in the business school. The student body, both graduate and undergraduate, was overwhelmingly if not exclusively male (I did not set eyes on, and never taught, a single female student there), and, befitting my place in the general scheme of things, these young men called me either Mrs. Berscheid or "Blondie" (as in "Hey, Blondie, what'd I get on the test?"). I look back on my business school job with nostalgia, for it was my good fortune, no doubt the result of my being a temporary alien, that I was left almost entirely alone. I was not invited to attend department meetings, for example, or to serve on college and university committees, or asked to do any of those things for discipline, God, and country that young professors are required to do today, sapping vast quantities of their time and their energy.

Unfortunately, the beginning of the end of my halcyon days at the business school came about a year later when, waiting for the elevator one day, I casually surveyed the business school's employment bulletin board and noticed an advertisement for a "market research analyst" at the company where I briefly had held such a position. I was dismayed to read that the only "qualification" for the job, entered on the appropriate blank on the business school's standard form, was "male." I removed the ad (politely, I thought) for reconsideration of the gender qualification, copying the business school's employment bureau. Moreover, I wrote letters to my Senators, at that time Eugene McCarthy and Hubert Humphrey telling them that it had become apparent to me that women did not have the same opportunities as men did in the workplace and asking what, if anything, they were doing about it. I then forgot about the whole episode, having discharged my duties as I saw them, and so I was truly surprised when a week or so later, I received a curt summons to appear "immediately" in the office of the associate dean. There, I found an agitated man who, venting his anger with the coarsest of language, told me that my actions had jeopardized scholarships and other monies donated to the school by the company in question and that he intended to bring charges against me. When I asked him what the charge was going to be, he replied, "It is against the law to mutilate University property, and by removing that ad, you mutilated our employment bulletin board."

Fortunately, several things happened to allow me to leave the business school quietly, and each event reflected the times: First, it turned out that the reason the associate dean, rather than the dean, had handled the matter was because the dean had been in Chicago that week attending a national conference addressed to the topic "The Place of Women in Business." That was heartening because it at least assumed that women had a place, although it apparently was taking a great deal of deliberation to figure out exactly where that place might be. Second, several weeks later, a group of black students who were shortcutting through the building lobby (there were no black students at the school either) spied an ad on the employment bulletin board that, under qualifications, listed "Caucasian." Their response was to douse the board with gasoline and set it afire, thereby leaving a rather large black hole where the employment bulletin board used to be for the remainder of the academic year. Third, the senior business school faculty rallied in my support and called a special meeting where impassioned speeches were made decrying the vulgar language and ungentlemanly behavior of the associate dean toward their lady professor and demanding that he apologize. No one mentioned the advertisement. Although an apology was subsequently made, when Elaine Hatfield left her research position with the Student Activities Bureau in the office of the Dean of Students to take a "real" psychology professorship at the University of Rochester, she arranged for me to be offered her job in the Bureau and I accepted it, believing it to be a safer foxhole than the business school. (For one thing, the Dean was a personal friend of Leon Festinger's, who had been Elaine Hatsfield's doctoral adviser as well as Elliot Aronson's, who had been my own adviser.) A year or so later, I too, was able to join a psychology department, when John G. Darley, the powerful and wily chair of the Minnesota department, called a faculty meeting for a Saturday morning after a violent snowstorm during spring break and made a motion that I be hired; when he later informed me that I was going to be transferred to the psychology department, Darley professed himself to have been "terribly pleased" that his motion had received the "unanimous" support of all who had attended the faculty meeting.

As all this suggests, in 1965 few people, including myself, and few institutions were aware that the word *sex* had been inserted at the last minute into Title VII of the 1964 Civil Rights Act. Indeed, it may have been the case that even some members of Congress were yet to become aware of what they had voted for, as neither of the replies I received from Senators Mc-Carthy and Humphrey made reference to that piece of legislation, although each man personally assured me that he was laboring mightily to improve working conditions for women. (Because one of the letters was addressed to "Dr. Allen Berscheid" and began "Dear Sir," I wasn't entirely convinced.) The word *race* had been noticed, of course, being the focus of the legislation, but as the business school's employment bulletin board reflected, most employers were still conducting business as usual. Martin Luther King's freedom marches, however, were keeping the issue in the headlines and on our minds. In fact, Elaine Hatfield had the wit to send Rev. King copies of our studies (e.g., "When Does a Harm-Doer Compensate a Victim?" [Berscheid & Walster, 1967]), in the hope that he could make some use of them. To our surprise, he wrote back to express his appreciation for the information, commenting that he was sure that there were many other studies in the social science literature that would be helpful to him if only he knew where they were. In 1965, that was wishful thinking on his part.

But that was then. Now, and just as I was preparing these remarks, my colleague, Gene Borgida, dropped on my desk a reprint of an article (that has since appeared in the *American Psychologist;* Fiske, Bersoff, Borgida, Deaux, & Heilman, 1991) entitled "Social Science Research on Trial: The Use of Sex Stereotyping Research in *Price Waterhouse* v. *Hopkins.*" As I picked it up and read how social psychological research on the antecedent conditions, indicators, consequences, and remedies of stereotyping played a crucial role at each stage of Hopkins's litigation, a lengthy judicial process that included a Supreme Court decision and ended with Hopkins winning her case of sex discrimination, I unabashedly admit that my eyes dampened with pride in social psychology. Twenty-five years ago, few of us could have imagined that there soon would be an army of social psychologists who would give the problem of stereotypes a full-court press in theory and research and that well within our lifetime, the fruits of our own discipline would be used to strike a landmark legal blow against sex discrimination.

WOMEN IN SOCIAL PSYCHOLOGY

In my personal view, then, one of the biggest changes that has taken place in the past 25 years has been the increase in the number of women social psychologists and the dramatic improvement in our working conditions (improvement but not yet equality, according to Brush, 1991). In fact, my guess is that the proportional increase of women into research positions in social psychology was greater than in any other subarea of psychology. (Unfortunately, the APA does not have the appropriate statistics, identifying researchers and nonresearchers, that would allow documentation of this point.)

There are several possible reasons for the influx of women into social psychology, but one that should be noted on an anniversary occasion is that the men who were influential in social psychology in 1965—and they were all men, as the identities of the founding fathers of SESP reflect—were far more egalitarian in outlook and values than those in any other area of psychology. The overlap in membership between Divisions 8 (the Society of Personality and Social Psychology) and 9 (the Society for the Psychological Study of Social Issues) of the APA, as well as the pervasive influence of Kurt Lewin, his students, and such other important early social psychologists as Gordon Allport, would suggest that women and minorities could expect a warmer reception in social psychology than in other domains of psychology. And, for the most part, we did. Many of these men are still alive and active today, and their extra-curricular contribution to social psychology through training their own female students and through the other professional roles they played at the time should be acknowledged. In addition to those who trained us and gave us jobs, one also immediately thinks of such people as Bill McGuire, then editor of *JPSP*, and Bob Krauss, then editor of the *Journal of Experimental Social Psychology*, who made special efforts to include women in the research review and editorial enterprise, as well as the rapidity (1967) with which SESP put women on its program. It is important to note that these efforts to encourage women to join the mainstream of social psychology were made long before such actions were regarded as socially chic, politically correct, or legally mandated. In short, the "culture" of social psychology in 1965 was well ahead of its time.

It can be argued that the relatively rapid entry of women into social psychology had a number of salutary consequences for the development of the field. Perhaps the most important of these was to keep the caliber of talent high while social psychology was undergoing enormous growth. By allowing the other half of the human race to participate in the enterprise—a half equal to the other in what we graduate students used to call "raw g"—the intellectual talent devoted to social psychological problems was not diluted in quality as it expanded in quantity, as appears to have been the case in certain other subareas of psychology that shall remain nameless here but whose graduate student applicants' Graduate Record Examination scores and GPA records at Minnesota over the years tell the tale.

Second, the influx of women into social psychology influenced the approach taken to many traditional research questions in the field. In this regard, it should be noted that because women were admitted into the mainstream and thus worked on research questions central to discipline, there has been less "ghettoization" of women in social psychology than there has been in many other disciplines. Rather than an alternative and "feminist" view of social psychology, one that offers an opposing view of the discipline's dominant knowledge domain, there has evolved, by and large, a single social psychology that has integrated, and has been enriched by, the different experiences and views that female social psychologists have brought to their work. Because examples of such enrichment abound, they perhaps are unnecessary, but one spontaneously remembers the sighs of recognition that greeted the Deaux and Emswiller (1974) article, whose subtitle, "What Is Skill for the Male Is Luck for the Female," said it all for many of us. The work of Alice Eagly and her colleagues also quickly comes to mind, for when I began teaching in 1965, it was a "fact," duly reported in the social psychology texts of the day, that women were more influenceable (read "gullible," "childlike," and "uninformed") than men, a finding that seemed to fit nicely into a constellation of data said to document the submissive and dependent nature of women. Those of us using those texts could only caution our students that not all women were easily influenceable (namely, their very own instructor) and once again drag out our all-purpose and over-used example of Golda Meir—the then Prime Minister of Israel and first female political leader of a major country in modern times, whom the daily news was revealing to be no docile "Mrs. Nice Guy"—as an illustration of the hazards of generalizing to the individual case. Sistrunk and McDavid (1971), of course, dealt the first empirical blow to the idea of women's innate influenceability but it was Eagly's (e.g., Eagly, 1978) work that buried it.

That work, in fact, turned up a subsidiary finding with important implications for the development of the social and behavioral sciences, both then and now. Pursuing the question of women's special influenceability with the then-new technique of meta-analysis, Eagly and Carli (1981) found an association between the sex of the researcher and the outcome of the experiment, such that both male and female researchers were more likely to find results favorable to their own sex. A tendency to produce findings favorable to groups intimately associated with the researcher's own identity, through intentional and as yet unidentified mechanisms, argues that diversification of the researcher population—apart from moral, legal, and human resource utilization considerations—serves an important scientific goal: Diversification protects against unintended and unidentified bias in any knowledge domain that purports to be applicable to all humans.

Ironically, the concern today seems to be that the discipline of psychology is tilting again but in the other direction. According to the APA newsletter *Advancing the Public Interest* (J. M. Jones, 1991), the profession of psychology currently consists of 60% men and 40% women. That number is likely to reach parity soon, for in 1989 56% of the graduates with doctoral degrees in psychology were women. Curiously, this movement toward gender parity has been popularly termed, not the *demasculinization* nor even the *degenderization* of our discipline but, rather, the *feminization of psychology*. However, in terms of the knowledge domain that we disseminate to the world—and this surely is where it counts—it is questionable whether psychology will be feminized soon. The critical issue concerns the extent to which the current 60:40 ratio holds in the research arena where psychological knowledge is produced. Only a small fraction of those who receive doctorates ever contribute to the knowledge base of their discipline, and, according to the National Research Council's recent report (Gerstein, Luce, Smelser, & Sperlich, 1988), this figure is not only lower for the social and behavioral sciences than it is for other science and engineering doctorates, but also "even at its highest point, campus strength in behavioral and social sciences research was well short of what one might expect on the basis of the numbers of trained personnel available" (p. 205). My guess is that the percentage of men in the population of researchers in psychology at the present time is higher than 60%. Supporting that hypothesis are figures cited by Bernadine Healy (1992), the new director of the National Institutes of Health. Although women's share of research grant money from the National Institutes of Health has doubled since 1981, and women's success rates for competing research grants is now equal to men's, women submitted and received only 19% of these awards, accounting for "a mere 16% of funds for research project grants" (1992, p. B5).[1]

---

[1]Some data relevant to the hypothesis that men are overrepresented in the researcher population was provided by a special breakdown I requested of the APA research office on the 16,194 persons who completed work activity forms in the 1989 APA Directory Survey and 1990–1991 new member updates: Of those who indicated that they performed at least some research activities, over 66% were men. Only those who identified their major field as developmental psychology came close to gender parity, with 44% male researchers (this was also the only area in which there

Women, accounting as they do for half of humankind, constituted the biggest and most obvious boulder to be moved on the road to diversification, but we have become more sophisticated over the past few decades about what true diversification means. And there is yet no reason for celebration. With respect to ethnic minorities, for example, E. E. Jones (1990) recently reported that ethnic minorities account only for about 3%–4% of APA membership and only about 8% of new doctorates. When one considers that these figures include African-Americans, Native Americans, Hispanics, and Asian-Americans—people who, collectively, soon will comprise one third of the population in this country—it is clear that no subarea of psychology can claim it has a diversified research arm.

INCREASE IN THE STATUS AND CENTRALITY OF SOCIAL PSYCHOLOGY WITHIN PSYCHOLOGY

Rivaling in importance the increase in the number of women within social psychology over the past quarter century has been the increase in the status and centrality of social psychology within psychology. As Zimbardo (1992) recently observed, social psychology was "long relegated to a subordinate position within psychology's status hierarchy" (p. xiv), a delicate way of saying that back in 1965, and for many years after, social psychologists were the lowest of the low. When I went off to the business school, social psychologists were having a tough time in departments of psychology. The reigning prima dons were the "experimentalists" in learning psychology, easily recognized as they flapped through the halls in their white lab coats stained with rat urine and pigeon droppings. Searching for universal laws of behavior that would span millions of years of evolutionary time, from earthworms to Homo sapiens, and often using precise mathematical models to represent their hypotheses and findings (many of which later turned out to be much ado about not very much of enduring interest), the experimental psychologists, one much admit, were doing a fine job of imitating their acknowledged betters in the "hard" sciences, especially their much admired colleagues in classical physics (most of whom, ironically, were already dead in 1965 or in a deep funk and paralyzed into inactivity by the epistemological conundrums posed by the new physics; see, for example, Capra, 1982).

It was out from the wings and onto this stage where the experimental psychologists were busily performing their classical scientific ballet, that the new social psychologists came clomping in their concrete overshoes. With live humans as our subjects and complex social phenomena as our focus, some of our early attempts to join in the dance were ungraceful at best and downright ludicrous at worst. One thinks, for example, of George Homans's (1961) treatise, *Social Behavior: Its Elementary Forms,* which, while it proved valuable to social psychology for other reasons, was a textbook illustration of the popular game played in most social psychology parlors of the day: "Let's find the Reinforcer!" (of this or that social behavior).

was a gender reversal). The figure for social psychology was 69% male. A better index may be authorship of articles in archival journals: for *JPSP* and *Personality and Social Psychology Bulletin* in the years 1989 and 1990, and eliminating the 39 authors whose gender was "hard to tell" by virtue of first name alone, 63% of the 1,263 authors appear to have been men.

Unfortunately, the dominant learning theories of those times had been developed primarily with animals missing an upper cortex, and their raw application to humans in social situations often had a rather surreal quality to them (e.g., one thinks back to those experiments in which bright college students, treated like rats, would look up puzzled each time they heard a penny come rattling down the chute before them as they performed their laboratory task). But we, too, wanted to be real scientists. And so, looking to our superiors for guidance, we spent time doing things we might not have done had we had more confidence in our unique mission. I recall, for example, the months we spent debating the perfect equation to represent such social phenomena as interpersonal equity (e.g., Walster, Berscheid, & Walster, 1973), and none of us will forget the meticulous precision of the "law of interpersonal attraction" (e.g., Byrne, 1971; Byrne & Nelson, 1965).

Despite our efforts to ape our betters in the world of psychology, and no doubt sometimes because of them, social psychologists were frequently the objects of laughter and derision; we were regarded as soft-headed and sloppy, an embarrassment, in fact, to "serious" psychologists. No one was immune. For example, even though the Laboratory for Research in Social Relations at Minnesota was among the first and most prestigious training grounds for social psychologists, with the likes of Leon Festinger, Stanley Schachter, Hal Kelley, and Elliot Aronson as psychology faculty in residence in its early years, when we left the lab to attend our psychology classes, we frequently heard social psychology ridiculed from the lectern. As an assistant professor, in fact, the first question the then-president of the local American Association of University Professors (AAUP) asked when we were introduced was "Why do you social psychologists take the abuse?" Embarrassed that word of our parish status had seeped out of Elliott Hall into the wider world, I retorted, "Because tomorrow belongs to us!" The bravado of that reply owed as much to the fact that I had seen the movie *Cabaret* as it did to my faith in the future, for at that time we social psychologists were haunted by dark nights of the soul and afflicted with wrenching "crises of confidence" (e.g., McGuire, 1973). Now, from the distance of 25 years and a cool look back at the hostile context in which social psychology was developing, it seems no wonder that we were frequently driven to contemplate our collective navel and to question whether we had a place in the scientific universe.

But it wasn't just our hostile academic environment that bedeviled us. We had most of the problems any new field has. We suffered from an identity problem, for example. Though still very much apparent in 1965, that problem at least was beginning to abate. In his review of the three new social psychology texts that had just blossomed (the original Roger Brown, 1965, text; the Secord & Backman, 1964, text; and a text by Newcomb, Turner, & Converse, 1965), Brewster Smith (1966) observed that earlier social psychology texts, reflecting the marginal status of social psychology between the disciplines of psychology and sociology, had devoted much space to the competing claims of each discipline and to trying to resolve, unsuccessfully, the conflicts between them. But Smith could now report that

> None of the [current] books pays attention to the earlier quarrels of sociology and psychology over the lineage and legitimacy of their offspring. Indeed, for two of them (Brown and Secord-Backman), the field that they survey or sample is to be defined only by academic and scientific convention: what social psychologists have been curious and busy about. (p. 110)

These three books broke a 13-year hiatus in social psychology texts (with only the Krech, Crutchfield, & Ballachey, 1962, revision of the 1948 Krech and Crutchfield text appearing in this time). The Brown and the Secord and Backman texts, along with the E. E. Jones and Gerard (1967) classic that was to appear shortly, were signal landmarks in social psychology for several reasons, but especially because they gave shape and direction to the field. They not only finessed questions of genealogy, but also their surveys of "what social psychologists were curious and busy about. Moreover, they systematically infused those doings with heavy doses of theory and findings from psychology proper, making useful interpretations and translations to social behavior (e.g., from object perception to social perception). In addition, by this time there were enough concrete findings to report that the empirical quality of the field was emerging clearly, putting armchair philosophizing in retreat. In this regard, and given the blizzards of findings that social psychologists today routinely attempt to assimilate, it is amusing to read Brewster Smith's plaint back in 1966:

> For myself, I am proud of the real gains in the course of the thirteen years since my last comparative review, but I am not too happy about the clogged state of our journals, filled with the products of project-supported business, in which fad and fashion, methodological fetishism, and what I remember Gordon Allport to have called "itsy-bitsy empiricism" make it easy to lose direction and significance. (p. 117)

In bypassing questions of identity, and in moving social psychology toward its psychological and Lewinian heritage, the appearance of these texts also was a godsend to those of us who had to fend off perennial attempts to eject us (all two of us at Minnesota, until 1976) from the psychology department; around budget time, we came to expect that someone would come up with the wonderful idea of creating two new line items for the psychology department by making us the wards of the sociology department and ask us if we didn't think it was a wonderful idea, too. In writing our annual "we shall not be moved" statement, the psychological content and orientation of these texts, which we used in our social psychology classes but which the sociological social psychologists did not, were invaluable.[2]

---

[2]In commenting on this article, Sidney Rosen, an observer of the fortunes of social psychologists within sociology over the past 25 years, noted that Herbert Simon addressed a sociological convention some years ago in which he offered a translation of Homans's (1961) propositions into a set of mathematical equations and wondered whatever happened to them, a rather telling question. Rosen then made the following fascinating points: "We might add the observation of a cultural lag distinguishing sociology and psychology. One relevant aspect of this lag was that theoretical sociology started to become attracted to formalization at about the time that such a preoccupation began to lose favor in psychology. Another relevant aspect of this lag is that sociological social psychology is still struggling to establish its identity within sociology. In this regard, Felson wrote the following, in the Winter 1992 newsletter of the social psychology section of ASA: 'Why did the status of social psychology in sociology decline in the last 20 years: I believe that one reason is ideological: social psychology is not politically correct (p. 3). Suffice it to say here that he meant political correctness from the perspective of traditional sociology." It should also be mentioned that sociological social psychologists are still represented in SESP, although their proportion to the total membership has declined radically over the past 25 years, and that sociological social psychologists as well as sociologists concerned with marriage and the family currently are core contributors to the emerging interdisciplinary science of interpersonal relationships.

Apart from who we were and where we belonged in the academy, serious questions and allegations were frequently raised about the value of our activities. I shall mention only one of these charges and that because, first, it struck at the heart of our claim to scientific status; second, because we were relatively defenseless against it 25 years ago when the field was young in age and few in number; and third, because it retained its currency long after it should have. Although the allegation was made by many, it perhaps was stated most persuasively and succinctly by my Minnesota colleague, Paul Meehl (1978):

> I consider it unnecessary to persuade you that most so-called "theories" in the soft areas of psychology (clinical, counseling, social, personality, community, and school psychology) are scientifically unimpressive and technologically worthless. . . . In the developed sciences, theories tend either to become widely accepted and built into the larger edifice of well-tested human knowledge or else they suffer destruction in the face of recalcitrant facts and are abandoned. . . . But in fields like personology and social psychology, this seems not to happen. There is a period of enthusiasm about a new theory, a period of attempted application to several fact domains, a period of disillusionment as the negative data come in, a growing bafflement about inconsistent and inexplicable empirical results, multiple resort to ad hoc excuses, and then finally people just sort of lose interest in the thing and pursue other endeavors. . . . It is simply a sad fact that in soft psychology theories rise and decline, come and go, more as a function of baffled boredom than anything else; and the enterprise shows a disturbing absence of that *cumulative* character that is so impressive in disciplines like astronomy, molecular biology, and genetics. (pp. 806–807)

Today, the charge of noncumulativeness against social psychology has a musty odor to it. In his article, "How Hard Is Hard Science, How Soft Is Soft Science? The Empirical Cumulativeness of Research," Hedges (1987) distinguished between *theoretical cumulativeness* and *empirical cumulativeness;* the latter being defined as the "degree of agreement among replicated experiments or the degree to which related experimental results fit into a simple pattern that makes conceptual sense" (p. 443). Comparing the consistency of research results in physics and in psychology using a sample of reviews of empirical findings from each domain, Hedges found that the results of physical experiments were not strikingly more consistent than those of social or behavioral experiments and, thus, that "the 'obvious' conclusion that the results of physical science experiments are more cumulative than those of social science experiments does not have much empirical support" (p. 443). For social psychology in particular, there is specific evidence of the empirical cumulativeness of the field. In their analysis of "Publication Trend in *JPSP*: A Three-Decade Review," Reis and Stiller (1992) reported that, since 1968, published articles have become progressively longer, they present more procedural information and tables, they cite more prior literature, they report research based on more studies, they use more subjects per study, and they use more complex statistical methods. These changes, the authors persuasively argued, reflect social psychologists' focus on increasingly complex theoretical issues as well as the field's demand for higher and higher standards of evidence as it has matured.

As Hedges (1987) observed, the assessment of empirical cumulativeness, although possessing the virtue of some objectivity, is also a narrower index of the cumulativeness of a discipline than is its theoretical cumulativeness, or the degree to which the field's "empirical laws and theoretical structures build on one another so that later developments extend and unify earlier work" (p. 443). Subjective though such an assessment must be, the evidence that can be mustered for the theoretical cumulativeness of social psychology in the past quarter century could easily pass the eyeball test of social psychology's severest critic.

In 1965 social psychology was already theory rich, but it remained to be seen whether these theories would provide the muscle and sinew the field needed to develop. Festinger (1954, 1957) had offered his theory of social comparison processes a decade earlier (in 1954), and his theory of cognitive dissonance (in 1957) was already turning the field's attention away from "groupy" phenomena (see Steiner, 1974) to matters that today would fall under the general rubric of "social cognition." Heider (1958) had already published *The Psychology of Interpersonal Relations,* which elaborated his balance theory (sketched over a decade earlier in his hard-to-read 1946 article "Attitudes and Cognitive Organization" that had purportedly influenced Festinger's concept of cognitive dissonance, although Asch, 1946, also had started people thinking about consistency as a principle of cognitive organization). In this seminal work, Heider also discussed his observation that people often try to attribute causes to events, and E. E. Jones and Davis (1965) had already begun to flesh out attribution theory. Thibaut and Kelley (1959) already had published the first version of their theory of interdependence; Homans (1961) had presented his idea of "distributive justice" in social relationships, which shortly was to be elaborated in equity theories; Newcomb (1956) already had drawn attention to problems in the prediction of interpersonal attraction in his APA presidential address and had recently published his study of *The Acquaintance Process* (Newcomb, 1961); and Schachter (1959) had presented both *The Psychology of Affiliation* and his article "The Interaction of Cognitive and Physiological Determinants of Emotional State" (Schachter, 1964). Moreover, Asch's (1946) empirical studies of conformity phenomena and of social perception were well-known, and the "Yale school's" work on attitude change (e.g., Hovland, Janis, & Kelley, 1953) had been around for a decade, with its "incentive motivation" view currently dueling with dissonance theory on the pages of the journals. There was much more, of course, but suffice it to say that, today, the names and the content of these theories will not strike even an undergraduate in social psychology as unfamiliar. Although some of these theories and the findings they produced may have been baffling from time to time, they were never boring, and they were never wholly abandoned. All were to prove to be vital building blocks for later theorists and investigators. And all have remained alive in the sense that they have been revised frequently in response to new findings—or they have been incorporated into other theories—or the findings they spawned have remained important in themselves or have played important roles in further theory development.

Perhaps the most impressive example of the cumulative nature of social psychology lies in the attribution area. From the theoretical outlines originally sketched by Heider (1958) to E. E. Jones and Davis's (1965) formulation to Kelley's (1967) rendering of "Attribution Theory in Social Psychology" two years later, the attributionists have patiently and systematically pursued their phenomena along a very long and winding road. A powerful chronicle of attribution theory and research over the past 25 years is presented in E. E. Jones's (1990) book, *Person Perception.* If social psychology is ever again required to defend itself against the charge of noncumulativeness, submission into evidence of this book alone would get the prosecution laughed out of court. And the attributionists aren't done yet; in fact, the best may be just around the bend, for two new and highly integrative theories of person perception recently have been offered, one by Susan Fiske and her colleagues (e.g., Fiske & Neuberg, 1990) and the other by Marilynn Brewer (1988).

Not only have social psychologists not been faddish about their theories, they haven't been flighty in their selection of the social behaviors they've sought to understand. In addition to the previously mentioned work on stereotypes and prejudice, begun in social psychology's infancy with the work of Gordon Allport and Kurt Lewin, and which now constitutes a theoretically impressive and practically useful body of knowledge (e.g., see Hamilton, 1981) that continues to be the subject of much current research (e.g., Swim, Borgida, Maruyama, & Myers, 1989), social comparison is still an active research area (e.g., Wheeler & Miyake, 1992), with its fruits extended over the years to illuminate other social phenomena of interest (e.g., Tesser, Millar, & Moore, 1988). Interpersonal attraction, that rock pile of theory and research on which some of us labored as graduate students, now helps form the core of the burgeoning interpersonal relationships wing of social psychology, where the cumulative and interdisciplinary nature of the work performed in this area over the past 3 decades was traced recently by George Levinger (1990) in his address to the International Society of the Study of Personal Relationships at Oxford University. Progress in this area can be illustrated by the fact that at the University of Minnesota we have graduated from Dr. Gregor Zilstein's (a.k.a. Stanley Schachter) frightening coeds with the prospect of electric shock, from Elaine Hatfield's designing computer dances for the Student Activities Bureau's freshman orientation week, and from Elliot Aronson's engineering pratfalls for otherwise competent people, to the construction of a free-standing doctoral minor in Interpersonal Relationships Research. This new program will join the forces of scholars in psychology, the Institute of Child Development, family social science, sociology, that old business school (now spiffily named the Carlson School of Management), several colleges and departments in the health sciences, and more to train graduate students and facilitate research on interpersonal relationships. As this illustrates, social psychologists not only have burrowed ever more deeply into the social phenomena that were of interest 25 years ago, but another quality of our discipline has been revealed as it's matured: its boundary-spanning nature.

Social psychologists have expanded their knowledge domain in virtually every direction. Surveying the thousands of books submitted to *Contemporary Psychology* for review consideration these past several years for example, we were continually surprised by the number of areas in which social psychologists are currently contributing theory and research. Reflecting this state of affairs, social psychology now often finds itself hyphenated to reflect its alliances with other subareas of psychology: social-developmental, social-clinical, social-personality, social psychology and law, social-health, social-organizational, social-educational, social-environmental, and social-community for examples. Few subareas of psychology interface with and inform so many other scholarly endeavors within psychology as well as in those disciplines located on psychology's perimeter.

It has become apparent, in fact, that social psychology has emerged as a central pivot for much of contemporary psychology. In this regard, it is interesting to note that even those prognosticators of the future of psychology who see it vanishing as a discipline, with many of its current internal domains being absorbed by other disciplines, do not foresee such a fate for social psychology. Scott (1991), for example, who subscribes to the notion that psychology as we know it will disintegrate, predicted that

> Social psychology will continue to expand its strong experimental base, and will increasingly ful-fill its promise to address society's most vexing problems. The solutions that emerge from social psychology laboratories will inform gender and racial issues and permeate the workplace, the in-ner city, and the home. Social psychology will become more practice oriented, affiliating with or creating its own professional schools . . . (p. 976)

If Scott is correct, it may fall to social psychologists to carry psychology's banner into the 21st century.

In sum, contemporary social psychology, with its dynamic, ever-changing and -expanding character, is an exemplar of all the social and behavioral sciences as they have been charac-terized by the National Research Council:

> Taking into consideration the dynamics of specialization, the development of data, theoretical shifts, and interdisciplinary activity—and the interactions of all of these with one another—the behavioral and social sciences resemble not so much a map as a kaleidoscope, with continuous growth, shifting boundaries, and new emphases and highlights. (Adams, Smelser & Treiman, 1982, p. 26)

Dynamic. And cumulative. Could anyone have asked more of social psychology 25 years ago?

IF WE'RE SO SMART, WHY AREN'T WE RICH?

Not everything has improved over the past 25 years. We still do not have an epistemology well suited to our endeavors (e.g., see Berscheid, 1986), which makes people uneasy when they think about it, which isn't very often anymore. Good minds have addressed the painful issues here over the years (e.g., Gergen, 1973; Harre & Secord, 1973) but with little practical effect and resolution. Fortunately, the field's momentum is such that we routinely walk on water in the faith that what we are doing is useful and important; it is only when we look down, and are reminded that the philosophy of science that supported classical physics cannot support us, do we sometimes sink and suffer yet another crisis of confidence.

There are other problems, but the most worrisome one, which brings me to the third and last change I wish to highlight, is the decrease in social psychology's funding per capita re-searcher. In 1965, the social and behavioral sciences were enjoying the "golden age" of re-search funding, and social psychology shared in the good times. Today, the amount of time talented researchers, both young and old, spend writing grant proposals only to be told that their ideas—though meritorious—must wither for lack of funds, is disheartening. A great many facts and figures have been published documenting our inadequate research support environment, so there is no need to repeat the dreary tale here, except to say that changes in support for all of the behavioral and social sciences have been "starkly different" (as the situ-ation is characterized in Appendix A, "Trends in Support for Research in the Behavioral and

Social Sciences," of the National Research Council's 1988 report) from those of other scientific disciplines, whose federal funding increased substantially over the past 15 years.

Ever pragmatic and fleet of foot, however, social psychologist have coped. And it perhaps is not too Panglossian to say that they have done so in ways that have protected the discipline and even strengthened it along several dimensions. As Zimbardo (1992) observed, "social psychologists have become the vanguard of the movement to extend the boundaries of traditional psychology into realms vital to contributing solutions for real-world problems, the areas of health, ecology, education, law, peace and conflict resolution, and much more" (p. xiv). As funding for basic research became more and more scarce, and funding for very specific social problems—such as alcohol and drug abuse, acquired immunodeficiency syndrome (AIDS), aging, and so forth—became available, social psychologists increasingly took their theories and their methodological tools out of the laboratory and into the world of pressing societal problems. In doing so, they have broken down the wall between basic and applied research that was apparent 25 years ago when basic and applied research were seen as parallel, rather than intertwined, research tracks. During the recent funding drought, social psychologists discovered anew the truth of Lewin's dictum that "there is nothing so practical as a good theory!" and have reunited the two faces of social psychology's research coin. We must continue to hope, however, that those who successfully use the tools and theory of social psychology in their applied enterprises never forget their way back home and the necessity for putting something back in the basic theory and research pot during the hard times of inadequate support for the discipline.

Having acknowledged some of the benefits of a harsh environment for the evolutionary development of social psychology, it must also be recognized that in addition to inadequate support for basic research and theory development, funding inadequacies have affected the field in other troubling ways. One of these is our inability to take advantage of the technological marvels that have become available over the past few decades to facilitate our research. A look at our journals today reveals that, just as it was back in 1965, social psychology is very much a pencil-and-paper enterprise. It may be even more of a pencil-and-paper enterprise today than it was then, for the use of self-report questionnaires and written treatments of independent variables seems to have increased; running subjects in large groups and handing out questionnaires is much cheaper, of course, than setting up elaborate treatment scenarios possessing high internal validity and spending one or two hours per subject to collect a single datum, and it is also much less expensive than going out into naturalistic settings to observe behavior.

One of the many unfortunate consequences of our being a pencil-and-paper field is that to those observers who still confuse technology with science—and there are many, both within the academy and without—social psychology still doesn't look like much of a science. In this, however, we are not much different from many of the other social and behavioral sciences. As the National Research Council (Gerstein et al., 1988) observed, "There is a persisting view that behavioral and social sciences research can operate as a virtually equipment-free enterprise, a view that is completely out of date for research in may areas" (p. 214). Needless to say, social psychology is very prominently one of those areas. Even equipment that has been shown to be useful to the exploration of many different social phenomena (e.g., physiological and facial measures of affect) are not routinely available in social psychological laboratories. Moreover, unobtrusive devices to measure important social psychological variables outside of the laboratory, with extremely reactive subjects who range freely over large habitats, still appear only in our dreams. The inability of researchers in social psychology to take advantage of the many technological developments that would facilitate our empirical research and broaden our theoretical horizons currently constitutes a particularly frustrating stumbling block as other, better funded, disciplines increasingly capitalize from rapid technological advances. For now, we can only pray that the lead mines fueling our pencils don't run dry before our funding prospects improve.

In this regard, there now is reason to hope, and hope for the future is always a good place to end a look at the past. As all who keep up with the events that affect the fortunes of psychology now know, a separate directorate for the behavioral and social science disciplines is being formed at the National Science Foundation (e.g., NSF Directorate: Yes!, 1991), the agency social psychologists look to for most of our basic research support. That reorganization, according to knowledgeable observers, should increase funding for all of the social and behavioral sciences and, on that score alone, social psychology's boat should lift along with the others. But beyond that general effect, we surely have reason to be confident that even the most jaundiced observer of social psychology's development and record of contribution over the past 25 years must conclude that social psychology has been faithful to its promise to the society that supports it and that society thus has a vested interest in keeping social psychologists as busy and as curious over the next quarter century as they've been over the last.

REFERENCES

Adams, R. Mc., Smelser, D. J. & Trieman, D. J. (1982). *Behavioral and social science research: A national resource (Part I)*. Washington, DC: National Academy Press. p 30.

Asch, S. E. (1946). Forming impressions of personality. *Journal of Abnormal and Social Psychology, 41*, 258–290.

Berscheid, E. (1986). Mea culpas and lamentations: Sir Francis, Sir Isaac, and "The slow progress of soft psychology." In R. Gilmour & S. Duck (Eds.), *The emerging field of personal relationships* (pp. 267–286). Hillsdale, NJ: Erlbaum.

Berscheid, E., & Walster [Hatfield], E. (1967). When does a harm-doer compensate a victim? *Journal of Personality and Social Psychology, 6*, 435–441.

Brewer, M. (1988). A dual process model of impression formation. In T. K. Srull & R. S. Wyer (Eds.), *Advances in social cognition* (Vol. 1, pp. 1–36). Hillsdale, NJ: Erlbaum.

Brown, R. (1965). *Social psychology*. New York: Free Press.

Brush, S. G. (1991, September–October). Women in science and engineering. *American Scientist, 79*, 404–419.

Byrne, D. (1971). *The attraction paradigm*. San Diego, CA: Academic Press.

Byrne, D., & Nelson, D. (1965). Attraction as a linear function of proportion of positive reinforcements. *Journal of Personality and Social Psychology, 1*, 659–663.

Capra, F. (1982). *The turning point: Science, society and the rising culture*. New York: Simon & Schuster.

Deaux, K., & Emswiller, T. (1974). Explanation of successful performance on sex-linked tasks: What is skill for the male is luck for the female. *Journal of Personality and Social Psychology, 29*, 80–85.

Eagly, A. H. (1978). Sex differences in influenceability. *Psychological Bulletin, 85,* 86–116.

Eagly, A. H., & Carli, L. L. (1981). Sex of researchers and sex-typed communications as determinants of sex differences in influenceability: A meta-analysis of social influence studies. *Psychological Bulletin, 90,* 1–20.

Festinger, L. (1954). A theory of social comparison processes. *Human Relations, 7,* 117–140.

Festinger, L. (1957). *A theory of cognitive dissonance.* Evanston, IL: Row, Peterson. p 31.

Fiske, S. T., Bersoff, D. N., Borgida, E., Deaux, & Heilman, M. E. (1991). Social science research on trial: Use of sex stereotyping research in *Price Waterhouse v. Hopkins. American Psychologist, 46,* 1049–1060.

Fiske, & Neuberg, S. L. (1990). A continuum of impression formation, from category-based to individuating processes: Influences of information and motivation on attention and interpretation. In M. P. Zanna (Ed.), *Advances in experimental social psychology* (Vol. 23, pp. 1–74). San Diego, CA: Academic Press.

Gergen, K. J. (1973). Social psychology as history. *Journal of Personality and Social Psychology, 26,* 309–320.

Gerstein, D. R., Luce, R. D., Smelser, N. J., & Sperlich, S. (Eds.). (1988). *The behavioral and social sciences: Achievements and opportunities.* Washington, DC: National Academy Press.

Hamilton, D. L. (Ed.). (1981). *Cognitive processes in stereotyping and intergroup behavior.* Hillsdale, NJ: Erlbaum.

Harre, R., & Secord, P. F. (1973). *The explanation of social behaviour.* Totowa, NJ: Littlefield Adams.

Healy, B. (1992, March 25). Quotable: "The astonishing thing is that young women pursue careers in science and medicine at all!" *The Chronicle of Higher Education,* March 25, p. 135.

Hedges, L. V. (1987). How hard is hard science, how soft is soft science? The empirical cumulativeness of research. *American Psychologist, 42,* 443–455.

Heider, F. (1958). *The psychology of interpersonal relations.* New York: Wiley.

Hollander, E. P. (1968). The Society of Experimental Social Psychology: An historical note. *Journal of Personality and Social Psychology, 9,* 280–282.

Homans, G. C. (1961). *Social behavior: Its elementary forms.* New York: Harcourt, Brace & World.

Hovland, C. I., Janis, I. L., & Kelley, H. H. (1953). *Communication and persuasion.* New Haven, CT: Yale University Press.

Jones, E. E. (1990). *Person perception.* Hillsdale, NJ: Erlbaum.

Jones, E. E., & Davis, K. E. (1965). From acts to dispositions: The attribution process in person perception. In L. Berkowitz (Ed.), *Advances in experimental social psychology* (Vol. II, pp. 219–266). San Diego, CA: Academic Press.

Jones, E. E., & Gerard, H. B. (1967). *Foundations of social psychology.* New York: Wiley.

Jones, J. M. (1991, July). The greening of psychology. *Advancing the Public Interest, 3,* 7–8.

Kelley, H. H. (1967). Attribution theory in social psychology. In D. Levine (Ed.), *Nebraska Symposium on Motivation* (Vol. 13, pp. 192–214). Lincoln: University of Nebraska Press.

Krech, D., & Crutchfield, R. S. (1948). *Theory and problems of social psychology.* New York: McGraw-Hill.

Krech, D., Crutchfield, R. S., & Ballachey, E. L. (1962). *Individual in society: A textbook of social psychology.* New York: McGraw-Hill.

Levinger, G. (1990, July). *Figure versus ground: Micro and macro perspectives on personal relationships.* Invited address to the International Society for the Study of Interpersonal Relationships, Oxford University, Oxford, England.

McGuire, W. J. (1973). The yin and yang of progress in social psychology: Seven koan. *Journal of Personality and Social Psychology, 26,* 446–456.

Meehl, P. E. (1978). Theoretical risks and tabular asterisks: Sir Karl, Sir Ronald, and the slow progress of soft psychology. *Journal of Consulting and Clinical Psychology, 46,* 806–834.

Newcomb, T. M. (1956). The prediction of interpersonal attraction. *American Psychologist, 11,* 575–586.

Newcomb, T. M. (1961). *The acquaintance process.* New York: Holt, Rinehart & Winston.

NEWCOMB, T. M., TURNER, R. H., & CONVERSE, P. E. (1965). *Social psychology: The study of human interaction.* New York: Holt, Rinehart & Winston.

NSF directorate: Yes! (1991, November). *APS Observer, 4,* 1, 28–31.

REIS, H. T., & STILLER, J. (1992). Publication trends in *JPSP:* A three-decade review. *Personality and Social Psychology Bulletin, 18,* 465–472.

SCHACHTER, S. (1959). *The psychology of affiliation: Experimental studies of the sources of gregariousness.* Stanford, CA: Stanford University Press.

SCHACHTER, S. (1964). The interaction of cognitive and physiological determinants of emotional state. In L. Berkowitz (Ed.), *Advances in experimental social psychology* (Vol. 1, pp. 49–80). San Diego, CA: Academic Press.

SCOTT, T. R. (1991). A personal view of the future of psychology departments. *American Psychologist, 46,* 975–976.

SECORD, P. F., & BACKMAN, C. W. (1964) *Social psychology.* New York: McGraw-Hill.

SISTRUNK, F., & McDAVID, J. W. (1971). Sex variable in conformity behavior. *Journal of Personality and Social Psychology, 17,* 200–207.

SMITH, M. B. (1966). Three textbooks: A special review. *Journal of Experimental Social Psychology, 2,* 109–118.

STEINER, I. D. (1974). Whatever happened to the group in social psychology? *Journal of Experimental Social Psychology, 10,* 93–108.

SWIM, J., BORGIDA, E., MARUYAMA, G., & MYERS, D. G. (1989). Joan McKay versus John McKay: Do gender stereotypes bias evaluations? *Psychological Bulletin, 105,* 409–429.

TESSER, A., MILLAR, M., & MOORE, J. (1988). Some affective consequences of social comparison and reflection processes: The pain and pleasure of being close. *Journal of Personality and Social Psychology, 54,* 49–61.

THIBAUT, J. W., & KELLEY, H. H. (1959). *The social psychology of groups.* New York: Wiley.

WALSTER, E., BERSCHEID, E., & WALSTER, G. W. (1973). New directions in equity. *Journal of Personality and Social Psychology, 25,* 151–176.

WHEELER, L., & MIYAKE, K. (1992). Social comparison in everyday life. *Journal of Personality and Social Psychology, 62,* 760–773.

ZIMBARDO, P. G. (1992). Foreword. In S. S. Brehm (Ed.), *Intimate relationships* (pp. xiv–xvi). New York: McGraw-Hill.

QUESTIONS

1. With respect to gender equality, how did social psychology compare to other areas of psychology in the late 1960s? How does Berscheid explain this?

2. Including women within the mainstream of social psychology was obviously morally and legally important. Why does Berscheid believe that it was also scientifically important?

3. Why does Berscheid consider the publication of four new textbooks in 1964–1967 so important to the field? How did this help resolve the identity crisis that social psychology was facing?

4. How does Berscheid respond to charges that social psychology is faddish and flighty? Does she think that the criticism was valid in 1965? Does she feel that it is valid today?

5. Explain how the shrinking availability of funds may have improved the quality of social psychological research.

PART II

SOCIAL COGNITION:
PERCEIVING THE SOCIAL
WORLD

❖ CHAPTER 2 ❖

SOCIAL COGNITION: PERCEIVING AND UNDERSTANDING INDIVIDUALS

Reading 3: Classic

How Do People Perceive the Causes of Behavior?

Edward E. Jones

As Ellen Berscheid mentions in the previous reading, attribution theory is among the most successful social psychological theories developed in recent years. It is also one of the first theories in the field that attempted to explain the mechanisms involved when people think about their social environment. In other words, it is one of the first social cognitive theories.

Attribution theory attempts to explain how people make sense of behavior, both their own and that of others. Interestingly, one major finding in this area is that the types of attributions (i.e., explanations) that people come up with when trying to explain their own behavior differ from those they use when trying to explain the behavior of another. This phenomenon became known as the actor-observer effect.

In this article, Edward Jones, the preeminent researcher in attribution theory, discusses the actor-observer effect. He admits that when he and his colleagues first proposed the phenomenon there was very little empirical support. Over the next few years that quickly changed as dozens of studies in many different labs confirmed Jones's prediction. In a very fundamental way, the same behavior looks very different when we perform it than when someone else does.

❖

Finding the causes for behavior is a fundamental enterprise of the psychologist. But it is an enterprise he shares with the man on the street. Our responses to others are affected by the reasons, or *attributes*, we assign for their behavior. At least this is the basic assumption of the attributional approach in social psychology, an approach that concerns itself with phenomenal causality—the conditions affecting how each of us attributes causes for his own and others' behavior. The hope is that if we can better understand how people perceive the causal structure of their social world, we can better predict their responses to that world. If *A* attributes *B*'s anger to the fact that *B* has lost his job, *A* is less likely to reciprocate. If a teacher attributes a student's poor performance to lack of motivation, he is more likely to express open disappointment than if his attribution were to lack of ability. A supervisor's appreciation of a subordinate's compliments is more or less alloyed by his attribution of ulterior motives.

Source: Jones, E. E. (1976, May/June). How do people perceive the causes of behavior? *American Scientist*, 300–305.

The attributional approach (Jones et al. 1972) is essentially a perspective, or a framework rather than a theory. The perspective owes much of its current prominence to the seminal writings of Fritz Heider. However, propositional statements have been spawned within the framework, and there are some identifiable theoretical positions. Davis and I outlined a theory of *correspondent inferences* in 1965 which is especially concerned with inferences about the dispositions and intentions of a person drawn from observing his behavior in particular contexts. Simply put, the theory states that casual attribution will be made to an actor to the extent that he is not bound by circumstances and is therefore free to choose from a number of behavioral options. If a person has choice, and if his actions depart in any way from expectations, the perceiver-attributor should gain information about his motives and personality. Under these conditions, we might say that the person reveals himself in his actions. We can make a correspondent inference that ties an act to a causal disposition: "He dominated the meeting because he is dominant"; "He cries because he is in pain"; "He voted for ERA because he believes in full civil liberties for women."

Two years later, Kelley proposed a comprehensive theory of *entity attribution* which was the complement of correspondent-inference theory. Whereas Davis and I wanted to explain how attributions to the person can be made by ruling out environmental explanations, Kelley wanted to show how we decide whether an actor's response is caused by the entity to which it is directed rather than by some idiosyncratic bias on his part. Both approaches accepted the division of person and situation as reflecting the terms in which the naive attributor is supposed to make his casual allocations.

In 1971, Nisbett and I rather recklessly proposed that actors and observers make divergent attributions about behavioral causes. Whereas the actor sees his behavior primarily as a response to the situation in which he finds himself, the observer attributes the same behavior to the actor's dispositional characteristics. This proposition had grown out of a number of informal observations as well as a sequence of experiments on attitude attribution. Let me digress for a moment to summarize briefly this line of research.

LABORATORY EXPERIMENTS

Nine separate experiments were run within the same general paradigm with college undergraduates from widely separated universities. Each followed a procedure in which subjects were given a short essay or speech favoring a particular position and were asked to infer the underlying attitude of the target person who produced it. In one experiment the statement was presented as an answer to an examination question; in another it was identified as the preliminary statement of a debater; in still others the statement was attributed to paid volunteers recruited for personality research (cf. Jones and Harris 1967). The statements used in each experiment involved a particular social issue such as the viability of Castor's Cuba, marijuana legalization, desegregation and busing, liberalized abortion, or socialized medicine.

The experimental conditions were created by varying whether the target person could choose which side of the issue to write or speak on, and whether or not the side was the expected or popular position. Some subjects were informed that the target person was assigned to defend a particular side of the issue (by his instructor, the debating coach, or the experimenter). Others were told he had been free to choose either side. The statement itself took one or the other side of the issue. In the typical experiment, then, there were four experimental groups: pro-position with choice, anti-position with choice, pro-position with no choice, and anti-position with no choice. For any given sample of subjects, one of the sides (pro or anti) was more popular or expected than the other.

All of the experiments showed remarkable stability in supporting the predictions one would make from correspondent inference theory. Attitudes in line with behavior were more decisively attributed to the target person in the choice than in the no-choice condition, but degree of choice made a greater difference if the essay or speech ran counter to the expected or normative position. This is illustrated in Figure 2–1, which presents the results from an early study (1967) dealing with attitudes toward Fidel Castro. Subjects read an essay presumably written as an opening statement by a college debater, but actually it was scripted beforehand as an unremarkable pro or anti summary, the kind of thing an undergraduate debater might write after minimal study of the issue. The subject was also told either that the target person had been directed by the team advisor to argue a specific side of the debate or that he was given his choice of sides.

After digesting the essay and noting the context in which it was produced, each subject was instructed to rate the target person's true attitude toward the Castor regime. From Figure 2–1 it is apparent that choice has an effect, but only in the pro-Castro condition, where the debater's position was not in line with the expected attitude of a college student in the late sixties.

For our present purposes, what is most interesting is a finding that could not have been predicted by correspondent inference theory: even in the no-choice conditions, subjects tended to attribute attitudes in line with the speech. They seemed to attach too little weight to the situation (the no-choice instructions) and too much to the person. Although several alternative explanations quickly suggested themselves, these were effectively ruled out by additional experiments (Jones et al. 1971; Snyder and Jones 1974). I became and remain convinced that we are dealing with a robust phenomenon of attributional bias and that persons as observers are all too ready to infer underlying dispositions, like attitudes, from behaviors, like opinion statements, even when it is obvious that the statements are produced under constraint.

Although these results were compatible with the hypothesis that actors and observers have divergent perspectives, they said nothing, of course, about the actor. But there is abundant evidence from other social psychological experiments that actors do not adjust their attitudes to make them consistent with their behavior if they are required (given little or not choice but) to defend the opposite of their initial position on an issue (cf. Aronson 1969; Bem 1972). Their behavior can be adequately explained by an attribution to the situation.

Nisbett and his associates (1973) set out to test the actor-observer proposition more directly. They found in a questionnaire study that people assign more traits to others than to themselves, a finding quite consistent with the notion that observers see personal dispositions in others but believe their own behavior depends primarily on the situation. Nisbett and his group also conducted an experiment in which some subjects were turned into actors and some into observers. The actors were asked to volunteer to take distinguished visitors around the Yale campus, while observers monitored the actors' responses to the volunteering request. Ac-

FIGURE 2–1

In this attitude-attribution experiment, target persons presented short speeches either for or against the Castro regime in Cuba. Some were said to have chosen which side to support (choice condition); others were said to have been required to take the position endorsed (no-choice condition). Observers then rated what they felt was each target person's true attitude toward Castro; the possible range was from 10 (extreme anti) to 70 (extreme pro). Observers rating pro-Castro target persons in the "choice" condition saw their true attitude as more decisively in favor of Castro than observers rating Castro supporters in the no-choice condition. Choice was a negligible factor when the speech opposed the Castro regime. At the time the experiment was conducted, most subjects—both target persons and observers—held anti-Castro views. Data from Jones and Harris (1967).

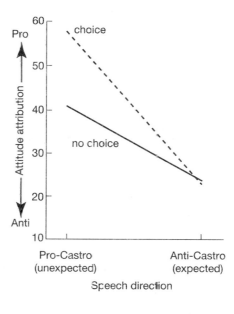

tors who volunteered were judged by the observers to be more likely to agree to canvass for the United fund (an instance of response generalization implying a "volunteering trait") than those who did not volunteer. There was a slight reversal in this trend when the actors themselves were asked whether they would volunteer to canvass. By inference, then, the observers assumed that someone who volunteers in one setting will volunteer in others—they attributed a volunteering disposition to the actor.

Nisbett and I (1971) incorporated these data and tried to elucidate some of the reasons why the actor-observer divergence might occur. As a starting point, it may be helpful to consider the observer's orientation. In the attitude-attribution paradigm, and in the volunteering experiments, we confront the observer with a brief sample of behavior produced in a particular setting. The actor is aware of a history of his prior actions in similar settings and is likely to compare the present behavior to previous behavior. Differences in his behavior over time can readily be attributed to the situation. The observer, on the other hand, is typically ignorant about details of the actor's history and is likely to take a cross-sectional, or normative, view, asking himself, "How do this person's reactions differ from those I would expect from others, from the average, from the norm?" Thus the observer's orientation is individuating; he seeks out (and exaggerates?) differences among people, perhaps because this gives him a feeling of control against the unexpected. His error seems to lie in failing to see the situation as a completely sufficient cause of the behavior observed. Heider (1958) must have had something similar in mind when he talked about the tendency for behavior to "engulf the field." Behavior belongs to the person; the "field" acts on everyone.

In addition to the observer's relative poverty of information, it is also true that the same information will be processed differently by actors and observers. For the observer, in general, action is dynamic, changing, unpredictable, and therefore *salient*. In the attitude-attribution paradigm, the essay appears to stand out as the unique product of the writer. It must, since it is the only concrete information the perceiver has about the writer, reflect the writer's characteristics in a number of ways. That is what "the experiment" is about: the subject is in the position of wondering how good he is at estimating a person's true attitudes. The actor who writes a counterattitudinal essay has faced situational pressure and succumbed to it. The observer knows in some intellectual sense that the pressure was there, but he is so drawn to the essay as the focus of his judgment task that he infers too much about the individual and his uniqueness.

There is good evidence, finally, that *perceptual focusing* leads to attribution (Duncker 1938; Wallach 1959). Of special relevance here is a study by Storms (1973). He set out to investigate whether observers and actors could be induced to exchange perspective with the aid of videotape replay. As is the case with most important experiments, the design was elegantly simple. Two experimental subjects (actors) held a brief get-acquainted conversation while two other subjects were each assigned to observe a different actor. Television cameras were pointed at each actor, but after the conversation the experimenter appeared to notice that only one had been working properly.

During the next phase of the experiment, all subjects observed the intact videotape replay of the conversation (focusing on one of the actors) and then made a series of attributional judgments. Thus, one actor had the same orientation toward the other actor that he had in the conversation—he was looking at the other on the video replay. The other actor was looking at himself on the replay. He had become a self-observer. When asked to account for the target person's behavior in terms of the contributions of personal characteristics and characteristics of the situation, the actors observing themselves were much more inclined to attribute their behavior to dispositional influences. Attributions by the two observers varied depending on their new orientation. The original observer of the nontaped actor was asked to account for his target person's behavior after looking at the other actor. In this changed orientation, he attributed his target person's behavior to situational factors. The other observer, who watched the taped subject originally as well as in phase two, assigned much greater dispositional influence to his target person.

To summarize these findings, then, attribution seems to follow along with perceptual focus, or perspective. It appears that we attribute causality to whatever or whomever we look at, at least when we are asked. The implications of this fact for persistent interpersonal misunderstandings are obvious. In a persuasive communication setting, for example, the communicator thinks he is describing reality, whereas the target person thinks he is expressing his personal biases.

The results of Storms' experiment also suggest that seating arrangements might be extremely important in a discussion group. In fact, this has been demonstrated by Taylor and Fiske (1975). In their experiment, subjects observing a two-person "get-acquainted" discussion between two confederates of the experimenter were seated in such a way that some faced one discussant, some faced the other, and some observed both from a 90° angle. These differences in literal perception strongly affected the observer-subjects' attributions of causality for various aspects of the conversation. Specifically, the discussant directly in the observer's line of sight was assigned greater personal causality. When the discussants were both observed from the side, equal personal causality was assigned.

In an even more subtle manipulation of perspective, Hansen et al. (unpublished) presented videotaped shots of a person solving a jigsaw puzzle or playing chess. The shots either viewed the puzzle or chessboard from the point of view of the actor or from an angle perpendicular to that of the actor. Once again, the observer focusing on the actor attributed greater behavioral causality to him. The observer with the same angle of vision as the actor attributed the game outcome to the situation.

These experiments essentially converted observers into actors by letting them literally see what the actor saw. Could the same result be achieved by a shift in *psychological* perspective? Regan and Totten (1975) showed college women a videotaped "getting-acquainted" discussion, telling half of them to empathize with discussant A (the target person) and to try to imagine how A felt as she engaged in the conversation. The remaining subjects were given no such instructions. Using the same measures that Storms had used, Regan and Totten confirmed their hypothesis that empathy-inducing instructions produce a shift toward attributing behavior causation to the situation. This was especially true in a condition where the subject could see only the target person on the tape, though she could hear the other discussant as well. Thus, the authors agree, the divergence of perspective between actors and observers is founded in more than differences in available information. It derives at least in part, from differences in the ways in which the same information is processed.

Arkin and Duval (1975) have also found that the subjects' attention can be manipulated to affect their causal attributions. Actors in a picture-judging experiment attributed their preferences more to various features of the situation that to themselves (whereas observers were more inclined to attribute the preferences to the actor as a person). However, these differences were reversed when actors felt that they were being videotaped. The self-consciousness induced by the presence of a TV camera apparently shifted the causal assignment from the situation to the self. This is quite in line with the Duval and Wicklund (1972) theory of *objective self-awareness,* which suggests that an actor's causal attributions are a function of whether or not his attention is focused on himself.

FIELD STUDIES

It is quite apparent that something interesting is happening here, and the evidence that perceptual perspective influences causal attribution seems reliable and replicable. But, the reader might demur, is this one of those hothouse laboratory phenomena that is overwhelmed by other variables in the more chaotic and complex natural environment? Obviously, we should not expect to find a quick answer to this question, but a recent study by West et al. (1975) shows the predicted basic pattern of actor-observer differences in a dramatic field experiment simulating the Watergate burglary attempt.

Undergraduate criminology majors at a state university were contacted by a man whom they knew as a local private investigator. He arranged a meeting with each subject at which detailed plans of a business burglary were presented. The subject was asked to participate in breaking into the offices of a local firm to microfilm a set of records. In one condition of the experiment, the subjects were told that a competing local firm had offered $8,000 for a copy of designs prepared by the first firm. The subjects were told that they would be paid $2,000 for their participation in the crime. In other conditions, the experimenter presented himself as working for the Internal Revenue Service and said that the records would allegedly show that the firm was trying to defraud the U.S. government. Of the subjects exposed to the IRS cover story, half were told that there would be no immunity. After an elaborate and convincing presentation of the plan, subjects were asked to come to a final planning meeting. Their assent or refusal was the major dependent measure of the experiment. Once the subjects either agreed or did not agree to participate in the burglary, the experiment was then over and they were given extensive debriefing concerning the deceptions involved and the purpose of the experiment. (Readers interested in the ethical problems of this experiment will find a considered view presented by West and his colleagues, 1975, and comments by Cook, 1975, who tries to place the experiment in the more general framework of ethical problems in psychological research.)

Not surprisingly, whether the subject thought he or she would be granted immunity if caught was a crucial determinant of the frequency of compliance. Nearly half (45 percent) of the subjects in the immunity condition agreed to attend the final planning session. It is somewhat surprising that only 1 out of 20 subjects in the IRS no-immunity condition complied, whereas 4 out of 20 subjects in the reward condition agreed, although this difference was not statistically significant.

In addition to the involved subjects, a large sample of role-playing "observers" were asked to imagine themselves in the situation of the subject. They were given a very detailed description of experimental events in the condition to which they were assigned and asked whether they would or would not comply. About 18 percent of these observer-subjects said that they would have agreed, and there was no difference as a function of the various conditions. Of special interest in the present context, all subjects (actors and role-players) were asked to explain *why* they did or did not agree to move closer toward the burglary. Whether the actors were compliers or noncompliers, they attributed their decision to environmental factors more than to personal dispositions. The role-playing observers, on the other hand, were much more likely to attribute the decision of a complying or a noncomplying actor. Thus the actor-observer divergence in this case is not simply a matter of the actor's being inclined to rationalize his "criminal" behavior by blaming the situation.

In another, less dramatic, field study McGee and Snyder (1975) followed their hunch that there are interesting attributional differences between those who salt before and those who salt after tasting their food. Restaurant patrons were approached after placing themselves in one of these two categories by their salting behavior, and were asked to rate themselves on a series of polar adjectives like realistic-idealistic, cautious-bold, and energetic-relaxed. Each adjective pair was followed by another option, "it depends on the situation." As predicted, the before-tasting salters tended to check more traits as characteristic of themselves than the after-tasting salters, who were much more inclined to check "it depends on the situation." (It should be emphasized that none of the traits made any reference to eating behavior, taste, and so on.) When asked why they salted their food, the two types also diverged: the before-salters explained their behavior in terms of personal characteristics, whereas the after-salters tended to refer to the food.

Snyder and Monson (in press) have also shown that subjects classified as high "self-monitors" expect themselves to behave variably across different hypothetical situations. Low "self-monitors," on the other hand, expect to show greater cross-situational consistency. The authors classified their subjects by means of the score attained on a self-descriptive questionnaire. . . . On another questionnaire, describing different hypothetical situations, low self-monitors expected their behavior and environment in these different situations to be much more stable than did the high self-monitors. There is some evidence, then, that Nisbett's and my proposition must be qualified: *some* actors tend to attribute their actions to themselves, whereas others—more faithful to the proposition—typically make situational attributions.

There are other experimental results which seem more drastically at odds with out proposition. Most of these studies (e.g. Wolosin et al. 1975) involve the perception of behavioral freedom as the main dependent variable. Under some conditions, at least, actors will rate themselves as freer of situational influence than observers would rate them. Thus, if the attributional question is phrased in terms of whether the situation has *required* the actor to behave in a certain way, or if it strongly implies the giving up of his freedom and control, actors will claim greater freedom and responsibility whereas observers will see them as relatively constrained. If the question is more neutral with regard to relinquishing control, however, actors will see their behavioral decisions as responses appropriate to the opportunities and constraints of the environment (cf. Bell 1973).

There is an important philosophical distinction between "reasons" and "causes" (discussed at length by Beck, 1975) that is relevant here. Apparently, under most conditions, actors do not like to think that their behavior is *caused* by either the environment or the personality. At the less deterministic level of *reasons*, however, they are more likely to attribute their behavior to situational rather than to personal factors, thought to some extent we all realize that both factors are involved.

Monson and Snyder (unpublished) raise a caveat that deserves to be mentioned. They point out that most actor-observer studies have been laboratory experiments in which the actor's behavior is, in fact, "controlled" by a situational manipulation. Thus, Nisbett and his colleagues (1973) induced actors to volunteer to lead sightseeing tours by offering to pay them. In such a case, it is not surprising that the actor—who, most would agree, is more sensitive to situational variations—tends to attribute his behavior to the setting. He is right. The monetary incentive was "responsible" for his behavior. On the other hand, Monson and Snyder point out that in the natural environment people are not placed in situations so much as they choose them. Or, as Wachtel (1973) has argued, the situational forces to which actors respond are often of their own making. To the extent that this is true, actors may see their behavior, even though it varies from situation to situation, as dispositionally caused, whereas observers who see only the variation with situations may, if anything, underestimate the dispositional role.

This is an intriguing point, and it has some support in empirical data. For example, experimental evidence supports the fact that actors attribute their choice *among* situations to personal, dispositional factors. Once in the situation, however they see their behavior as controlled by its salient cues (cf. Gurwitz and Panciera 1975). It remains true, however, that even in the natural environment we often find ourselves in situations which we may have long ago selected but which we do not control in any detail. We should be wary of an easy translation from the laboratory to real life, but we should be equally careful not to assume that the laboratory is some irrelevant microcosm.

WIDER IMPLICATIONS OF THE THEORY

I think the balance of the evidence provides rather remarkable support for our "reckless" proposition. To say that actors attribute to situations what observers assign to dispositions is obviously not a law of behavioral science. But it is a useful guiding hypothesis that holds under a surprising range of conditions. The proposition can be subverted by special motivational factors (such as wanting to claim personal responsibility for a success) or by special knowledge on the part of the actor that he selected among many situations the one to which he now exposes himself. In the absence of these special conditions, however, our proposition seems to be robust and quite general. The proposition derives its validity in part from differences in perceptual perspective and in part from differences in the information available to actors and observers.

The major implication of the observer bias in attitude-attribution studies is that such a bias sows the seeds for interpersonal misunderstandings. It seems reasonable to assume that the more two people get to know each other, the more capable they become of taking each other's perspective: there should be a gradual merging of actor-observer orientations. In more transient interactions, however, we may all be victims of a tendency to misread role for personality. If our research has any generalization value at all, it is very likely that we assign to another's personality what we should be viewing as a complex interaction between person and situation. Particular roles within society or within an organization may call for certain patterns of behavior that are then used as a clue to what the role player is really like. What the reviewed research shows is that people make some allowance for the determining significance of roles and other situational pressures, but the allowance undershoots the mark. As a consequence, people who may be arbitrarily assigned to a group role, or assigned to a role on the basis of some initial response to strong environmental pressures, may have attributed to them a set of unwarranted personality characteristics to explain the role-induced behavior. Furthermore, once the group members make these attributions, their behavior toward the target person may constrain him to meet their expectations by "taking on" the personality they have assigned him. This is in the nature of a self-fulfilling prophecy: I expect John to behave in a certain way, and I give off subtle cues to ensure that he does.

In recent years a number of social scientists have pointed to and commented on the tendency in the field of psychology toward overattribution to the person. Mischel (1968, 1969) has essentially argued that there is not enough personal consistency across situations to warrant the personality psychologist's confident attribution of traits and attitudes to individual subjects or clients. Anthropologists D'Andrade (1974) and Shweder (1975) have also criticized individual difference psychology, claiming (with supportive evidence) that personality impressions follow the conceptual logic of the perceiver but do not fit the behavior of the persons being judged. The present research results point in the same direction by at least hinting at the pervasiveness of personal overattribution.

One final question might be raised: If such a pervasive attributional bias does exist, how come we get along as well as we do in the world? And how come the tendency doesn't get corrected by feedback and eventually drop out? One answer to the first question is, Maybe we don't get along so well. The Peter Principle (1969) is a striking example of attributional bias. A man gets promoted to his level of incompetence because the manager doesn't realize that a good performer in one setting may be incompetent in another. There may be other human costs incurred by the person who is misread by others, costs associated with the strain of meeting false expectations.

Perhaps one reason the bias persists uncorrected is that predictions from personality often overlap with or converge on predictions from situations. Much of our social life is more highly structured than we realize. Because we often see particular others in a restricted range of settings, cross-situational consistence is not an issue. Furthermore, we as observers are always a constant in the situation, which gives a further impetus to behavioral consistency. In situations restricted to a standard setting it makes no difference whether the prediction of behavioral continuity is based on attributions about personality or perceptions of situational requirements. There is no opportunity for corrective feedback. It is also the case that social behavior is notoriously ambiguous as feedback, and many an observer can tailor his perceptions of behavior to previously made personality attributions. We are probably all rather adept at maintaining trait inferences in the face of disconfirming behavioral evidence. When practiced by some psychoanalytic writers, the maneuvering can be truly breathtaking.

REFERENCES

Arkin, R. M., & Duval, S. (1975). Focus of attention and causal attributions of actors and observers. *Journal of Experimental Social Psychology, 11,* 427–438.

Aronson, E. (1969). The theory of cognitive dissonance: A current perspective. In Leonard Berkowitz (Ed.), *Advances in experimental social psychology: Vol. 4* (pp. 1–34). New York: Academic Press.

Beck, L. W. (1975). *The actor and the spectator.* New Haven, CT: Yale University Press.

Bell, L. G. (1973). *Influence of need to control on differences in attribution of causality by actors and observers.* Doctoral dissertation, Duke University.

Bem, D. J. (1972). Self-perception theory. In Leonard Berkowitz (Ed.). *Advances in experimental social psychology: Vol. 6* (pp. 2–62). New York: Academic Press.

Cook, S. W. (1975). A comment on the ethical issues involved in West, Gunn, and Chernicky's "Ubiquitous Watergate: An attributional analysis." *Journal of Personality and Social Psychology, 32,* 66–68.

D'Andrade, R. (1974). Memory and the assessment of behavior. In Hubert M. Blalock (Ed.), *Measurement in the social sciences.* Chicago: Aldine.

DUNCKER, K. (1938). Induced motion. In Willis D. Ellis (Ed.), *A sourcebook of Gestalt psychology,* (pp. 161–172). New York: Harcourt, Brace.

DUVAL, S., & WICKLUND, R. A. (1972). *A theory of objective self-awareness.* New York: Academic Press.

GURWITZ, S. B., & PANCIERA, L. (1975). Attributions of freedom by actors and observers. *Journal of Personality and Social Psychology, 32,* 31–39.

HANSEN, R. D., RUHLAND, D. J., & ELLIS, C. L. *Actor versus observer: The effect of perceptual orientation on causal attributions for success and failure.* Unpublished manuscript.

HEIDER, F. (1958). *The psychology of interpersonal relations.* New York: Wiley.

JONES, E. E., & DAVIS, K. E. (1965) A theory of correspondent inferences: From acts to dispositions. In Leonard Berkowitz (Ed.), *Advances in experimental social psychology: Vol. 2* (pp. 219–66). New York: Academic Press.

JONES, E. E. & HARRIS, V. A. (1967). The attribution of attitudes. *Journal of Experimental Social Psychology, 3,* 1–24.

JONES, E. E., KANOUSE, D. E., KELLEY, H. H., NISBETT, R. E., VALINS, S., & WEINER, B. (1972). *Attribution: Perceiving the causes of behavior.* Morristown, NJ: General Learning.

JONES, E. E., & NISBETT, R. E. (1971). *The actor and the observer: Divergent perceptions of the causes of behavior.* New York: General Learning.

JONES E. E., WORCHEL, S., GOETHALS, G. R., & GRUMET, J. (1971). Prior expectancy and behavioral extremity as determinants of attitude attribution. *Journal of Experimental Social Psychology, 7,* 59–80.

KELLEY, H. H. (1967). Attribution theory in social psychology. In David Levine (Ed.), *Nebraska Symposia on Motivation,* (pp. 192–240). Lincoln: University of Nebraska Press.

McGEE, M. G., & SNYDER, M. (1975). Attribution and behavior: Two field studies. *Journal of Personality and Social Psychology, 32,* 185–90.

MISCHEL, W. (1968). *Personality and assessment.* New York: Wiley.

MISCHEL, W. (1969). Continuity and change in personality. *American Psychologist, 24,* 1012–1018.

MONSON, T. C., & SNYDER, M. *Actors, observers and the attribution process: Toward a reconceptualization.* Unpublished manuscript.

NISBETT, R. E., CAPUTO, C., LEGANT, P., & MARACEK, J. (1973). Behavior as seen by the actor and as seen by the observer. *Journal of Personality and Social Psychology, 27,* 154–65.

PETER, L. J., & HULL, R. (1969). *The Peter Principle.* New York: Morrow.

REGAN, D. T., & TOTTEN, J. (1975). Empathy and attribution: Turning observers into actors. *Journal of Personality and Social Psychology, 32,* 850–856.

SNYDER, M., & JONES, E. E. (1974). Attitude attribution when behavior is constrained. *Journal of Experimental Social Psychology, 10,* 585–600.

SNYDER, M., & MONSON, T. C. (in press). Persons, situations, and the control of social behavior. *Journal of Personality and Social Psychology.*

STORMS, M.D. (1973). Videotape and the attribution process: Reversing actors' and observers' points of view. *Journal of Personality and Social Psychology, 27,* 165–75.

SHWEDER, R. A. (1975). How relevant is an individual difference theory of personality? *Journal of Personality, 43,* 455–484.

TAYLOR, S. E., & FISKE, S. T. (1975). Point of view and perceptions of causality. *Journal of Personality and Social Psychology, 32,* 439–445.

WACHTEL, P. (1973). Psychodynamics, behavior therapy, and the implacable experimenter: An inquiry into the consistency of personality. *Journal of Abnormal Psychology, 82,* 324–334.

WALLACH, H. (1959). The perception of motion. *Scientific American, 201,* 56–60.

WEST, S.G., GUNN, S.P., & CHERNICKY, P. (1975). Ubiquitous Watergate: An attributional analysis. *Journal of Personality and Social Psychology, 32,* 55–65.

WOLOSIN, R. J., ESSER, J., & FIND, G. A. (1975). Effects of justification and vocalization on actors' and observers' attributions of freedom. *Journal of Personality, 43,* 612–33.

QUESTIONS

1. What are the two types of attributions that people make to explain behavior? Are the two types mutually exclusive—that is, can people make both types about the same behavior?

2. In general, how do the attributions of actors differ from those of observers? In line with this, should people assign more stable personality traits to themselves or to others?

3. What is the role of salience and perceptual focus on the actor-observer effect? By perspective, does Jones mean just visual perspective?

4. How does the personality trait of self-monitoring influence the attributions of actors? How might it affect the attributions of observers?

5. In a sense, psychologists are the ultimate observers. How might this influence the types of theories that they propose?

Reading 4: Contemporary

Roots of Reason

Bruce Bower

In many ways, the early attribution theorists were the first social cognitivists. Their aim was to un-
derstand how people reason and make sense of their social world. Their theories were not meant
to explain all of human reasoning, just that part that was used when thinking about social prob-
lems. In other words, they believed that the cognitive processes involved in solving social prob-
lems differed from those involved in more abstract problems, such as math and statistics.

Today many social psychologists are challenging the assumption that social cognition (that is,
thinking about social problems) constitutes a subset of the more general cognitive processes
available for nonsocial cognition (for example, math and statistics). In fact, many would like to
turn this assumption completely around and argue that the mind did not develop in order to solve
the complex and often abstract problems faced by humans today, but to solve the immediate and
largely social problems faced by our prehistoric ancestors.

Today social psychologists studying social cognitive process are at the forefront of the quest
to understand human reasoning. For example, years of research on the pitfalls of social thought
are no longer seen as the consequences of applying nonsocial thought processes to social prob-
lems, but as important clues to understanding all of human thought. In the following article Bruce
Bower reviews attempts to understand human problem-solving skills and finds social psychology
at every turn.

❖

Suppose an astrologer offered you this advice: If a person is a Leo, that person is brave. As a confirmed skeptic, you want to debunk such a starry-eyed notion, but how might you go about it?

First, you would probably look for exceptions to the rule by assessing the bravery of people you know whose birthdates qualify them as Leos. Then you might look for Leos among
individuals of unquestioned valor. However, the latter tactic leaves the astrologer's claim un-
scratched, since not all brave people need to possess the same astrological sign. A clutch of
heroic Virgos, for example, could coexist with all those courageous Leos.

What's worse, you—like all people who attempt to solve an experimental version of this
task—probably fail to consider the astrological credentials of cowards. A card-carrying Leo
who cringes at his own shadow would clearly violate the astrologer's rule. Now consider a more
down-to-earth problem. Imagine yourself as a bartender who can legally serve alcohol only to
people age 21 or older. At your bar sit four customers, each quaffing a beverage. You know that

Source: Bower, B. (1994, January 29). Roots of reason. *Science News, 145,* 72–75.

one nurses a beer, another sips a soda, and an adult and a teenager make up the rest of the group. What do you need to know to determine whether your liquor license is in jeopardy?

In contrast to the astrologer's challenge, about three-quarters of those who ponder this problem in experiments correctly realize that the bartender must find out the beer drinker's age and what the teenager has in his glass.

The astrologer and bartender quandaries share an underlying structure summarized as "if p (in these cases, a Leo or a liquor drinker), then q (brave or at least 21 years old, respectively)." Yet over the past decade, an increasing number of studies has charted large differences in the ease with which people resolve various "if-then" questions. These results have inspired competing scientific reassessments of how people reason and solve problems. Moreover, related research has fueled an escalating debate over the nature of routine decision making, in which we often base judgments on ambiguous and incomplete bits of information.

One group of researchers argues that millions of years of evolution have endowed humans with a multitude of "reasoning instincts" that automatically coordinate the way we think about important day-to-day problems that echo those faced repeatedly by our Stone Age ancestors. In their view, people generally deal best with such challenges, which include finding food and mates, assessing threats, and exchanging goods and services. Much recent research has focused on a reasoning instinct that may aid in identifying individuals who cheat on social obligations, such as underage drinkers.

Moreover, the same scientists assert that humans rely on evolved brain mechanisms to estimate the frequency with which pairs of events in our immediate surroundings occur together. Frequency judgments of this sort pave the way for relatively accurate inductions, or inferences generated from the particulars of daily life. According to this theory, decisions occur so fluidly that they get taken for granted. Take, for example the jogger who—based on many previous encounters—intuitively knows which dogs to avoid during a run. Other investigators agree that people reason in specialized ways depending on what they think about and the context in which thinking occurs. But they argue that various situations evoke sets of rules, called "pragmatic reasoning schemas," which cover a far broader range than, say, a mechanism for detecting cheaters. One proposed reasoning schema guides inferences about whether a specific event or action causes another; a second orchestrates reasoning about permitted behavior in different contexts, which includes cheater detection; and a third handles thinking about obligation in various situations.

Some scientists, however, see no need to invoke instincts or rules that specialize in solving particular kinds of problems. Instead they theorize that individuals make specific inferences from rough guidelines, or reason deductively, by constructing "mental models" that keep track of conclusions compatible with the information at hand and any relevant background knowledge. The mental model that provides the best fit between the premises of a problem and an acceptable conclusion wins out in this approach.

In another bow to mental models, influential studies conducted over the past 20 years have focused on general principles that help us patch together decisions out of incomplete or ambiguous threads of information. Investigators of these judgmental shortcuts, or "heuristics," view the human mind as a good, yet often fallible, reasoning device that falls prey to certain "cognitive illusions," just as our senses sometimes produce perceptual illusions. From this perspective, people apply mental heuristics to single problems of concern and make little note of how frequently two events are associated with each other.

The evolutionary approach to reason sparks much passion and polemic. Two researchers at the University of California, Santa Barbara—Leda Cosmides, a psychologist, and John Tooby, an anthropologist—have for the past decade applied Charles Darwin's theory of natural selection to their proposed revision of how scientists conceptualize human thinking. Cosmides and Tooby reject the widespread opinion among psychologists that the human brain harbors at most a few flexible mechanisms for reasoning about all sorts of problems and situations.

In fact, since the 17th century, a number of influential philosophers have proposed that people achieve rational conclusions by invoking abstract principles, or a "universal calculus" of logic embedded in the mind.

The Santa Barbara scientists instead take inspiration from early experimental psychologists such as William James, who proposed more than 100 years ago that human intelligence surpasses that of other animals because our minds include a constellation of "faculties," or instincts," that directs learning, reasoning, and behavior.

"The human mind contains specialized mechanisms that evolved to reason about important problems posed by the social world of our ancestors," Cosmides contends. "The mind is probably more like a Swiss army knife than an all-purpose blade. It's saturated with mechanisms that solve adaptive problems well."

According to this approach, we reason most poorly when faced with problems that our evolutionary forebears never worried about, such as demonstrating that not all people born under the sign of Leo are brave. Psychologists have often tested responses to evolutionarily novel problems, a tactic that makes people look illogical and irrational, the two researchers maintain.

Cosmides and Tooby summarize their work on reasoning about social exchange in the 1992 book *The Adapted Mind* (J. H. Barkow, L. Cosmides, and J. Tooby, editors, Oxford University Press).

Evolutionary biologists refer to social exchange as "reciprocal altruism," a fancy phrase for "I'll scratch your back if you scratch mine." Mathematical analyses of reciprocal altruism have employed the Prisoner's Dilemma, in which two players receive varying rewards and punishments for either cooperating with each other or acting selfishly. Success at this task hinges on the rapid detection of partners who fail to return favors (*Science News*: 7/3/93, p. 6).

To test whether people make special types of inferences to ferret out social cheaters, Cosmides and Tooby turned to the Wason test, a reasoning experiment introduced in 1966 by Peter Wason, a psychologist at University College, London. Volunteers administered a Wason test check the veracity of a hypothesis posed in the form of "if p, then q." Each participant views four cards that, respectively, show cases corresponding to p, not-p, q, and not-q. They are told that each card contains values for the corresponding part of the hypothesis on its opposite side.

Standard logic dictates that the rule is violated when p is true but q is false. Thus, a volunteer should turn over p and not-q (which might have p on its back).

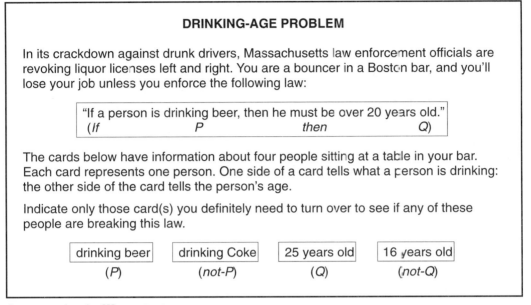

An example of a Wason test.

For instance, one version of the Wason test asks for verification of the rule, "If a card has a D on one side, then it must have a 3 on the other side." Volunteers view four cards displaying D, F, 3, and 7, respectively. To determine if the rule has been violated, they must turn over D (corresponding to *p*) and 7 (corresponding to not-*q*).

Although Wason expected people to excel at picking out breaches of arbitrary if-then rules, he and many other researchers found that fewer than one-quarter of those tested offer logically correct answers. Most commonly, participants fail to choose the not-*q* card, a misstep comparable to omitting cowards from an evaluation of the claim that all Leos exhibit bravery.

Yet people detect violations of if-then rules much more easily and accurately if the situation calls for enforcement of a social contract, exemplified by "If you take the benefit then you pay the cost," Cosmides and Tooby argue. In these instances, finding people who cheat on the contract assumes paramount importance. Even if such cheating occurs in unfamiliar or bizarre situations, from 70 percent to 90 percent of volunteers accurately pick out cheaters on a Wason test, according to the researchers.

For instance, in experiments Cosmides and Tooby administered to Stanford University undergraduates, one Wason test described a fictitious tribe in which a chief called Big Kiku decrees that "If you get a tattoo on your face, then I'll give you a cassava root." Other tests presented arbitrary rules devoid of any social-exchange implications such as "If you eat duiker meat, then you have found an ostrich eggshell."

About three-quarters of the students turned over the correct cards to determine whether Big Kiku lived up to his word. But only about one-quarter succeeded in figuring out whether arbitrary rules had been violated.

Elaboration of these findings comes from a study conducted by Gerd Gigerenzer of the University of Chicago and Klaus Hug of the University of Salzburg in Austria. Logical responses on Wason tests involving social contracts vary with one's perspective on cheating, Gigerenzer and Hug report in the May 1992 *Cognition*.

In one trial, college students search for cheaters on the following social contract: "If an employee works on the weekend, then that person gets a day off during the week." They could turn over cards bearing the statements "worked on the weekend," "did not work on the weekend," "did get a day off," and "did not get a day off." Some participants adopted the perspective of the employer, while others took an employee's view of the situation.

When looking for cheats, most "employees" worried about whether a comrade had worked on the weekend but did not get a day off; thus, they turned over cards corresponding to p ("worked on the weekend") and not-q ("did not get a day off"), the logically correct answer to a typical Wason test. But "employers" looked for whether an employee cheated by taking a weekday off in spite of not working on the weekend; thus, they most often looked under cards corresponding to not-p ("did not work on the weekend") and q ("did get a day off"), the most logical choices given their perspective.

Another study employing Wason tests, published in the August 1993 *Cognition,* also finds that adults more often solve problems that link a cost to a benefit. But one's perspective on cheating actually adds little to this effect, argue Richard D. Platt and Richard A. Griggs, both psychologists at the University of Florida in Gainesville. Good reasoning occurs most often when volunteers receive clear statements about a rule violation, such as "If you take the benefit you *must pay* the cost," they conclude.

In Gigerenzer and Hug's study, students may have tried to figure out whether the rule about the benefits of weekend work was correct or not rather than whether a violation of the rule had occurred, the Florida researchers maintain.

Whatever the case, a specific mental mechanism keeps tabs on social contracts and stays alert for cheats, Cosmides contends.

Further Wason tests devised by the Santa Barbara researchers provide preliminary support for two additional reasoning instincts. One regulates precautions taken in hazardous situations, and the other assesses aggressive threats, such as bluffs and double crosses.

A universal network of reasoning instincts governs social exchange, Cosmides and Tooby theorize; different parts of the network emerge from one situation to another within a culture, as well as between cultures.

Keith J. Holyoak and Patricia W. Cheng, both psychologists at the University of California, Los Angeles, view a reasoning mechanism devoted only to the costs and benefits of social contracts as far too narrow. Instead, they contend, a general set of "permission schemas," or rules, allows people to assess whether others conform to all sorts of contractual agreements, of which paying the costs for particular benefits makes up only a small part.

In permission schemas, satisfaction of a precondition bestows the right to take a regulated action. Consider the drinking-age rule. The permission schema focuses attention on the case in which the action occurs (check alcohol drinkers to make sure they meet the age precondition) and the case in which the precondition is not met (make sure teenagers are not drinking alcohol). These cases correspond to p and not-q cards on a Wason test—the logically correct responses.

Moreover, a set of "obligation schemas" allows individuals to judge situations in which satisfaction of a precondition imposes a duty to take a certain action, according to the UCLA investigators. For instance, participants typically perform well on Wason tests that describe an obligation for those who treat AIDS patients: "If you clean up spilled blood, then you must wear rubber gloves." The test mentions no specific benefit for which one must pay a cost, Cheng notes.

Permission and obligation schemas work in complementary ways that can explain Gigerenzer and Hug's observation of perspective effects on reasoning, Cheng and Holyoak maintain. For the rule "If an employee works on the weekend, then that person gets a day off during the week," employees concentrate on the employer's duty following weekend work and their own rights to a day off, whereas employers focus on employees' duty to meet weekend-work obligation and the bosses' right to deny a day off to those who hadn't done so. This leads to contrasting responses on a Wason test, the UCLA researchers hold.

Unconscious reasoning instincts favored by Cosmides and Tooby cannot explain the "explicit," or conscious, strategies that foster human creativity, the ability to imagine alternative solutions, and planning for the future, Holyoak adds. Explicit reasoning often deals with problems far removed from our evolutionary past, he asserts. Its purpose appears to revolve around "helping us adapt the environment to us."

Evolved reasoning instincts allow us to think about the world in ways that give rise to explicit reasoning, Cosmides responds.

As this debate proceeds, some researchers simply reject the need for content-specific rules in favor of more flexible "mental models" that help individuals choose the best available solution to Wason tests or other reasoning tasks.

Philip N. Johnson-Laird, a psychologist at Princeton University, has for more than a decade promoted mental models as keys to deductive reasoning.

His latest research, conducted with Princeton colleague Malcolm I. Bauer and published in the November 1993 *Psychological Science*, finds that certain types of diagrams help people track the various elements that make up a complex problem and, in turn, to reason about that problem more successfully.

In one test, 24 college students grappled with the following mind-bender:

Raphael is in Tacoma or Julia is in Atlanta, or both.

Julia is in Atlanta or Paul is in Philadelphia, or both.

What follows?

Not surprisingly, fewer than half of the students deduced a valid conclusion, such as "Julia is in Atlanta, or both Raphael is in Tacoma and Paul is in Philadelphia."

Yet three-quarters of another group of 24 students solved the same problem when the researchers supplied a diagram that showed shapes corresponding to Julia and her cohorts, each of which could fit into a similarly shaped slot corresponding to the appropriate city. These reasoners also reached their conclusions more quickly than those who simply read about the potential whereabouts of the puzzle's far-flung protagonists.

Visual images apparently reduce the amount of verbal information that reasoners must keep track of and speed up the process of inference, Johnson-Laird argues.

Enigmatic puzzles such as that above may seem bizarre, but they magnify a common problem in reasoning, he adds: As the number of possibilities suggested by a problem increases, so does confusion in reasoners. In high-pressure situations, this can lead to disastrous decisions. For instance, Johnson-Laird points out, just prior to malfunctions at Three Mile Island, operators concluded that a leak caused the high temperature at a relief valve and overlooked the possibility that the valve was struck open.

Reasoning aids that, like Johnson-Laird's mental models, offer a framework for problem solving influence much research on how people reach routine decisions. Although these handy mental shortcuts prove indispensable for making sense of often confusion snippets of information, they also lead judgments astray in a number of situations, according to many studies.

"People use mental approximations to understand an uncertain world," argues Amos Tversky, a psychologist at Stanford University. "As a result, we make certain types of errors in judgment."

In a 1974 *Science* article, Tversky and psychologist Daniel Kahneman of the University of California, Berkeley, described 11 "cognitive biases" produced by mental heuristics. A cascade of related research by Tversky, Kahneman, and others soon followed.

Gigerenzer, joined by Cosmides and Tooby, now challenges the widespread emphasis on reasoning shortcuts and their shortcomings. Gigerenzer, building on a theory proposed by German psychologist Egon Brunswick in the 1960s, views the human brain as an "intuitive statistician" immersed in unconscious calculations of the frequency with which pairs of phenomena occur together in one's immediate surroundings.

"Evolution has tuned the way we think to frequencies of co-occurrences, as with the hunter who remembers the area where he has had the most success killing game," Gigerenzer asserts. "When we take frequency thinking into account, we can make cognitive biases disappear."

This dispute reflects a division that has existed in statistics and probability theory for more than 300 years. Bayesians—named for 18th century British mathematician Thomas Bayes—consider probability a measure of subjective certainty about single events; for instance, "I'm 70 percent certain that my favorite baseball team will win today." In contrast, frequentists view probability as the long-term recurrence of events; say, "My favorite baseball team won 7 out of its last 10 games when today's pitcher started the game."

People reason cognitive biases right out of existence when faced with frequentist rather than Bayesian versions of the same problem, Gigerenzer contends.

Exhibit number one: the "conjunction fallacy." In one test conducted by Tversky and Kahneman, volunteers read about a single, outspoken woman described as a former philosophy major who as a student took part in antinuclear protests and still holds liberal political views. Participants almost always consider it more probable that the woman is both a bank teller and an activist in the feminist movement than that the woman is simply a bank teller. But the probability of a conjunction of the two circumstances cannot exceed the probability of one of those circumstances occurring by itself. Thus, the woman more likely works at the bank—period.

Yet according to Gigerenzer, about three out of four people correctly solve this problem when they read about the woman and respond to a frequentist question: How many of 100 people who fit this description are bank tellers, and how many are bank tellers and active in the feminist movement?

In the October 1991 *Psychological Review,* Gigerenzer also takes on the "overconfidence bias." When asked a general-knowledge question, such as "Which city has more inhabitants, Hyderabad or Islamabad?" groups of volunteers tend to think they know the answer more often than they actually do. Gigerenzer and his colleagues find that after college students answer a series of such questions, they accurately estimate their total number of correct responses, even though they feel overconfident about answers to particular queries.

And in a study slated to appear in *Cognition,* Cosmides and Tooby confront a cognitive bias known as the "base-rate fallacy." As an illustration, they cite a 1978 study in which 60 staff and students at Harvard Medical School attempted to solve this problem: "If a test to detect a disease whose prevalences is 1/1,000 has a false positive rate of 5%, what is the chance that a person found to have a positive result actually has the disease, assuming you know nothing about the person's symptoms or signs?"

Nearly half the sample estimated this probability as 95 percent; only 11 gave the correct response of 2 percent. Most participants neglected the base rate of the disease (it strikes 1 in 1,000 people) and formed a judgment solely from the characteristics of the test.

Cosmoses and Tooby rephrased the medical problem in frequentist terms for several groups of college students. After stating the base rate of the disease, their description says that "out of every 1,000 people who are perfectly healthy, 50 of them test positive for the disease." For a random group of 1,000 people, "how many who test positive for the disease will actually have the disease?"

This version yielded a correct response from three out of four participants, the psychologists contend.

Overall, the data suggest that people automatically compute frequencies of events that occur together time and again in their environments, Gigerenzer holds. Given limited knowledge about a specific problem and a restricted amount of attention to devote to its solution, frequency estimates provide a foundation for planning and decision making.

Tversky and Kahneman take strong exception to Gigerenzer's critique. They note that their research has long distinguished between an "inside" focus on the details of a particular problem and an "outside" view of long-term frequencies in a reference class of related problems. Although the latter information greatly improves the quality of judgments, people generally ignore it in favor of an inside perspective, Tversky and Kahneman maintain.

An example of this tendency appears in the November 1993 *Psychological Science*. Robyn M. Dawes, a psychologist at Carnegie Mellon University in Pittsburgh, and his co-workers asked college students to provide estimates of the frequency with which their peers endorsed certain personality characteristics alone and in combinations, such as "I enjoy doing things which challenge me" and "I spend a good deal of my time just having fun."

Volunteers tended to ignore their base-rate predictions of how often students cited single characteristics and provided inflated estimates of the proportion of their peers reporting pairs of personality features, Dawes' team concludes.

"I'm sympathetic with the frequentist approach to statistics, but not to life," Tversky says. "Single-case thinking is far more common, and we see about as many errors in frequency judgments as in single-case judgments."

In one study of faulty thinking about frequencies, he notes, volunteers incorrectly asserted that more words exist that end in the letters "ing" than contain "n" as their next-to-last letter.

Mistakes inevitably occur when dealing with frequencies, Gigerenzer acknowledges. But fewer appear, he contends, if a person has experienced a representative sample of relevant co-occurrences in the environment (such as the approximate size of various cities), as opposed to less salient cues (such as the number of words harboring certain letter combinations).

The debate over single-case and frequency thinking appears destined to take some unusual turns. In an unpublished study of how people reason about causes and effects, UCLA's Patricia Cheng—a staunch critic of reasoning instincts proposed by Cosmides and Tooby—elicits support for their frequentist position.

Cheng and UCLA colleague Angela Fratianne offered volunteers feedback as they attempted to figure out a cause-effect relationship, such as whether any of three hypothetical chemicals in a fertilizer caused a fungus to grow on plant roots. Those showing data outlining the frequency of fungus growth in the absence of a particular chemical (the effect's base rate), as well the frequency in the presence of the same substance, more easily and accurately identified the fungus-fomenting culprits.

"It's plausible that people [unconsciously] use information about the frequency of an effect in the absence of a cause to test causal hypotheses," Cheng contends.

Keith Holyoak, Cheng's UCLA collaborator, downplays the role of frequency computations in reasoning, although he sees a place for mental heuristics. More important, he argues, people achieve inductive insights by relying on clusters of related rules or principles that make sense of available information in flexible ways. For example, "If it's four-legged, furry, and has a wet nose, it's a dog"; but "If it also has black rings around its eyes and emerges from the woods, it's a raccoon."

A series of computer simulations supporting this theory appears in the 1986 book co-authored by Holyoak, *Induction: Processes of Inference, Learning, and Discovery* (J. H. Holland et al., MIT Press).

One conclusion, articulated by Amos Tversky, resonates among all researchers exploring the roots of reason. "At this point, nobody has a complete theory of judgment and decision making."

QUESTIONS

1. Explain the concepts of heuristics and of mental illusions. How does the evolutionary approach explain the development of heuristics, given that they often lead to mental illusions?

2. How does the view of rational thought differ in the two knife analogies: the mind as an all-purpose blade, and the mind as a Swiss army knife? Which analogy would William James, the father of American psychology, prefer?

3. Why do people have more difficulty solving the astrology problem than the bartender problem? Do both apply the same logical rule? Which model of reason (that is, which knife analogy) does this phenomenon support?

4. In general, are people better at solving frequency or probability problems? List three biases that commonly result when people attempt to solve probability problems.

5. According to social psychologists Tversky and Kahneman, how good are people at correctly using frequency reasoning in real life?

❖ CHAPTER 3 ❖

PREJUDICE, DISCRIMINATION, AND STEREOTYPES: PERCEIVING AND UNDERSTANDING GROUPS

Reading 5: Classic

The Robber's Cave Experiment: Intergroup Conflict and Cooperation

Muzafer Sherif, O. J. Harvey, B. Jack White, William E. Hood, and Carolyn W. Sherif

The hallmark of social psychology, what separates it from other areas of psychology, is a focus on social groups. For example, some of the earliest research in social psychology investigated the dynamics of individuals when interacting with other group members. On a different level of analysis, social psychologists are also concerned with how entire groups behave when interacting with other groups. Moving to this broader level of analysis enables social psychologists to study intergroup conflict.

The study of intergroup conflict is a complicated matter. Just as the dynamics within two groups are never exactly alike, the dynamics between two groups are also never exactly alike. Not satisfied with simply describing conflict between two particular groups, social psychologist Muzafer Sherif wanted to find the universals of intergroup conflict. To this end, he decided to create two new groups and carefully observe the dynamics of each: first in isolation of each other, later in situations designed to foster hostility between the groups, and finally in situations designed to foster cooperation and to eliminate hostility between the groups. Sherif hoped the results would be the discovery of universal principles for fostering better intergroup relations.

Most social psychologists today believe that Sherif was successful. In the following reading, excerpted from his seminal book, Sherif provides an overview of his now famous Robber's Cave study outlining the concept of superordinate goals and how they can be used to reduce tension between any two antagonistic groups.

❖

A. THE PRESENT APPROACH

The word "group" in the phrase "intergroup relations" is not a superfluous label. If our claim is the study of relations between two or more groups or the investigation of intergroup

Source: Sherif, M., Harvey, O. J., White, B. J., Hood, W. E., & Sherif, C. W. (1961). *The Robber's Cave experiment: Intergroup conflict and cooperation.* Norman: University of Oklahoma Book Exchange.

attitudes, we have to bring into the picture the properties of the groups and the consequences of membership for the individuals in question. Otherwise, whatever we may be studying, we are not, properly speaking, studying intergroup problems.

Accordingly, our first concern was an adequate conception of the key word "group" and clarification of the implications of an individual's membership in groups. A definition of the concept improvised just for the sake of research convenience does not carry us far if we are interested in the validity of our conclusions. The actual properties of groups which brought them to the foreground in the study of serious human problems have to be spelled out.

The task of defining groups and intergroup relations can be carried out only through an *interdisciplinary approach*. Problems pertaining to groups and their relations are not studied by psychologists alone. They are studied on various levels of analysis by men in different social sciences. In the extensive literature on relations within and between small groups, we found crucial leads for a realistic conception of groups and their relations.

Abstracting the recurrent properties of actual groups, we attained a definition applicable to small groups of any description. A *group* is a social unit which consists of a number of individuals who, at a given time, stand in more or less definite interdependent status and role relationships with one another, and which explicitly or implicitly possesses a set of norms or values regulating the behavior of the individual members, at least in matters of consequence to the group.

Intergroup relations refer to relations between groups thus defined. Intergroup attitudes (such as prejudice) and intergroup behavior (such as discriminatory practice) refer to the attitudes and the behavior manifested by members of groups collectively or individually. The characteristic of an intergroup attitude or an intergroup behavior is that it is related to the individual's membership in a group. In research the relationship between a given attitude and facts pertaining to the individual's role relative to the groups in question has to be made explicit.

Unrepresentative intergroup attitudes and behavior are, to be sure, important psychological facts. But attitude and behavior unrepresentative of a group do not constitute the focal problem of intergroup relations, nor are they the cases which make the study of intergroup relations crucial in human affairs. The central problem of intergroup relations is not primarily the problem of *deviate behavior*.

In shaping the reciprocal attitudes of members of two groups toward one another, the limiting determinant is the nature of functional relations between the groups. The groups in question may be competing to attain some goal or some vital prize so that the success of one group necessarily means the failure of the other. One group may have claims on another group in the way of managing, controlling or exploiting them, in the way of taking over their actual or assumed rights or possessions. On the other hand, groups may have complementary goals, such that each may attain its goal without hindrance to the achievement of the other and even aiding this achievement.

Even though the nature of relations between groups is the limiting condition, various other factors have to be brought into the picture for an adequate accounting of the resulting intergroup trends and intergroup products (such as norms for positive or negative treatment of the other group, stereotypes of one's own group and the other group, etc.). Among these factors are the kind of leadership, the degree of solidarity, and the kind of norms prevailing within each group. Reciprocal intergroup appraisals of their relative strengths and resources, and the intellectual level attained in assessing their worth and rights in relation to others, need special mention among these factors. The frustrations, deprivations and the gratifications in the life histories of the individual members also have to be considered.

Theories of intergroup relations which posit single factors (such as the kind of leadership, national character, or individual frustrations) as sovereign determinants of intergroup conflict or harmony have, at best, explained only selectively chosen cases.

Of course leadership counts in shaping intergroup behavior; the prevailing norms of social distance count; so do the structure and practices within the groups, and so do the personal frustrations of individual members. But none of these singly determines the trend of intergroup behavior at a given time. They all contribute to the structuring of intergroup behavior, but with different relative weights at different times. Intergroup behavior at a given time can be explained only in terms of the entire frame of reference in which all these various factors function interdependently. This approach, here stated briefly, constituted the starting point of our experiments on intergroup relations. The approach was elaborated fully in out previous work, *Groups in Harmony and Tension*.

The relative weights of various factors contributing to intergroup trends and practices are not fixed quantities. Their relative importance varies according to the particular set of conditions prevailing at the time. For example, in more or less closed, homogeneous or highly organized groups, and in times of greater stability and little change, the prevailing social distance scale and established practices toward out-group which have been standardized in the past for group members will have greater weight in determining the intergroup behavior of individual members. But when groups are in greater functional interdependence with each other and during periods of transition and flux, other factors contribute more heavily. In these latter cases, there is a greater discrepancy between attitude and intergroup behavior in different situations, attributable to situational factors, as insistently noted by some leading investigators in this area of research. Alliances and combinations among groups which seem strange bedfellows are not infrequent in the present world of flux and tension.

Because of their influence in social psychology today, two other approaches to intergroup behavior deserve explicit mention. A brief discussion of them will help clarify the conception of the experiment reported in this book.

One of these approaches advances frustration suffered in the life history of the individual as the main causal factor and constructs a whole explanatory edifice for intergroup aggression on this basis. Certainly aggression is *one* of the possible consequences of frustration experienced by the individual. But, in order that individual frustration may appreciably affect the course of intergroup trends and be conducive to standardization of negative attitudes toward an out-group, the frustration has to be shared by other group members and perceived *as an issue* in group interaction. Whether interaction focuses on matters within a group or between groups, group trends and attitudes of members are not crystallized from thin air. The problem of intergroup behavior, we repeat, is not primarily the problem of the behavior of one or a few deviate individuals. The realistic contribution of frustration as a factor can be studied only within the framework of in-group and intergroup relations.

The other important approach to intergroup relations concentrates primarily on processes within the groups in question. It is assumed that measures introduced to increase cooperativeness and harmony *within* the groups will be conducive to cooperativeness and harmony in intergroup relations. This assumption amounts to extrapolating the properties of in-group relations to intergroup relations, as if in-group norms and practices were commodities easily transferable. Probably, when friendly relations already prevail between groups, cooperative and harmonious in-group relations do contribute to solutions of joint problems among groups. However there are numerous cases showing that in-group cooperativeness and harmony may contribute effectively to intergroup competitiveness and conflict when interaction between groups is negative and incompatible.

The important generalization to be drawn is that the properties of intergroup relations cannot be extrapolated either (1) from individual experiences and behavior or (2) from the properties of interaction within groups. The limiting factor bounding intergroup attitudes and behavior is the nature of relations between groups. Demonstration of these generalizations has been one of the primary objectives of our experiment.

B. THE EXPERIMENT

The Design in Successive Stages

Experimental Formation of Groups. In order to deal with the essential characteristics of intergroup relations, one prerequisite was the production of two distinct groups, each with a definite hierarchical structure and a set of norms. The formation of groups whose natural histories could thus be ascertained has decided advantage for experimental control and exclusion of other influences. Accordingly, *Stage 1* of the experiment was devoted to the formation of autonomous groups under specified conditions. A major precaution during this initial stage was that group formation proceed independently in each group without contacts between them. This separation was necessary to insure that the specified conditions introduced, and not intergroup relations, were the determining factors in group formation. Independent formation of distinct groups permitted conclusions to be drawn later from observations on the effects of intergroup encounters and engagements upon the group structure.

The distinctive features of our study are Stages 2 and 3 pertaining to intergroup relations. The main objective of the study was to find effective measures for reducing friction between groups and to discover realistic steps toward harmonious relations between them. If we had attempted to get two groups to cooperate without first bringing about a state of friction between them, there would have been no serious problem to be solved. The great task that social scientists, practitioners and policy-makers face today is the reduction of prevailing intergroup frictions.

Intergroup Conflict. After formation of definite in-groups, we introduced a period of intergroup relations as *Stage 2* of the experiment. During this stage, the two experimentally formed groups came into contact under conditions which were competitive, so that the victory of one group meant loss for the other. This series of encounters was conducive to successive frustrations whose causes were experienced as coming from the other group.

Only after an unmistakable state of friction between the two groups was manifested in hostile acts and derogatory stereotypes was the stage of reducing intergroup friction introduced.

Reduction of Intergroup Hostility. Various measures could have been tried in this experimental attempt toward the reduction of intergroup friction. One possible measure is the introduction of a "common enemy." Exposed to a common enemy, groups may join hands to do away with the common threat. This measure was not resorted to because it implies intergroup conflict on a larger scale.

Another possible approach is through dissemination of specific information designed to correct prevailing group stereotypes. This measure was not seriously considered because of the large body of research showing that discrete information, unrelated to central concerns of a group, is relatively ineffective in changing attitudes. Stereotypes crystallized during the eventful course of competition and conflict with the out-group are usually more real in the experience of the group members than bits of information handed down to them.

The alternative of channeling competition for highly valued rewards and prizes along individualized directions may be effective in reducing intergroup friction by breaking down group action to individual action. This measure may be practicable for small groups and is attempted at times by supervisors in classroom and recreational situations. However frictions and conflicts of significant consequence in life and the problem of their resolution are in terms of group demarcations and alignments.

The initial phase of *Stage 3* was devoted to testing the effects of intergroup contact involving close physical proximity in activities that were satisfying in themselves, such as eating meals or seeing a movie. This initial phase was introduced with the objective of clarifying the blanket term "contact" as applied to intergroup relations.

The alternative chosen as the most effective measure for reducing intergroup friction was the introduction of a series of *superordinate goals,* in line with the hypothesis stated prior to the experiment. Superordinate goals are goals of high appeal value for both groups, which cannot be ignored by the groups in question, but whose attainment is beyond the resources and efforts of any one group alone.

Research Methods

The methods used in this experiment to bring about the formation and subsequent change of attitude and behavior in directions predicted by the hypotheses were neither lecture method nor discussion method. Instead, the procedure was to place the members of respective groups in demanding problem situations, the specifications of which met the criteria established for the experimental state in question. The problem situations concerned activities, objects or materials which we knew, on the basis of the expressed preferences of the individuals or the state of their organisms, were highly appealing to them at the time. Facing a problem situation which is immediate, which must be attended to, which embodies a goal that cannot be ignored, group members do initiate discussion, do plan, do make decisions and do carry through the plans by word and deed until the objective is achieved. In this process, the discussion becomes *their* discussion, the plan becomes *their* plan, the decision becomes *their* decision, and the action becomes *their* action. In this process, discussion has its place, planning has its place, action has its place and when occasion arises, lecture has its place, too. The sequence of these related activities need not be the same in all cases. In many instances, we observed two or three of them carried on simultaneously.

Thus, problem situations introduced in *Stage 1* embodied goals of immediate appeal value to all members within a group, and the goals required their concerted activity or coordinated division of labor for attainment. The problem situations of *Stage 2* offered goals whose attainment by one group necessarily meant failure for the other group. Intergroup conflict was generated in the course of such engagements. The main part of *Stage 3* consisted of introducing a series of situations conducive to superordinate goals requiring joint action by both groups towards common ends. In every stage, changes in attitudes and action were not attempted through a single problem situation, but through the cumulative effect of a series of varied activities which, during each stage, had the distinctive characteristics summarized here.

All problem situations were introduced in a naturalistic setting and were in harmony with activities usually carried out in such a setting. The individuals participating in the study were not aware that each step was especially designed to study a particular phase of group relations. Once the problem situation was introduced under specified conditions and at a specified time, the initiative, discussion and planning were theirs, of course within bounds insuring health, security and well-being of the individuals studied.

Every effort was made that the activities and the flow of interaction in these activities appear natural to the subjects. Yet these activities and the interaction in them were *experimental:* Problem situations were chosen for each stage according to specified criteria . . . and were introduced under specified conditions (including the place, terrain, time, arrangement of facilities, stimulus materials available, etc.) The choice of an isolated site made it possible to restrict interaction situations and the individuals involved in them to those appropriate during each experimental stage.

Techniques of data collection were also determined by the theoretical approach and methodological considerations briefly stated above. The subjects were not aware that behavioral trends reflecting favorable or unfavorable, friendly or hostile intergroup attitudes were being studied. Knowing that one is under constant observation cannot help becoming a factor in structuring experience and behavior, particularly when the observation is related to our status concerns, our acceptance or rejection by others, our good or bad intentions toward others.

To the subjects, the participant observers appeared to be personnel of a usual camp situation. They were introduced as senior counselors. In this capacity they were close to their respective groups in a continuing way. True to their announced roles, the participant observers jotted down relevant observations out of the subjects' sight, and then expanded their notes later each day.

When the technique of observation is adapted to the flow of interaction, there is danger of being selective in the choice of events to be recorded. The effective remedy against possible selectivity is using a *combination of methods* to check finding obtained with one method against those obtained by other methods.

The events which revealed stabilization and shifts in statuses, and crystallization of negative and then positive intergroup attitudes, were recurrent and so striking that one could not help observing them. However, in testing our main hypotheses, we supplemented the observational method with sociometric and laboratory-like methods. One distinctive feature of this study was introducing, at choice points, laboratory-like techniques to assess emerging attitudes through indirect, yet precise indices. Such laboratory-like assessment of attitudes is based on the finding that under relevant conditions, simple judgments or perceptions reflect major concerns, attitudes and other motives of man.

Reliability of observation and observer ratings was checked by comparing those of the participant observer with independent observations by others in crucial test situations. One such test situation illustrates the technique. When the status hierarchy in one group became stabilized toward the end of Stage 1, a problem situation was introduced which, like other problem situations of this stage, required initiative and coordination of the membership. A staff member who was not with the group regularly and who had not rated the status positions from day to day observed the group interaction in this situation. On this basis he made the independent ratings of the status hierarchy, which were significantly correlated with those of the participant observer of that group.

C. MAIN CONCLUSIONS

Individual Characteristics and Intergroup Behavior

In this experiment, the rigorous criteria and painstaking procedures for selecting subjects ruled out explanations of hostile or friendly intergroup attitudes in terms of differences in socioeconomic, ethnic, religious, or family backgrounds. Similarly, the criteria for subject selection insured against explanations on the basis of unusual individual frustrations, failures, maladjustment or instability.

The subjects came from families who were established residents of the same city. They were stable families composed of natural parents and siblings. No subjects came from broken homes. Their religious affiliations were similar. They were from the middle socioeconomic class. They were of the same chronological and educational level. They had all made satisfactory progress academically; none had failed in school. In school and neighborhood, their social adjustment was above average. None was a behavior problem in home, neighborhood or school. In short, they were normal, healthy, socially well-adjusted boys who came from families with the same or closely similar socioeconomic, ethnic, and religious backgrounds.

Since none of the individuals was personally acquainted with others prior to the experiment, pre-existing positive or negative interpersonal relations did not enter into the rise of intergroup attitudes.

The conclusion that explanations of the intergroup trends and attitudes on the basis of individual characteristics are ruled out in this experiment should not be construed to mean that the relative contributions of individuals within their own groups and intergroup relationships are unimportant. Individuals do contribute differentially both in shaping and carrying on the trend of group relationships. This experiment does indicate, however, that intergroup attitudes are not merely products of severe individual frustrations or background differences brought to the situation.

Formation of Group Organization and Norms

When the individuals interacted in a series of situations toward goals with common appeal value which required interdependent activity for their attainment, definite group structures arose. These groups developed stable, but by no means immutable *status hierarchies* and *group norms* regulating experience and behavior of individual members.

More concretely, a pattern of leader-follower relations evolved within each group as members faced compelling problem situations and attained goals through coordinated action. As group structure was stabilized, it was unmistakably delineated as an "in-group." Certain places and objects important in group activities were incorporated as "ours." Ways of doing things, of meeting problems, of behaving under certain conditions were standardized, permitting variation only within limits. Beyond the limits of the group norms, behavior was subject to group sanctions, which ranged from ridicule, through ignoring the offender and his behavior, to threats, and occasionally to physical chastisement.

In-Group Cooperativeness Is Not Directly Transferable

When two groups met in competitive and reciprocally frustrating engagements, in-group solidarity and cooperativeness increased. Toward the end of the intergroup friction (Stage 2), in-group solidarity became so strong that when the groups were taken to a public beach crowded with outsiders and affording various distractions, our groups stuck almost exclusively to activities within their respective in-groups. Psychologically, other people did not count as far as they were concerned. In the presence of so many people and distractions, this intensive concentration of interests and activities within the group atmosphere would have been impossible had the groups gone there before attaining such a high degree of solidarity.

This heightened in-group solidarity and cooperativeness were observed at the very time when intergroup hostility was at its peak, during the period when the groups asserted emphatically that they would not have anything more to do with each other. This can only mean that the nature of intergroup relations cannot be extrapolated from the nature of in-group relations. In-group solidarity, in-group cooperativeness and democratic procedures need not necessarily be transferred to the out-group and its members. Intergroup relations cannot be improved simply by developing cooperative and friendly attitudes and habits within groups.

Consequential Intergroup Relations Affect In-Group Relations

Special note should be made of a related finding, namely that consequential intergroup relations have an impact on the in-group organization.

When it became evident that certain members of one group, including the leader, were not living up to the responsibilities expected of them by other members during the eventful course of intergroup competition, leadership changed hands. Those individuals who distinguished themselves by giving a good account for their group rose in the status hierarchy. Internal shifts in status were observed again during the cooperative intergroup activities of Stage 3. Functional relations between groups which are of consequence tend to bring about changes in the pattern of in-group relations.

Limiting Conditions for Intergroup Attitude and Behavior

We have seen that the individuals studied in this experiment were selected in ways which rule out explanations for the direction of intergroup behavior on the basis of differences in their backgrounds or on the basis of their individual frustrations, instabilities and the like. In the preceding sections, we have seen evidence that in-group properties were affected by consequential intergroup relations. Thus the intergroup hostility and its reduction cannot be explained merely by the nature of relationships within the groups.

Our findings indicate that the limiting condition determining friendly or hostile attitudes between groups is the nature of functional relations between them, as defined by analysis of their goals. When the groups competed for goals which could be attained by only one group, to the dismay and disappointment of the other, hostile deeds and unflattering labels developed in relation to one another. In time, derogatory stereotypes and negative attitudes toward the out-group were crystallized. These conclusions are based on observations made independently by observers of both groups and other staff members. Sociometric indices pointed to the overwhelming preponderance of friendship choices for in-group members. Experimental assessment of intergroup attitudes showed unmistakable attribution of derogatory stereotypes to the villainous out-group and of favorable qualities to the in-group. Laboratory-type judgments of performance showed the tendency to overestimate the performance attributed to fellow group members and to minimize the performance of members of the out-group.

What Kind of Contact Between Groups Is Effective?

The novel step in this experiment was Stage 3, in which intergroup friction was reduced. We have already stated why we discarded certain procedures in this stage, such as introducing a "common enemy" or disseminating information. In order to clarify the term "contact," we tried the method of bringing the groups into close proximity in a series of activities. Most of these contact situations involved activities which were satisfying in themselves, such as eating good food in the same room, attending a movie together, or engaging in an exciting activity like shooting fireworks. But none of them created a state of interdependence between the groups. Such contact situations did not prove effective in reducing friction. Instead contact situations not conducive to interdependence were used by our groups for overt acts of hostility and further exchanges of unflattering invectives.

The ineffectiveness of contacts during which hostile groups engaged, while in close physical contiguity, in activities which were themselves satisfying to each individual has obvious implications for psychological theorizing.

The Introduction of Superordinate Goals

During the final period of the experiment, the prevailing friction between groups was reduced. Reduction of the conflict and hostility was observed in reciprocally cooperative and helpful intergroup actions, in friendly exchanges of tools, in developing standard procedures for alternating responsibilities and in meeting problems. The change in behavior and patterns of interaction between the groups was striking to all observers. The reliability of these observations is established by sociometric indices which showed increases of friendship choices for the erstwhile antagonists and also in the sharp decrease of unfavorable stereotypes toward the outgroup. Favorable conceptions of the out-group developed, so that ratings of the in-group and out-group were no longer a set of contrasted polarities.

The end result was obtained through introduction of a series of superordinate goals which had compelling appeal value for both groups but which could not be achieved by the efforts and resources of one group alone. When a state of interdependence between groups was produced for the attainment of superordinate goals, the groups realistically faced common problems. They took them up as common problems, jointly moving toward their solution, proceeding to plan and to execute the plans which they had jointly envisaged.

In this experiment, the setting and circumstances for the introduction of superordinate goals were elaborately prepared by the experimenters. But beyond setting the scene, the methods followed, the discussion necessary for the solution, the plans to be made and executed were left to the groups themselves. Faced with superordinate goals, the groups carried on discussion when necessary, listened to the advice and suggestions of members of both groups who were resourceful, made decisions, and even combined discussion, decision and deeds simultaneously when the goal was attained more effectively this way.

Cumulative Effects of Superordinate Goals

If the hostile attitudes generated during intergroup friction had any stability, it could not be expected that one or two situations embodying superordinate goals could wipe them out. Indeed intergroup antagonisms did not disappear in one stroke. At first, cooperative interaction involving both groups developed in specific situations in response to common problems and goals, only to be followed by a renewal of sharply drawn group lines and intergroup friction after the challenge had been met. Patterns and procedures for intergroup cooperation were laid down at first on a small scale in specific activities. Only during interaction in a series of situations involving superordinate goals did intergroup friction begin to disappear and the procedures for intergroup reciprocity developed in specific situations extend spontaneously to widening areas of activity.

In the sequential events of Stage 3, it was abundantly evident that the series of activities conducive to superordinate goals provided opportunities for members of the two groups to work out and develop procedures for cooperation in various spheres of action. Once a cooperative pattern was effective in a specific activity, it was extended by members of both groups to related actions. In the face of successful functioning of such procedures, the occasional dissident member who preferred the old days of intergroup strife or self-imposed separation found it more difficult to make his voice count in his own group.

Some procedures successful in intergroup interaction had previously been used by the groups in meeting problems within their own groups. But their transfer to intergroup interaction involved a significant step: the tacit recognition that the procedures now involved groups of individuals and not merely so many individual members within a group. Each individual within his group had been expected and encouraged by others to contribute to group efforts to the best of his abilities. Now, each group expected the other to contribute its share to meeting intergroup problems. While previously solutions were experienced as equitable or not relative to the individual's expectations and contributions within his group, now justice was also evaluated relative to equitable participation and opportunity for the groups as well.

The Same Tools May Serve Intergroup Conflict or Cooperation

In planning and working towards superordinate goals, there were times when the groups used jointly the tools and techniques which had been used by one or both groups separately in the service of fights during the intergroup conflict. Tools and techniques can be put to the service of harmony and integration as well as of deadly competition and conflict. Tools, in themselves, are not opposed to cooperation among individuals using them. It is the individuals as group members who put the tool to use in their opposition to other groups.

Even the proprietary pride that a place, a technique, a tool is "ours" takes on a different significance when the trend in intergroup relations is cooperation toward superordinate goals. Use of the technique or the tool in intergroup activities now implies a contribution toward a goal common to both groups—a contribution by the group in which members may take personal pride and which can be reciprocated by the other group equally enjoying its benefits through its own contributions at that or future occasions.

Superordinate Goals Alter The Significance of Other Influences

Contacts between groups in the course of actions towards superordinate goals are effective. They are used for developing plans, making decisions, and for pleasant personal exchanges. *Information* about the out-group becomes a matter of interest to group members and is actually sought in the course of interactions between members of the two groups. *Leaders* find that the trend toward intergroup cooperation in activities involving superordinate goals widens the spheres in which they may take positive steps toward working out procedures for joint endeavors and planning future contacts. Mingling with members of the other group and sharing in activities with them is no longer perceived by in-group members as "betrayal" or "treason." Similarly, the out-group member who engages in activities with the in-group is no longer seen by them as a strange and threatening figure in "our midst." On the contrary, intermingling of persons from different groups becomes a joint opportunity to work towards goals shared by both groups.

These are products of interaction towards goals superordinate to all group, which are genuinely appealing to all, whose attainment requires equitable participation and contributions from all groups in interdependent activities.

QUESTIONS

1. What two methods of reducing intergroup friction did the experimenters choose not to attempt? Why?

2. What two methods did the experimenters use to reduce friction between the two groups? Which method did they expect to be more successful?

3. Briefly describe the methodology of this experiment. How did the experimenters control for possible bias in their observations?

4. What do the authors mean by "in-group"? How are the dynamics of in-groups affected by the presence of another group? What is the relation between in-group solidarity and intergroup solidarity?

5. Describe the effect on intergroup relations of allowing the two groups to engage in intrinsically satisfying activities. How does this contact differ from that brought about by superordinate goals?

Reading 6: Contemporary

Race and the Schooling of Black Americans

Claude M. Steele

One of the strengths of social psychology is its focus on everyday social issues and problems. It is not surprising, then, that the study of prejudice and discrimination has received considerable attention from social psychologists for many years. Recall that in the 1960s, social psychology escaped an identity crisis, in part, by focusing more on applied issues. Fortunately, this coincided with an unprecedented awareness in our culture of the social evils of sexism and racism. As a result, social psychologists have given these topics a great deal of attention.

Three decades later, social psychologists continue to grapple with these important issues. As Claude Steele discusses in the following article, the problems of racism have been more pernicious than many first imagined. Today, after the removal of explicit barriers, African-Americans continue to fare poorly in school. This occurs even in the absence of overt racism. What, then, is going on?

Steele believes that the difficulty faced by African-American students today is the result of a more subtle form of racism. Our school system, he argues—indeed, our whole culture— expects that African-Americans will not succeed in academics. This message is communicated to teachers, it is communicated to African-American students themselves, subtly encouraging them to turn away from education. In this article, Steele addresses the problems and a possible solution: to make schools "wise."

❖

My former university offered minority students a faculty mentor to help shepherd them into college life. As soon as I learned of the program, I volunteered to be a mentor, but by then the school year was nearly over. Undaunted, the program's eager staff matched me with a student on their waiting list—an appealing nineteen-year-old black woman from Detroit, the same age as my daughter. We met finally in a campus lunch spot just about two weeks before the close of her freshman year. I realized quickly that I was too late. I have heard that the best way to diagnose someone's depression is to note how depressed you feel when you leave the person. When our lunch was over, I felt as gray as the snowbanks that often lined the path back to my office. My lunchtime companion was a statistic brought to life, a living example of one of the most disturbing facts of racial life in America today: the failure of so many black Americans to thrive in school. Before I could lift a hand to help this student, she had decided to do what 70 percent of all black Americans at four-year colleges do at some point in their academic careers—drop out.

Source: Steele, C. M. (1992, April). Race and the schooling of Black Americans. *The Atlantic Monthly*, 68–80.

I sense a certain caving-in of hope in America that problems of race can be solved. Since the sixties, when race relations held promise for the dawning of a new era, the issue has become one whose persistence causes "problem fatigue"—resignation to an unwanted condition of life.

This fatigue, I suspect, deadens us to the deepening crisis in the education of black Americans. One can enter any desegregated school in America, from grammar school to high school to graduate or professional school, and meet a persistent reality: blacks and whites in largely separate worlds. And if one asks a few questions or looks at a few records, another reality emerges: these worlds are not equal, either in the education taking place there or in the achievement of the students who occupy them.

As a social scientist, I know that the crisis has enough possible cause to give anyone problem fatigue. But at a personal level, perhaps because of my experience as a black in American schools, or perhaps just as the hunch of a myopic psychologist, I have long suspected a particular culprit—a culprit that can undermine black achievement as effectively as a lock on a schoolhouse door. The culprit I see is *stigma*, the endemic devaluation many blacks face in our society and schools. This status is its own condition of life, different from class, money, culture. It is capable, in the words of the late sociologist Erving Goffman, of "breaking the claim" that one's human attributes have on people. I believe that its connection to school achievement among black Americans has been vastly underappreciated.

This is a troublesome argument, touching as it does on a still unhealed part of American race relations. But it leads us to a heartening principle: if blacks are made less racially vulnerable in school, they can overcome even substantial obstacles. Before the good news, though, I must at least sketch in the bad: the worsening crisis in the education of black Americans.

Despite their socioeconomic disadvantages as a group, blacks begin school with test scores that are fairly close to the test scores of whites their age. The longer they stay in school, however, the more they fall behind; for example, by the sixth grade blacks in many school districts are two full grade levels behind whites in achievement. This pattern holds true in the middle class nearly as much as in the lower class. The record does not improve in high school. In 1980, for example, 25,500 minority students, largely black and Hispanic, entered high school in Chicago. Four years later only 9,500 graduated, and of those only 2,000 could read at grade level. The situation in other cities is comparable.

Even for blacks who make it to college, the problem doesn't go away. As I noted, 70 percent of all black students who enroll in four-year colleges drop out at some point, as compared with 45 percent of whites. At any given time nearly as many black males are incarcerated as are in college in this country. And the grades of black college students average half a letter below those of their white classmates. At one prestigious university I recently studied, only 18 percent of the graduating black students had grade averages of B or above as compared with 64 percent of the whites. This pattern is the rule, not the exception, in even the most elite American colleges. Tragically, low grades can render a degree essentially "terminal" in the sense that they preclude further schooling.

Blacks in graduate and professional schools face a similarly worsening or stagnating fate. For example, from 1977 to 1990, though the number of Ph.D.'s awarded to other minorities increased and the number awarded to whites stayed roughly the same, the number awarded to

American blacks dropped from 1,116 to 828. And blacks needed more time to get those degrees.

Standing ready is a familiar set of explanations. First is societal disadvantage. Black Americans have had, and continue to have, more than their share: a history of slavery, segregation, and job ceilings; continued lack of economic opportunity; poor schools; and the related problems of broken families, drug-infested communities, and social isolation. Any of these factors—alone, in combination, or through accumulated effects—can undermine school achievement. Some analysts point also to black American culture, suggesting that, hampered by disadvantage, it doesn't sustain the values and expectations critical to education, or that it fosters learning orientations ill suited to school achievement, or that it even "opposes" mainstream achievement. These are the chestnuts, and I had always thought them adequate. Then several facts emerged that just didn't seem to fit.

For one thing, the achievement deficits occur even when black students suffer no major financial disadvantage—among middle-class students on wealthy college campuses and in graduate school among black students receiving substantial financial aid. For another thing, survey after survey shows that even poor black Americans value education highly, often more than whites. Also, as I will demonstrate, several programs have improved black school achievement without addressing culturally specific learning orientations or doing anything to remedy socioeconomic disadvantage.

Neither is the problem fully explained, as one might assume, by deficits in skill or preparation which blacks might suffer because of background disadvantages. I first doubted that such a connection existed when I saw flunk-out rates for black and white students at a large, prestigious university. Two observations surprised me. First, for both blacks and whites the level of preparation, as measured by Scholastic Aptitude Test scores, didn't make much difference in who flunked out; low scorers (with combined verbal and quantitative SATs of 800) were no more likely to flunk out than high scorers (with combined SATs of 1,200 to 1,500). The second observation was racial: whereas only two percent to 11 percent of the whites flunked out, 18 percent to 33 percent of the blacks flunked out, even at the highest levels of preparation (combined SATs of 1,400). Dinesh D'Souza has argued recently that college affirmative-action programs cause failure and high dropout rates among black students by recruiting them to levels of college work for which they are inadequately prepared. That was clearly not the case at this school; black students flunked out in large numbers even with preparation well above average.

And, sadly, this proved the rule, not the exception. From elementary school to graduate school, something depresses black achievement *at every level of preparation, even the highest.* Generally, of course, the better prepared achieve better than the less prepared, and this is about as true for blacks as for whites. But given any level of school preparation (as measured by tests and earlier grades), blacks somehow achieve less in subsequent schooling than whites (that is, have poorer grades, have lower graduation rates, and take longer to graduate), no matter how strong that preparation is. Put differently, the same achievement level requires better preparation for blacks than for whites—far better: among students with a C+ average at the university I just described, the mean American College Testing Program (ACT) score for blacks was at the 98th percentile, while for whites it was at only the 34th percentile. This pattern has been documented so broadly across so many regions of the country, and by so many investigations (literally hundreds), that it is virtually a social law in this society—as well as a racial tragedy.

Clearly, something is missing from our understanding of black underachievement. Disadvantage contributes, yet blacks underachieve even when they have ample resources, strongly value education, and are prepared better than adequately in terms of knowledge and skills. Something else has to be involved. That something else could be of just modest importance—a barrier that simply adds its effect to that of other disadvantages—or it could be pivotal such that were it corrected, other disadvantages would lose their effect.

That something else, I believe, has to do with the process of identifying with school. I offer a personal example:

I remember conducting experiments with my research adviser early in graduate school and awaiting the results with only modest interest. I struggled to meet deadlines. The research enterprise—the core of what one does as a social psychologist—just wasn't *me* yet. I was in school for other reasons—I wanted an advanced degree, I was vaguely ambitious for intellectual work, and being in graduate school made my parents proud of me. But as time passed, I began to like the work. I also began to grasp the value system that gave it meaning, and the faculty treated me as if they thought I might even be able to do it. Gradually I began to think of myself as a social psychologist. With this change in self-concept came a new accountability; my self-esteem was affected now by what I did as a social psychologist, something that hadn't been true before. This added a new motivation to my work; self-respect, not just parental respect, was on the line. I noticed changes in myself. I worked without deadlines. I bored friends with applications of arcane theory to their daily lives. I went to conventions. I lived and died over how experiments came out.

Before this transition one might have said that I was handicapped by my black working-class background and lack of motivation. After the transition the same observer might say that even though my background was working-class, I had special advantages: achievement-oriented parents, a small and attentive college. But these facts alone would miss the importance of the identification process I had experienced: the change in self-definition and in the activities on which I based my self-esteem. They would also miss a simple condition necessary for me to make this identification: treatment as a valued person with good prospects.

I believe that the "something else" at the root of black achievement problems is the failure of American schooling to meet this simple condition for many of its black students. Doing well in school requires a belief that school achievement can be a promising basis of self-esteem, and that belief needs constant reaffirmation even for advantaged students. Tragically, I believe the lives of black Americans are still haunted by a specter that threatens this belief and the identification that derives from it at every level of schooling.

THE SPECTER OF STIGMA AND RACIAL VULNERABILITY

I have a good friend, the mother of three, who spends considerable time in the public school classrooms of Seattle, where she lives. In her son's third-grade room, managed by a teacher of unimpeachable good will and competence, she noticed over many visits that the extraordinary artwork of a small black boy named Jerome was ignored—or, more accurately perhaps, its significance was ignored. As genuine art talent has a way of doing—even in the third grade—his stood out. Yet the teacher seemed hardly to notice. Moreover, Jerome's reputation, as it was passed along from one grade to the next, included only the slightest mention of his talent. Now, of course, being ignored like this could happen to anyone—such is the overload in our public schools. But my friend couldn't help wondering how the school would have responded to this talent had the artist been one of her own, middle-class white children.

Terms like "prejudice" and "racism" often miss the full scope of racial devaluation in our society, implying as they do that racial devaluation comes primarily from the strongly prejudiced, not from "good people" like Jerome's teacher. But the prevalence of racists—deplorable though racism is—misses the full extent of Jerome's burden, perhaps even the most profound part.

He faces a devaluation that grows out of our images of society and the way those images catalogue people. The catalogue need never be taught. It is implied by all we see around us: the kinds of people revered in advertising (consider the unrelenting racial advocacy of Ralph Lauren ads) and movies (black women are rarely seen as romantic partners, for example); media discussions of whether a black can be President; invitation lists to junior high school birthday parties; school curricula; literary and musical canons. These details create an image of society in which black Americans simply do not fare well. When I was a kid, we captured it with the saying "If you're white you're right, if you're yellow you're mellow, if you're brown stick around, but if you're black get back."

In ways that require no fueling from strong prejudice or stereotypes, these images expand the devaluation of black Americans. They act as mental standards against which information about blacks is evaluated: that which fits these images we accept; that which contradicts them we suspect. Had Jerome had a reading problem, which fits these images, it might have been accepted as characteristic more readily than his extraordinary artwork, which contradicts them.

These images do something else as well, something especially pernicious in the classroom. They set up a jeopardy of double devaluation for blacks, a jeopardy that does not apply to whites. Like anyone, blacks risk devaluation for a particular incompetence, such as a failed test or a flubbed pronunciation. But they further risk that such performances will confirm the broader racial inferiority they are suspected of. Thus, from the first grade through graduate school, blacks have the extra fear that in the eyes of those around them their full humanity could fall with a poor answer or a mistaken stroke of the pen.

Moreover, because these images are conditioned in all of us, collectively held, they can spawn racial devaluation in all of us, not just in the strongly prejudiced. They can do this even in blacks themselves: a majority of black children recently tested said they like and prefer to play with white rather than black dolls—almost fifty years after Kenneth and Mamie Clark, conducting similar experiments, documented identical findings and so paved the way for *Brown v. Topeka Board of Education.* Thus Jerome's devaluation can come from a circle of people in his world far greater than the expressly prejudiced—a circle that apparently includes his teacher.

In ways often too subtle to be conscious but sometimes overt, I believe, blacks remain devalued in American schools, where, for example, a recent national survey shows that through

high school they are still more than twice as likely as white children to receive corporal punishment, be suspended from school, or be labeled mentally retarded.

Tragically, such devaluation can seem inescapable. Sooner or later it forces on its victims
two painful realizations. The first is that society is preconditioned to see the worst in them.
Black students quickly learn that acceptance, if it is to be won at all, will be hard-won. The
second is that even if a black student achieves exoneration in one setting—with the teacher
and fellow students in one classroom, or at one level of schooling for example—this approval
will have to be rewon in the next classroom, at the next level of schooling. Of course, individual characteristics that enhance one's value in society—skills, class status, appearance, and
success—can diminish the racial devaluation one faces. And sometimes the effort to prove
oneself fuels achievement. But few from any group could hope to sustain so daunting and ever-
lasting a struggle. Thus, I am afraid, too many black students are left hopeless and deeply vulnerable in America's classrooms.

"DISIDENTIFYING" WITH SCHOOL

I believe that in significant part the crisis in black Americans' education stems from the power
of this vulnerability to undercut identification with schooling, either before it happens or after it has bloomed.

Jerome is an example of the first kind. At precisely the time when he would need to see
school as a viable source of self-esteem, his teachers fail to appreciate his best work. The de-
valuated status of his race devalues him and his work in the classroom. Unable to entrust his
sense of himself to this place he resists measuring himself against its values and goals. He lan-
guishes there, held by the law, perhaps even by his parents, but not allowing achievement to
affect his view of himself. This psychic alienation—the act of not caring—makes him less vulnerable to the specter of devaluation that haunts him. Bruce Hare, an educational researcher,
has documented this process among fifth-grade boys in several schools in Champaign, Illinois.
He found that although the black boys had considerably lower achievement-test scores than
their white classmates, their overall self-esteem was just as high. This stunning impervious-
ness to poor academic performance was accomplished, he found, by their deemphasizing
school achievement as a basis of self-esteem and giving preference to peer-group relations—a
domain in which their esteem prospects were better. They went where they had to go to feel
good about themselves.

But recall the young student whose mentor I was. She had already identified with school,
and wanted to be a doctor. How can racial vulnerability break so developed an achievement
identity? To see, let us follow her steps onto campus: Her recruitment and admission stress
her minority status perhaps more strongly than it has been stressed at any other time in her
life. She is offered academic and social support services, further implying that she is "at risk"
(even with qualifications well above the threshold for whites). Once on campus, she enters a
socially circumscribed world in which blacks—still largely separate from whites—have lower
status; this is reinforced by a sidelining of minority material and interest in the curriculum and
in university life. And she can sense that everywhere in this new world her skin color places

her under suspicion of intellectual inferiority. All of this gives her the double vulnerability I spoke of: she risks confirming a particular incompetence, at chemistry or a foreign language, for example; but she also risks confirming the racial inferiority she is suspected of—a judgment that can feel as close at hand as a mispronounced word or an ungrammatical sentence. In reaction, usually to some modest setback, she withdraws, hiding her troubles from instructors, counselors, even other students. Quickly, I believe, a psychic defense takes over. She *disidentifies* with achievement; she changes her self-conception, her outlook and values, so that achievement is no longer so important to her self-esteem. She may continue to feel pressure to stay in school—from her parents, even from the potential advantages of a college degree. But now she is psychologically insulated from her academic life, like a disinterested visitor. Cool, unperturbed. But, like a painkilling drug, disidentification undoes her future as it relieves her vulnerability.

The prevalence of this syndrome among black college students has been documented extensively, especially on predominantly white campuses. Summarizing this work, Jacqueline Fleming, a psychologist, writes, "The fact that black students must matriculate in an atmosphere that feels hostile arouses defensive reactions that interfere with intellectual performance. . . . They display academic demotivation and think less of their abilities. They profess losses of energy." Among a sample of blacks on one predominantly white campus, Richard Nisbett and Andrew Reaves, both psychologists, and I found that attitudes related to disidentification were more strongly predictive of grades than even academic preparation (that is, SATs and high school grades).

To make matters worse, once disidentification occurs in a school, it can spread like the common cold. Blacks who identify and try to achieve embarrass the strategy by valuing the very thing the strategy denies the value of. Thus pressure to make it a group norm can evolve quickly and become fierce. Defectors are called "oreos" or "incognegroes." One's identity as an authentic black is held hostage, made incompatible with school identification. For black students, then, pressure to disidentify with school can come from the already demoralized as well as from racial vulnerability in the setting.

Stigmatization of the sort suffered by black Americans is probably also a barrier to the school achievement of other groups in our society, such as lower-class whites, Hispanics and women in male-dominated fields. For example, at a large Midwestern university I studied, women match men's achievement in the liberal arts, where they suffer no marked stigma, but underachieve compared with men (get lower grades than men with the same ACT scores) in engineering and premedical programs, where they, like blacks across the board, are more vulnerable to suspicions of inferiority.

"WISE" SCHOOLING

> *When they approach me they see . . . everything and anything except me . . . [this] invisibility . . . occurs because of a peculiar disposition of the eyes. . . .*
>
> —Ralph Ellison, *Invisible Man*

Erving Goffman, borrowing from gays of the 1950s, used the term "wise" to describe people who don't themselves bear the stigma of a given group but who are accepted by the group.

These are people in whose eyes the full humanity of the stigmatized is visible, people in whose eyes they feel less vulnerable. If racial vulnerability undermines black school achievement, as I have argued, then this achievement should improve significantly if schooling is made "wise"—that is, made to see value and promise in black students and to act accordingly.

And yet, although racial vulnerability at school may undermine black achievement, so many other factors seem to contribute—from the debilitations of poverty to the alleged dysfunctions of black American culture—that one might expect "wiseness' in the classroom to be of little help. Fortunately, we have considerable evidence to the contrary. Wise schooling may indeed be the missing key to the schoolhouse door.

In the mid-seventies black students in Philip Uri Treisman's early calculus courses at the University of California at Berkeley consistently fell to the bottom of every class. To help, Treisman developed the Mathematics Workshop Program, which, in a surprisingly short time, reversed their fortunes, causing them to outperform their white and Asian counterparts. And although it is only a freshman program, black students who take it graduate at a rate comparable to the Berkeley average. Its central technique is group study of calculus concepts. But it is also wise; it does things that allay the racial vulnerabilities of these students. Stressing their potential to learn, it recruits them to a challenging "honors" workshop tied to their first calculus course. Building on their skills, the workshop gives difficult work, often beyond course content, to students with even modest preparation (some of their math SATs dip to the 300s). Working together, students soon understand that everyone knows something and nobody knows everything, and learning is speeded through shared understanding. The wisdom of these tactics is their subtext message: "You are valued in this program because of your academic potential—regardless of your current skill level. You have no more to fear than the next person, and since the work is difficult, success is a credit to your ability, and a setback is a reflection only of the challenge." The black students' double vulnerability around failure—the fear that they lack ability, and the dread that they will be devalued—is thus reduced. They can relax and achieve. The movie *Stand and Deliver* depicts Jaime Escalante using the same techniques of assurance and challenge to inspire advanced calculus performance in East Los Angeles Chicano high schoolers. And, explaining Xavier University's extraordinary success in producing black medical students, a spokesman said recently, "What doesn't work is saying, 'You need remedial work.' What does work is saying, 'You may be somewhat behind at this time but you're a talented person. We're going to help you advance at an accelerated rate."

The work of James Comer, a child psychiatrist at Yale, suggests that wiseness can minimize even the barriers of poverty. Over a fifteen-year period he transformed the two worst elementary schools in New Haven, Connecticut, into the third and fifth best in the city's thirty-three-school system without any change in the type of students—largely poor and black. His guiding belief is that learning requires a strongly accepting relationship between teacher and student. "After all," he notes, "what is the difference between scribble and a letter of the alphabet to a child? The only reason the latter is meaningful, and worth learning and remembering, is because a *meaningful* other wants him or her to learn and remember it." To build these relationships Comer focuses on the overall school climate, shaping it not so much to transmit specific skills, or to achieve order per se, or even to improve achievement, as to establish a valuing and optimistic atmosphere in which a child can—to use his term—"identify" with learning.

Responsibility for this lies with a team of ten to fifteen members, headed by the principal and made up of teachers, parents, school staff, and child-development experts (for example, psychologists or special-education teachers). The team develops a plan of specifics: teacher training, parent workshops, coordination of information about students. But at base I believe it tries to ensure that the students—vulnerable on so many counts—get treated essentially like middle-class students, with conviction about their value and promise. As this happens, their vulnerability diminishes, and with it the companion defenses of disidentification and misconduct. They achieve, and apparently identify, as their achievement gains persist into high school. Comer's genius, I believe, is to have recognized the importance of these vulnerabilities as barriers to *intellectual* development, and the corollary that schools hoping to educate such students must learn first how to make them feel valued.

These are not isolated successes. Comparable results were observed, for example, in a Comer-type program in Maryland's Prince Georges County, in the Stanford economist Henry Levin's accelerated-schools program, and in Harlem's Central Park East Elementary School, under the principalship of Deborah Meier. And research involving hundreds of programs and schools points to the same conclusion: black achievement is consistently linked to conditions of schooling that reduce racial vulnerability. These include relatively harmonious race relations among students; a commitment by teachers and schools to seeing minority-group members achieve; the instructional goal that students at all levels of preparation achieve; desegregation at the classroom as well as the school level; and a de-emphasis on ability tracking.

That erasing stigma improves black achievement is perhaps the strongest evidence that stigma is what depresses it in the first place. This is no happy realization. But it lets in a ray of hope: whatever other factors also depress black achievement—poverty, social isolation, poor preparation—they may be substantially overcome in a schooling atmosphere that reduces racial and other vulnerabilities, not through unrelenting niceness or ferocious regimentation but by wiseness, by *seeing* value and acting on it.

WHAT MAKES SCHOOLING UNWISE

But if wise schooling is so attainable, why is racial vulnerability the rule, not the exception, in American schooling?

One factor is the basic assimilationist offer that schools make to blacks: You can be valued and rewarded in school (and society), the schools say to these students, but you must first master the culture and ways of the American mainstream, and since that mainstream (as it is represented) is essentially white, this means you must give up many particulars of being black—styles of speech and appearance, value priorities, preferences—at least in mainstream settings. This is asking a lot. But it has been the "color-blind" offer to every immigrant and minority group in our nation's history, the core of the melting-pot ideal, and so I think it strikes most of us as fair. Yet nonimmigrant minorities like blacks and Native Americans have always been here, and thus are entitled, more than new immigrants, to participate in the defining images of the society projected in school. More important, their exclusion from these images denies their contributive history and presence in society. Thus, whereas immigrants can tilt toward assimilation in pursuit of the opportunities for which they came, American blacks may find it harder to assimilate. For them, the offer of acceptance in return for assimilation carries a primal insult: it asks them to join in something that has made them invisible.

Now, I must be clear. This is not a criticism of Western civilization. My concern is an omission of image-work. In his incisive essay "What America Would Be Like Without Blacks," Ralph Ellison showed black influence on American speech and language, the themes of our finest literature, and our most defining ideals of personal freedom and democracy. In *The World They Made Together,* Mechal Sobel described how African and European influences shaped the early American South in everything from housing design and land use to religious expression. The fact is that blacks are not outside the American mainstream but, in Ellison's words, have always been "one of its major tributaries." Yet if one relied on what is taught in America's schools, one would never know this. There blacks have fallen victim to a collective self-deception, a society's allowing itself to assimilate like mad from its constituent groups while representing itself to itself as if the assimilation had never happened, as if progress and good were almost exclusively Western and white. A prime influence of American society on world culture is the music of black Americans, shaping art forms from rock and roll to modern dance. Yet in American schools, from kindergarten through graduate school, these essentially black influences have barely peripheral status, are largely outside the canon. Thus it is not what is taught but what is *not* taught, unwiseness in American schooling, and keeps black disidentification on full boil.

Deep in the psyche of American educators is a presumption that black students need academic remediation, or extra time with elemental curricula to overcome background deficits. This orientation guides many efforts to close the achievement gap—from grammar school tutoring to college academic-support programs—but I fear it can be unwise. Bruno Bettelheim and Karen Zelan's article "Why Children Don't Like to Read" comes to mind: apparently to satisfy the changing sensibilities of local school boards over this century, many books that children like were dropped from school reading lists; when children's reading scores also dropped, the approved texts were replaced by simpler books; and when reading scores dropped again, these were replaced by even simpler books, until eventually the children could hardly read at all, not because the material was too difficult but because they were bored stiff. So it goes, I suspect, with a great many of these remediation efforts. Moreover, because so many such programs target blacks primarily, they virtually equate black identity with substandard intellectual status, amplifying racial vulnerability. They can even undermine students' ability to gain confidence from their achievement, by sharing credit for their successes while implying that their failures stem from inadequacies beyond the reach of remediation.

The psychologist Lisa Brown and I recently uncovered evidence of just how damaging this orientation may be. At a large prestigious university we found that whereas the grades of black graduates of the 1950s improved during the students' college years until they virtually matched the school average, those of blacks who graduated in the 1980s (we chose only those with above-average entry credentials, to correct for more-liberal admissions policies in that decade) worsened, ending up considerably below the school average. The 1950s graduates faced outward discrimination in everything from housing to the classroom, whereas the 1980s graduates were supported by a phalanx of help programs. Many things may contribute to this pattern. The Jackie Robinson, "pioneer" spirit of the 1950s blacks surely helped them endure. And in a pre-affirmative-action era, they may have been seen as intellectually more deserving. But one cannot ignore the distinctive fate of 1980s blacks: a remedial orientation put their abilities under suspicion, deflected their ambitions, distanced them from their successes, and painted them with their failures. Black students on today's campuses may experience far less overt prejudice than their 1950s counterparts but, ironically, may be more racially vulnerable.

THE ELEMENTS OF WISENESS

For too many black students school is simply the place where, more concertedly, persistently, and authoritatively than anywhere else in society, they learn how little valued they are.

Clearly, no simple recipe can fix this, but I believe we now understand the basics of a corrective approach. Schooling must focus more on reducing the vulnerabilities that block identification with achievement. I believe that four conditions, like the legs of a stool, are fundamental.

- If what is meaningful and important to a teacher is to become meaningful and important to a student, the student must feel valued by the teacher for his or her potential and as a person. Among the more fortunate in society, this relationship is often taken for granted. But it is precisely the relationship that race can still undermine in American society. As Comer, Escalante, and Treisman have shown, when one's students bear race and class vulnerabilities, building this relationship is the first order of business— at all levels of schooling. No tactic of instruction, no matter how ingenious, can succeed without it.
- The challenge and the promise of personal fulfillment, not remediation (under whatever guise), should guide the education of these students. Their present skills should be taken into account, and they should be moved along at a pace that is demanding but doesn't defeat them. Their ambitions should never be scaled down but should instead be guided to inspiring goals even when extraordinary dedication is called for. Frustration will be less crippling than alienation. Here psychology is everything: remediation defeats challenge strengthens—affirming their potential, crediting them with their achievements, inspiring them.

    But the first condition, I believe, cannot work without the second, and vice versa. A valuing teacher-student relationship goes nowhere without challenge, and challenge will always be resisted outside a valuing relationship. (Again, I must be careful about something: in criticizing remediation I am not opposing affirmative-action recruitment in the schools. The success of this policy, like that of school integration before it, depends, I believe, on the tactics of implementation. Where students are valued and challenged, they generally succeed.)
- Racial integration is a generally useful element in this design, if not a necessity. Segregation, whatever its purpose, draws out group differences and makes people feel

more vulnerable when they inevitably cross group lines to compete in the larger society. This vulnerability, I fear, can override confidence gained in segregated schooling unless that confidence is based on strongly competitive skills and knowledge—something that segregated schooling, plagued by shortages of resources and access, has difficulty producing.

• The particulars of black life and culture—art, literature, political and social perspective, music—must be presented in the mainstream curriculum of American schooling, not consigned to special days, weeks, or even months of the year, or to special-topic courses and programs and aimed essentially at blacks. Such channeling carries the disturbing message that the material is not of general value. And this does two terrible things: it wastes the power of this material to alter our images of the American mainstream—continuing to frustrate black identification with it—and it excuses in whites and others a huge ignorance of their own society. The true test of democracy, Ralph Ellison has said, "is . . . the inclusion—not assimilation—of the black man."

Finally, if I might be allowed a word specifically to black parents, one issue is even more immediate: our children may drop out of school before the first committee meets to accelerate the curriculum. Thus, although we, along with all Americans, must strive constantly for wise schooling, I believe we cannot wait for it. We cannot yet forget our essentially heroic challenge: to foster in our children a sense of hope and entitlement to mainstream American life and schooling, even when it devalues them.

QUESTIONS

1. What percentage of whites and blacks[1] attending a four-year college drop out? What two explanations are most frequently given to explain blacks' poorer school performance?

2. According to Steele, what jeopardy do all students risk by failing a test in school? What additional concern adds to this risk for blacks, creating a "jeopardy of double devaluation"?

3. Explain the concept of disidentification. What is the main benefit and the main cost to those who use it? Why does Steele liken disidentification to the common cold?

4. Explain the technique developed by educators such as Treisman, Escalante, and Comer to improve the academic performance of minority students. Why does Steele believe that the technique is so successful?

5. Why do blacks have more difficulty than other racial minorities in identifying with mainstream educational values? In what ways do some of our current attempts to aid black students have the opposite effect?

---

[1]We use the term "black" here instead of "African-American" to be consistent with author Claude Steele's terminology.

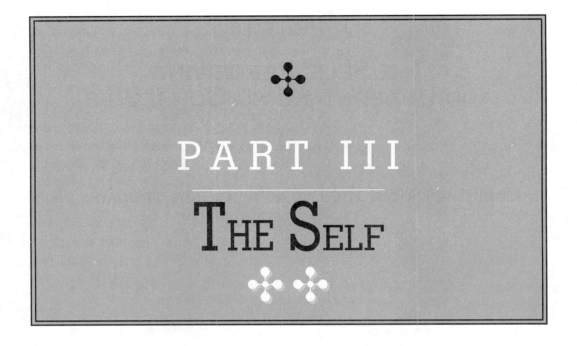

PART III
THE SELF

✛ CHAPTER 4 ✛

THE SELF: PERCEIVING AND UNDERSTANDING OURSELVES

Reading 7: Classic

Cognitive, Social and Physiological Determinants of Emotional State

Stanley Schachter and Jerome E. Singer

Emotions are unquestionably among the most important phenomena in human life. Although it is our ability for abstract thought that distinguishes us from other animals, it is emotions that give meaning to our lives. You may wonder what business social psychologists have in studying emotions. After all, emotions are a deeply personal experience—an individual experience, not a social experience.

On the contrary, many psychologists believe that the functions of emotions are primarily social. People don't just get angry, they get angry at someone. We don't just like and love, we like and love other people. As these examples suggest, emotional responses serve to inform us about our social environment.

Yet the specific processes that lead to emotions are not clearly understood. Although experienced as a simple experiential reaction, emotions involve physiological components (arousal), cognitive components (perceptions of the situation), and social components (facial expressions). The interplay between these many parts creates a complex and confusing situation for psychologists.

Despite the complexity of emotions, social psychologists have made important steps in understanding them. One classic study, conducted by Stanley Schachter and Jerome Singer, is reported in the following article. To try to understand how arousal, cognitions, and social environment interact to produce emotions, Schachter and Singer manipulated each element independently of the other. Their results may surprise you.

✛

The problem of which cues, internal or external, permit a person to label and identify his own emotional state has been with us since the days that James (1890) first tendered his doctrine that "the bodily changes follow directly the perception of the exciting fact, and that our feeling of the same changes as they occur *is* the emotion" (p. 449). Since we are aware of a variety of feeling and emotion states, it should follow from James' proposition that the various

Source: Schachter, S., & Singer, J. E. (1962). Cognitive, social, and physiological determinants of emotional state. *Psychological Review, 69*, 379–399.

emotions will be accompanied by a variety of differentiable bodily states. Following James' pronouncement, a formidable number of studies were undertaken in search of physiological differentiators of the emotions. The results, in these early days, were almost uniformly negative. All of the emotional states experimentally manipulated were characterized by a general pattern of excitation of the sympathetic nervous system, but there appeared to be no clear-cut physiological discriminators of the various emotions. This pattern of results was so consistent from experiment to experiment that Cannon (1929) offered, as one of the crucial criticisms of the James-Lange theory, the fact that "the same visceral changes occur in very different emotional states and in nonemotional states" (p. 351).

More recent work, however, has given some indication that there may be differentiators. Ax (1953) and Schachter (1957) studied fear and anger. On a large number of indices both of these states were characterized by a similarly high level of autonomic activation, but on several indices they did differ in the degree of activation. Wolf and Wolff (1947) studied a subject with a gastric fistula and were able to distinguish two patterns in the physiological responses of the stomach wall. It should be noted, though, that for many months they studied their subject during and following a great variety of moods and emotions and were able to distinguish only two patterns.

Whether or not there are physiological distinctions among the various emotional states must be considered an open question. Recent work might be taken to indicate that such differences are at best rather subtle and that the variety of emotion, mood, and feeling states are by no means matched by an equal variety of visceral patterns.

This rather ambiguous situation has led Ruckmick (1936), Hunt, Cole, and Reis (1958), Schachter (1959) and others to suggest that cognitive factors may be major determinants of emotional states. Granted a general pattern of sympathetic excitation as characteristic of emotional states, granted that there may be some differences in pattern from state to state, it is suggested that one labels, interprets, and identifies this stirred-up state in terms of the characteristics of the precipitating situation and one's apperceptive mass. This suggests, then, that an emotional state may be considered a function of a state of physiological arousal and of a cognition appropriate to this state of arousal. The cognition, in a sense, exerts a steering function. Cognitions arising from the immediate situation as interpreted by past experience provide the framework within which one understands and labels his feelings. It is the cognition which determines whether the state of physiological arousal will be labeled as "anger," "joy," "fear," or whatever.

In order to examine the implications of this formulation let us consider the fashion in which these two elements, a state of physiological arousal and cognitive factors, would interact in a variety of situations. In most emotion-inducing situations, of course, the two factors are completely interrelated. Imagine a man walking alone down a dark alley; a figure with a gun suddenly appears. The perception-cognition "figure with a gun" in some fashion initiates a state of physiological arousal; this state of arousal is interpreted in terms of knowledge about dark alleys and guns and the state of arousal is labeled "fear." Similarly a student who unexpectedly learns that he has made Phi Beta Kappa may experience a state of arousal which he will label "joy."

Let us now consider circumstances in which these two elements, the physiological and the cognitive, are, to some extent, independent. First, is the state of physiological arousal alone sufficient to induce an emotion? Best evidence indicates that it is not. Marañon (1924), in a fascinating study (which was replicated by Cantril & Hunt, 1932, and Landis & Hunt, 1932), injected 210 of his patients with the sympathomimetic agent adrenaline and then simply asked them to introspect. Seventy-one percent of his subjects simply reported physical symptoms with no emotional overtones; 29% of the subjects responded in an apparently emotional fashion. Of these the great majority described their feelings in a fashion that Marañon labeled "cold" or "as if" emotions, that is they made statements such as "I feel *as if* I were afraid" or "*as if* I were awaiting a great happiness." This is a sort of emotional "déjà vu" experience; these subjects are neither happy nor afraid, they feel "as if" they were. Finally a very few cases apparently reported a genuine emotional experience. However, in order to produce this reaction in most of these few cases, Marañon (1924) points out:

> One must suggest a memory with strong affective force but not so strong as to produce an emotion in the normal state. For example, in several cases we spoke to our patients before the injection about their sick children or dead parents and they responded calmly to this topic. The same topic presented later, during the adrenal commotion, was sufficient to trigger emotion. This adrenal commotion places the subject in a situation of "affective imminence" (pp. 307–308).

Apparently, then, to produce a genuinely emotional reaction to adrenaline, Marañon was forced to provide such subjects with appropriate cognition.

Though Marañon (1924) is not explicit on his procedure, it is clear that his subjects knew that they were receiving an injection and in all likelihood knew that they were receiving adrenaline and probably had some order of familiarity with its effects. In short, though they underwent the pattern of sympathetic discharge common to strong emotional states, at the same time they had a completely appropriate cognition or explanation as to why they felt this way. This, we would suggest, is the reason so few of Marañon's subjects reported any emotional experience.

Consider now a person in a state of physiological arousal for which no immediately explanatory or appropriate cognitions are available. Such a state could result were one covertly to inject a subject with adrenaline or, unknown to him, feed the subject a sympathomimetic drug such as ephedrine. Under such conditions a subject would be aware of palpitations, tremor, face flushing, and most of the battery of symptoms associated with a discharge of the sympathetic nervous system. In contrast to Marañon's (1924) subjects he would, at the same time, be utterly unaware of why he felt this way. What would be the consequence of such a state?

Schachter (1959) has suggested that precisely such a state would lead to the arousal of "evaluative needs" (Festinger, 1954); that is, pressures would act on an individual in such a state to understand and label his bodily feelings. His bodily state grossly resembles the condition in which it has been at times of emotional excitement. How would he label his present feelings? It is suggested, of course, that he will label his feelings in terms of his knowledge of the immediate situation. Should he at the time be with a beautiful woman he might decide that he was wildly in love or sexually excited. Should he be at a gay party, he might, by comparing himself to others, decide that he was extremely happy and euphoric. Should he be arguing with his wife, he might explode in fury and hatred. Or, should the situation be completely inappropriate he could decide that he was excited about something that had recently happened to him or, simply, that he was sick. In any case, it is our basic assumption that emotional states are a function of the interaction of such cognitive factors with a state of physiological arousal.

This line of thought, then, leads to the following propositions:

1. Given a state of physiological arousal for which an individual has no immediate explanation, he will "label" this state and describe his feelings in terms of the cognitions available to him. To the extent that cognitive factors are potent determiners of emotional states, it could be anticipated that precisely the same state of physiological arousal could be labeled "joy" or "fury" or "jealousy" or any of a great diversity of emotional labels depending on the cognitive aspects of the situation.

2. Given a state of physiological arousal for which an individual has a completely appropriate explanation (e.g., "I feel this way because I have just received an injection of adrenaline") no evaluative needs will arise and the individual is unlikely to label his feelings in terms of the alternative cognitions available.

   Finally, consider a condition in which emotion inducing cognitions are present but there is no state of physiological arousal. For example, an individual might be completely aware that he is in great danger but for some reason (drug or surgical) remain in a state of physiological quiescence. Does he experience the emotion "fear"? Our formulation of emotion as a joint function of a state of physiological arousal and an appropriate cognition, would, of course, suggest that he does not, which leads to our final proposition.

3. Given the same cognitive circumstances, the individual will react emotionally or describe his feelings as emotions only to the extent that he experiences a state of physiological arousal.

PROCEDURE

The experimental test of these propositions requires (a) the experimental manipulation of a state of physiological arousal, (b) the manipulation of the extent to which the subject has an appropriate or proper explanation of his bodily state, and (c) the creation of situations from which explanatory cognitions may be derived.

Manipulating Arousal

In order to manipulate physiological arousal, subjects were given one of two injections. Some subjects were given epinephrine, a type of adrenaline, which increases autonomic arousal. Other subjects were given a placebo . . .

Manipulating an Appropriate Explanation

By "appropriate" we refer to the extent to which the subject has an authoritative, unequivocal explanation of his bodily condition. Thus, a subject who had been informed by the physician that as a direct consequence of the injection he would feel palpitations, tremor, etc. would be considered to have a completely appropriate explanation. A subject who had been informed only that the injection would have no side effects would have no appropriate explanation of his state. This dimension of appropriateness was manipulated in three experimental conditions which shall be called: Epinephrine Informed (Epi Inf), Epinephrine Ignorant (Epi Ign), and Epinephrine Misinformed (Epi Mis) . . .

Producing An Emotion Inducing Cognition

Our initial hypothesis has suggested that given a state of physiological arousal for which the individual has no adequate explanation, cognitive factors can lead the individual to describe his feelings with any of a diversity of emotional labels. In order to test this hypothesis, it was decided to manipulate emotional stress which can be considered quite different—euphoria and anger.

There are, of course, many ways to induce such states. In our own program of research, we have concentrated on social determinants of emotional states and have been able to demonstrate in other studies that people do evaluate their own feelings by comparing themselves with others around them (Schachter 1959; Wrightsman 1960). In this experiment we have attempted again to manipulate emotional state by social means. In one set of conditions, the subject is placed together with a stooge who has been trained to act euphorically. In a second set of conditions the subject is with a stooge trained to act in an angry fashion . . .

In summary, this is a seven-condition experiment which, for two different emotional states, allows us (a) to evaluate the effects of "appropriateness" on emotional inducibility and (b) to begin to evaluate the effects of sympathetic activation on emotional inducibility. In schematic form the conditions are the following:

Euphoria	*Anger*
Epi Inf	Epi Inf
Epi Ign	Epi Ign
Epi Mis	Placebo
Placebo	

The Epi Mis condition was not run in the Anger sequence. This was originally conceived as a control condition and it was felt that its inclusion in the Euphoria conditions alone would suffice as a means of evaluating the possible artifactual effect of the Epi Inf instructions.

Measurement

Two types of measures of emotional state were obtained. Standardized observation through a one-way mirror was the technique used to assess the subject's behavior. To what extent did he act euphoric or angry? Such behavior can be considered in a way as a "semiprivate" index of mood, for as far as the subject was concerned, his emotional behavior could be known only to the other person in the room—presumably another student. The second type of measure was self-report in which, on a variety of scales, the subject indicated his mood of the moment. Such measures can be considered "public" indices of mood for they would, of course, be available to the experiment and his associates . . .

Subjects

The subjects were all male, college students taking classes in introductory psychology at the University of Minnesota. Some 90% of the students in these classes volunteer for a subject pool for which they receive two extra points on their final exam for every hour that they serve as experimental subjects. For this study the records of all potential subjects were cleared with the Student Health Service in order to insure that no harmful effects would result from the injections.

Evaluation of the Experimental Design

The ideal test of our propositions would require circumstances which our experiment is far from realizing. First, the proposition that: "A state of physiological arousal for which an individual has no immediate explanation will lead him to label this state in terms of the cognitions available to him" obviously requires conditions under which the subject does not and cannot have a proper explanation of his bodily state. Though we toyed with such fantasies as ventilating the experimental room with vaporized adrenaline, reality forced us to rely on the disguised injection of Suproxin—a technique which was far from ideal for no matter what the experimenter told them, some subjects would inevitably attribute their feelings to the injection. To the extent that subjects did so, differences between the several appropriateness conditions should be attenuated.

Second, the proposition that: "Given the same cognitive circumstances the individual will react emotionally only to the extent that he experiences a state of physiological arousal" requires for its ideal test the manipulation of states of physiological arousal and of physiological quiescence. Though there is no question that epinephrine effectively produces a state of arousal, there is also no question that a placebo does not prevent physiological arousal. To the extent that the experimental situation effectively produces sympathetic stimulation in placebo subjects, the proposition is difficult to test, for such a factor would attenuate differences between epinephrine and placebo subjects.

Both of these factors, then, can be expected to interfere with the test of our several propositions. In presenting the results of this study, we shall first present condition by condition results and then evaluate the effect of these two factors on experimental differences. . . .

RESULTS

Effects of the Manipulations on Emotional State

Euphoria. *Self-report*. The effects of the several manipulations on emotional state in the euphoria conditions are presented in Table 1. The scores recorded in this table are derived, for each subject, by subtracting the value of the point he checks on the irritation scale from the

TABLE 1   SELF-REPORT OF EMOTIONAL STATE
IN THE EUPHORIA CONDITIONS

Condition	N	Self-Report Scales	Comparison	p
Epi Inf	25	0.98	Epi Inf vs. Epi Mis	<.01
Epi Ign	25	1.78	Epi Inf vs. Epi Ign	.02
Epi Mis	25	1.90	Placebo vs. Epi Mis, Ign, or Inf	ns
Placebo	26	1.61		

All p values reported throughout paper are two-tailed.

value of the point he checks on the happiness scale. Thus, if a subject were to check the point "I feel a little irritated and angry" on the irritation scale and the point "I feel very happy and good" on the happiness scale, his score would be + 2. The higher the positive value, the happier and better the subject reports himself as feeling. Though we employ an index for expositional simplicity, it should be noted that the two components of the index each yield results completely consistent with those obtained by use of this index.

Let us examine first the effects of the appropriateness instructions. Comparison of the scores for the Epi Mis and Epi Inf conditions makes it immediately clear that the experimental differences are not due to artifacts resulting from the informed instructions. In both conditions the subject was warned to expect a variety of symptoms as a consequence of the injection. In the Epi Mis condition, where the symptoms were inappropriate to the subject's bodily state, the self-report score is almost twice that in the Epi Inf condition, where the symptoms were completely appropriate to the subject's bodily state. It is reasonable, then, to attribute differences between informed subjects and those in other conditions to differences in manipulated appropriateness rather than to artifacts such as introspectiveness or self-examination.

It is clear that, consistent with expectations, subjects were more susceptible to the stooge's mood and consequently more euphoric when they had no explanation of their own bodily states than when they did. The means of both the Epi Ign and Epi Mis conditions are considerably greater than the mean of the Epi Inf condition.

It is of interest to note that Epi Mis subjects are somewhat more euphoric than are Epi Ign subjects. This pattern repeats itself in other data shortly to be presented. We would attribute this difference to differences in the appropriateness dimension. Though, as in the Epi Ign condition, a subject is not provided with an explanation of his bodily state, it is, of course, possible that he will provide one for himself which is not derived from his interaction with the stooge. Most reasonably he could decide for himself that he feels this way because of the injection. To the extent that he does so he should be less susceptible to the stooge. It seems probable that he would be less likely to hit on such an explanation in the Epi Mis condition than in the Epi Ign condition, for in the Epi Mis condition both the experimenter and the doctor have told him that the effects of the injection would be quite different from what he actually feels. The effect of such instructions is probably to make it more difficult for the subject himself to hit on the alternative explanation described above. There is some evidence to support this analysis. In open-end questions in which subjects described their own mood and state, 28% of the subjects in the Epi Ign condition made some connection between the injection and their bodily state compared with the 16% of subjects in the Epi Mis condition who did so. It could be considered, then, that these three conditions fall along a dimension of appropriateness, with the Epi Inf condition at one extreme and the Epi Mis condition at the other.

Comparing the placebo to the epinephrine conditions, we note a pattern which will repeat itself throughout the data. Placebo subjects are less euphoric than either Epi Mis or Epi Ign subjects but somewhat more euphoric than Epi Inf subjects. These differences are not, however, statistically significant. We shall consider the epinephrine-placebo comparisons in detail in a later section of this paper following presentation of additional relevant data. For the moment, it is clear that by self-report, manipulating appropriateness has had a very strong effect on euphoria.

Behavior. Let us next examine the extent to which the subject's behavior was affected by the experimental manipulations. To the extent that his mind has been affected, one should expect that the subject will join in the stooge's whirl of manic activity and initiate similar activities of his own. The relevant data are presented in Table 2. The column labeled "Activity Index" presents summary figures on the extent to which the subject joined in the stooge's activity. This is a weighted index which reflects both the nature of the activities in which the subject engaged and the amount of time he was active. The index was devised by assigning the following weights to the subject's activities: 5—hula hooping; 4—shooting with slingshot; 3—paper airplanes; 2—paper basketballs; 1—doodling; 0—does nothing. Pretest scaling on 15 college

TABLE 2   BEHAVIORAL INDICATIONS OF EMOTIONAL STATE
IN THE EUPHORIA CONDITIONS

Condition	N	Activity Index	Mean Number of Acts Initiated
Epi Inf	25	12.72	.20
Epi Ign	25	18.28	.56
Epi Mis	25	22.56	.84
Placebo	26	16.00	.54

p Value

Comparison	Activity Index	Initiates
Epi Inf vs. Epi Mis	.05	.03
Epi Inf vs. Epi Ign	*ns*	.08
Plac vs. Epi Mis, Ign, or Inf	*ns*	*ns*

Tested by χ^2 comparison of the proportion of subjects in each condition initiating new acts.

students ordered these activities with respect to the degree of euphoria they represented. Arbitrary weights were assigned so that the wilder the activity, the heavier the weight. These weights are multiplied by an estimate of the amount of time the subject spent in each activity, and the summed products make up the activity index for each subject. This index may be considered a measure of behavioral euphoria. It should be noted that the same between-condition relationships hold for the two components of this index as for the index itself.

The column labeled "Mean Number of Acts Initiated" presents the data on the extent to which the subject deviates from the stooge's routine and initiates euphoric activities of his own.

On both behavioral indices, we find precisely the same pattern of relationships as those obtained with self-reports. Epi Mis subjects behave somewhat more euphorically than do Epi Ign subjects, who in turn behave more euphorically than do Epi Inf subjects. On all measures, then there is consistent evidence that a subject will take over the stooge's euphoric mood to the extent that he has no other explanation of his bodily state.

Again it should be noted that on these behavioral indices, Epi Ign and Epi Mis subjects are somewhat more euphoric than placebo subjects but not significantly so.

Anger. *Self-report.* Before presenting data for the anger conditions, one point must be made about the anger manipulation. In the situation devised, anger, if manifested, is most likely to be directed at the experimenter and his annoyingly personal questionnaire. As we subsequently discovered, this was rather unfortunate, for the subjects, who had volunteered for the experiment for extra points on their final exam, simply refused to endanger these points by publicly blowing up, admitting their irritation to the experimenter's face or spoiling the questionnaire. Though as the reader will see, the subjects were quite willing to manifest anger when they were alone with the stooge, they hesitated to do so on material (self-ratings of mood and questionnaire) that the experimenter might see and only after the purposes of the experiment had been revealed were many of these subjects willing to admit to the experimenter that they had been irked or irritated.

This experimentally unfortunate situation pretty much forces us to rely on the behavioral indices derived from observation of the subject's presumably private interaction with the stooge. We do, however, present data on the self-report scales in Table 3. These figures are derived in the same way as the figures presented in Table 1 for the euphoria conditions, that is,

TABLE 3 SELF-REPORT OF EMOTIONAL STATE
IN THE ANGER CONDITIONS

Condition	N	Self-Report Scales	Comparison	p
Epi Inf	22	1.91	Epi Inf vs. Epi Ign	.08
Epi Ign	23	1.39	Placebo vs. Epi Ign or Inf	*ns*
Placebo	23	1.63		

the value checked on the irritation scale is subtracted from the value checked on the happiness scale. Though, for the reasons stated above, the absolute magnitude of these figures (all positive) is relatively meaningless, we can, of course, compare condition means within the set of anger conditions. With the happiness-irritation index employed, we should, of course, anticipate precisely the reverse results from those obtained in the euphoria conditions; that is, the Epi Inf subjects in the anger conditions should again be less susceptible to the stooge's mood and should, therefore, describe themselves ad in a somewhat happier frame of mind than subjects in the Epi Ign condition. This is the case; the Epi Inf subjects average 1.91 on the self-report scales while the Epi Ign subjects average 1.39.

Evaluating the effects of the injections, we note again that, as anticipated, Epi Ign subjects are somewhat less happy than Placebo subjects but, once more, this is not a significant difference.

Behavior. The subject's responses to the stooge during the period when both were filling out their questionnaires were systematically coded to provide a behavioral index of anger. The coding scheme and the numerical values attached to each of the categories have been described in the methodology section. To arrive at an "Anger index" the numerical value assigned to a subject's responses to the stooge is summed together for the several units of stooge behavior. In the coding scheme used, a positive value to this index indicates that the subject agrees with the stooge's comment and is growing angry. A negative value indicates that the subject either disagrees with the stooge or ignores him.

The relevant data are presented in Table 4. . . . We must, of course, anticipate that subjects in the Epi Ign condition will be angrier than subjects in the Epi Inf condition. This is indeed the case. The Anger index for the Epi Ign condition is positive and large, indicating that these subjects have become angry, while in the Epi Inf condition the Anger index is slightly negative in value, indicating that these subjects have failed to catch the stooge's mood at all. It seems clear that providing the subject with an appropriate explanation of his bodily state

TABLE 4 BEHAVIORAL INDICATIONS OF EMOTIONAL STATE IN THE ANGER CONDITIONS

Condition	N	Anger Units
Epi Inf	22	−0.18
Epi Ign	23	+2.28
Placebo	22[a]	+0.79

Comparison For Anger Units	p
Epi Inf vs. Epi Ign	<.01
Epi Ign vs. Placebo	<.05
Placebo vs. Epi Inf	ns

[a]For one subject in this condition the sound system went dead and the observer could not, of course, code his reactions.

greatly reduces his tendency to interpret his state in terms of the cognitions provided by the stooge's angry behavior.

Finally, on this behavioral index, it can be seen that subjects in the Epi Ign condition are significantly angrier than subjects in the Placebo condition. Behaviorally, at least, the injection of epinephrine appears to have led subjects to an angrier state than comparable subjects who received placebo shots.

DISCUSSION

Let us summarize the major findings of this experiment and examine the extent to which they support the propositions offered in the introduction of this paper. It has been suggested, first, that given a state of physiological arousal for which an individual has no explanation, he will label this state in terms of the cognitions available to him. This implies, of course, that by manipulating the cognitions of an individual in such a state we can manipulate his feelings in diverse directions. Experimental results support this proposition, for following the injection of epinephrine, those subjects who had no explanation for the bodily state thus produced gave behavioral and self-report indications that they had been readily manipulable into the disparate feeling states of euphoria and anger.

From this first proposition, it must follow that given a state of physiological arousal for which the individual has a completely satisfactory explanation, he will not label this state in terms of the alternative cognitions available. Experimental evidence strongly supports this expectation. In those conditions in which subjects were injected with epinephrine and told precisely what they would feel and why, they proved relatively immune to any effects of the manipulated cognitions. In the anger condition, such subjects did not report or show anger; in the euphoria condition, such subjects reported themselves as far less happy than subjects with an identical bodily state but no adequate knowledge of why they felt the way they did.

Finally, it has been suggested that given constant cognitive circumstances, an individual will react emotionally only to the extent that he experiences a state of physiological arousal. Without taking account of experimental artifacts, the evidence in support of this proposition is consistent but tentative. When the effects of "self-informing" tendencies in placebo subjects are partialed out, the evidence strongly supports the proposition.

The pattern of data, then, falls neatly in line with theoretical expectations. . . . .

REFERENCES

Ax, A. F. (1953). Physiological differentiation of emotional states. *Psychosomatic Medicine, 15,* 433–442.

Cannon, W. B. (1929). *Bodily changes in pain, hunger, fear and rage* (2nd ed.). New York: Appleton.

Cantril, H., & Hunt, W. A. (1932). Emotional effects produced by the injection of adrenaline. *American Journal of Psychology, 44,* 300–307.

Festinger, L. (1954). A theory of social comparison processes. *Human Relations, 7,* 114–140.

Hunt, J. McV., Cole, M. W., & Reis, E. E. (1958). Situational cues distinguishing anger, fear, and sorrow. *American Journal of Psychology, 71,* 136–151.

James, W. (1890). *The principles of psychology.* New York: Holt.

Landis, C., & Hunt, W. A. (1932). Adrenaline and emotion. *Psychology Review, 39,* 467–485.

Marañon, G. (1924). Contribution a l'étude de l'action émotive de l'adrénaline. *Revue Francaise d'Endocrinologie, 2,* 301–325.

Ruckmick, C. A. (1936). *The psychology of feeling and emotion.* New York: McGraw-Hill.

Schachter, J. (1957). Pain, fear, and anger in hypertensives and normotensives: A psychophysiologic study. *Psychosomatic Medicine, 19,* 17–29.

Schachter, S. (1959). *The psychology of affiliation.* Stanford, CA: Stanford University Press.

Wolf, S., & Wolff, H. G. (1947). *Human gastric function.* New York: Oxford University Press.

Wrightsman, L. S. (1960). Effects of waiting with others on changes in level of felt anxiety. *Journal of Abnormal and Social Psychology, 61,* 216–222.

QUESTIONS

1. Briefly describe the James-Lange theory of emotion. On what grounds did Cannon criticize this theory?

2. Outline the process by which the authors believe emotions are felt. What similarities does this theory share with the James-Lange theory?

3. What physiological, cognitive, and social manipulations were required to test the experimental hypotheses?

4. How did the authors measure subjects' angry responses? Which measure did not produce the expected results?

5. How did subjects in the placebo condition behave in this study? Like which other group were they predicted to behave? Which other group does their behavior most resemble?

Reading 8: Contemporary

The Pursuit of Happiness

David G. Myers and Ed Diener

Many people believe that the job of health professionals is to fix problems. Just as medical doctors are trained to understand illness, psychologists have devoted considerable attention to understanding psychological disorders such as depression and anxiety. The logic of studying medical and psychological problems is straightforward: If you understand the problem, you can fix it. However, in recent years social psychologists, as well as practitioners in a new branch of psychology known as "health psychology," have suggested an alternative approach that focuses on health rather than illness.

For social psychologists, one important aspect of health is subjective well-being. As you will see in this next reading, subjective well-being is a combination of happiness and satisfaction. The authors of this article are not concerned with temporary states of happiness, such as joy after accomplishing an important goal. Instead, they are interested in understanding a form of happiness that is more global and stable—the kind of happiness people use to describe how they feel about their life as a whole.

In the following reading, social psychologists David Myers and Ed Diener review the findings of many recent studies of subjective well-being. They find that most people are reasonably happy about their lives. When they next try to uncover why some people are happier than others, they make some surprising discoveries. After reading their report, you may discover that many of your intuitions about the secrets of happiness are wrong.

❖

Compared with misery, happiness is relatively unexplored terrain for social scientists. Between 1967 and 1994, 46,380 articles indexed in *Psychological Abstracts* mentioned depression, 36,851 anxiety, and 5,099 anger. Only 2,389 spoke of happiness, 2,340 life satisfaction, and 405 joy.

Recently we and other researchers have begun a systematic study of happiness. During the past two decades, dozens of investigators throughout the world have asked several hundred thousand representatively sampled people to reflect on their happiness and satisfaction with life—or what psychologists call "subjective well-being." In the U.S. the National Opinion Research Center at the University of Chicago has surveyed a representative sample of roughly 1,500 people a year since 1957; the Institute for Social Research at the University of Michigan has carried out similar studies on a less regular basis, as has the Gallup Organization. Government-funded efforts have also probed the moods of European countries.

Source: Myers, D. G., & Diener, E. (1996, May). The pursuit of happiness. *Scientific American*, 70–72.

We have uncovered some surprising findings. People are happier than one might expect, and happiness does not appear to depend significantly on external circumstances. Although viewing life as a tragedy has a long and honorable history, the responses of random samples of people around the world about their happiness paint a much rosier picture.

In the University of Chicago surveys, three in 10 Americans say they are very happy, for example. Only one in 10 chooses the most negative description, "not too happy." The majority describe themselves as "pretty happy." (The few exceptions to global reports of reasonable happiness include hospitalized alcoholics, new inmates, new psychotherapy clients, South African blacks during apartheid, and students living under conditions of economic and political oppression.)

How can social scientists measure something as hard to pin down as happiness? Most researchers simply ask people to report their feelings of happiness or unhappiness and to assess how satisfying their lives are. Such self-reported well-being is moderately consistent over years of retesting. Furthermore, those who say they are happy and satisfied seem happy to their close friends and family members and to a psychologist-interviewer. Their daily mood ratings reveal more positive emotions, and they smile more than those who call themselves unhappy. Self-reported happiness also predicts other indicators of well-being. Compared with the depressed, happy people are less self-focused, less hostile and abusive, and less susceptible to disease.

We have found that the even distribution of happiness cuts across almost all demographic classifications of age, economic class, race and educational level. In addition, almost all strategies for assessing subjective well-being—including those that sample people's experience by polling them at random times with beepers—turn up similar findings.

Interviews with representative samples of people of all ages, for example, reveal that no time of life is notably happier or unhappier. Similarly, men and women are equally likely to declare themselves "very happy" and "satisfied" with life, according to a statistical digest of 146 studies by Marilyn J. Haring, William Stock and Morris A. Okun, all then at Arizona State University. Alex Michalos of the University of Northern British Columbia and Ronald Inglehart of the University of Michigan, summarizing newer surveys of 18,000 university students in 39 countries and 170,000 adults in 16 countries, corroborate these findings.

Knowing someone's ethnicity also gives little clue to subjective well-being. African-Americans are only slightly less likely than European-Americans to feel very happy. The National Institute of Mental Health found that rates of depression and alcoholism among blacks and whites are roughly equal. Social psychologists Jennifer K. Crocker of the University of Michigan and Brenda Major of the University of California at Santa Barbara assert that people in disadvantaged groups maintain self-esteem by valuing things at which they excel, by making comparisons within their own groups and by blaming problems on external sources such as prejudice.

WHAT MONEY CAN'T BUY

Wealth is also a poor predictor of happiness. People have not become happier over time as their cultures have become more affluent. Even though Americans earn twice as much in today's dollars as they did in 1957, the proportion of those telling surveyors from the National Opinion Research Center that they are "very happy" has declined from 35 to 29 percent.

Even very rich people—those surveyed among *Forbes* magazine's 100 wealthiest Americans—are only slightly happier than the average American. Those whose income has increased over a 10-year period are not happier than those whose income is stagnant. Indeed, in most nations the correlation between income and happiness is negligible—only in the poorest countries, such as Bangladesh and India, is income a good measure of emotional well-being.

Are people in rich countries happier, by and large, than people in not so rich countries? It appears in general that they are, but the margin may be slim. In Portugal, for example, only one in 10 people reports being very happy, whereas in the much more prosperous Netherlands the proportion of very happy is four in 10. Yet there are curious reversals in this correlation between national wealth and well-being—the Irish during the 1980s consistently reported greater life satisfaction than the wealthier West Germans. Furthermore, other factors, such as civil rights, literacy and duration of democratic government, all of which also promote reported life satisfaction, tend to go hand in hand with national wealth. As a result, it is impossible to tell whether the happiness of people in wealthier nations is based on money or is a by-product of other felicities.

HABITS OF HAPPY PEOPLE

Although happiness is not easy to predict from material circumstances, it seems consistent for those who have it. In one National Institute on Aging study of 5,000 adults, the happiest people in 1973 were still relatively happy a decade later, despite changes in work, residence and family status.

In study after study, four traits characterize happy people. First, especially in individualistic Western cultures, they like themselves. They have high self-esteem and usually believe themselves to be more ethical, more intelligent, less prejudiced, better able to get along with others, and healthier than the average person. (Such findings bring to mind Sigmund Freud's joke about the man who told his wife, "If one of us should die, I think I would go live in Paris.")

Second, happy people typically feel personal control. Those with little or no control over their lives—such as prisoners, nursing home patients, severely impoverished groups or individuals, and citizens of totalitarian regimes—suffer lower morale and worse health. Third, happy people are usually optimistic. Fourth, most happy people are extroverted. Although one might expect that introverts would live more happily in the serenity of their less stressed, contemplative lives, extroverts are happier—whether alone or with others.

The causal arrows for these correlations are uncertain. Does happiness make people more outgoing, or are outgoing people more likely to be happy, perhaps explaining why they marry sooner, get better jobs and make more friends? If these traits indeed predispose their carriers to happiness, people might become happier by acting in certain ways. In experiments, people who feign high self-esteem report feeling more positively about themselves, for example.

Whatever the reason, the close personal relationships that characterize happy lives are also correlated with health. Compared with loners, those who can name several intimate friends are healthier and less likely to die prematurely. For more than nine out of 10 people, the most significant alternative to aloneness is marriage. Although broken marital relationships can cause much misery, a good marriage apparently is a strong source of support. During the 1970s and 1980s, 39 percent of married adults told the National Opinion Research Center they were "very happy," as compared with 24 percent of those who had never married. In other surveys, only 12 percent of those who had divorced perceived themselves to be "very happy." The happiness gap between the married and the never-married was similar for women and men.

Religiously active people also report greater happiness. One Gallup survey found that highly religious people were twice as likely as those lowest in spiritual commitment to declare themselves very happy. Other surveys, including a 16-nation collaborative study of 166,000 people in 14 nations, have found that reported happiness and life satisfaction rise with strength of religious affiliation and frequency of attendance at worship services. Some researchers believe that religious affiliation entails greater social support and hopefulness.

Students of happiness are now beginning to examine happy people's exercise patterns, world views and goals. It is possible that some of the patterns discovered in the research may offer clues for transforming circumstances and behaviors that work against well-being into ones that promote it. Ultimately, then, the scientific study of happiness could help us understand how to build a world that enhances human well-being and to aid people in getting the most satisfaction from their circumstances.

QUESTIONS

1. According to psychologists Jennifer Crocker and Brenda Major, why may members of advantaged and disadvantaged groups report similar levels of happiness?

2. How does happiness change over the life span? How is this change different for people who become increasingly wealthy over time? What two explanations have been given for the finding that people in wealthier countries tend to be happier than people in not so wealthy countries?

3. What four traits characterize happy people in Western cultures? Do you think that extroversion causes happiness or that happiness leads to extroversion?

4. What role does self-efficacy have in happiness? Based on your reading of this article, who would be happier—people who are high self-monitors or those who are low self-monitors?

5. After reading this article, what advice could you give to help someone become happier?

❖ CHAPTER 5 ❖

Well-Being and Health: Caring for the Self

Reading 9:   Classic

Confronting a Traumatic Event: Toward an Understanding of Inhibition and Disease

James W. Pennebaker and Sandra Klihr Beall

The next reading is not a classic in terms of when it was published, in 1986. But in a very short time it has become a modern classic. It has achieved this status because it addresses an issue that has interested psychologists for over 100 years. Freud's first major work in psychology investigated the physical consequences of traumatic events. In this article, James Pennebaker and Sandra Beall breathe new life into Freud's well-known notion of catharsis.

In the following article, Pennebaker and Beall describe a study they conducted over 4 consecutive days in which subjects wrote about either a traumatic event or a trivial one. Subjects who noted traumatic events wrote about either the facts of the event, the emotions they felt during the event, or about both facts and emotions. Although important differences were observed in how the subjects in each group felt immediately following the essay sessions, more impressive was how they felt 6 months later.

The following empirical article is divided into four main sections. In the introduction, the authors discuss the previous literature, going all the way back to Freud, and the psychology of confronting trauma. In the second section, a brief overview of the experimental method is provided. In the third section, the authors discuss in detail the results of the study. (Don't worry too much about deciphering the statistical analysis reported.) Finally, the authors discuss the implications of this work.

❖

Individuals seek to understand major upheavals in their lives. Although a natural way of understanding trauma is by talking with others, many upsetting events cannot easily be discussed. For example, victims of family or sexual abuse, or perpetrators of illegal or illicit acts are often reticent to divulge these experiences because of guilt or fear of punishment. In order not to betray their true feelings or experiences, they must inhibit their overt behaviors, facial expressions and language. In addition to the work of inhibiting behavior following a

---

Source: *Pennebaker, J. W., & Beall, S. K. (1986). Confronting a traumatic event: Toward an understanding of inhibition and disease. Journal of Abnormal Psychology, 95, 274–281.*

trauma, individuals may actively attempt not to think about aspects of the concealed information because of its aversive and unresolved nature. In short, individuals who are unable to confide in others about extremely upsetting events must work to inhibit their behaviors, thoughts and feelings.

In recent years, evidence has accumulated indicating that not disclosing extremely personal and traumatic experiences to others over a long period of time may be related to disease processes. For example, across several surveys, college students and adults who have reported having experienced one of several types of childhood traumatic events (e.g., sexual or physical abuse, death or divorce of parents) were more likely to report current health problems if they had not disclosed the trauma to others than if they had divulged it (Pennebaker & Hoover, 1986, Susman, 1986). These results were obtained independent of measures of social support (See Pennebaker, 1985, for review). Similarly, a survey of spouses of suicide and accidental-death victims revealed that those individuals most likely to become ill in the year following the death were the ones who had not confided in others about their experiences (Pennebaker & O'Heeron, 1984). Survey results indicate that the less individuals confided, the more they ruminated about the death.

A question that emerges from these studies is, What aspects of confiding a traumatic event reduce physiological levels and disease rates? On a strict impersonal level, discussing a trauma allows for social comparison (e.g., Wortman & Dunkel-Schetter, 1979) and coping information from others (e.g., Lazarus, 1966). From a cognitive perspective, talking about or in some way confronting a traumatic event may help the individual to organize (Meichenbaum, 1977), assimilate (Horowitz, 1976), or give meaning to (Silver & Wortman, 1980) the trauma. These approaches assume that a major upheaval undermines the world view of the person. Confronting the event, then, should help the individual categorize the experience into a meaningful frame work.

Many investigators have argued that discussing an event may also serve a cathartic function (e.g., Scheff, 1979). In one of the few well-controlled clinical studies examining catharsis, Nichols (1974) found that patients undergoing somatic-emotional discharge therapy (in which subjects actively express emotions) were more likely to achieve their therapeutic goals than were matched control subjects who received traditional insight therapy. Other studies that have employed venting, in which subjects hit a pillow or write about fantasies associated with aggression, have produced mixed results in subsequent reports of anger (see Nichols & Zax, 1977, for review).

Catharsis and the cathartic method, as developed by Freud (1904/1954) and Breuer and Freud (1895/1966), stress the fundamental links between cognition and affect surrounding a significant or threatening experience. If the experience is particularly disturbing, the memory or ideation may be suppressed, whereas the emotion or affect associated with the event continues to exist in consciousness in the form of anxiety. The cathartic method, or talking cure, was effective in that the forgotten memories were recalled and linked to the anxiety. Breuer and Freud (1895/1966) noted that hysterical symptoms were most likely to disappear after the patient had described the event in fine detail. Although very few studies have directly tested the original catharsis ideas, some recent work suggests that the linking of the cognitive and affective components of a given phobia helps to reduce the magnitude of the phobia (Tesser, Leone, & Clary, 1978).

Our own views assume that to inhibit one's behavior requires physiological work. To not talk about or otherwise confront major upheavals that have occurred in one's life is viewed as a form of inhibition. Actively inhibiting one's behavior, thoughts, and/or feelings over time places cumulative stress on the body and thus increases the probability of stress-related diseases (cf. Selye, 1976). It would follow that if individuals actively inhibit divulging personal or traumatic events, or both, allowing them to do so in a benign setting could have the positive effect of reducing long-term stress and stress-related disease. The original purpose of the present project was to learn if merely writing about a given traumatic event would reduce stress associated with inhibition in both the short run and over time. Our second purpose was to attempt to evaluate the aspects of dealing with a past trauma that were most effective in reducing stress.

Because we were interested in examining the effects of divulging traumatic events independent of social feedback, subjects in the present experiment were required to write rather than talk about upsetting experiences. On 4 consecutive nights, subjects wrote about either a trivial preassigned topic (control condition) or a traumatic experience in their own life from one of three perspectives. Analogous to the venting view of catharsis, trauma-emotion subjects were instructed to write each night about their feelings concerning their traumatic experiences without discussing the precipitating event. In line with a strict cognitive approach, the trauma-fact subjects were required to write about traumatic events without discussing their feelings. Similar to the cathartic method, the trauma-combination subjects wrote about both the traumatic events and their feelings about them. Heart rate, blood pressure, and self-reports were collected during each session. Finally, health center records and mail-back surveys were collected from 4 to 6 months following the experiment in order to determine long-term health consequences of the study.

METHOD

Overview

Within the 4 × 4 (Condition × Session) between-within design, 46 undergraduates were randomly assigned to write one of four types of essays for 15 minutes each night for 4 consecutive evenings. Those in the control condition ($n = 12$) were assigned different trivial topics each night; those in the trauma-emotion cell ($n = 12$) wrote about their feelings associated with one or more traumas in their life; trauma-fact subjects ($n = 11$) wrote about the facts surrounding traumatic events; and trauma-combination subjects ($n = 11$) wrote about both their feeling and the facts surrounding the traumas. Before and following the writing of each essay, subjects had their blood pressure, heart rate, and self-reported moods, and physical symptoms collected. Four months after completion of the study, subjects completed questionnaires about their health and general views of the experiment. In addition, records for both prior to and 6 months following the experiment were collected from the health and counseling centers. . . .

RESULTS

Overall, the study has four general classes of variables. The first class dealt with the essays themselves, including what the subjects wrote about, the way they approached the essays, and their perceptions of the essays. The second type of variable relates to the subjects' responses to the essays. That is, we sought to learn about changes in the subjects' physiological levels, moods, and symptom reports from before to after writing each essay across the 4 days. The third broad issue concerned the long-term effects of the experiment. For example, did the study influence the various health-related variables or have any lasting psychological or behavioral impact, or both? A final group of variables of interest includes several individual difference factors, such as sex of subject, and measures of anxiety, symptom-reporting, and so forth. Specifically, we sought to learn if any of these variables relate to any of our manipulated factors. . . .

Content of Essays

. . . . Of the 127 trauma essays, 27% dealt with the death of a close friend, family member, or pet; 20% involved boyfriend/girlfriend problems (usually the breaking of a relationship); and 16% centered on fights among or with parents or friends. Other percentages of topics were, major failure, such as not being elected cheerleader (8%); public humiliation, such as overhearing friends laughing about them (8%); leaving home to go to college (7%); being involved in car accident (5%); their own health problems (4%); sexual abuse, such as incest or rape (3%); and other, or unclassifiable (13%). The percentages total more than 100% because some of the topics could be classified in two separate categories. One-way ANOVAs [ANOVA stands for analysis of variance] comparing the three trauma conditions indicated no consistent differences in type of topics written about. Note, however, that a significantly higher percentage of trauma-emotion essays could not be categorized ($p = .03$). The only individual difference variable related to essay topic was sex of subject: women were more likely to write about losing a boyfriend/girlfriend; men were more likely to focus on death of a pet (both $ps < .05$).

It is difficult to convey the powerful and personal nature of the majority of trauma condition essays with statistical analyses. One woman wrote about teaching her brother to sail; on his first solo outing, he drowned. The father of a male subject separated from his mother when the subject was about 9 years old. Prior to leaving home, the father told the subject that the divorce was the subject's fault (because his birth had disrupted the family). When she was 10 years old, one female subject had been asked to clean her room because her grandmother was to be visiting that night. The girl did not do so. That night, the grandmother tripped on one of the girl's toys, broke her hip, and died of complications during surgery a week later. Another subject depicted her seduction by her grandfather when she was about 12 years old. Another, who had written about relatively trivial topics during the first sessions, admitted during the last evening that she was gay. A male subject reported that he had considered suicide because he thought that he had disappointed his parents.

Two additional observations are in order. First, there was no discernible pattern about the depth or emotionality of the subject's topic from one night to another. For some subjects, the first session produced the most profound essay, whereas for others the final session did. Often a particularly emotional essay would be followed by a startlingly superficial one. No individual difference measures were related to patterning or overall depth of the essay topic. Second, a mere reading of the topics by each subject overlooks the person's reaction to it. For example, approximately one third of the essays dealing with the death of a close friend of family member indicated that the subjects were not particularly upset by the loss of the person. Rather, the death made them aware of their own mortality.

Responses to Essays

Before and after each day's essay writing, the heart rate and blood pressure of each of the subjects were measured by the experimenter. Also before and after writing the essay, subjects completed a brief questionnaire that assessed the degree to which they were experiencing each of nine physical symptoms and eight moods.

Physiological Measures. Because heart rate and systolic and diastolic blood pressure reflect a general cardiovascular response, all three measures were simultaneously subjected to a $4 \times 4 \times 2 \times 3$ (Condition $\times$ Session $\times$ Pre-versus Post-Essay Reading $\times$ Physiological Index [heart rate, systolic and diastolic blood pressure]) between-within repeated measures multivariate analysis of variance (MANOVA). Across all three physiological indexes, a Condition $\times$ Session $\times$ Pre-Post interaction attained significance, $F(9, 116) = 1.99$, $p = 0.46$. In addition, the type of physiological index interacted with both session, $F,(6, 37) = 11.7, p < .001$, and Condition $\times$ Pre-Post, $F(6, 80) = 2.26, p < 0.46$. No other main effects or interactions were significant.

Separate repeated measures ANOVAs on each of the physiological measures indicated that all of the above effects were attributable to changes in systolic blood pressure. That is, a $4 \times 4 \times 2$ (Condition $\times$ Session $\times$ Pre-Post) between-within ANOVA yielded a significant session main effect indicating a general lowering of blood pressures over the course of the experiment for subjects in all conditions, $F(3, 40) = 16.6, p < .001$. In addition, a marginally significant Condition $\times$ Pre-Post interaction, $F(3, 42) = 2.56, p \times 0.68$, and a Condition $\times$ Session $\times$ Pre-Post interaction, $F(9, 116) = 2.23, p = .025$, were obtained. As depicted in Table 1, the Condition $\times$ Pre-Post interaction reflects the fact that subjects in the control and trauma-fact cells demonstrated significantly larger decreases in blood pressure following the writing sessions. The triple interaction is primarily attributable to the trauma-combination condition subjects, who initially evidenced a large increase in blood pressure from before to after the essay. After the first session, however, the trauma-combination subjects demonstrated moderate decreases in blood pressure from before to after the writing session. Separate repeated measures ANOVAs on heart rate and diastolic blood pressure yielded no significant condition main effects or interactions.

Self-Reports. Before and after each essay, subjects responded to a questionnaire asking them to rate the degree to which they were currently experiencing each of nine symptoms and eight moods—ranging from *not at all* (1) to *a great deal* (7). Because previous research has

TABLE 1 MEANS OF ESSAY-RELATED VARIABLES BY CONDITION

| Variables | CONDITION | | | |
	Control	Trauma-Emotion	Trauma-Fact	Trauma-Combination
Essay-related dimensions				
Personal	2.8_a	5.2_b	4.4_b	4.9_b
Reveal emotion	2.5_a	5.3_b	2.5_a	5.4_b
Subjects writing personal essay				
previously not discussed (%)	16.6_a	75.0_b	63.6_b	54.6_b
Words per essay	252_a	301_{ab}	296_{ab}	340_{ab}
Self-references per essay (%)	2.4_a	11.3_b	7.1_c	8.4_c
Self-report and physiological measures				
Systolic blood pressure change	-3.9_a	-0.8_{ab}	-3.0_a	$+0.4_b$
Negative moods change	-1.0_a	$+1.7_{bc}$	$+0.6_{ab}$	$+3.8_c$
N	12	12	11	11

Note: The personal and reveal emotion means are based on subjects' self-reports of their own essays averages all four sessions. Ratings were based on 7-point scales, where 7 = *essay was personal or revealed emotion to a great extent.* Change scores are computed by subtracting the pre-essay score from the post-essay score. A positive number, then, indicates an increase in blood pressure or negative emotion following the essay. For none of the above variables are there significant initial differences. Means with different subscripts are different at $p \leq .05$.

indicated that the symptoms (racing heart, upset stomach, headache, backache, dizziness, shortness of breath, cold hands, sweaty hands, pounding heart) such as these are correlated, the items were summed to yield an overall symptom index (see Pennebaker, 1982 for scalar properties of comparable symptom and mood indexes). Similarly, the summed mood items (nervous, sad, guilty, not happy, not contented, fatigued, anxious) composed a general negative mood index.

A $4 \times 4 \times 2$ (Condition × Session × Pre-versus Post-Essay) repeated measures ANOVA on the self-reported symptom index yielded no main effects or interactions. A comparable analysis on the negative mood index resulted in a significant pre-post main effect, $F(1, 42) = 4.49$, $p = .04$, such that subjects tended to report more negative moods after writing each day's essay. In addition, a significant Pre-Post × Session interaction emerged, $F(3, 40) = 3.07$, $p = .04$, such that over time, subjects' negative moods increased after writing each essay. Finally, the Condition × Pre-Post interaction attained significance, $F(3, 42) = 2.83, p = .05$. As seen in Table 1, these effects reflect the fact that subjects in the trauma conditions reported more negative moods after writing the essays, whereas control subjects typically felt more positive.

The means presented in Table 1 depict the general changes in blood pressure and self-reported negative moods from before to after writing each day's essay. It is of interest that across each of these measures the means of the trauma-emotion and trauma-combination conditions are similar, as are the trauma-fact and control cells. Indeed, contrasts using the mean-square error term comparing these two sets of cells indicate that they are all significantly different.

Further, in referring back to Table 1, this general pattern holds for the degree to which subjects revealed emotions and the percentage of self-references used in their essays. The implications of these similarities in response to a relatively brief stimulus are discussed later.

Long-Term Effects

At the conclusion of the school year, Student Health Center personnel recorded the number of times that each subject had visited the health center for each of the following reasons: illness, injury, check-up, psychiatric, or other. The number of visits were recorded separately for number of visits prior to the experiment (i.e., from the beginning of the school year in late August to mid-November) and following the experiment (mid-November through mid-May). Counseling center records were recorded for number of visits for psychological versus other reasons (e.g., vocational) for both prior to and following the experiment. Approximately 4 months following the completion of the laboratory study, subjects were mailed a questionnaire that included a number of health and health-related items that had been assessed on the beginning day of the experiment. The items on the follow-up survey asked subjects about health problems that had occurred since the completion of the laboratory study. Finally, two additional questions were included that asked subjects how much they had thought about and had been affected by their participation in the study. Further, subjects were encouraged to write, in their own words, their perceptions of the experiment. All but four of the subjects completed and returned the questionnaire.

Health and Counseling Center Visits. The number of visits to the health center for illness was subjected to a 4×2 (Condition $\times$ Before versus After the Experiment) repeated measures ANOVA. Although neither main effect approached significance, the predicted Condition $\times$ Before-After interaction was obtained, $F(3, 42) = 2.74$, $p = .055$. As can be seen in Table 2, the change in health center visits for illness was due to an overall increase in all conditions except the trauma-combination cell. Separated repeated measures ANOVA for the number of health center visits due to injury, psychiatric, or other reasons yielded no significant effects. Over the course of the year, only 1 subject visited the counseling center for psychological reasons and 2 for vocational help. Analyses of variance on these data produced no significant effects.

Follow-up Questionnaire Data. Although only 42 of the original 46 subjects returned the follow-up questionnaires, their health data were similar to the health center findings. Subjects were asked at the beginning of the experiment in November and on the follow-up questionnaire to report the number of days their activities had been restricted due to illness (since the beginning of school, during the November administration, and since the experiment for the follow-up questionnaire). A repeated measures ANOVA yielded a trend for the Condition $\times$ Time interaction, $F(3, 38) = 2.19$, $p = .10$, suggesting that those in the control condition reported the most days and those in the trauma-combination the fewest (see Table 2). On both administrations of the questionnaire, subjects were asked to check if they had

TABLE 2 SUMMARY OF LONG-TERM EFFECTS

Variables	Control	Trauma-Emotion	Trauma-Fact	Trauma-Combination
		CONDITION		
No. of health center visits				
Prior to study	0.33	0.33	0.27	0.54
Following study	1.33$_{ab}$	1.58$_a$	1.45$_{ab}$	0.54$_b$
Change in visits	1.00$_a$	1.25$_a$	1.18$_a$	0.00$_b$
Self-reported health measures				
Change in No. of days restricted activity for illness	4.00$_a$	1.18$_{ab}$	1.90$_{ab}$	0.70$_b$
Change in no. of illnesses	0.18$_a$	−0.73$_b$	0.10$_a$	−0.60$_b$
Amount of thought about study	1.82$_a$	2.73$_b$	1.40$_a$	2.70$_b$
Degree of long-lasting effects	1.36	2.45	1.70	2.40

Note: The health center visit means are based on all subjects ($N = 46$). All other variables are based on follow-up self-reports ($n = 42$). See text for significance levels of one-way analyses of variance. Means with different subscripts are significantly different, $p \leq .05$. No significant initial differences by condition were obtained for any of the above variables.

experienced each of eight specific health problems (ulcers, high blood pressure, constipation/diarrhea, colds or flu, migraine headaches, acne or skin disorders, heart problems, or other major difficulties). The summed health problem index was then subjected to a repeated measures ANOVA. Overall, subjects in the trauma-combination and trauma-emotion conditions reported reductions in health problems relative to those in control and trauma-fact cells, $F(3, 38) = 3.05$, $p = .04$. For none of the above measures were there significant condition effects at Time 1. In addition, subjects were asked about several health-related behaviors, such as aspirin consumption, and alcohol, tobacco, and caffeine use for both prior to and following the experiment. No significant differences were obtained on any measure

All of the subjects were asked to rate the degree to which they had thought about or had been affected by the experiment. In response to the question, "Since the end of the experiment back in November, how much have you thought about what you wrote," on a scale ranging from *not at all* (1) to *a great deal* (7), a marginally significant condition main effect was obtained, $F(3, 38) = 2.58$, $p = .06$. As seen in Table 2, those in the trauma-emotion and trauma-combination conditions were more likely to have thought about their essays than those in the trauma-facts or control cells.

Finally, subjects responded to the question, "Looking back on the experiment, do you feel as if it has had any long-lasting effects? Please answer this in your own words as well as rating it on a 1 to 7 scale." Although the overall one-way ANOVA was not statistically significant, $F(3, 38) = 1.43$, $p = .25$, the Means × Condition interactions is presented in the table. Overall, 7 of the 31 trauma subjects rated the long-lasting effect as 4 or higher along the 7-point scale. The responses to the open-ended question were uniformly positive. Because of the potentially sensitive nature of this paradigm, we feel that it is useful to present the responses of each of these subjects:

Trauma-emotion subjects. It helped me think about what I felt during those times. I never realized how it affected me before.

It helped to write things out when I was tense, so now when I'm worried I sit and write it out . . . later I feel better.

I had to think and resolve past experiences . . . One result of the experiment is peace of mind, and a method to relieve emotional experiences. To have to write emotions and feelings helped me understand how I felt and why.

Trauma-fact subject. It made me think a little deeper about some of the important parts of my life.

Trauma-combination subjects. It made me think a lot—But I'm still in the same situation.

If one writes down things that worry one, there is a tendency to feel better.

Although I have not talked with any one about what I wrote, I was finally able to deal with it, work through the pain instead of trying to block it out. Now it doesn't hurt to think about it.

DISCUSSION

The results of the experiment should be viewed as promising rather than definitive. Writing about earlier traumatic experience was associated with both short-term increases in physiological arousal and long-term decreases in health problems. Although these effects were most pronounced among subjects who wrote about both the trauma and their emotions associated with the trauma, there was substantial overlap in effects with those subjects who wrote only about their emotions associated with traumatic events. Subjects who were instructed to write only about previous traumatic events—without referring to their own emotions—were similar to control condition subjects on most physiological, health, and self-report measures.

Despite the general pattern of results, several weaknesses underscore the importance of future replication. Some of the measures yielded contradictory or only marginally significant effects. The number of subjects was quite small. Subjects were not selected in any way for having a debilitating undisclosed past trauma: therefore, it was impossible to evaluate the degree to which such subjects carried the results. In addition, two possible confounds associated with demand characteristics and changes in coping strategies may have influenced the health center data. These alternative explanations, as well as a number of issues surrounding catharsis, self-disclosure, coping strategies, and behavioral inhibition, are discussed next.

Recall that subjects were debriefed following the final essay-writing session. Although subjects were told about the experimental design, we were honest in admitting that we had no idea which, if any, condition would be most related to health. It is possible that subjects regulated their health center visits and follow-up questionnaire reports to some degree on the basis of our debriefing information.

One unforeseen mechanism that may also have affected the results was that we apparently provided some subjects with a new strategy for coping with both traumatic and significant daily events. It was clear that among those subjects who responded in writing to our follow-up questionnaire, some had begun writing about their experiences on their own after having participated in the experiment. Although we suspect that this behavior occurred with greater frequency in the trauma-emotion and trauma-combination cells, we cannot evaluate its direct impact on health.

Although these alternative explanations must be considered seriously, several of the experimental findings offer important directions for future research. For all but the objective health center data, the trauma-emotion and trauma-combination subjects were strikingly similar. Both groups evidenced higher blood pressure and more negative moods, relative to the other groups, each day after writing the essay; and both groups thought a great deal about the study in the months following the study. The results from both of these conditions cause one to argue against simple venting or discharge theory of catharsis, which would predict that the expression of emotion should make the person more relaxed or happy or both. Despite these relatively brief negative effects, both groups showed some long-term benefits. For example, self-reports concerning the change in number of different illnesses reported indicated in improvement in health for both groups. Similar trends emerged for self-reported days of restricted activity due to illness. Unfortunately, we cannot evaluate whether the long-term similarity between the two groups for these self-report measures reflects expectancy effects or true self-perceptions. Clearly, writing about the emotional side of a traumatic event was upsetting and physiologically arousing. However, the arousal per se may not have produced any long-term changes.

Perhaps one of the more unexpected findings was that having subjects write about the objective aspects of the traumatic events alone was neither arousing nor particularly upsetting. Indeed, this is reminiscent of the finding with subjects in studies by Lazarus and colleagues (e.g., Lazarus, Opton, Nomikos, & Rankin, 1965), in which hearing a nonemotional and/or intellectual description of an upsetting scene greatly reduced physiological responses to that event. Despite the fact that there were no short-term adverse effects from writing the nonemotional description of one's own traumatic experiences, there appear to be few, if any, long-term benefits in any objective of subjective indexes of health. It should be emphasized that these results are not necessarily inconsistent with the view of theorists who argue that the resolution of a trauma is associated with the cognitive work of organizing, assimilating, or finding meaning to the events surrounding the trauma (e.g., Horowitz, 1976; Silver, Boon, & Stones, 1983; Swann & Predmore, 1985). Rather, our findings point to the importance of emphasizing the emotions that coincide with the objective (or, at least, perceived) trauma.

Although the results of the experiment support what has been hypothesized by theorists in psychology and psychosomatics for decades, the exact mechanisms linking confiding and disease have not been sufficiently identified. The early ideas of Freud and Breuer were partially confirmed, in that tying both the cognitions and affect surrounding traumatic events was optimally effective in maintaining long-term health. Unlike their early claims, however, these effects were not immediate. It must be admitted, however, that subjects wrote only briefly each night. Either longer writing times or collecting our self-reports and physiological measures several minutes or hours after each night's essay, or both, may have demonstrated different results.

An interesting variation on this idea, posited by Jourard (1971) argues that self-disclosure allows for one's feelings and thoughts to become more concrete, which ultimately results in greater self-knowledge. Disease results, according to Jourard, when the motive toward self-understanding is blocked. Although we cannot evaluate the role of a possible blocked motive related to understanding, the concept of making thoughts and feelings concrete may be critically important. In this study, subjects did not receive social support or social comparison information. In none of the essays did subjects write about developing some type of coping strategies for the future. No love, positive feedback, or other mechanism commonly used to explain psychotherapy was at work.

The ideas of Jourard closely parallel many of our ideas abut behavioral inhibition. We have argued that the act of inhibiting behavior is psychologically stressful (cf. Pennebaker & Chew, 1985). Previous surveys indicate that not confiding in others about a traumatic event—which we view as a form of behavioral inhibition—is associated with disease. As our study has indicated, one need not orally confide to another. Rather, the mere act of writing about an event and the emotions surrounding it is sufficient to reduce the long-term work of inhibition.

We have raised more questions than we have answered. The general pattern of results—although promising—must be replicated under more stringent conditions. Further, the role of inhibition must be demonstrated more precisely. Although writing about traumas appears to have positive long-term health effects, we must pinpoint the aspect of this exercise that is beneficial. Possibilities include making an event concrete, linking the affective and cognitive aspects, the reduction of forces associated with behavioral inhibition over time, and so forth. The ultimate resolution of these issues should have direct bearing on our understanding of social, cognitive, and psychosomatic processes.

REFERENCES

BREUER, J., & FREUD, S. (1966). *Studies on hysteria.* New York: Avon. (Original work published 1895)

FREUD, S. (1954). *The origins of psychoanalysis.* New York: Basic Books. (Original work published 1904)

HOROWITZ, M. J. (1976). *Stress response syndromes.* New York: Jacob Aronson.

JOURARD, S. M. (1971). *Self-disclosure: An experimental analysis of the transparent self.* New York: Wiley.

LAZARUS, R., (1966). *Psychological stress and the coping process.* New York: McGraw-Hill.

LAZARUS, R., OPTON, E., NOMIKOS, M., & RANKIN, N. (1965). The principle of short-circuiting of threat: Further evidence. *Journal of Personality, 33,* 622–635.

MEICHENBAUM, D. (1977). *Cognitive-behavior modification: An integrative approach.* New York: Plenum.

NICHOLS, M. P. (1974). Outcome of brief cathartic psychotherapy. *Journal of Consulting and Clinical Psychology, 42,* 403–410.

NICHOLS, M. P., & ZAX, M. (1977). *Catharsis in psychotherapy.* New York: Gardner Press.

PENNEBAKER, J. W. (1982). *The psychology of physical symptoms.* New York: Springer-Verlag.

PENNEBAKER, J. W. (1985). Traumatic experience and psychosomatic disease: Exploring the roles of behavioral inhibition, obsession, and confiding. *Canadian Psychology, 26,* 82–95.

PENNEBAKER, J. W., & CHEW, C. H. (1985). Deception, electrodermal activity, and inhibition of behavior. *Journal of Personality and Social Psychology, 49,* 1427–1433.

PENNEBAKER, J. W., & HOOVER, C. W. (1986). Inhibition and cognition: Toward an understanding of trauma and disease. In R. J. Davidson, G. E. Schwartz & D. Shapiro (Eds.), *Consciousness and self-regulation* (Vol. 4, pp. 107–136).New York: Plenum.

PENNEBAKER, J. W., & O'HEERON, R. C. (1984). Confiding in others and illness rates among spouses of suicide and accidental-death victims. *Journal of Abnormal Psychology, 93,* 473–476.

SCHEFF, T. J. (1979). *Catharsis in healing, ritual, and drama.* Berkeley: University of California Press.

SELYE, H. (1976). *The stress of life.* New York: McGraw-Hill.

SILVER, R. L., BOON, C., & STONES, M. H. (1983). Searching for meaning in misfortune: Making sense of incest. *Journal of Social Issues, 39,* 81–102.

SILVER, R. L., & WORTMAN, C. B. (1980). Coping with undesirable life events. In J. Garber & M. E. P. Seligman (Eds.), *Human helplessness: Theory and applications* (pp. 279–375). New York: Academic Press.

SUSMAN, J. R. (1986). *The relationship of expressiveness styles and elements of traumatic experiences to self-reported illness.* Unpublished master's thesis, Southern Methodist University.

SWANN, W. B., & PREDMORE, S. C. (1985). Intimates as agents of social support: Sources of consolation or despair? *Journal of Personality and Social Psychology, 49,* 1609–1617.

TESSER, A., LEONE, C., & CLARY, E. G. (1978). Affect control: Process constraints versus catharsis. *Cognitive Therapy and Research, 2,* 265–274.

WORTMAN, C. B., & DUNKEL-SCHETTER, C. (1979). Interpersonal relationships and cancer: A theroetical analysis. *Journal of Social Issues, 35,* 120–155.

QUESTIONS

1. According to Pennebaker and Beall, what are the health consequences of not confiding traumatic events? Briefly list a social, cognitive, and emotional explanation that has been given for this relationship. Where does the cathartic explanation fit in?

2. What are the authors' own views about the relationship between confiding traumatic events and health? Which of the three types of traditional explanations does this study investigate?

3. According to the physiological measure taken immediately before and after subjects wrote essays, which group seems to benefit the most from the essay writing?

4. Which group showed the best overall health in the 6 months following the study? Did these subjects also feel better immediately after the essay sessions?

5. Considering all of the data discussed in this article, which of the four original hypotheses (social, cognitive, emotional, cathartic) were supported?

Reading 10: Contemporary

Can Your Mind Heal Your Body?

Editors of Consumer Reports

Arguments over how the mind and body are related are as old as recorded history. Whereas some people and cultures see mind and body as one tightly interwoven unit, others believe that the two operate entirely separately from each other. In contemporary Western society, our view seems to be somewhat one-directional. While allowing that biological processes affect mental processes in many ways (e.g., physical pain, alcohol and drugs), we are more reluctant to accept the idea that mental processes affect biological ones.

This unidirectional view has dominated Western medicine throughout the twentieth century. However, other cultures, most notably Eastern cultures, hold a different view. In these societies, meditation and other mental techniques have a long history of helping people cope with physical problems. Recently these techniques have made their way into the West and are winning many supporters.

Unfortunately, our understanding of mental healing techniques is still limited. The confusion over exactly what the mind can do to help and hurt the body led the editors of Consumer Reports *to investigate which techniques work and which do not. In the following article they review the latest evidence, both medical and psychological, and suggest that "the power of 'mind/body medicine' may be greater than you think."*

❖

No one would deny that the mind can affect the body's health. The ancient Greeks knew it. So did Sir William Osler, the great 19th-century physician who was the father of modern medicine. ("The care of tuberculosis," said Osler, "depends more on what the patient has in his head than what he has in his chest.") In our own century, too, physicians have been intrigued by the mind/body connection, and have explored it under the rubric of "psychosomatic" medicine. But this venerable tradition has coexisted with a much more questionable one: a tradition of self-styled healers, some true believers and some outright charlatans, who have proclaimed that the mind has almost miraculous power to cure disease.

Recently, physicians have developed a new interest in the mind's role in health—and so have the entrepreneurs. Ads for books and tapes promise that these products can "Trigger Your Body's Own Natural Immunities! For 21 Days Absolutely Free!" or claim that "Control of the Immune System Comes Into Your Hands!" One best-selling author now offers a tape of "Meditations for Enhancing Your Immune System."

Source: Can your mind heal your body? (1993, February). *Consumer Reports*, 108–115.

Even worse is the dark side to these optimistic claims: If good thoughts can make you well, the logic goes, then bad thoughts might kill you. Several popular writers have implied that people become ill because of their emotional problems, or even because they have "wished" themselves to be sick. This blame-the-victim philosophy has been particularly common—and particularly destructive—when it comes to cancer. One book of self-help tips for healing claims that cancer comes from "deep hurt . . . resentment [and] carrying hatreds." And some healers tell patients to ask themselves, "Why did I need this cancer?" as a standard exercise— one that can easily turn into an exercise in guilt.

In fact, the mind is neither a miracle cure nor a lethal weapon. There is no good evidence that any kind of emotional distress predisposes people to cancer. And conversely, there is no evidence that meditating or listening to a special audiotape will make a tumor go away. Such claims are little more than wishful thinking about positive thinking.

But these distortions mask an important medical reality. The evidence is rapidly growing that thoughts, beliefs, and emotions can have a major impact on physical health. And research is showing that relaxation, meditation, hypnosis, biofeedback, support groups, and psychotherapy may affect the course of physical illness. The result is a new synthesis in medical theory and practice that's coming to be known as mind/body medicine.

Today's upsurge of interest in mind/body medicine dates back to the mid-1970s, when a series of experiments deepened the scientific understanding of the ways in which the mind and emotions may affect physical health. In particular, those experiments showed that the mind can influence the immune system, along with other systems and organs in the body. The immune system plays a central role in health and illness; it defends the body against both cancerous cells and external invaders such as bacteria or viruses.

As this research has advanced, clinicians and medical researchers have begun testing ways to use the power of the mind to help their patients. At the Stanford University School of Medicine, for example, a psychiatrist is using supportive group therapy for women with advanced breast cancer—an approach that his research has shown to lengthen the lives of such women significantly. At Duke University Medical Center, men and women with cardiovascular disease are being taught to control their feelings of hostility and anger, in the hope that those emotional changes will benefit their hearts. And at Harvard Medical School, a simple technique for eliciting the body's "relaxation response" is being used to help patients with problems as diverse as hypertension, headaches, and infertility.

Because laypeople can't easily distinguish the responsible, innovative clinicians and researchers from the New Age healers whose credentials and claims are often questionable, anyone who wants to explore this promising field would benefit from expert guidance in telling the two apart. Unfortunately, your own physician will probably not be as helpful a guide as you'd like.

Although mind/body medicine has become a more credible field in recent years, most physicians are still unlikely to be aware of current research in this area—even if they follow the medical literature. Much of the research in mind/body medicine has been published in journals of psychiatry or psychology, or in journals that cover individual medical specialties. It is only recently that mind/body research papers have been published in the most widely read journals, such as *The Lancet* and *The New England Journal of Medicine.*

In addition, many physicians may be leery of mind/body approaches because they are not completely understood. There is still no comprehensive, unifying theory to explain just how the mind affects the body—nothing that is the equivalent of the germ theory of disease, or even close to it.

Nevertheless, there is emerging scientific evidence from three converging areas of research:

- Physiological research, which investigates the connections between the brain and nervous system and the rest of the body.
- Epidemiological research, which measures various correlations between psychological factors and illness in the population at large.
- Clinical research, which tests the effectiveness of mind/body approaches in treating specific diseases.

Taken together, these different kinds of research are beginning to show a coherent picture—like a jigsaw puzzle that still has many pieces missing, but that is starting to form a recognizable image.

TRACING THE CONNECTIONS

The physiological research behind mind/body medicine began early in this century, when Harvard physiologist Walter B. Cannon described the fight-or-flight response. Faced with a threat, he discovered, the body produces adrenaline and other "stress hormones" that trigger a cascade of physiological changes: Heart rate, blood pressure, and muscle tension all rise sharply, and the blood sugar level rises for quick energy.

Those changes marshal the body to readiness, as if preparing it to fight or run. But while this fight-or-flight response was essential to survival in a time when human beings faced physical threats, it's not so helpful for dealing with the stresses of the modern world. And if your stress hormones are chronically elevated by high-pressure situations—working under constant deadlines, say, or having ongoing arguments with your spouse—the impact on your body can raise the risk that you will become ill.

Although these basic aspects of the stress response have been known for many years, the current research in mind/body medicine was kindled by a discovery made in 1974. In that year, Robert Ader, an experimental psychologist at the University of Rochester School of Medicine and Dentistry, first found evidence that the nervous system and the immune system are intimately connected. His work suggested that the interaction between mind and body might be more intricate, more sophisticated, and more constant than the primitive fight-or-flight response suggested.

Ader and his colleagues had been doing a series of experiments with rats in classical behavioral conditioning and found some unusual results that led the researchers to pursue a new direction. They gave rats saccharin-laced water together with an injection of a drug that suppresses the immune system; shortly after the rats tasted the sweet water, key cells in their immune systems declined in number. The researchers then showed that giving the same rats saccharin water alone later on produced the same effect: Their bodies had "learned" to respond to a sweet taste with a drop in immune function.

Until Ader's experiments, anatomists, physicians, and biologists believed that the brain and the immune system were separate entities, neither able to influence the other. Those experiments have now been repeated successfully, however, and scientists are finding that there are, indeed, many connections between these systems. Nerve endings have been found in the tissues that produce, develop, and store immune-system cells—the thymus, lymph nodes, spleen, and bone marrow—and immune-system cells have been shown to respond to chemical signals produced by the nervous system. These findings have generated the new field known as psychoneuroimmunology, PNI: "psycho" for mind, "neuro" for the neuroendocrine system (the nervous and hormonal systems), and "immunology" for the immune system.

The working hypothesis for much research in PNI is that psychological distress can suppress the immune system enough to increase the risk of physical illness. Just in the last decade, researchers have begun to study the effects of normal stressful events on the human immune system. At the Ohio State University College of Medicine, for example, Janice Kiecolt-Glaser (a psychologist) and Ronald Glaser (an immunologist) have shown declines in the activity of immune-system cells in several groups of people under stress: medical students taking final exams, people caring for loved ones with Alzheimer's disease, and women who have recently gone through a difficult divorce.

A key question now is whether changes like those the Glasers have measured are great enough to affect physical health. That chain of connection between stress, immune function, and illness is still unproven. However, many studies over the last three decades have shown that stress, and the way a person deals with it, can have a major effect on the risk of illness.

WHO GETS SICK?

Many epidemiological researchers have studied the links between stress, psychological factors, and patterns of illness in large groups of people. One classic study, done in the early 1960s for the U.S. Navy, showed that men who had gone through serious life changes—a divorce, move, job loss, or the like—had an increased chance of becoming seriously ill in the months that followed those upsets. The researchers found that even occasions for celebrations, like retirement or marriage, can take a toll because of the change they entail.

Many more-recent studies, however, have failed to find such a direct connection between stressful events and illness. That doesn't meant that stress is irrelevant, only that its effects on health may be more complex than anyone realized at first. The reaction to stressful events varies tremendously among individuals: Faced with the same challenges, one person will get sick and another won't.

A variety of psychological factors—including personality characteristics, mood, and coping style—can affect the way a person deals with stress and thus affect physical health. For example, Dr. Redford Williams at Duke University has shown that people who are chronically angry are more likely to be affected by the stresses of life—and more likely to develop heart disease. . . . Other studies have now shown that people who have an optimistic outlook on life—as measured by various psychological tests—are healthier than pessimists overall.

Recent research has focused on the ways that social networks affect the ability to cope with stress, and thus affect physical health. There is much suggestive evidence that support from family and friends—and even the emotional benefits of having a pet—can reduce the risk of illness, and boost recovery for people who do get sick.

The next step will be to go beyond such population studies to examine the link between stress and illness in careful, well-controlled experiments. In 1991, Sheldon Cohen, a psychologist at Carnegie Mellon University, reported on one of the first studies of this kind. Dr. Cohen and his colleagues had given volunteers measured doses of a cold virus and then waited to see who got sick. Result: The chance that a volunteer would get a cold or respiratory infection was directly proportional to the amount of stress he said he had experienced during the past year. This landmark study, published in *The New England Journal of Medicine,* provided the first well-controlled demonstration that stress can increase the risk of infection.

WHAT TREATMENTS CAN HELP?

If stress can make you sick, will learning to cope with stress boost your immune system? Right now, that's a central question in the field of mind/body medicine—both for researchers and for the general public. "The public wants very badly to believe that people can control their immune responses with their minds," notes Dr. Steven Locke, a psychiatrist at Harvard Medical School who has done research in mind/body medicine and reviewed recent studies in the field.

According to Dr. Locke, "More than 40 published studies have looked at the ability of human beings to alter some aspect of immunity using some mental strategy—biofeedback, guided imagery, meditation, hypnosis, and so on. Most of them report some positive outcome. But while there are some excellent studies, there are also some pretty sloppy ones. Most important, the studies that have been done are still so different from each other that we don't have a clear understanding of what's going on and how it happens."

While their effects on immune function are still uncertain, however, mind/body approaches have other physiological effects that can have an impact on health. Many researchers are now testing the value of these approaches in treating a variety of conditions.

BASIC RELAXATION

Probably the most widely used mind/body approach is simple relaxation. The basic goal of relaxation is to counteract the physical changes associated with stress—such as muscle tension, high blood pressure, and hormonal changes—while also calming the mind.

Fighting the stress response isn't simply a matter of telling your body to calm down. The sympathetic nervous system, which regulated the fight-or-flight response, operates outside the realm of conscious control. But the body also has a *para*sympathetic nervous system, which helps compensate for periods of high stress—for example, by lowering heart rate, blood pressure, and muscle tension. A basic goal of relaxation is to trigger the parasympathetic nervous system in a positive way.

Some techniques for doing this go back many decades. A method called progressive muscle relaxation, developed in the 1920s, involves tensing and then relaxing all of the body's major muscle groups, in sequence. Another method, called autogenic training, entails scanning the body mentally and imagining different parts of the body becoming heavy and relaxed.

Perhaps the most widely used relaxation technique, however is a set of steps used to elicit the "relaxation response" that was described by Dr. Herbert Benson of Harvard Medical School in the early 1970s. Instructions for producing the relaxation response are simple, and it is easy for people to learn on their own. . . .

Benson and his colleagues, as well as many other researchers, have now studied the medical uses of various methods that produce the relaxation response. While much of this research is still preliminary, as a whole it suggests that relaxation may help at least some people with a wide range of medical problems. Among them:

Chronic Pain

Muscle relaxation can help control stress-related pain, including some types of headache and low-back pain, by preventing muscle spasms and reducing muscle tension. A recent review of several studies showed that various forms of relaxation training produced on average a 38 percent improvement for people with migraine headaches and a 45 percent improvement for those people with tension headaches. (Improvement was measured on a scale that took the intensity, frequency, and duration of headaches into account.)

Hypertension

High blood pressure, or hypertension, is most often of unknown cause—so-called "essential" hypertension. In some people with hypertension, stress can be an important trigger—for example, a person may have "white-coat hypertension," and have high blood pressure only under the stress of a visit to the doctor. Because it is sometimes hard to separate stress-related cases of hypertension from those that are not, some studies have failed to find an overall beneficial effect of relaxation when all sorts of people with high blood pressure are studied together. When it is effective, however, relaxation can lower systolic and diastolic blood pressure by about 5 to 10 millimeters of mercury on average.

Diabetes

At Duke University Medical Center, psychologist Richard Surwit and his colleagues have shown that progressive muscle relaxation can help control blood sugar in many people with Type II (adult-onset) diabetes. As with hypertension, relaxation is effective for only some diabetics: those who are suffering from relatively high levels of stress and anxiety.

Infertility

Couples dealing with infertility often find that the problem is extremely stressful, and that stress, in turn, can complicate their medical treatment. Dr. Benson's group has found that practicing the relaxation response helps infertile women become less anxious and depressed, and the group has preliminary evidence that relaxation may improve the chance that in vitro fertilization will be successful.

Side Effects of Cancer Treatment

Various forms of relaxation therapy can help alleviate the anxiety and depression that often accompany chemotherapy or radiation treatment for cancer. Specifically, relaxation-based techniques can reduce the nausea that about a third of cancer patients develop in connection with their drug treatment; this "anticipatory" nausea can strike up to 24 hours before a scheduled session of chemotherapy.

Anxiety, Depression, and Insomnia

Many studies have shown that regular practice of the relaxation response can help people deal with psychological problems. In particular, recent research by Dr. Benson's group has shown that about four-fifths of people who have sleep-onset insomnia—difficulty in falling asleep initially—can become normal sleepers after they undergo training in relaxation.

BIOFEEDBACK

Unlike the other mind/body approaches, biofeedback relies on machinery. Electronic sensors are hooked up to measure aspects of your body's functioning that you would not otherwise be consciously aware of: muscle tension, skin temperature, sweat-gland activity, pulse rate, breathing patterns, or brain waves. The electronic information is then translated into a signal that can be easily perceived—for example, and audible tone that changes as skin temperature does—and "fed back" to you in that form.

Using this setup, a biofeedback therapist can help you learn to regulate a variety of bodily functions consciously. Since biofeedback can measure bodily reactions that reflect your level of stress, it is often used to help people relax.

In addition, a special virtue of biofeedback is that it can help people learn to control very specific biological processes. For example, biofeedback machines that measure skin temperature can help people with Raynaud's disease, a disorder in which constricted blood vessels lead to cold-induced pain and blanching of the fingers and toes. Through biofeedback, these people can learn to dilate their blood vessels and raise the skin temperature of their hands and feet. Biofeedback can help incontinent people regain control of their bladder and bowels by teaching them to tighten the appropriate muscles. It can help patients learn to reuse their leg and arm muscles after surgery, and help stroke patients learn to use alternative muscles to move a limb when the primary muscles can no longer do the job. Biofeedback is now even being used experimentally to teach hyperactive children to change their brain-wave patterns, which can help them change their behavior.

HYPNOSIS

Despite the popular stereotypes of swinging pocket watches and beady-eyed Svengalis, hypnosis is not magical or mysterious. Put most simply, it is a process of focusing attention that can be used to help people relax and to help them control the body's functions.

Hypnosis begins with relaxation. As you sit back with your eyes closed, a hypnotist gives you a series of suggestions that help you focus your attention and become more and more deeply relaxed. Once you are in a hypnotic state, however, you can use it to achieve more specific goals. Hypnosis is a state of high suggestibility, and suggestions given under hypnosis can be used to affect psychological processes in a number of different ways.

Almost invariably, hypnotic suggestions are given in the form of imagery—the person under hypnosis imagines seeing, hearing, smelling, tasting, or touching something. To relax, for example, you might imagine yourself lying on a warm beach, feeling the sun and listening to the sound of the ocean.

Hypnosis has been used successfully to decrease headache pain, reduce bleeding in hemophiliacs, control the severity of asthma attacks, reduce the discomfort of dental procedures, and ease labor for pregnant women. For many people with painful chronic conditions, hypnosis can be used to help them reduce the dosage of pain medication they need, or even eliminate their need for medication entirely. Hypnotic suggestion can also eradicate warts—a rather mysterious phenomenon that may involve the immune system, and that is now the subject of a major research study headed by Dr. Karen Olness at Case Western Reserve University . . .

In general, hypnosis is most effective when a person does not just rely on a hypnotherapist, but also practices self-hypnosis regularly for weeks or months. The most reliable way to learn self-hypnosis is by working with a professional, since different methods of hypnosis are most effective for different people.

Because they can't be tailored to the individual, commercial audiotapes that promise to teach self-hypnosis often give disappointing results. In particular, there is no good research behind the many "subliminal learning" tapes that are supposed to help you lose weight, improve your attitude, or sharpen your memory through hypnosis.

MINDFULNESS MEDITATION

One promising mind/body approach that has recently been applied to physical illness is known as mindfulness. Like the relaxation response, mindfulness is based on an ancient tradition of meditation, a Buddhist tradition in this case. But while the relaxation response involves training the mind on a single point of focus, such as a word or phrase, mindfulness involves focusing on whatever a person happens to be experiencing at the time—and learning to experience anything calmly, whether it is pleasant or not. People with chronic pain, for example, would not try to distract themselves from the pain, but would simply experience the pain without fear or anxiety (emotions that generally make the pain more intense).

Research into medical uses of mindfulness is just beginning. This approach has been developed at the Stress Reduction Clinic of the University of Massachusetts Medical Center, founded by Jon Kabat-Zinn, an associate professor of medicine. More than 6,000 patients with a wide range of medical problems have now gone through that program; the majority have kept practicing mindfulness for years afterward, and say that is has helped them. Research at the clinic has already shown benefits for patients with chronic pain, and Kabat-Zinn and his colleagues are now doing clinical studies of patients with panic disorder, emphysema, and psoriasis.

SUPPORT GROUPS

Many studies have shown that people with strong social-support networks are healthier than others, and researchers are now trying to find out whether joining a support group could also improve a person's health. Dr. David Spiegel's work with support groups for women with breast cancer at Stanford has become the model for new research in this area. . . . Several other researchers working with cancer patients are now trying to replicate Spiegel's work, and still others are using support groups with patients with heart disease.

Many stress-management programs now combine support groups with relaxation training, instruction in diet and exercise, and other lifestyle changes. While the combined approach is often effective, however, it makes it difficult to find out just how much of a program's benefits come from the social support of people in the group and how much is due to other factors.

PSYCHOTHERAPY

Psychotherapy can be valuable in helping people deal with serious physical illness. Such people are often made anxious or depressed by their disease—and those emotional problems can make their illness worse. Studies show that patients hospitalized for medical reasons have longer hospital stays if they are also suffering psychologically. And just as psychological problems can hurt a patient's medical prognosis, psychotherapy can improve it.

That was shown recently in a study done by Dr. James Strain and his colleagues at New York's Mount Sinai Medical Center, together with a team at Northwestern University Medical School. The team evaluated elderly hip-fracture patients when they entered the hospital, and offered to help anyone with serious emotional problems. (Hip-fracture patients are especially likely to become depressed when they find themselves immobilized.) A control group of patients was not given psychotherapy. The patients who received therapy left the hospital two days earlier than the control group on average; they also spent fewer days in rehabilitation, and were less likely to be rehospitalized.

Even when psychotherapy does not have a direct impact on physical health, it can help people cope with the emotional fallout of a serious illness. According to Dr. Strain, several medical conditions are particularly likely to involve emotional distress: AIDS, bone-marrow transplantation, heart or liver transplantation, severe burns, end-stage kidney disease, open-heart surgery, and plastic surgery (as well as hip fracture). Patients dealing with those conditions may benefit especially from psychological care.

Psychotherapy is also the treatment of choice for somatizers: people with physical symptoms that appear to be signs of a medical problem, but that are actually caused by unconscious emotional conflicts. Unless they get effective therapy, somatizers can spend huge amounts of time and money in a fruitless search for a medical solution to their problems.

PUTTING IT ALL IN PERSPECTIVE

Mind/body medicine is still far from being an exact science; many perplexing questions remain. But a growing number of well-designed studies are now under way, testimony to the scientific excitement the field has generated in a short time.

For most people, the question is not whether mind/body medicine is a legitimate field for research (it is), or whether its potential has yet been fully defined and proven (it hasn't). The immediate, practical question is whether mind/body medicine as it now stands can be of value to patients dealing with a range of serious illness and to people under stress who want to stay healthy.

Although mind/body medicine is still evolving, enough is now known to make it applicable in a number of situations. Even in cases where mind/body approaches don't offer a clear physical benefit for people with medical problems, they can greatly improve the quality of life. For example, relaxation methods, hypnosis, psychotherapy, and support groups can all help cancer patients deal effectively with their fears and anxieties about the disease and the treatments they must take. Psychological approaches can also help many people with arthritis, gastrointestinal disorders, and other chronic conditions to deal with their symptoms.

Finally, mind/body techniques pose virtually no physical or emotional risks. Even if some of their benefits are still hypothetical, no one is likely to be harmed by giving these approaches a try—as long as he or she doesn't choose to use them in place of conventional medicine. And there's no need to even consider that choice; mind/body approaches are perfectly compatible with conventional medical care.

QUESTIONS

1. Do the authors believe that it is relatively easy or difficult for the average person to distinguish between genuine mind/body clinicians and New Age charlatans? Why might your doctor not be able to help?

2. What is the importance of the discovery of nerve endings in the thymus, lymph nodes, spleen, and bone marrow? What piece of the mind/body puzzle does this provide?

3. What have most recent studies of the relationship between stress and illness discovered? What other factors are important in this relationship?

4. Can the mind help as well as harm the body? List six medical problems that may benefit from relaxation therapy.

5. Some mental techniques help reduce physical symptoms, while others allow people to accept their symptoms without anxiety or depression. Divide the techniques described in this article into these two categories.

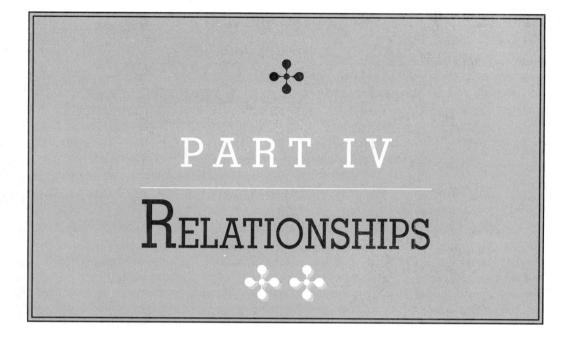

PART IV

RELATIONSHIPS

❖ CHAPTER 6 ❖

INTERPERSONAL ATTRACTION: OUR LIKING FOR OTHERS

Reading 11: Classic

Physical Attractiveness

Ellen Berscheid and Elaine Hatfield

Romantic love is considered by most contemporary Western cultures as one of the most mean-ingful aspects of life. Yet surprisingly, it is an issue that social scientists largely ignored for decades. Social psychologists were no exception, and paid love only minor attention until the late 1960s.

Interestingly, the first theories of "mate selection" tended to downplay the importance of phys-ical attractiveness. Discussing the absence of this intuitively important construct, Elliot Aronson, a prominent social psychologist, suggested that psychologists were afraid of what they might find. We would all like to believe that people are judged by others on the basis of their character, not superficial looks. Perhaps psychology's omission of this construct in its research was moti-vated by the desire not to discover that physical attractiveness does, in fact, greatly influence how others perceive us.

As Ellen Berscheid and Elaine Hatfield discuss in this excerpted selection, Aronson may have been correct. Subsequent research indicates that physical attractiveness has an enormous impact on dating choices. Although both men and women typically report that physical attractiveness is only moderately important to them in selecting dating partners, their behavior suggests otherwise.

❖

PHYSICAL ATTRACTIVENESS AND HETEROSEXUAL ATTRACTION: THE LURE OF THE PHYSICALLY ATTRACTIVE

Despite democratic notions of fairness and equal opportunity, and the taint of the morpho-logical, those interested in the antecedents of opposite-sex attraction could not long ignore the demand to recognize the physical attractiveness variable. Insight into the potency of physical attractiveness initially emerged from experiments designed to test the hypothesis that men and women of similar levels of social desirability tend to "pair off" in courtship and marriage.

Source: Berscheid, E., & Hatfield, E. (1974). Physical attractiveness. In L. Berkowitz (Ed.), *Advances in experimen-tal social psychology* (Vol. 7, pp. 157–215). New York: Academic Press.

A. The Matching Hypothesis

The "matching hypothesis" was first suggested by the sociologist Erving Goffman, who said, "A proposal of marriage in our society tends to be a way in which a man sums up his social attributes and suggests to a woman that hers are not so much better as to preclude a merger or a partnership in these matters" [1952, p. 456]. The sum of a person's social attributes is presumably determined by his level of social skills, his intelligence, his access to such material resources as money and prestige, his physical attractiveness, and his possession of other socially valued characteristics.

The hypothesis of matching in social choice was initially tested by Walster, Aronson, Abrahams, and Rottmann (1966), who formally derived their prediction from Level of Aspiration Theory (cf. Lewin, Dembo, Festinger, & Sears, 1944). They reasoned that one's romantic aspirations are influenced by the same factors that influence one's level of aspiration in other areas—the desirability of the goal and the perceived probability of attaining it. While socially desirable people ought to be preferred by everyone, the perceived probability of obtaining their attention and esteem ought to vary with the person's own social desirability. Thus, for romantic liaisons people should select, and like best, those of their own social desirability level.

To test their hypothesis, Walster *et al.* conducted a "computer dance" for college freshman, where purchase of a ticket ensured a date for the dance. It was impossible for the investigators to make a precise determination of the "sum" of each student's social attributes, but they reasoned that scores on personality, intelligence, social skill, and physical attractiveness measures would provide an index. (Each student's physical attractiveness level was quickly and roughly assessed at the box office as he or she purchased a ticket to the dance.)

All the men and women who signed up for the dance were paired on a random basis with but one restriction. The informal but apparently cardinal rule of dating, that the man be taller than the woman, was never violated. It was hypothesized that those students who obtained, by chance, dates of their own social desirability levels (whether high or low) would like each other more than those who received dates whose social desirability levels were inferior or superior to their own.

It was fortunate that the investigators suspected that a student's physical attractiveness level might be an important component of each student's social desirability. Questionnaires which were administered at the intermission of the dance to determine how well the partners had hit it off revealed that the only apparent determinant of how much each person liked his or her date, how much he or she wanted to see the partner again, and (it was determined later) how often the man actually did ask his partner for subsequent dates, was simply how physically attractive the partner was. The more physically attractive the date, the more he or she was liked. Every effort to find additional factors which might possibly predict attraction failed. Students with exceptional social skills and intelligence levels, for example, were not liked any better than those less fortunately endowed.

The apparently inordinate importance of physical attractiveness as a determinant of attraction, at least in blind date settings, has been substantiated by other investigators. Brislin and Lewis (1968) found a correlation of .89 between the perceived physical attractiveness of a computer dance date and a desire to date the partner again; Tesser and Brodie (1971) found a correlation of .69 between these two variables. In both studies the partner's *perception* of the physical attractiveness of the date (physical attractiveness was not independently assessed) correlated higher with the "desire to date again" response than did any of the other perceived characteristics of the partner, including perception of "similar interests," "character," etc.

Although Walster *et al.* failed to find support for the matching principle—everyone seemed to prefer the highly attractive man or woman—subsequent investigators argued that the computer dance situation was not an optimal setting for the test of the hypothesis. The matching hypothesis as derived from Level of Aspiration Theory predicts that an individual will choose a date of approximately his own level of social desirability when making a *realistic,* as opposed to *idealistic,* social choice. Realistic choices, according to Level of Aspiration Theory, are influenced not only by the objective desirability of the choice alternative (as in idealistic choices), but also by the individual's perception of his probability of attaining the goal. An underlying assumption of the matching hypothesis, then, is that people of lesser social desirability feel that they are likely to meet with rejection when they attempt to contact a person of higher social desirability.

Berscheid, Dion, Walster, and Walster (1971) reasoned that the salience of the possibility of social rejection by one's choice, while ever-present in most informal dating situations, was minimized in the Walster *et al.* computer dance setting. Dates had been assigned, and those who by chance secure more attractive dates than themselves were assured not only of social contact, but of the fruits of social courtesy norms for the duration of the dance. In addition, those who had achieved their ideal goal of a physically attractive partner may have shown more interest in *retaining* it then they might have shown in trying to *attain* it initially.

Berscheid *et al.* conducted two experiments to determine if the matching principle would reveal itself when the individual was required to actively *choose* a dating partner (rather than evaluate one already secured) and to discover if matching was especially likely when the salience of possible rejection by the chosen date was emphasized. In both experiments, the physical attractiveness of each *S* was independently assessed by judges, the salience of possible rejection by the dating choice was varied, and the physical attractiveness level of the date *S* desired was examined.

The results of both experiments found support for the matching principle. As in Walster *et al.,* physically attractive dates were markedly preferred by everyone. *Within* this general trend, however, it was clear that men and women of lesser attractiveness did tend to choose less attractive dates than did highly attractive individuals.

Both experimental attempts to ascertain whether the degree of matching would vary with the probability of acceptance or rejection by the chosen date failed. *Ss* in these experiments appeared to operate on the matching principle equally whether the possibility of acceptance or rejection by the chosen person was salient. Thus, although a matching effect was found, there was no evidence of its presumed mediator—high probability of rejection by those of higher social desirabilities.

A recent study conducted by Huston (1973), however, does demonstrate that men do perceive their chances of social acceptance to be less with attractive women and, further, that their subjective probability of rejection may influence attempts to approach them. Huston's *Ss* were asked to choose a date from an array of women representing three levels of physical attractiveness. Half of the men were assured that each of the women had previously indicated that she would accept a date with him; to the remainder, it was left unclear whether their chosen date would accept or reject them. As well as making their choices, the latter group was asked to indicate the likelihood that each woman would accept them as a date.

Huston found the ubiquitous effect that, overall, the men generally preferred to date the most physically attractive women. This was most pronounced, however, when they were assured of acceptance by them. Ss who were not guaranteed acceptance believed that the highly physically attractive women would be significantly less likely to want them as a date than would either the moderately attractive or the unattractive women. In addition, each man's rating of his own physical attractiveness level was related to perceived chance of acceptance by each of the potential dates. Those men who believed themselves to be highly attractive estimated their chances of acceptance as better than did those who considered themselves relatively unattractive.

Although Huston found no evidence that self-ratings of physical attractiveness corresponded to the chosen date's physical attractiveness level, others have demonstrated a positive relationship. Stroebe, Insko, Thompson, and Layton (1971), for example, found that men and women who believed themselves to be unattractive were more likely to consider dating unattractive others, and less likely to consider attractive others, than were people who had a more favorable opinion of their physical attractiveness.

These studies indicate that while physically attractive men and women are strongly preferred in heterosexual dating relationships, within this overall tendency, a person's own physical attractiveness level acts as a moderating influence on date selection. Further, there is suggestive evidence that differential probabilities of rejection associated with attractive and unattractive dates mediate the matching effect.

B. Matching, FAIT ACCOMPLI

If it is true that men and women of equal levels of social desirability tend to pair off in courtship and marriage, and if it is also true that one's degree of physical attractiveness plays an extremely important role in determining both a man's and a woman' social desirability level, then couples who have formed viable affectional relationships should appear to outside observers to be of approximately equal levels of physical attractiveness.

The question of *fait accompli* matching was addressed by Silverman (1971), who examined the degree of similarity in attractiveness exhibited by couples observed in naturalistic dating settings. Teams of observers (two males and two females each) went to such dating habitats as bars, social events, and theater lobbies where they could watch couples unobtrusively. The couples, according to Silverman, were predominantly in the 18- to 22-year range and were unmarried. Each observer rated the dating partner of the opposite sex on a 5-point scale, independently and without knowledge of the ratings made by the other observers.

Silverman and his associates found an extraordinarily high degree of similarity in physical attractiveness between the dating partners. While the distribution of attractiveness scores of the men and women ranged from 1 to 5 in intervals of .5, Silverman found that for 60% of the couples, partners were not separated by more than half a scale point, and no couple was disparate by more than 2.5 scale points.

In addition to rating the physical attractiveness level of the dating partners, the observers recorded whether the couple engaged in intimate touching (such as holding hands, walking arm-in-arm, etc.) during the period of observation. Silverman hypothesized that couples more similar in attractiveness would seem to be happier with each other as reflected by their degree of physical intimacy. The data revealed that 60% of the couples who were highly similar in physical attractiveness level were engaged in intimate physical contact of some kind, as compared to 46% of the moderately similar couples and 22% of those in the lowest similarity group.

Silverman's evidence of *fait accompli* matching along the physical attractiveness dimension is not as unequivocal as one would like. Despite the fact that observers did not know how the other observers rated the attractiveness of the other member of the dating pair, they did, of course, see the dating partners. Thus, it is possible that a "halo" emanating from one dating partner and influencing perception of the other may have produced artifactually similar ratings of dating pairs. This possibility seems especially cogent, since Sigall and Landy (in press) have recently demonstrated that the favorability of the overall impression a man makes on outside observers is affected by the physical attractiveness level of a women with whom he is romantically associated. Although knowledge of romantic association did not specifically appear to affect the rating of the man's physical attractiveness level, the pervasiveness of its effect along a number of other dimensions suggests that the *fait accompli* matching hypothesis might be best tested under conditions in which attractiveness judges are not aware of who is paired with whom.

A further problem with Silverman's data is that no analyses were undertaken to determine whether the degree of matching observed was significantly above that which might be expected by chance. As Udry (1971) points out, "the frequency of distribution of individual ratings indicates that most individuals were rated between 2 and 4, with two out of three females and half of the men receiving ratings between 2.5 and 3.5. Under these circumstances, random matings would produce most similarly rated couples" [p. 23].

Murstein (1972), avoiding both these difficulties, examined the correspondence between the physical attractiveness levels of 99 couples who were engaged or going steady. The degree of matching exhibited by the dating couples was compared to that of a control group of couples which was formed by randomly paring the physical attractiveness scores of the 99 men and women with each other. Photographs were taken of each of the dating couples, and ratings of the physical attractiveness of each member of each couple were made. According to Murstein, judges did not know which partner belonged to whom when they made their attractiveness judgments.

Murstein found evidence of matching along the physical attractiveness dimension; the physical attractiveness level of the engaged or steadily dating couples was significantly less discrepant than those of the artificially paired couples. Murstein concluded, "Individuals with equal market value for physical attractiveness are more likely to associate in an intimate relationship such as premarital engagement than individuals with disparate values" [p. 11].

C. Sex Differences in the Importance of Physical Attractiveness in Heterosexual Choice

The data provided by the preceding studies not only tend to support the matching hypothesis but indicate that physical attractiveness is of major significance for both sexes' dating choices. They also suggest that physical attractiveness may be of even more importance to men in making their dating choices than it is to women. Walster *et al.* (1966) devised a Self-Report Popularity index which included the question "How popular are you with the opposite sex?" and "How many dates have you had in the last six months?" Physical attractiveness and popularity correlated .46 for women and .31 for men. Both coefficients are significantly different from each other, and both are significantly different from 0. Berscheid *et al.* (1971) also found a significant difference between men and women in the strength of correspondence between physical attractiveness and dating popularity. Physical attractiveness and number of dates within the past year correlated .61 for females; the correspondence for males was only .25.

These findings, which indicate that physical attractiveness is more strongly related to a woman's dating popularity than to a man's, are compatible with the results of several studies which have examined the factors college students report to be important in making dating choices (e.g., Coombs & Kenkel, 1966; Hewitt, 1958, Williamson, 1966; Vail & Staudt, 1950). Males, in comparison with females, consistently report that they place more importance on physical attractiveness in making dating choices. Whether these stated preferences are translated into action may be another matter. Byrne, Ervin, and Lamberth (1970) found that, although men reported that the physical attractiveness of their assigned date was a more important factor in determining their attraction for the date than women did, the date's physical attractiveness correlated .60 with the attraction responses of female Ss and only .39 for male Ss.

D. Summary

The investigators who went hunting for evidence of matching in social choice not only caught their quarry but found the imposing tracks of bigger game. If the "sum" of a person's social desirability in the dating and mating market were composed of a wide variety of components, each with its individual weight and unique mode of interaction with the other components, life would have been much more complex for the matching researchers. The discovery that matching could be observed considering only the physical attractiveness component, as well as the repeated observance of large main effects in choice along the physical attractiveness dimension, provides consistent and convincing evidence that physical attractiveness is a factor which cannot be ignored in the prediction of date and mate selection.

REFERENCES

BERSCHEID, E., DION, K. K., WALSTER, E., & WALSTER, G. W. (1971) Physical attractiveness and dating choice: A test of the matching hypothesis. *Journal of Experimental Social Psychology, 7*, 173–189.

BRISLIN, R. W., & LEWIS, S. A. (1968) Dating and physical attractiveness: Replication. *Psychological Reports, 22,* 976.

BYRNE, D., ERVIN, C. R., & LAMBERTH, J. (1970) Continuity between the experimental study of attraction and real-life computer dating. *Journal of Personality and Social Psychology, 16,* 157–165.

COOMBS, R. H., & KENKEL, W. F. (1966) Sex differences in dating aspirations and satisfaction with computer-selected partners. *Journal of Marriage and Family, 28(1),* 62–66.

GOFFMAN, E. (1952) On cooling the mark out: Some aspects of adaptation to failure. *Psychiatry, 15,* 451–463.

HEWITT, L. E. (1958) Student perceptions of traits desired in themselves as dating and marriage partners. *Marriage and Family Living, 20,* 344–349.

HUSTON, T. L. (1973) Ambiguity of acceptance, social desirability, and dating choice. *Journal of Experimental Social Psychology, 9(1),* 32–42.

LEWIN, K., DEMBO, T., FESTINGER, L., & SEARS, P. (1944) Level of aspiration. In J. McV. Hunt (Ed.), *Personality and the behavior disorders.* Vol. 1. New York: Ronald Press.

MURSTEIN, B. I. (1972) Physical attractiveness and marital choice. *Journal of Personality and Social Psychology, 22(1),* 8–12.

SIGALL, H., & LANDY, D. (in press) Radiating beauty: The effects of having a physically attractive partner on person perception. *Journal of Personality and Social Psychology.*

SILVERMAN, I. (1971, September) Physical attractiveness and courtship. *Sexual Behavior, 22–25.*

STROEBE, W., INSKO C. A., THOMPSON, V. D., & LAYTON, B. D. (1971) Effects of physical attractiveness, attitude similarity, and sex on various aspects of interpersonal attraction. *Journal of Personality and Social Psychology, 18,* 79–91.

TESSER, A., & BRODIE, M. (1971) A note on the evaluation of a "computer date." *Psychonomic Science, 23,* 300.

UDRY, J. R. (1971, September) Commentary. *Sexual Behavior, 23.*

VAIL, J. P., & STAUDT, V. M. (1950) Attitudes of college students toward marriage and related problems: I. Dating and mate selection. *Journal of Psychology, 30,* 171–182.

WALSTER, E., ARONSON, V., ABRAHAMS, D., & ROTTMANN, L. (1966) Importance of physical attractiveness in dating behavior. *Journal of Personality and Social Psychology, 4(5),* 508–516.

WILLIAMSON, R. L. (1966) *Marriage and family relations.* New York: Wiley.

QUESTIONS

1. Explain the matching hypothesis. What is being "matched"? What role does physical attractiveness play according to this hypothesis?

2. Did the "computer dance" study done by Walster et al. confirm the predictions of the matching hypothesis? How do Berscheid and Walster explain this?

3. What do Silverman's "fait accompli" data suggest about the matching hypothesis? Why are Berscheid and Walster hesitant to accept these data?

4. What differences have been found in the importance that men and women place on their partners' attractiveness?

5. Contrary to Goffman's prediction, it appears that people tend to try to date the most attractive person they can. Can you reconcile this with Silverman's evidence of "fait accompli" matching?

Reading 12: Contemporary

The Biology of Beauty

Geoffrey Cowley

In the previous reading, Berscheid and Hatfield convincingly argued for the importance of physical attraction in dating choices. They were less able, however, to explain why people are so influenced by attractiveness. Further, they were unable to specify precisely what features people considered attractive. Both of these issues are addressed in the next reading by Geoffrey Cowley, who writes about psychology for Newsweek magazine.

It is obvious to anyone who has ever seen the standards of beauty portrayed in classic works of art from previous centuries that these standards have changed. For example, women in the paintings of the Flemish master Rubens bear little resemblance to contemporary supermodels. Clearly, what people consider beautiful is not universal. But, according to some researchers, beautiful people from all ages, including Rubens's and our own, do share some important qualities in common. These commonalities may point to universal features of beauty, features that have their basis in human biology.

❖

When it comes to choosing a mate, a female penguin knows better than to fall for the first creep who pulls up and honks. She holds out for the fittest suitor available—which in Antarctica means one chubby enough to spend several weeks sitting on newly hatched eggs without starving to death. The Asian jungle bird *Gallus gallus* is just as choosy. Males in that species sport gaily colored head combs and feathers, which lose their luster if the bird is invaded by parasites. By favoring males with bright ornaments, a hen improves her odds of securing a mate (and bearing offspring) with strong resistance to disease. For female scorpion flies, beauty is less about size or color than about symmetry. Females favor suitors who have well-matched wings—and with good reason. Studies show they're the most adept at killing prey and at defending their catch from competitors. There's no reason to think that any of these creatures understands its motivations, but there's a clear pattern to their preferences. "Throughout the animal world," says University of New Mexico ecologist Randy Thornhill, "attractiveness certifies biological quality."

Is our corner of the animal world different? That looks count in human affairs is beyond dispute. Studies have shown that people considered attractive fare better with parents and teachers, make more friends and more money, and have better sex with more (and more beautiful) partners. Every year, 400,000 Americans, including 48,000 men, flock to cosmetic

Source: Cowley, G. (1996, June 3). The biology of beauty. *Newsweek, 127,* 61–66.

surgeons. In other lands, people bedeck themselves with scars, lip plugs or bright feathers. "Every culture is a 'beauty culture'," says Nancy Etcoff, a neuroscientist who is studying human attraction at the MIT Media Lab and writing a book on the subject. "I defy anyone to point to a society, any time in history or any place in the world, that wasn't preoccupied with beauty." The high-minded may dismiss our preening and ogling as distractions from things that matter, but the stakes can be enormous. "Judging beauty involves looking at another person," says University of Texas psychologist Devendra Singh, "and figuring out whether you want your children to carry that person's genes."

It's widely assumed that ideals of beauty vary from era to era and from culture to culture. But a harvest of new research is confounding that idea. Studies have established that people everywhere—regardless of race, class or age—share a sense of what's attractive. And though no one knows just how our minds translate the sight of a face or a body into rapture, new studies suggest that we judge each other by rules we're not even aware of. We may consciously admire Kate Moss's legs or Arnold's biceps, but we're also viscerally attuned to small variations in the size and symmetry of facial bones and the placement of weight on the body.

This isn't to say that our preferences are purely innate—or that beauty is all that matters in life. Most of us manage to find jobs, attract mates and bear offspring despite our physical imperfections. Nor should anyone assume that the new beauty research justifies the biases it illuminates. Our beautylust is often better suited to the Stone Age than to the Information Age; the qualities we find alluring may be powerful emblems of health, fertility and resistance to disease, but they say nothing about people's moral worth. The human weakness for what Thornhill calls "biological quality" causes no end of pain and injustice. Unfortunately, that doesn't make it any less real.

No one suggests that points of attraction never vary. Rolls of fat can signal high status in a poor society or low status in a rich one, and lip plugs go over better in the Kalahari than they do in Kansas. But local fashions seem to rest on a bedrock of shared preferences. You don't have to be Italian to find Michelangelo's David better looking than, say, Alfonse D'Amato. When British researchers asked women from England, China and India to rate pictures of Greek men, the women responded as if working from the same crib sheet. And when researchers at the University of Louisville showed a diverse collection of faces to whites, Asians and Latinos from 13 countries, the subjects' ethnic background scarcely affected their preferences.

To a skeptic, those findings suggest only that Western movies and magazines have overrun the world. But scientists have found at least one group that hasn't been exposed to this bias. In a series of groundbreaking experiments, psychologist Judith Langlois of the University of Texas, Austin, has shown that even infants share a sense of what's attractive. In the late '80s, Langlois started placing 3- and 6-month-old babies in front of a screen and showing them pairs of facial photographs. Each pair included one considered attractive by adult judges and one considered unattractive. In the first study, she found that the infants gazed significantly longer at "attractive" white female faces than at "unattractive" ones. Since then, she has repeated the drill using white male faces, black female faces, even the faces of other babies, and the same pattern always emerges. "These kids don't read *Vogue* or watch TV," Langlois says. "They haven't been touched by the media. Yet they make the same judgments as adults."

What, then, is beauty made of? What are the innate rules we follow in sizing each other up? We're obviously wired to find robust health a prettier sight than infirmity. "All animals are attracted to other animals that are healthy, that are clean by their standards and that show signs of competence," says Rutgers University anthropologist Helen Fisher. As far as anyone knows, there isn't a village on earth where skin lesions, head lice and rotting teeth count as beauty aids. But the rules get subtler than that. Like scorpion flies, we love symmetry. And though we generally favor average features over unusual ones, the people we find extremely beautiful share certain exceptional qualities.

When Randy Thornhill started measuring the wings of Japanese scorpion flies six years ago, he wasn't much concerned with the orgasms and infidelities of college students. But sometimes one thing leads to another. Biologists have long used bilateral symmetry—the extent to which a creature's right and left sides match—to gauge what's known as developmental stability. Given ideal growing conditions, paired features such as wings, ears, eyes, and feet would come out matching perfectly. But pollution, disease and other hazards can disrupt development. As a result, the least resilient individuals tend to be the most lopsided. In chronicling the scorpion flies' daily struggles, Thornhill found that the bugs with the most symmetrical wings fared best in the competition for food and mates. To his amazement, females preferred symmetrical males even when they were hidden from view; evidently, their smells are more attractive. And when researchers staring noting similar trends in other species, Thornhill turned his attention to our own.

Working with psychologist Steven Gangestad, he set about measuring the body symmetry of hundreds of college-age men and women. By adding up right-left disparities in seven measurements—the breadth of the feet, ankles, hands, wrists and elbows, as well as the breadth and length of the ears—the researchers scored each subject's overall body asymmetry. Then they had the person fill out a confidential questionnaire covering everything from temperament to sexual behavior, and set about looking for connections. They weren't disappointed. In a 1994 study, they found that the most symmetrical males had started having sex three to four years earlier than their most lopsided brethren. For both men and women, greater symmetry predicted a larger number of past sex partners.

That was just the beginning. From what they knew about other species, Thornhill and Gangestad predicted that women would be more sexually responsive to symmetrical men, and that men would exploit that advantage. To date, their findings support both suspicions. Last year they surveyed 86 couples and found that women with highly symmetrical partners were more than twice as likely to climax during intercourse (an event that may foster conception by ushering sperm into the uterus) than those with low-symmetry partners. And in separate surveys, Gangestad and Thornhill have found that, compared with regular Joes, extremely symmetrical men are less attentive to their partners and more likely to cheat on them. Women showed no such tendency.

It's hard to imagine that we even notice the differences between people's elbows, let alone stake our love lives on them. No one carries calipers into a singles bar. So why do these measurements predict so much? Because, says Thornhill, people with symmetrical elbows tend to have "a whole suite of attractive features." His findings suggest that besides having attractive (and symmetrical) faces, men with symmetrical bodies are typically larger, more muscular and more athletic than their peers, and more dominant in personality. In a forthcoming study, researchers at the University of Michigan find evidence that facial symmetry is also associated with health. In analyzing diaries kept by 100 students over a two-month period, they found that the least symmetrical had the most physical complaints, from insomnia to nasal congestion, and reported more anger, jealously and withdrawal. In light of all Thornhill and Gangestad's findings, you can hardly blame them.

If we did go courting with calipers, symmetry isn't all we would measure. As we study each other in the street, the office or the gym, our beauty radars pick up a range of signals. Oddly enough, one of the qualities shared by attractive people is their averageness. Researchers discovered more than a century ago that if they superimposed photographs of several faces, the resulting composite was usually better looking than any of the images that went into it. Scientists can now average faces digitally, and it's still one of the surest ways to make them more attractive. From an evolutionary perspective, a preference for extreme normality makes sense. As Langlois has written, "Individuals with average population characteristics should be less likely to carry harmful genetic mutations."

So far, so good. But here's the catch: while we may find average faces attractive, the faces we find most beautiful are not average. As New Mexico State University psychologist Victor Johnston has shown, they're extreme. To track people's preferences, Johnston uses a computer program called FacePrints. Turn it on, and it generates 30 facial images, all male or all female, which you rate on a 1–9 beauty scale. The program then "breeds" the top-rated faces with one of the others to create two digital offspring, which replace the lowest-rated faces in the pool. By rating round after round of new faces, you create an ever more beautiful population. The game ends when you award some visage a perfect 10. (If you have access to the World Wide Web, you can take part in a collective face-breeding experiment by visiting http://www-psych.nmsu.edu/~vic/faceprints/.)

For Johnston, the real fun starts after the judging is finished. By collecting people's ideal faces and comparing them to average faces, he can measure the distance between fantasy and reality. As a rule, he finds that an ideal female has a higher forehead than an average one, as well as fuller lips, a shorter jaw and a smaller chin and nose. Indeed, the ideal 25-year-old woman, as configured by participants in a 1993 study, had a 14-year-old's abundant lips and an 11-year-old's delicate jaw. Because her lower face was so small, she also had relatively prominent eyes and cheekbones.

The participants in that study were all college kids from New Mexico, but researchers have since shown that British and Japanese students express the same bias. And if there are lingering doubts about the depth of that bias, Johnston's latest findings should dispel them. In a forthcoming study, he reports that male volunteers not only consciously prefer women with small lower faces but show marked rises in brain activity when looking at pictures of them. And though Johnston has yet to publish specs on the ideal male, his unpublished findings suggest that a big jaw, a strong chin and an imposing brow are as prized in a man's face as their opposites are in a woman's.

Few of us ever develop the heart-melting proportions of a FacePrints fantasy. And if it's any consolation, beauty is not an all-or-nothing proposition. Madonna became a sex symbol despite her strong nose, and Melanie Griffith's strong jaw hasn't kept her out of the movies. Still, special things have a way of happening to people who approximate the ideal. We pay them huge fees to stand on windblown bluffs and stare into the distance. And past studies have found that square-jawed males not only start having sex earlier than their peers but attain higher rank in the military.

None of this surprises evolutionary psychologists. They note that the facial features we obsess over are precisely the ones that diverge in males and females during puberty, as floods of sex hormones wash us into adulthood. And they reason that hormonal abundance would have been a good clue to mate value in the hunter-gatherer world where our preferences evolved. The tiny jaw that men favor in women is essentially a monument to estrogen—and obliquely, to fertility. No one claims that jaws reveal a woman's odds of getting pregnant. But like breasts, they imply that she could.

Likewise, the heavy lower face that women favor in men is a visible record of the surge in androgens (testosterone and other male sex hormones) that turns small boys into 200-pound spear-throwers. An oversized jaw is biologically expensive, for the androgens required to produce it tend to comprise the immune system. But from a female's perspective, that should make jaw size all the more revealing. Evolutionists think of androgen-based features as "honest advertisements" of disease resistance. If a male can afford them without falling sick, the thinking goes, he must have a superior immune system in the first place.

No one has tracked the immune responses of men with different jawlines to see if these predictions bear out (Thornhill has proposed a study that would involve comparing volunteers' responses to a vaccine). Nor is it clear whether penis size figures into these equations. Despite what everyone thinks he knows on the subject, scientists haven't determined that women have consistent preferences one way or the other.

Our faces are our signatures, but when it comes to raw sex appeal, a nice chin is no match for a perfectly sculpted torso—especially from a man's perspective. Studies from around the world have found that while both sexes value appearance, men place more stock in it than women. And if there are social reasons for that imbalance, there are also biological ones. Just about any male over 14 can produce sperm, but a woman's ability to bear children depends on her age and hormone levels. Female fertility declines by two thirds between the ages of 20 and 44, and it's spent by 54. So while both sexes may eyeball potential partners, says Donald Symons, an anthropologist at the University of California in Santa Barbara, "a larger proportion of a woman's mate value can be detected from visual cues." Mounting evidence suggests there is no better cue than the relative contours of her waist and hips.

Before puberty and after menopause, females have essentially the same waistlines as males. But during puberty, while boys are amassing the bone and muscle of paleolithic hunters, a typical girl gains nearly 35 pounds of so-called reproductive fat around the hips and thighs. Those pounds contain roughly the 80,000 calories need to sustain a pregnancy, and the curves they create provide a gauge of reproductive potential. "You have to get very close to see the details of a woman's face," says Devendra Singh, the University of Texas psychologist. "But you can see the shape of her body from 500 feet, and it says more about mate value."

Almost anything that interferes with fertility—obesity, malnutrition, pregnancy, menopause—changes a woman's shape. Healthy, fertile women typically have waist-hip ratios of .6 to .8, meaning their waists are 60 to 80 percent the size of their hips, whatever their actual weight. To take one familiar example, a 36-25-36 figure would have a WHR of .7. Many women outside this range are healthy and capable of having children, of course. But as researchers in the Netherlands discovered in a 1993 study, even a slight increase in waist size relative to hip size can signal reproductive problems. Among 500 women who were attempting in vitro fertilization, the odds of conceiving during any given cycle declined by 30 percent with every 10 percent increase in WHR. In other words, a woman with a WHR of .9 was nearly a third less likely to get pregnant than one with a WHR of .8, regardless of her age or weight. From an evolutionary perspective, it's hard to imagine men not responding to such a revealing signal. And as Singh has shown repeatedly, they do.

Defining a universal standard of body beauty once seemed a fool's dream; common sense said that if spindly Twiggy and Rubens's girthy *Three Graces* could all excite admiration, then nearly anyone could. But if our ideals of size change from one time and place to the next, our taste in shapes is amazingly stable. A low waist-hip ratio is one of the few features that a long, lean Barbie doll shares with a plump, primitive fertility icon. And Singh's findings suggest that fashion won't change any time soon. In one study, he compiled the measurements of *Playboy* centerfolds and Miss America winners from 1923 to 1990. Their bodies got measurably leaner over the decades, yet their waist-hip ratios stayed within the narrow range of .68 to .72. (Even Twiggy was no tube; at the peak of her fame in the 1960s, the British model had a WHR of .73).

The same pattern holds when Singh generates line drawings of different female figures and asks male volunteers to rank them for attractiveness, sexiness, health and fertility. He has surveyed men of various backgrounds, nationalities and ages. And whether the judges are 8-year-olds or 85-year-olds, their runaway favorite is a figure of average weight with a .7 WHR. Small wonder that when women were liberated from corsets and bustles, they took up girdles, wide belts and other waist-reducing contraptions. Last year alone, American women's outlays for shape-enhancing garments topped a half-billion dollars.

To some critics, the search for a biology of beauty looks like a thinly veiled political program. "It's the fantasy life of American men being translated into genetics," says poet and social critic Katha Pollitt. "You can look at any feature of modern life and make up a story about why it's genetic." In truth, says Northwestern University anthropologist Micaela di Leonardo, attraction is a complicated social phenomenon, not just a hard-wired response. If attraction were governed by the dictates of baby-making, she says, the men of ancient Greece wouldn't have found young boys so alluring, and gay couples wouldn't crowd modern sidewalks. "People make decisions about sexual and marital partners inside complex networks of friends and relatives," she says. "Human beings cannot be reduced to DNA packets."

Homosexuality is hard to explain as a biological adaptation. So is stamp collecting. But no one claims that human beings are mindless automatons, blindly striving to replicate our genes. We pursue countless passions that have no direct bearing on survival. If we're sometimes attracted to people who can't help us reproduce, that doesn't mean human preferences lack any coherent design. A radio used as a doorstop is still a radio. The beauty mavens' mission—and that of evolutionary psychology in general—is not to explain everything people do but to unmask our biases and make sense of them. "Our minds have evolved to generate pleasurable experiences in response to some things while ignoring other things," says Johnston. "That's why sugar tastes sweet, and that's why we find some people more attractive than others."

The new beauty research does have troubling implications. First, it suggests that we're designed to care about looks, even though looks aren't earned and reveal nothing about character. As writer Ken Siman observes in his new book, "The Beauty Trip," "the kind [of beauty] that inspires awe, lust, and increased jeans sales cannot not be evenly distributed. In a society where everything is supposed to be within reach, this is painful to face." From acne to birth defects, we wear our imperfections as thorns, for we know the world sees them and takes note.

A second implication is that sexual stereotypes are not strictly artificial. At some level, it seems, women are designed to favor dominant males over meek ones, and men are designed to value women for youthful qualities that time quickly steals. Given the slow pace of evolutionary change, our innate preferences aren't likely to fade in the foreseeable future. And if they exist for what were once good biological reasons, that doesn't make them any less nettlesome. "Men often forgo their health, their safety, their spare time and their family life in order to get rank," says Helen Fisher, the Rutgers anthropologist, "because unconsciously, they know that rank wins women." And all too often, those who can trade cynically on their rank do.

But do we have to indulge every appetite that natural selection has preserved in us? Of course not. "I don't know any scientist who seriously thinks you can look to nature for moral guidance," says Thornhill. Even the fashion magazines would provide a better compass.

QUESTIONS

1. Describe the relationship between beauty and averageness in facial features. Is this relationship linear or curvilinear?

2. Why is the evidence from studies of very young children important in understanding whom adults find attractive?

3. According to the article, one of evolution's "goals" was to make women attracted to men, and vice versa. How might this have affected men's and women's preference for facial features? How can this view explain same-sex attraction?

4. How might the same general biological and social mechanisms combine to lead people to find excessive body fat attractive in one culture and unattractive in another?

5. Which of the phenomena discussed in this article are supported by evidence from many different modern cultures? How do opponents of biological theories respond to this type of evidence? Of the many findings discussed in this article, which do you believe makes the strongest evidence in support of some biological basis of beauty?

CHAPTER 7

CLOSE RELATIONSHIPS: THE NATURE OF INTIMATE RELATIONS

Reading 13: Classic

A Social Psychological Perspective on Marital Dissolution

George Levinger

As discussed in the two previous readings, research on love relationships has been an important part of social psychology for over half a century. Much of this research has focused on the beginnings of relationships—for example, initial attraction. Other research has focused on mature, ongoing relationships. Social psychologist George Levinger has given considerable attention to a third stage of relationships—their dissolution.

In order to understand why married couples either do or don't stay together, Levinger uses concepts from research on larger groups. He suggests that in any group, the members' level of commitment, or cohesiveness, depends on three factors: (1) attraction to the group, which derives from the net sum of all of one's positive and negative experiences in it; (2) barriers against leaving it, which stem from the cost of ending one's membership; and (3) one's alternative attractions, which refer to one's positive and/or negative feelings about joining an alternative, comparable group.

The next reading is an excerpt from Levinger's important 1976 paper that reviews the then-current literature on the forces that hold marital groups together or help pull them apart. The article analyzes how attractions, either to the marriage itself or to its best alternative, depend on a complex set of material, symbolic, and affectional rewards. Barriers, which is the main focus of the present excerpt, are categorized in terms of their "material," their "symbolic," and their "affectional" costs. You may be surprised to discover how factors that seem entirely outside a marriage relationship may strongly influence the likelihood of whether or not it will endure.

✜

The cycle of life is inexorable. What rises eventually descends. What grows eventually perishes. Closely knit interpersonal attachments, too, sooner or later dissolve.

Why do couple relationships dissolve? The grounds are often complex. Determinants of disruption vary on a continuum ranging from entirely voluntary to entirely involuntary. At the involuntary extreme is death. At the voluntary end, either or both partners may clearly

---

Source: Levinger, G. (1976). A social psychological perspective on marital dissolution. *Journal of Social Issues, 32,* 21–47.

choose to break the bond, as occurs in some instances of withdrawal, estrangement, separation, or divorce.

Divorce generally seems to be the end product of a process of estrangement (Goode, 1956; McCall & Simmons, 1966). It is often preceded by numerous little acts that cool the relationship. Before the actual breakup, a sensitive observer can note stepwise detachments or withdrawals:

> The parties to a progressively less rewarding relationship are allowed simply to give it correspondingly less salience in their respective agendas. . . . The two parties thus begin to fade out of each other's lives. (McCall & Simmons, 1966, pp. 198–199)

Intimate relationships are not easily broken. If they do break, however, they seem already to have declined to a point where one or both partners see an alternative state that is more attractive. The more attractive alternative is not necessarily another lover; it may be going it alone or living in groups other than a nuclear family.

There are few actual data on processes of dissolution. Existing data about the afflicted system are generally based on retrospective reports of single spouses or ex-spouses (Goode, 1956; Weiss, 1976) or of ex-members of premarital pairs (Hill, Rubin, & Peplau, 1976). Process data about couple interaction are difficult to obtain, and neither researchers nor couple members themselves are in a position to view such pair processes objectively.

Most instances of pair dissolution, however, contain a mixture of perceived volition and coercion through circumstance. Events inside the relationship, such as poor communication or intermember coordination, are usually only partly accountable for its breakup; external events also exert powerful effects. Discussions of marital disruption must recognize such external factors. For example, one indirect contributor to the increase in voluntary marital separation during the past century has been the decrease of involuntary separation through death (Bane, 1976). Spouses today see only a distant prospect of death parting an unsatisfying union; thus they may have a greater need to consider other forms of separation. External determinants can also be the source of marital conflict or deficiency. One important source is inadequate income; low family income has been a significant correlate of divorce (Cutright, 1971; Norton & Glick, 1976). The private lives of marriage partners are intertwined with events in their surrounding social and economic environment.

A SOCIAL PSYCHOLOGICAL PERSPECTIVE

This discussion of divorce will view the marriage relationship as a special case of pair relationships in general. In doing so, it builds on two lines of my earlier work—a decade-old integrative review of the literature on marital cohesiveness and dissolution (Levinger, 1965) and a more recent conceptualization of the development of attraction in dyadic relationships (Levinger 1974; Levinger & Snoek, 1972). Although cognizant that the events affecting marital durability emerge out of the broader sociocultural matrix, I here consider the marital relationship mainly as a dyad. And even though most data about marriage and divorce derive from the work of demographers and family sociologists, the present view will be mainly social psychological.

Thus, the conceptual framework focuses more on the marital dyad than on the subtleties of its context. Its constructs are simple, and the complexities of existing data do not arrange themselves easily into its structure. Nevertheless, the approach serves as a heuristic strategy [with] weaknesses as well as strengths. . . .

Cohesiveness of the Marriage Pair

One approach to the determinants of marital breakup is to conceive the marriage pair as a special case of all other social groups, and to consider its continuation in terms of its cohesiveness:

> The marriage pair is a two-person group. It follows, then, that marital cohesiveness is analogous to group cohesiveness and can be defined accordingly. Group cohesiveness is "the total field of forces which act on members to remain in the group" [Festinger, Schachter, & Back, 1950]. Inducements to remain in any group include the attractiveness of the group itself and the strength of the restraints against leaving it; inducements to leave a group include the attractiveness of alternative relationships and the restraints against breaking up such existing relationships. (Levinger, 1965, p. 19)

A second approach focuses on gradations of interpersonal relationship. Pair relationships are distinguished according to degrees of interpersonal involvement, from the unilateral impression of another to the deeply mutual attraction (Levinger, 1974; Levinger & Snoek, 1972). Consider, in particular, the continuum of interpersonal involvement ranging from superficial contact to profound closeness—as indicated by varying degrees of cognitive, behavioral, and emotional interdependence.

Most pair dissolutions occur long before two acquaintances ever reach any appreciable depth, but data about dissolution pertain almost entirely to the breakup of established pairs. The ending of superficial encounters offers few research problems. In contrast, the phenomena of marital separation and divorce pertain to couples who have had high involvement, sufficient for them to enter into a long-term commitment; yet, at the moment of breakup such involvement may be either low or charged with negativity. My social psychological perspective does not make categorical assumptions about the phenomena of separation or divorce. Without knowing a pair's location on a continuum of relatedness, one can say little about the meaning of its breakup.

An Image of the Pair. Figure 7–1 depicts a relationship between Person (P) and Other (O), interpretable according to the above two views. The size of the intersection between P's and O' s life circles refers to the degree of their interdependence—substantial in this instance. It refers to a complex of joint property, joint outlook or knowledge, capacities, behaviors, feelings, joint memories and anticipations.

The arrows marked "+," "−," and "b" pertain to different aspects of pair cohesiveness. The positive and negative arrows refer to forces that drive a person toward either or away from a relationship—positive "attractions" such as feelings of comfort or admiration, and negative "attractions" such as discomfort or irritation. It is assumed that one usually has both positive

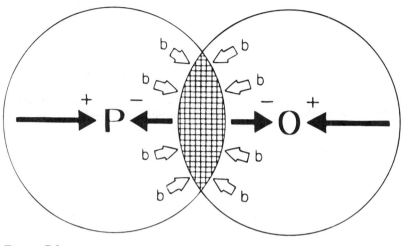

Figure 7-1
Schema of Person-Other relationship.

and negative feelings toward an intimate partner. P's net positive attraction tends to be higher, the larger the size of the P-O intersection. Nonetheless, we can imagine persons who feel large interdependence with their partner, but whose feelings are predominantly negative. Resentment or hatred are also forms of bondage or conversely, being forced to remain together may itself raise negative feelings.

The "b" arrows in Figure 7–1 refer to barrier forces that act to contain the P-O relationship. Barriers—or psychological restraining forces" (Lewin, 1951)—affect one's behavior only if one wishes to leave the relationship. In a marriage one's feelings of obligation to the contract or one's fear of community disapproval at its termination are each examples of psychological barriers against breakup. . . .

Barriers

Discussions of cohesiveness have usually ignored the existence of restraining forces. As originally proposed by Lewin (1951, p. 259), a restraining force affects a person only when he approaches the boundary of a psychological region; he is not restrained unless and until he attempts to cross the boundary. Restraining forces that derive from barriers between people act to keep them apart: barriers around relationships act to keep people together.

Barriers are important for keeping long-term relationships intact. An example is the partnership contract, legitimated by the norms of society. Barriers lessen the effect of temporary fluctuations in interpersonal attraction; even if attraction becomes negative, barriers act to continue the relationship.

If there is little delight in a relationship, however, the existence of strong barriers creates a prison. Such a marital relationship has been called an "empty shell" marriage:

The atmosphere is without laughter or fun, and a sullen gloom pervades the household. Members do not discuss their problems or experiences with each other, and communication is kept to a minimum. . . . Their rationalization for avoiding a divorce is, on the part of one or both, sacrifice for the children, neighborhood respectability, and a religious conviction that divorce is morally wrong. . . . The hostility in such a home is great, but arguments focus on the small issues, not the large ones. Facing the latter would, of course, lead directly to separation or divorce, but the couple has decided that staying together overrides other values, including each other's happiness and the psychological health of their children. (Goode, 1961, pp. 441–442)

The metaphor of an empty shell marriage evokes contrasting images of "full shell" and "no shell" pairs. A "full shell" marriage would be one in which not only the boundaries but also both partners' attractions are strong.

The left column of Figure 7–2 shows two distinct instances of "no shell" relationships which differ in their attractiveness. The top left corner refers to premarital or nonmarital relationships between partners who care deeply for one another, but who have not formalized any commitment. The bottom cell refers to partners who are estranged; divorced pairs are significant instances. Figure 7–2, then, describes a range of instances along two important interpersonal continua: fullness-emptiness of attraction and strength-weakness of boundaries. . . .

Material Barriers

Divorce or separation are expensive. Two places of residence are less economical than one. And if there are children, complications in seeing them or providing for them usually requires additional time and money.

Both high- and low-income partners who separate will have added financial cost. Fixed costs, such as for filing a divorce application or for legal services, affect the poor relatively more than the rich. Sliding costs, especially those for separate maintenance of wife and children, affect the rich more than the poor; a high-income husband is likely to pay proportionately more.

| | BARRIERS | |
	None (or Weak)	Strong
Highly Positive	premarital pairs; uncommitted lovers	attracted and mutually committed marriages
Low or Negative	strangers; pairs that are now divorced	"empty shell" marriages; apathetic and dulled dyads

(ATTRACTIONS, shown vertically at left)

Figure 7-2
Varying patterns of pair attractions and barriers.

In some societies, divorce rates vary inversely with the size of the dowry, which the husband must return to the ex-wife (Goode, 1964). In matrilineal societies where an ex-husband must leave his children and property if he returns to his own kin, the divorce rate is rather low (Swift, 1958). The desire not to break up family financial assets becomes a significant restraint against marital dissolution when those assets are sufficiently large. Furthermore, the wife of a well-to-do husband who herself has little independent income tends to suffer a significant reduction of financial support; in contrast if a husband's current support is already low, there is no such deprivation.

Symbolic Barriers

Marriage is important not only as an arrangement of property, but also as a symbolic acknowledgment of one's place in a culture and in a kin network. This latter meaning of marriage—so important along tribal cultures—seems to have changed most during the past century. Symbols taken for granted in other cultures and at earlier times have changed.

> In the past hundred years, Americans have redefined the nature of marriage . . . as an arrangement of mutual gratification. Once this redefinition is made, it becomes impossible to marshal social pressure against divorce. Conditions are provided which allow couples to see divorce as a natural solution for marital difficulty. (Udry, 1974, p. 404)

Obligation Toward Marital Bond. A firmly committed spouse does not yearn for separation and may never even think of divorce. Other spouses feel less obligation toward keeping their marriage intact. It is difficult to obtain direct measures of such feelings, but contributing factors may be posited.

Length of acquaintance before marriage has frequently been found to be a significant correlate of its durability (Goode, 1956). Partners who wait long before making a formal commitment probably take it more seriously and later feel more invested in it than those who wait little time. Quickie marriages of convenience or necessity, particularly those with a premarital adolescent pregnancy (Furstenberg, 1976), are especially divorce-prone. Furthermore, the longer an existing marriage has lasted, the less likely it is to dissolve (Jacobson, 1959). Here too the strength of spouses' mutual obligations is pertinent.

The probability of divorce is heightened by either spouse's experience of divorce in a previous marriage (Goode, 1956; Monahan, 1952). Previously divorced persons appear more prone than persons in their first marriage to consider divorce as a solution to conflict, or to be members of groups that find it acceptable.

Finally, a history of divorce between the parents of either spouse appears to contribute to divorce proneness (Goode, 1956; Landis, 1949; Pope & Mueller, 1976). A person's continued tolerance for his or her own marital difficulty would be lower if he or she previously experienced mutual intolerance in the parental family.

Religious Constraints. The wedding ceremony and the marriage covenant are in many cultures tied to deep-seated religious beliefs. Nevertheless, both cultures and religions vary greatly in how much they constrain the perpetuity of the marriage tie.

Intrafaith marriages have had lower rates of marital separation than interfaith marriages, yet among intrafaith marriages there tend to be differences across religious denominations. Jewish couples have been found to have the least instability, Protestants the highest, with Catholics in between (Bumpass & Sweet, 1972). Further, couples married at a religious ceremony have been found less likely to get divorced than those joined by a civil ceremony (Christensen & Meissner, 1953).

Like-faith couples who attend church regularly have been found less likely to break up their marriage than those who do not (Chesser, 1957; Goode, 1956; Locke, 1951). Aside from their joint adherence to a general moral standard, such couples are members of a network of connected affiliations; membership in such a net is itself a source of cohesive pressure. At a time of weakened religious orthodoxy, however, today other sources of social integration are coming to exert more powerful effects on marital durability.

If partners differ in their religious affiliation, new forces seem to emerge. Religious dissimilarity is not only the source of attitudinal dissimilarity, but it also can have disjunctive effects on either spouse's obligation toward [his or her] own nuclear family and parental kin. And religious faiths differ in the strength of their prescriptive pressures.

Landis's (1949) study of divorce rates in Catholic-Protestant marriages showed that mixed-faith unions were less durable than same-faith marriages. Furthermore, Catholic-Protestant marriages were three times as likely to break up when the wife was Protestant than when the husband was Protestant. Given that wives are the plaintiffs in about three quarters of all divorce filing, the simplest explanation for Landis's findings is that Catholic wives in mixed-faith unions were less likely to ask for a divorce than were Protestant wives.[1]

A parallel finding to Landis's is reported by Boekestijn (1963) in his comparison of 1951–1955 divorce rates among same- and mixed-faith couples in Holland. Mixed-faith marriages showed divorce rates that were four to five times higher than those of same-faith marriages. Within the same-faith sample, the more "relevant" the religion, the lower the rate. The lowest divorce rates were found for marriages in which both partners were Calvinists, next lowest were for both Catholics, next were both Dutch Reform, and highest was the rate among both "no church." Most interesting was the finding in the mixed-faith sample that, in each of six independent comparisons, marriages where the wife rather than the husband belonged to the more "relevant" of the two religions showed significantly lower divorce rates. Boekestijn's Dutch data thus support Landis's earlier United States findings.

Pressures from Primary Groups. Violation of the standards of church or other communal institutions is merely one potential source of termination costs. Affiliation with kinfolk seems more important, though less measurable.

---

[1]A more complicated explanation (Levinger, 1965) assumes that women's identifications with their religion are generally stronger than men's, that mothers have greater responsibility for child-rearing than do fathers, and that parents in Catholic-Protestant marriages have generally felt obligated to raise their children as Catholics. The Protestant mother in such a marriage would feel greater conflict about religion that would a Protestant father.

Ackerman (1963) hypothesized that divorce rates vary across different cultures to the extent that cultures encourage conjunctive rather then disjunctive affiliation with kin. In the conjunctive case, husband and wife share a common network of kinfolk and friends; in the disjunctive case, the spouses' loyalties go in different directions. Ackerman did indeed find that cultures encouraging competing primary group affiliations showed more divorce proneness than those discouraging such competing affiliations.

Other social anthropologists have also noted the importance of connected kinship and friendship networks for stabilizing a pair relationship even in the absence of strong intrapair affection (Bott, 1971). On the other hand, in such tightly knit networks the more that close kinfolk or friends express disapproval of the marriage, the greater is the likelihood of divorce (Goode, 1964; Locke, 1951).

Pressure from the Community. Another source of termination costs derives from community disapproval. Communal pressures are linked to a couple's social visibility; they are usually greater in small communities than in large ones, in rural areas than in urban one. Thus it is reasonable that rural divorce rates are substantially lower than urban ones (Carter & Plateris, 1963). But this rural-urban difference holds only for settled farmers and farm managers; farm laborers and migrants have among the highest rates of marital separation (Cutright, 1971).

Adherence to conventional social norms does not, of course, necessarily create a barrier against divorce. If a society should publicly encourage marital breakup, then adherence to prevailing norms would raise rather than lower divorce proneness. Instances of that occur in some sub-Saharan tribes (Goode, 1963) and are reported anecdotally for some California suburbs and in some communes (Jaffe & Kanter, 1976).

Affectional Barriers

The divorce of a childless couple is considered largely the couple's own private affair. For couples with dependent children, there is greater reluctance to sanction divorce. And husbands and wives with minor offspring themselves feel more restraint against breakup than those with no offspring. Findings from various sources do show that, with length of marriage controlled, childless couples have generally had higher separation rates than child-rearing couples, although the differences have decreased during recent decades (Carter & Plateris, 1963; Jacobson, 1959; Monahan, 1955).

One recent study reports that unsatisfied married couples usually mentioned "children" as their greatest or only marital satisfaction, while satisfied couples reported many other sources of gratification (Luckey & Bain, 1970). For unsatisfied pairs, children seem to have provided the major reason to remain together.

Even if marriage with and marriages without children had identical separation rates, one still could argue that the presence of dependent children exerts a significant barrier force. That is because American couples with children in the home tend to have lower marital satisfaction than those without children (Burr, 1970; Campbell, 1975). They have greater financial burdens and more interpersonal stress. On the basis of his recent national probability survey,

Campbell writes: "Almost as soon as a couple has kids, their happy bubble bursts. For both men and women, reports of happiness and satisfaction drop . . . , not to rise again until their children are grown and about to leave the nest" (1975, p. 39).

The crucial question is what obligation or affection do the parents in an unsatisfying marriage feel toward their children? And to what extent do they feel that a divorce would hurt them? If parents believe the damage to their children will be substantially greater than that from continuing their conflicted relationship, then the existence of children is indeed a psychological source or restraint; if not, such restraint may be negligible. The age (or dependency) of the children is inversely related to the parents' length of marriage, however, and it is exceedingly difficult to disentangle these opposing influences on cohesiveness (Jacobson, 1959, pp. 132–135). Thus it is hard to generalize about the effect of children on the durability of marriage (see also Bane, 1976; Furstenberg, 1976).

REFERENCES

ACKERMAN, C. (1963). Affiliations: Structural determinants of differential divorce rates. *American Journal of Sociology, 69,* 12–20.

BANE, M. J. (1976). Marital disruption and the lives of children. *Journal of Social Issues 32,* (1).

BOEKSTIJN, C. (1963). The significance of value-concordance and value-relevance for group cohesion. In M. Mulder (Ed.), *Mensen, groepen, en organisaties* (Deel 2). Van Gorcum: Assen.

BOTT, E. (1971). *Family and social network* (2nd ed.). London: Tavistock.

BUMPASS, L. L., & SWEET, J. A. (1972). Differentials in marital instability: 1970. *American Sociological Review, 37,* 754–766.

BURR, W. R. (1970). Satisfaction with various aspects of marriage over the life cycle. *Journal of Marriage and the Family, 32,* 26–37.

CAMPBELL, A. (1975, May). The American way of mating: Marriage si, children only maybe. *Psychology Today,* pp. 37–43.

CARTER, H., & PLATERIS, A. (1963, September). Trends in divorce and family disruption. *HEW Indicators,* pp. v–xiv.

CHESSER, E. (1957). *The sexual, marital, and family relationships of the English woman.* New York: Roy.

CHRISTENSEN, H. T., & MEISSNER, H. H. (1953). Studies in child spacing: Premarital pregnancy as a factor in divorce. *American Sociological Review, 18,* 641–644.

CUTRIGHT, P. (1971). Income and family events: Marital stability. *Journal of Marriage and Family, 33,* 291–306.

FESTINGER, L., SCHACHTER, S., & BACK, K. (1950). *Social pressures in informal groups.* New York: Harper.

FURSTENBERG, F. F., Jr. (1976). Premarital pregnancy and marital instability. *Journal of Social Issues,* 32(1).

GOODE, W. J. (1956). *After divorce.* Glencoe, IL: Free Press.

GOODE, W. J. (1961). Family disorganization. In R. K. Merton & R. A. Nisbet (Eds.), *Contemporary social problems.* New York: Harcourt Brace.

GOODE, W. J. (1963). *World revolution and family patterns.* New York: Free Press.

GOODE, W. J. (1964). *The Family.* Englewood Cliffs, NJ: Prentice Hall.

HILL, C. T., RUBIN, Z., & PEPLAU, L. A. (1976). Breakups before marriage: The end of 103 affairs. *Journal of Social Issues,* 32(1).

JACOBSON, P. H. (1959). *American marriage and divorce.* New York: Rinehart.

JAFFE, D. T., & KANTER, R. M. (1976). Couple strains in communal households: A four-factor model of the separation process. *Journal of Social Issues, 32* (1).

LANDIS, J. T. (1949). Marriages of mixed and non-mixed religious faith. *American Sociological Review, 14,* 401–406.

LEVINGER, G. (1965). Marital cohesiveness and dissolution: An integrative review. *Journal of Marriage and the Family, 27,* 19–28.

LEVINGER, G. (1974). A three-level approach to attraction: Toward an understanding of pair relatedness. In T. L. Huston (Ed.), *Foundations of interpersonal attraction.* New York: Academic Press.

LEVINGER, G., & SNOEK, J. D. (1972). *Attraction in relationship: A new look at interpersonal attraction.* Morristown, NJ: General Learning Press.

LEWIN, K. (1951). *Field theory in social science.* New York: Harper.

LOCKE, H. J. (1951). *Predicting adjustment in marriage: A comparison of a divorced and a happily married group.* New York: Holt.

LUCKEY, E. B., & BAIN, J. K. (1970). Children: A factor in marital satisfaction. *Journal of Marriage and the Family, 32,* 43–44.

MCCALL, G. J., & SIMMONS, J. L. (1966). *Identities and interactions.* New York: Free Press.

MONAHAN, T. P. (1952). How stable are remarriages? *American Journal of Sociology, 58,* 280–288.

MONAHAN, T. P. (1955). Divorce by occupation level. *Marriage and Family Living, 17,* 322–324.

NORTON, A. J., & GLICK, P. C. (1976) Marital instability: Past, present, and future. *Journal of Social Issues. 32*(1).

POPE, H., & MUELLER, C. W. (1976). The intergenerational transmission of marital instability: Comparisons by race and sex. *Journal of Social Issues, 32*(1).

SWIFT, M. G. (1958). A note on the durability of Malay marriages. *Man, 208,* 155–159.

UDRY, J. R. (1974). *The social context of marriage* (3rd ed.). Philadelphia: Lippincott.

WEISS, R. S. (1976) The emotional impact of marital separation. *Journal of Social Issues 32*(1).

QUESTIONS

1. What do the "−," "+," and "b" represent in Levinger's schema of a relationship? Give an example of each.

2. Levinger asserts that "events inside the relationship . . . are usually only partially accountable for its breakup." How, according to Levinger, can events not inside a relationship affect its breakup?

3. Using concepts from Levinger's model, explain "empty shell" marriages. How do they differ from "full shell" and "no shell" marriages?

4. Discuss briefly how religion acts as a marital barrier. In interfaith marriages, does the wife's or husband's faith appear to be a stronger barrier against breakup? Why might this be?

5. In what ways may the presence of children increase the likelihood of marital separation? In what ways may it decrease the likelihood of separation?

Reading 14: Contemporary

What Makes Marriage Work?

John Gottman

How can you tell if your relationship is thriving or struggling? For researchers in the area of close relationships, predicting which relationships will continue and which are likely to break up is an important goal. In the previous reading, George Levinger discussed factors outside of a relationship that affect its durability. For example, he cited evidence that relationships between people who are strongly religious are less likely to break up. In this next reading, John Gottman discusses one important factor within *a relationship that affects whether it is likely to end: conflict style.*

After years of research and hundreds of interviews, Gottman has discovered that how couples resolve conflict is an important indicator of how likely they are to stay together. Many people believe that any conflict will harm a relationship, but Gottman argues that this is incorrect. He believes that conflict is inevitable in any relationship, and that conflict often brings people closer together rather than further apart. In the following article, Gottman describes what he believes to be three healthy styles of conflict resolution. He then describes what happens to couples who don't resolve conflicts in a healthy way. Although Gottman's research focuses on married couples, his advice is likely to be equally important for people in less committed relationships.

❖

If you are worried about the future of your marriage or relationship, you have plenty of company. There's no denying that this is a frightening time for couples. More than half of all first marriages end in divorce; 60 percent of second marriages fail. What makes the numbers even more disturbing is that no one seems to understand *why* our marriages have become so fragile.

In pursuit of the truth about what tears a marriage apart or binds it together, I have found that much of the conventional wisdom—even among marital therapists—is either misguided or dead wrong. For example, some marital patterns that even professionals often take as a sign of a problem—such as having intense fights or avoiding conflict altogether—I have found can signify highly successful adjustments that will keep a couple together. Fighting, when it airs grievances and complaints, can be one of the *healthiest* things a couple can do for their relationship. If there's one lesson I've learned in my years of research into marital relationships—having interviewed and studied more than 200 couples over 20 years—it is that a lasting marriage results from a couple's ability to resolve the conflicts that are inevitable in any relationship. Many couples tend to equate a low level of conflict with happiness and believe

Source: Gottman, J. (1994, March/April). What makes marriage work: *Psychology Today,* 38–43, 68.

the claim "we never fight" is a sign of marital health. But I believe we grow in our relationships by reconciling our differences. That's how we become more loving people and truly experience the fruits of marriage.

Although there are other dimensions that are telling about a union, the intensity of argument seems to bring out a marriage's true colors. To classify a marriage, in my lab at the University of Washington in Seattle, I look at the frequency of fights, the facial expressions and physiological responses (such as pulse rate and amount of sweating) of both partners during their confrontations, as well as what they say to each other and in what tone of voice they interact verbally.

But there's much more to a successful relationship than knowing how to fight well. Not all stable couples resolve conflicts in the same way, nor do they mean the same thing by "resolving" their conflict. In fact, I have found that there are three different styles of problem solving into which healthy marriages tend to settle.

- *Validating.* Couples compromise often and calmly work out their problems to mutual satisfaction as they arise.
- *Volatile.* Conflict erupts often, resulting in passionate disputes.
- *Conflict-avoiding.* Couples agree to disagree, rarely confronting their differences head-on.

Previously, many psychologists might have considered conflict-avoiding and volatile marriages to be destructive. But my research suggests that *all three* styles are equally stable and bode equally well for the marriage's future.

"HEALTHY" MARRIAGE STYLES

One of the first things to go in a marriage is politeness. As laughter and validation disappear, criticism and pain well up. Your attempts to get communication back on track seem useless, and partners become lost in hostile and negative thoughts and feelings. Yet here's the surprise: There are couples whose fights are as deafening as thunder yet who have long-lasting, happy relationships.

The following three newly married couples accurately illustrate the three distinct styles of marriage.

Bert and Betty, both 30, both came from families that weren't very communicative, and they were determined to make communication a priority in their relationship. Although they squabbled occasionally, they usually addressed their differences before their anger boiled over. Rather than engaging in shouting matches, they dealt with their disagreements by having "conferences" in which each aired his or her perspective. Usually, they were able to arrive at a compromise.

Max, 40, and Anita, 25, admitted that they quarreled far more than the average couple. They also tended to interrupt each other and defend their own point of view rather than listen to what their partner was expressing. Eventually, however, they would reach some sort of accord. Despite their frequent tension, however, they seemed to take much delight in each other.

Joe, 29, and Sheila, 27, said they thought alike about almost everything and felt "an instant comfort" from the start. Although they spent a good deal of time apart, they still enjoyed each other's company and fought very rarely. When tension did arise, both considered solo jogging more helpful in soothing the waters than talking things out or arguing.

Not surprisingly, Bert and Betty were still happily married four years after I'd first interviewed them. However, so were Max and Anita, as well as Joe and Sheila. Marriages like Bert and Betty's, though, which emphasize communication and compromise, have long been held up as the ideal. Even when discussing a hot topic, they display a lot of ease and calm, and have a keen ability to listen to and understand each other's emotions.

That's why I call such couples "validators": In the midst of disagreement they still let their partners know that they consider his or her emotions valid, even if they don't agree with them. This expression of mutual respect tends to limit the number of arguments couples need to have.

Anita and Max take a different approach to squabbling than do Bert and Betty, yet their marriage remained just as solid over time. How can people who seem to thrive on skirmishes live happily together? The truth is that not every couple who fights this frequently has a stable marriage. But we call those who do "volatile." Such couples fight on a grand scale and have an even grander time making up.

More than the other types, volatile couples see themselves as equals. They are independent sorts who believe that marriage should emphasize and strengthen their individuality. Indeed, they are very open with each other about their feelings—both positive and negative. These marriages tend to be passionate and exciting, as if the marital punch has been spiked with danger.

Moving from a volatile to an avoidant style of marriage, like Joe and Sheila's, is like leaving the tumult of a hurricane for the placid waters of a summer lake. Not much seems to happen in this type of marriage. A more accurate name for them is "conflict minimizers," because they make light of their differences rather than resolving them. This type of successful coupling flies in the face of conventional wisdom that links marital stability to skillful "talking things out."

It may well be that these different types of couples could glean a lot from each other's approach—for example, the volatile couple learning to ignore some conflicts and the avoidant one learning how to compromise. But the prognosis for these three types of marriage is quite positive—they are each healthy adaptations to living intimately with another human being.

THE ECOLOGY OF MARRIAGE

The balance between negativity and positivity appears to be the key dynamic in what amounts to the emotional ecology of every marriage. There seems to be some kind of thermostat operating in healthy marriages that regulates this balance. For example, when partners get contemptuous, they correct it with lots of positivity—not necessarily right away, but sometime soon.

What really separates contended couples from those in deep marital misery is a healthy balance between their positive and negative feelings and actions toward each other.

Volatile couples, for example, stick together by balancing their frequent arguments with a lot of love and passion. But by balance I do not mean a 50–50 equilibrium. As part of my research I carefully charted the amount of time couples spend fighting versus interacting positively—touching, smiling, paying compliments, laughing, etc. Across the board I found there was a very specific ratio that exists between the amount of positivity and negativity in a stable marriage, whether it is marked by validation, volatility, or conflict avoidance.

That magic ratio is 5 to 1. As long as there is five times as much positive feeling and interaction between husband and wife as there is negative, the marriage was likely to be stable over time. In contrast, those couples who were heading for divorce were doing far too little on the positive side to compensate for growing negativity between them.

WARNING SIGNS: THE FOUR HORSEMEN

If you are in the middle of a troubled marriage, it can seem that your predicament is nearly impossible to sort out. But in fact unhappy marriages do resemble each other in one overriding way: they followed the same, *specific,* downward spiral before coming to a sad end.

Being able to predict what emotions and reactions lead a couple into trouble is crucial to improving a marriage's chances. By pinpointing how marriages destabilize, I believe couples will be able to find their way back to the happiness they felt when their marital adventure began.

The first cascade a couple hits as they tumble down the marital rapids is comprised of the "Four Horsemen"— four disastrous ways of interacting that sabotage your attempts to communicate with your partner. As these behaviors become more and more entrenched, husband and wife focus increasingly on the escalating sense of negativity and tension in their marriage. Eventually they become deaf to each other's efforts at peacemaking. As each new horseman arrives, he paves the way for the next, each insidiously overriding a marriage that started out full of promise.

THE FIRST HORSEMAN: CRITICISM

When Eric and Pamela married fresh out of college, it soon became clear that they had different notions of what frugality meant. Pamela found herself complaining about Eric's spending habits, yet as time passed she found that her comments did not lead to any change on her husband's part. Rather, something potentially damaging to their marriage soon began occurring: instead of complaining about his actions, she began to criticize *him*.

On the surface, there may not seem to be much difference between complaining and criticizing. But criticizing involves attacking someone's *personality* or character rather than a specific *behavior,*. usually with blame. When Pamela said things like "You always think about yourself," she assaulted Eric, not just his actions, and blamed him for being selfish.

Since few couples can completely avoid criticizing each other now and then, the first horseman often takes up long-term residence even in relatively healthy marriages. One reason is that criticizing is just a short hop beyond complaining, which is actually one of the *healthiest* activities that can occur in a marriage. Expressing anger and disagreement makes the marriage stronger in the long run than suppressing the complaint.

The trouble begins when you feel that your complaints go unheeded and your spouse repeats the offending habits. Over time, it becomes more and more likely that your complaints will pick up steam. With each successive complaint you're likely to throw in your inventory of prior, unresolved grievances. Eventually you begin blaming your partner and being critical of his or her personality rather than of a specific deed.

One common type of criticism is to bring up a long list of complaints. I call this "kitchen sinking": you throw in every negative thing you can think of. Another form is to accuse your partner of betraying you, of being untrustworthy: "I trusted you to balance the checkbook and you let me down! Your recklessness amazes me." In contrast, complaints don't necessarily finger the spouse as a culprit; they are more a direct expression of one's own dissatisfaction with a particular situation.

Criticisms also tend to be generalizations. A telltale sign that you've slipped from complaining to criticizing is if global phrases like "you never" or "you always" start punctuating your exchanges:

Complaint: "We don't go out as much as I'd like to."

Criticism: "You never take me anywhere."

Being critical can begin innocently enough and is often the expression of pent-up, unresolved anger. It may be one of those natural self-destruct mechanisms inherent in all relationships. Problems occur when criticism becomes so pervasive that it corrodes the marriage. When that happens it heralds the arrival of the next horseman that can drag you toward marital difficulty.

THE SECOND HORSEMAN: CONTEMPT

By their first anniversary, Eric and Pamela still hadn't resolved their financial differences. Unfortunately, their fights were becoming more frequent and personal. Pamela was feeling disgusted with Eric. In the heat of one particularly nasty argument, she found herself shrieking: "Why are you so irresponsible?" Fed up and insulted, Eric retorted, "Oh, shut up. You're just a cheapskate. I don't know how I ended up with you anyway." The second horseman—contempt—had entered the scene.

What separates contempt from criticism is the *intention* to insult and psychologically abuse your partner. With your words and body language, you're lobbing insults right into the heart of your partner's sense of self. Fueling these contemptuous actions are negative thoughts about the partner—he or she is stupid, incompetent, a fool. In direct or subtle fashion, that message gets across along with the criticism.

When this happened, they ceased being able to remember why they had fallen in love in the first place. As a consequence, they rarely complimented each other anymore or expressed mutual admiration or attraction. The focal point of their relationship became abusiveness.

What Pamela and Eric experienced is hardly uncommon. When contempt begins to overwhelm your relationship, you tend to forget your partner's positive qualities, at least while you're feeling upset. You can't remember a single positive quality or act. This immediate decay of admiration is an important reason why contempt ought to be banned from marital interactions.

Recognizing when you or your spouse is expressing contempt is fairly easy. Among the most common signs are:

- *Insults and name-calling*
- *Hostile humor*
- *Mockery*
- *Body language*—including sneering, rolling your eyes, curling your upper lip.

It is easy to feel overly critical at times, and it is human to state criticism in a contemptuous way now and then, even in the best relationships. Yet if abusiveness seems to be a problem in your relationship, the best way to neutralize it is to stop seeing arguments with your spouse as a way to retaliate or exhibit your superior moral stance. Rather, your relationship will improve if you approach your spouse with precise complaints rather than attacking your partner's personality or character.

THE THIRD HORSEMAN: DEFENSIVENESS

Once contempt entered their home, Eric and Pamela's marriage went from bad to worse. When either of them acted contemptuously, the other responded *defensively*, which just made matters worse. Now they both felt victimized by the other—and neither was willing to take responsibility for setting things right. In effect, they both constantly pleaded innocent.

The fact that defensiveness is an understandable reaction to feeling besieged is one reason it is so destructive—the "victim" doesn't see anything wrong with being defensive. But defensive phrases, and the attitude they express, tend to escalate a conflict rather than resolve anything. If you are being defensive, you are adding to your marital troubles. Familiarize yourself with the signs of defensiveness so you can recognize them for what they truly are:

- *Denying Responsibility.* No matter what your partner charges, you insist in no uncertain terms that you are not to blame.
- *Making Excuses.* You claim that external circumstances beyond your control forced you to act in a certain way.
- *Disagreeing with Negative Mind-Reading.* Sometimes your spouse will make assumptions about your private feelings, behavior, or motives (in phrases such as "You think it's a waste of time" or "I know how you hate it"). When this "mind-reading" is delivered in a negative manner, it may trigger defensiveness in you.
- *Cross-Complaining.* You meet your partner's complaint (or criticism) with an immediate complaint of your own, totally ignoring what your partner has said.
- *Repeating Yourself.* Rather than attempting to understand the spouse's point of view, couples who specialize in this technique simply repeat their own position to each other again and again. Both think they are right and that trying to understand the other's perspective is a waste of time.

The first step toward breaking out of defensiveness is to no longer see your partner's words as an attack but as information that is being strongly expressed. Try to understand

and empathize with your partner. This is admittedly hard to do when you feel under siege, but it is possible and its effects are miraculous. If you are genuinely open and receptive when your partner is expecting a defensive response, he or she is less likely to criticize you or react contemptuously when disagreements arise.

THE FOURTH HORSEMAN: STONEWALLING

Exhausted and overwhelmed by Pamela's attacks, Eric eventually stopped responding, even defensively, to her accusations. Their marriage went from being marred by poor communication to being virtually destroyed by none. Once Eric stopped listening to Pamela, their relationship became extraordinarily difficult to repair. Instead of arguing about specific issues, every confrontation degenerated into Pamela screaming at Eric that he was shutting her out: "You never say anything. You just sit there. It's like talking to a brick wall."

Stonewalling often happens while a couple is in the process of talking thing out. The stonewaller just removes himself by turning into a stone wall. Usually someone who is listening reacts to what the speaker is saying, looks at the speaker, and says things like "Uh huh" or "Hmmm" to indicate he is tracking. But the stonewaller abandons these messages, replacing them with stony silence.

Stonewallers do not seem to realize that it is a very powerful act: It conveys disapproval, icy distance, and smugness. It is very upsetting to speak to a stonewalling listener. This is especially true when a man stonewalls a woman. Most men don't get physiologically aroused when their wives stonewall them, but wives' heart rates go up dramatically when their husbands stonewall them.

The fourth horseman need not mark the end of a relationship. But if your interactions have deteriorated to this extent you are at great risk of catapulting even farther down the marital cascade—becoming so overwhelmed by the negativity in your relationship that you end up divorced, separated, or living lonely, parallel lives in the same home. Once the fourth horseman becomes a regular resident, it takes a good deal of hard work and soul-searching to save the marriage.

The four horsemen are not the end of the line. It is only after they turn a relationship sour that the ultimate danger arises: Partners seize on powerful thoughts and beliefs about their spouses that cement their negativity. Only if these inner thoughts go unchallenged are you likely to topple down the final marital cascade, one that leads to distance and isolation. However, if you learn to recognize what is happening to your once-happy marriage, you can still develop the tools you need to regain control of it.

QUESTIONS

1. What three conflict styles does Gottman believe can characterize a healthy marriage? Prior to reading this article, would you have thought that these three styles were equally healthy?

2. How does complaining differ from criticizing? When is a marriage partner likely to switch from one to the other?

3. How does contempt differ from criticizing? What are the common signs of contempt?

4. Is a relationship in which couples express more negativity always more unstable than a relationship in which couples express less negativity? Why or why not?

5. Describe how a person in a healthy relationship might respond to his or her spouse's criticism? How would a person whose relationship was in the third stage of dissolution (i.e., characterized by the "third horseman") respond? How would a person whose relationship was in the fourth stage of dissolution respond?

PART V

HELPING AND HURTING OTHERS

⁘ CHAPTER 8 ⁘

Prosocial Behavior

Reading 15: Classic

Models and Helping: Naturalistic Studies in Aiding Behavior

James H. Bryan and Mary Ann Test

In 1962, many people were shocked to learn that a woman named Kitty Genovese had been pursued and slowly killed outside her apartment. Most shocking was that her long, fatal ordeal occurred in full view of more than 30 neighbors, not one of whom lifted a finger to help her until it was too late.

Alarmed by the event, social psychologists began a wave of studies aimed at understanding when people do and do not help others. Armed with a social psychological perspective suggesting that situational factors, and not dispositional factors, are most important in determining whether a person in need will receive help, this research led to many interesting findings.

In this next article, social psychologists James Bryan and Mary Test describe research showing that people will be more likely to give help if they have recently seen another person doing so. Their methodological approach was simple yet elegant. This article begins with an overview of some previous research, which leads them to believe that modeling will increase helpful behavior. Next they describe in detail two studies in which they observed the modeling effect, and finally discuss the implications of their research.

⁘

Recently, concern has been evidenced regarding the determinants and correlates of altruistic behavior, those acts wherein individuals share or sacrifice a presumed positive reinforcer for no apparent social or material gain. Studies addressed to these behaviors have explored both individual differences in the tendency to be altruistic and situational determinants of such responses. Gore and Rotter (1963) found that students at a southern Negro college were more likely to volunteer for a social protest movement if they perceived sources of reinforcement as internally rather than externally guided. Subjects high on internal control were more likely to volunteer as freedom riders, marchers, or petition signers than subjects who perceived others as primary agents of reinforcement. Experimental evidence has been generated supporting the often-made assumption that guilt may serve as a stimulus to altruistic activity. Darlington and Macker (1966) found that subjects led to believe that they had harmed another through

Source: Bryan, J. H., & Test, M. A. (1967). Models and helping: Naturalistic studies in aiding behavior. *Journal of Personality and Social Psychology, 6,* 400–407.

incompetent performances on the experimental tasks (three paper-and-pencil tests) were more willing than control subjects to donate blood to a local hospital. . . .Midlarsky and Bryan (1967) found that children exposed to treatment conditions designed to produce empathy were more willing to donate M&M candies than subjects given control conditions while Handlon and Gross (1959), Ugurel-Semin (1952), Wright (1942), and Midlarsky and Bryan have found sharing to be positively correlated with age among school-age children. Lastly, Berkowitz and Friedman (1967) have demonstrated that adolescents of the working class and the bureaucratic middle class are less affected in their helping behaviors by interpersonal attraction than adolescents of the entrepreneur middle class.

Three hypotheses have emerged regarding the situational determinants of self-sacrificing behaviors. One suggests that individuals behave in an altruistic fashion because of compliance to a norm of reciprocity. That is, individuals are aware of the social debts and credits established between them, and expect that ultimately the mutual exchange of goods and services will balance (Gouldner, 1960). Berkowitz and Daniels (1964) have suggested that individuals might show a generalization of such obligatory feelings and thus aid others who had not previously assisted them.

A second hypothesis was put forth by Berkowitz and his colleagues (Berkowitz, 1966; Berkowitz & Daniels, 1963; Berkowitz, Klanderman, & Harris, 1964; Daniels & Berkowitz, 1963) who have postulated the social responsibility norm. They have contended that dependency on others evokes helping responses even under conditions where the possibility of external rewards for the helper are remote. Using supervisor's ratings of an unknown and absent other to produce dependency, and a box-construction task as the dependent variable, considerable support has been generated for the suggestion that dependency increases helping.

A third major determinant of helping may be the presence of helping (or nonhelping) models. While attention to the effects of models has generally been directed toward antisocial behaviors (cf. Bandura & Walters, 1963; Freed, Chandler, Mouton, & Blake, 1955; Lefkowitz, Blake, & Mouton, 1955), some recent evidence suggests that observation of self-sacrificing models may lead to subsequent succorant behavior by children. For example, Rosenhan and White (1967) have demonstrated that children are more likely to donate highly valued gift certificates to residents of a fictitious orphanage if they have seen an adult do so. Hartup and Coates[1] found that nursery school children who have been exposed to a self-sacrificing peer were more likely to be altruistic than children not so exposed. Test and Bryan[2] found that female college students were more likely to render aid to another in computing arithmetic problems if they saw other people so doing.

The present series of experiments was designed to test the effects of models in natural settings on subject samples other than college or high school students, and in contexts other than a schoolroom or university setting. The [two] experiments reported are concerned with the impact of observing helping models upon subsequent helping behaviors. . . .

[1]W. W. Hartup & B. Coates. Imitation of peers as a function of reinforcement from the peer group and rewardingness of the model. Unpublished manuscript, 1966.

[2]M. A. Test & J. H. Bryan. Dependency, models and reciprocity. Unpublished manuscript, 1966.

EXPERIMENT I: LADY IN DISTRESS: A FLAT TIRE STUDY

Few studies have been concerned with the effects of models upon adults, and fewer still with the impact of prosocial models upon them (Wheeler, 1966). Those that have been concerned with such behaviors have invariably employed college students as subjects. For example, Rosenbaum and Blake (1955) and Rosenbaum (1956) have found that college students exposed to a model who volunteered, upon the personal request of the experimenter, to participate in an experiment would be more likely to consent than subjects not exposed to such a model or than subjects who observed a model refuse to cooperate. Pressures toward conformity in these experiments were great, however, as the request was made directly by the experimenter and in the presence of a large number of other students.

Test and Bryan found that the observation of helping models significantly increased the subsequent offers of aid by observers. However, in that study, subjects were given the task of solving arithmetic problems and then rating their difficulty, a task ordinarily requiring autonomous efforts. Furthermore, the experiment was conducted within a university setting, a context where independence of thought is often stressed. The effects of the model may have been simply to increase the subjects' faith that assisting others was allowed. While questionnaire data of the study did not support this interpretation, such effects could not be ruled out entirely. Thus, it is possible that the model impact was simply a propriety-defining activity which reduced the inhibitions associated with such helping behavior.

In general, then, investigations of modeling that employ adults as subjects and that demand self-sacrifice on the part of subjects are limited in number, exploit strong pressures toward conformity, and rely upon college students as subjects. The present experiment was designed to assess the impact of models upon subsequent spontaneous offers of help in other than a university setting.

Method

The standard condition consisted of an undergraduate female stationed by a 1964 Ford Mustang (control car) with a flat left-rear tire. An inflated tire was leaned upon the left side of the auto. The girl, the flat tire, and the inflated tire were conspicuous to the passing traffic.

In the model condition, a 1965 Oldsmobile was located approximately 1/4 mile from the control car. The car was raised by jack under the left rear bumper, and a girl was watching a male changing the flat tire.

In the no-model condition, the model was absent; thus, only the control car was visible to the passing traffic.

The cars were located in a predominantly residential section in Los Angeles, California. They were placed in such a manner that no intersection separated the model from the control car. No turnoffs were thus available to the passing traffic. Further, opposite flows of traffic were divided by a separator such that the first U turn available to the traffic going in the opposite direction of the control car would be after exposure to the model condition.

The experiment was conducted on two successive Saturdays between the hours of 1:45 and 5:50 P.M. Each treatment condition lasted for the time required for 1000 vehicles to pass the control car. While private automobiles and trucks, motorscooters, and motorcycles were tallied as vehicles, commercial trucks, taxis, and buses were not. Vehicle count was made by a fourth member of the experiment who stood approximately 100 feet from the control car hidden from the passing motorists. On the first Saturday, the model condition was run first and lasted from 1:45 and 3:15 P.M. In order to exploit changing traffic patterns and to keep the time intervals equal across treatment conditions, the control car was moved several blocks and placed on the opposite side of the street for the no-model condition. The time of the no-model treatment was 4:00 to 5:00 P.M. On the following Saturday, counterbalancing the order and the location of treatment conditions was accomplished. That is, the no-model condition was run initially and the control car was placed in the same location that it had been placed on the previous Saturday during the model condition. The time of the no-model condition was 2:00 to 3:30 P.M. For the model condition, the control car was placed in that locale where it had been previously during the no-model condition. The time of the model condition was 4:30 to 5:30 P.M.

Individuals who had stopped to offer help were told by the young lady that she had already phoned an auto club and that help was imminent. Those who nonetheless insisted on helping here were told the nature of the experiment.

Results

The dependent variable was the number of cars that stopped and from which at least one individual offered help to the stooge by the control car. Of the 4000 passing vehicles, 93 stopped. With the model car absent, 35 vehicles stopped; with the model present, 58 halted. The difference between the conditions was statistically significant ($\chi^2 = 5.53$, corrected for continuity, $df = 1$, $p < .02$, two-tailed). Virtually all offers of aid were from men rather than women drivers.

The time of day had little impact upon the offering of aid. Fifty vehicles stopped during the early part of the afternoon; 43 during the later hours. Likewise, differences in help offers were not great between successive Saturdays, as 45 offers of aid were made on the first Saturday, 48 on the second Saturday.

The results of the present study support the hypothesis that helping behaviors can be significantly increased through the observation of others' helpfulness. However, other plausible hypotheses exist which may account for the findings. It is possible to account for the differences in treatment effects by differences in sympathy arousal. That is, in the model condition, the motorist observed a woman who had had some difficulty. Such observations may have elicited sympathy and may have served as a reminder to the driver of his own social responsibilities.

Another explanation of the findings revolves around traffic slowdown. It is possible that the imposition of the model condition served to reduce traffic speed, thus making subsequent stopping to help a less hazardous undertaking. While the time taken for 1000 autos to pass the control car was virtually identical in the model and no-model condition and thus not supportive of such an explanation, the "slowdown" hypothesis cannot be eliminated. Assuming the model effect to be real, one might still argue that it was not a norm of helping that was facilitated by the model, but rather that inhibitions against picking up helpless young ladies were reduced. That is, within the model condition, the passing motorists may have observed a tempted other and thus felt less constrained themselves regarding similar efforts. Indeed, the insistence of some people to help in spite of the imminent arrival of other aiders suggested the operation of motives other than simply helping. Indeed, while the authors did not index the frequency of pick-up attempts, it was clear that a rather large number were evidenced.

Because of the number of alternative explanations, the evidence supporting the hypothesis that the observation of helpers per se will increase subsequent aiding is weak. Experiment II was designed to test further the prediction that the perception of another's altruistic activity would elicit similar behavior on the part of the observer.

EXPERIMENT II: COINS IN THE KETTLE

The investigation was conducted on December 14th between the hours of 10:00 A.M. and 5:00 P.M. The subjects were shoppers at a large department store in Princeton, New Jersey. Observations made on the previous day indicated that the shoppers were overwhelmingly Caucasian females.

A Salvation Army kettle was placed on the sidewalk in front of the main entrance to the store. Two females, both in experimenter's employ, alternatively manned the kettle for periods of 25 minutes. One solicitor was a Negro, the other a Caucasian. Each wore a Salvation Army cape and hat. Although allowed to ring the Salvation Army bell, they were not permitted to make any verbal plea or to maintain eye contact with the passing shoppers, except to thank any contributor for his donation.

The model condition (M) was produced as follows: Once every minute on the minute, a male dressed as a white-collar worker would approach the kettle from within the store and contribute 5 cents. As the model donated, he started a stopwatch and walked from the kettle toward a parking lot as if searching for someone. He then returned to the store. The following 20-second period constituted the duration of the treatment condition.

Following a subsequent lapse of 20 seconds, the next 20-second period defined the no-model condition (NM). Within any one minute, therefore, both M and NM treatments occurred. There were 365 occasions of each treatment.

It should be noted that it was possible that some subjects in the NM condition observed the contribution of the model or a donor affected by the model. If that hypothesis is correct, however, the effects of such incidents would be to reduce rather than enhance the differences between treatments.

Results

The dependent variable was the number of people who independently donated to the Salvation Army. People obviously acquainted, as for example, man and wife, were construed as one potential donating unit. In such conditions, if both members of a couple contributed, they were counted as a single donor.

Since there were no differences in model effects for the Negro or Caucasian solicitor, data obtained from each were combined. The total number of contributors under the NM condition was 43; under the M condition, 69. Assuming that the chance distribution of donations would be equal across the two conditions, a chi-square analysis was performed. The chi-square equaled 6.01 ($p < .01$)[3]

In spite of precautions concerning the elimination of correlated observations within a treatment condition, it was possible for subjects in any one observational period to influence one another. Such influence may have been mediated through acquaintances not eliminated by our procedures or the observations of others as well as the model donating. A more conservative analysis of the data, insuring independent observation, was therefore made. Instead of comparing treatments by analyzing the number of donors, the analysis used, as the dependent variable, the number of observation periods in which there was a contribution, that is, those periods in which more than one donation occurred were scored identically to those in which only a single contribution was received. Occasions of donations equaled 60 in the M treatment, 43 in the NM condition. The chi-square equaled 2.89 ($p < .05$).

The results of Experiment II further support the hypothesis that observation of altruistic activity will increase such behavior among observers. But the matter is not yet entirely clear, for when the observer saw the model donate he saw two things: first, the actual donation, and second, the polite and potentially reinforcing interaction that occurred between the donor and solicitor. Conceivably, the observation of an altruistic model, per se, who was not socially reinforced for his behavior, would have little or no effect on an observer. . . .

DISCUSSION

The results of [these] [two] experiments clearly replicate those of Test and Bryan and extend the findings over a variety of subject populations, settings, and tasks. The results hold for college students, motorists, and shoppers; in the university laboratory, city streets, and shopping centers; and when helping is indexed by aiding others solve arithmetic problems, changing flat tires, or donating money to the Salvation Army. The findings then are quite consistent: the presence of helping models significantly increases subsequent altruistic behavior.

That generosity breeds generosity is interesting in light of the recent concern with helping behaviors in emergency contexts. Darley and Latané[4] and Latané and Darley[5] have found that subjects are less inclined to act quickly in emergency situations when in the presence of other potential helpers. Whether faced with a medical emergency (a simulated epileptic seizure) or a dangerous natural event (simulated fire), the rapidity with which students sought to aid was reduced by the presence of others. These findings have been interpreted in three ways: as reflecting the subjects' willingness to diffuse responsibility (others will aid); as reflecting their diffusion of blame (others didn't aid either); or as reflecting conformity to the nonpanicked stooges. It is clear that the results of [these] experiments in the present series

---

[3]All chi-square analyses were corrected for continuity and all tests of significance were one-tailed.

[4]J. Darley & B. Latané. Diffusion of responsibility in emergency situations. Unpublished manuscript, 1966.

[5]B. Latané & J. Darley. Group inhibition of bystander intervention in emergencies. Unpublished manuscript, 1966.

do not follow that which might be predicted by the diffusion concepts. A giving model apparently does not lend credibility to the belief that others than the self will make the necessary sacrifices. The helping other did not strengthen the observer's willingness to diffuse his social obligations, but rather stimulated greater social responsibility. In light of these results, the delayed reaction exhibited by the subjects tested by Darley and Latané might be best attributable to conformity behavior. As they have suggested, subjects, faced with a unique and stressful situation may have been either reassured by the presence of calm others or fearful of acting stupid or cowardly. Additionally, it is possible that diffusion of responsibility is only associated with anxiety-inducing situations. The current data fail to indicate that such diffusion occurs in nonstressful situations which demand fulfillment of social obligations.

While it appears clear that the behavior of the motorists and shoppers was not dictated by a variety of situational and social pressures usually associated with the study of modeling in adults or experiment in academic settings (Orne, 1962), the mechanisms underlying the effects are not obvious. While the presence of the model in the flat-tire study may have reminded the motorists as to the social responsibility norm, a hypothesis does not appear reasonable in accounting for the results in the coins-in-the-kettle [study]. The bell-ringing Salvation Army worker, with kettle and self placed squarely in the pathway of the oncoming pedestrian, would seem to be reminder enough to one's obligation toward charity. A priori, it would not appear necessary to superimpose upon that scene the donating other for purposes of cognitive curing (Wheeler, 1966).

One hypothesis to account for the model effect is that the observer is given more information regarding the consequences of such donation behavior. . . . It is possible that the model serves to communicate to the potential donor relevant information concerning the consequences of his act. That is, the model may demonstrate that an approach to the solicitor does not involve an unwanted interpersonal interaction (e.g., lectures on religion).

A second hypothesis to account for the data pertains to the shame-provoking capacities of the model. It is reasonable to assume that most people feel that they are, by and large, benevolent and charitable. Furthermore, it is likely that such a self-image is rarely challenged: first because charitable acts are not frequently required; second, at least in the street scenes employed in the current series of studies, solicitations are made in the context of many nongiving others. That is, a multitude of negative models—of uncharitable others—surround the solicitations in the current series of studies. Indeed, the contexts are such that most people are not helping; many more cars pass than stop to offer aid to the lady in distress; and there are many more people who refuse to put coins in the kettle than those who do. However, the witnessing of a donor, an individual who not only recognizes his social responsibility but in fact acts upon it, may produce a greater challenge to the good-self image of the observer. Acts rather than thoughts may be required of the observer in order to maintain the self-image of benevolence and charity. If such is the case, then the model characteristics most effective in producing prosocial behavior by socialized adults would be those directed toward shame or guilt production (e.g., donations from the poor), rather than those reflecting potential reinforcement power (e.g., donations from the high-status).

Whatever the mechanism underlying the model effect, it does appear quite clear that prosocial behavior can be elicited through the observation of benign others.

REFERENCES

BANDURA, A., & WALTERS, R. H. (1963). *Social learning and personality development.* New York: Holt, Rinehart & Winston.

BERKOWITZ, L. (1966). A laboratory investigation of social class and national differences in helping behavior. *International Journal of Psychology, 1,* 231–240.

BERKOWITZ, L., & DANIELS, L. (1963). Responsibility and dependency. *Journal of Abnormal and Social Psychology, 66,* 429–436.

BERKOWITZ, L., & DANIELS, L. (1964). Affecting the salience of the social responsibility norm: Effects of past help on the response to dependency relationships. *Journal of Abnormal and Social Psychology, 68,* 275–281.

BERKOWITZ, L., & FRIEDMAN, P. (1967). Some social class differences in helping behavior. *Journal of Personality and Social Psychology, 5,* 217–225.

BERKOWITZ, L., KLANDERMAN, S. B., & HARRIS, R. (1964). Effects of experimenter awareness and sex of subject and experimenter on reactions to dependency relationships. *Sociometry, 27,* 327–337.

DANIELS, L., & BERKOWITZ, L. (1963). Liking and response to dependency relationships. *Human Relations, 16,* 141–148.

DARLINGTON, R. B., & MACKER, C. E. (1966). Displacement of guilt-produced altruistic behavior. *Journal of Personality and Social Psychology, 4,* 442–443.

FREED, A., CHANDLER, P., MOUTON, J., & BLAKE, R. (1955). Stimulus and background factors in sign violation. *Journal of Personality, 23,* 449.

GORE, P. M., & ROTTER, J. B. (1963). A personality correlate of social action. *Journal of Personality, 31,* 58–64.

GOULDNER, A. (1960). The norm of reciprocity: A preliminary statement. *American Sociological Review, 25,* 161–178.

HANDLON, B. J., & GROSS, P. (1959). The development of sharing behavior. *Journal of Abnormal and Social Psychology, 59,* 425–428.

LEFKOWITZ, M., BLAKE, R., & MOUTON, J. (1955). Status factors in pedestrian violation of traffic signals. *Journal of Abnormal and Social Psychology, 51,* 704–706.

MIDLARSKY, E., & BRYAN, J. H. (1967). Training charity in children. *Journal of Abnormal and Social Psychology, 5,* 408–415.

ORNE, M. (1962). On the social psychology of the psychological experiment: With particular reference to demand characteristics and their implications. *American Psychologist, 17,* 776–783.

ROSENBAUM, M. (1956). The effect of stimulus and background factors on the volunteering response. *Journal of Abnormal and Social Psychology, 53,* 118–121.

ROSENBAUM, M. & BLAKE, R. (1955). Volunteering as a function of field structure. *Journal of Abnormal and Social Psychology, 50,* 193–196.

ROSENHAN, D., & WHITE, G. M. (1967). Observation and rehearsal as determinants of prosocial behavior. *Journal of Personality and Social Psychology, 5,* 424–431.

UGUREL-SEMIN, R. (1952). Moral behavior and moral judgment of children. *Journal of Abnormal and Social Psychology, 47,* 463–474.

WHEELER, L. (1966). Toward a theory of behavioral contagion. *Psychological Review, 73,* 179–192.

WRIGHT, B. A. (1942). Altruism in children and perceived conduct of others. *Journal of Abnormal and Social Psychology, 37,* 218–233.

QUESTIONS

1. What two norms do the authors suggest might encourage people to help others in need? Could both norms operate at the same time?

2. What third factor do the authors suggest will influence helping behavior? Do they cite previous empirical evidence to support this prediction? What is the authors' goal in this research?

3. Who are the subjects in the first experiment? In what two conditions did they participate?

4. What was the major finding in each of these studies? Which of the three factors influencing altruistic behavior, discussed at the beginning of the article, can explain the results of the first study? Which can explain the results of both studies?

5. What three explanations have been suggested to explain Darley and Latané's findings? Which of these explanations do the two current studies support?

Reading 16: Contemporary

Cities with Heart

Robert V. Levine

Most of us are familiar with the stereotype that people in big cities are not as friendly or helpful as people in small cities. Looking at statistics of crime and violence, it's clear that hurtful behaviors are indeed more common in larger cities. But what about helpful behaviors? Do indices of help-ful behavior show a similar pattern, with small towns being more helpful than larger cities? Or is it the case that big cities have more helpful as well as more hurtful people? Psychologist Robert Levine set out to answer these questions.

In 36 small, medium, and large cities across the United States, Levine and his colleagues set about to measure the helpfulness of city residents. In all, six areas were measured, ranging from per capita donations to the United Way to helping retrieve a stranger's dropped pen. The results of this study were sometimes surprising and sometimes not. For example, if people have ever told you that New York City was one of the least friendly places in the United States, they are, ac-cording to Levine, correct. However, Levine, a native of New York City, does not believe that the residents of such places are themselves less dispositionally helpful, only that they find themselves in an environment that discourages helpful behavior.

❖

Thomas Wolfe once wrote that city people "have no manners, no courtesy, no consideration for the rights of others, and no humanity." Here in post–Rodney King America, most of us would agree that urban residents see more than their share of human nature's nastier side. Am-ple evidence demonstrates that the rates of crime and violence rise with population density.

But what of the benevolent side of city people? While growing up in New York City, I was taught that big cities simply have more of everything, both good and bad. Of course, there were more criminals. But I was assured that beneath the seemingly harsh exteriors, you would find as many compassionate hearts as in any small town.

Over the past two years, my research group—students Todd Martinez, Garry Brase, Kerry Sorenson, and other volunteers—spent much of their summer vacations traveling nationwide conducting these experiments. We compared the frequency of helpful acts in various places to answer two basic questions. First how does overall helping compare from one city and re-gion to another? Second, which characteristics of communities best predict how helpful resi-dents are toward strangers?

Source: Levine, R. V. (1993, October). Cities with heart. *American Demographics*, 46–54.

WHERE DO PEOPLE HELP?

The team conducted six different experiments in 36 cities of various sizes in all four regions of the country:

Dropped A Pen

Walking at a moderate pace, the researcher approached a solitary pedestrian passing in the opposite direction. When 15 to 20 feet away, the researcher reached into his pocket, "accidentally" dropped his pen behind him, and continued walking. Helping was scored on a five-point scale, ranging from no help offered to picking up the pen and running back to hand it to the researcher.

Helping A Blind Person Across The Street

Researchers dressed in dark glasses and carrying white canes acted the role of blind persons needing help crossing the street. Just before the light turned green, they stepped up to the corner, held out their cane, and waited for help. A trial was terminated after 60 seconds or when the light turned red, whichever came first. Helping was measured on a two-point scale: helped or did not help.

A Hurt Leg

Walking with a heavy limp and wearing a large, clearly visible leg brace, researchers "accidentally" dropped and then unsuccessfully struggled to reach down for a pile of magazines as they came within 20 feet of a passing pedestrian. Helping was scored on a three-point scale ranging from no help to picking up the magazines and asking to be of further assistance.

Change For A Quarter

With a quarter in full view, researchers approached pedestrians passing in the opposite direction and asked politely if they could make change. Responses were scored on a four-point scale ranging from totally ignoring the request to stopping to check for change.

Lost Letter

A neat handwritten note reading, "I found this next to your car," was placed on a stamped envelope addressed to the researcher's home. The envelope was then left on the windshield of a randomly selected car parked at a meter in a main shipping area. The response rate was measured by the share of letters that later arrived because people were helpful enough to mail them.

United Way Contributions

As a general measure of charitable contributions, we looked at 1990 per capita contributions to United Way campaigns in each city.

Helping Behavior

Disregard for strangers seems to increase with population density and environmental stress.

(36 cities ranked by overall score for helping behavior, population density rank, environmental stress rank, and pace of life rank)

	Overall Helping Rank	Lowest Population Density	Least Environmental Stress	Fastest Pace of Life
1	Rochester, NY	Bakersfield, CA	East Lansing, MI	Boston, MA
2	East Lansing, MI	Fresno, CA	Indianapolis, IN	Buffalo, NY
3	Nashville, TN	Santa Barbara, CA	Worcester, MA	New York, NY
4	Memphis, TN	Shreveport, LA	Atlanta, GA	Salt Lake City, UT
5	Houston, TX	Chattanooga, TN	Buffalo, NY	Columbus, OH
6	Chattanooga, TN	Knoxville, TN	Memphis, TN	Worcester, MA
7	Knoxville, TN	Nashville, TN	San Francisco, CA	Providence, RI
8	Canton, OH	East Lansing, MI	Shreveport, LA	Springfield, MA
9	Kansas City, MO	Sacramento, CA	Springfield, MA	Rochester, NY
10	Indianapolis, IN	Kansas City, MO	Boston, MA	Kansas City, MO
11	St. Louis, MO	Rochester, NY	Kansas City, MO	St. Louis, MO
12	Louisville, KY	Columbus, OH	Nashville, TN	Houston, TX
13	Columbus, OH	Canton, OH	Providence, RI	Paterson, NJ
14	Detroit, MI	Indianapolis, IN	Rochester, NY	Bakersfield, CA
15	Santa Barbara, CA	Louisville, KY	Chicago, IL	Atlanta, GA
16	Dallas, TX	Memphis, TN	Louisville, KY	Detroit, MI
17	Worcester, MA	St. Louis, MO	Paterson, NJ	Youngstown, OH
18	Springfield, MA	Worcester, MA	Chattanooga, TN	Indianapolis, IN
19	San Diego, CA	Youngstown, OH	Columbus, OH	Chicago, IL
20	San Jose, CA	Springfield, MA	Dallas, TX	Philadelphia, PA
21	Atlanta, GA	Atlanta, GA	Knoxville, TN	Louisville, KY
22	Bakersfield, CA	Dallas, TX	Salt Lake City, UT	Canton, OH
23	Buffalo, NY	San Diego, CA	Detroit, MI	Knoxville, TN
24	Salt Lake City, UT	Houston, TX	Houston, TX	San Francisco, CA
25	Boston, MA	Salt Lake City, UT	Los Angeles, CA	Chattanooga, TN
26	Shreveport, LA	Buffalo, NY	Philadelphia, PA	Dallas, TX
27	Providence, RI	Providence, RI	San Jose, CA	Nashville, TN
28	Philadelphia, PA	Detroit, MI	Bakersfield, CA	San Diego, CA
29	Youngstown, OH	San Jose, CA	Fresno, CA	East Lansing, MI
30	Chicago, IL	Philadelphia, PA	New York, NY	Fresno, CA
31	San Francisco, CA	Boston, MA	Sacramento, CA	Memphis, TN
32	Sacramento, CA	San Francisco, CA	San Diego, CA	San Jose, CA
33	Fresno, CA	Los Angeles, CA	St. Louis, MO	Shreveport, LA
34	Los Angeles, CA	Paterson, NJ	Santa Barbara, CA*	Sacramento, CA
35	Paterson, NJ	Chicago, IL	Canton, OH*	Los Angeles, CA
36	New York, NY	New York, NY	Youngstown, OH*	Santa Barbara, CA*

Note: Boxes denote ties.
*data not available
Source: Environmental stress rank is based on Zero Population Growth, Environmental Stress Index, 1991; and author's research.

Towns With Pity

Overall Helping Rank	Dropped Pen	Hurt Leg	Make Change	Blind Person	Lost Letter	United Way
1	Rochester, NY	Springfield, MA	Chattanooga, TN	Louisville, KY	Kansas City, MO	San Diego, CA	Rochester, NY
2	East Lansing, MI	Santa Barbara, CA	Fresno, CA	Houston, TX	Knoxville, TN	Detroit, MI	Chattanooga, TN
3	Nashville, TN	East Lansing, MI	Nashville, TN	Knoxville, TN	Rochester, NY	East Lansing, MI	Columbus, OH
4	Memphis, TN	Louisville, KY	Sacramento, CA	Canton, OH	Bakersfield, CA	Indianapolis, IN	Indianapolis, IN
5	Houston, TX	San Francisco, CA	Shreveport, LA	Detroit, MI	Dallas, TX	Worcester, MA	St. Louis, MO
6	Chattanooga, TN	Memphis, TN	Memphis, TN	East Lansing, MI	Nashville, TN	Knoxville, TN	Kansas City, MO
7	Knoxville, TN	Dallas, TX	San Diego, CA	Boston, MA	Chicago, IL	Canton, OH	Philadelphia, PA
8	Canton, OH	Houston, TX	Providence, RI	Nashville, TN	Columbus, OH	Columbus, OH	Dallas, TX
9	Kansas City, MO	Salt Lake City, UT	San Jose, CA	Worcester, MA	East Lansing, MI	San Francisco, CA	Nashville, TN
10	Indianapolis, IN	Bakersfield, CA	Canton, OH	Santa Barbara, CA	Indianapolis, IN	San Jose, CA	Boston, MA
11	St. Louis, MO	Detroit, MI	Kansas City, MO	Buffalo, NY	St. Louis, MO	Chattanooga, TN	Springfield, MA
12	Louisville, KY	Canton, OH	Atlanta, GA	Kansas City, MO	Memphis, TN	Rochester, NY	Canton, OH
13	Columbus, OH	Knoxville, TN	Houston, TX	Rochester, NY	Buffalo, NY	Salt Lake City, UT	Atlanta, GA
14	Detroit, MI	Nashville, TN	Paterson, NJ	San Jose, CA	Houston, TX	St. Louis, MO	Worcester, MA
15	Santa Barbara, CA	St. Louis, MO	St. Louis, MO	Indianapolis, IN	Atlanta, GA	Los Angeles, CA	Louisville, KY
16	Dallas, TX	Indianapolis, IN	Bakersfield, CA	Chattanooga, TN	New York, NY	Louisville, KY	Memphis, TN
17	Worcester, MA	San Diego, CA	Youngstown, OH	Memphis, TN	Santa Barbara, CA	Memphis, TN	Buffalo, NY
18	Springfield, MA	Worcester, MA	Rochester, NY	Bakersfield, CA	Louisville, KY	Santa Barbara, CA	Detroit, MI

#							
19	San Diego, CA	Atlanta, GA	Santa Barbara, CA	Salt Lake City, UT	Canton, OH	Youngstown, OH	Houston, TX
20	San Jose, CA	Rochester, NY	Detroit, MI	Columbus, OH	Philadelphia, PA	Houston, TX	Knoxville, TN
21	Atlanta, GA	Fresno, CA	East Lansing, MI	Springfield, IL	Shreveport, LA	Sacramento, CA	San Jose, CA
22	Bakersfield, CA	Paterson, NJ	Salt Lake City, UT	St. Louis, MO	Providence, RI	Buffalo, NY	East Lansing, MI
23	Buffalo, NY	Kansas City, MO	Dallas, TX	Fresno, CA	Detroit, MI	Dallas, TX	Chicago, IL
24	Salt Lake City, UT	Los Angeles, CA	Springfield, IL	Shreveport, IL	Los Angeles, CA	Kansas City, MO	San Francisco, CA
25	Boston, MA	Sacramento, CA	Boston, MA	Youngstown, OH	San Jose, CA	Nashville, TN	Providence, RI
26	Shreveport, LA	Shreveport, LA	Worcester, MA	Dallas, TX	Worcester, MA	New York, NY	Santa Barbara, CA
27	Providence, RI	Chattanooga, TN	Chicago, IL	Los Angeles, CA	Chattanooga, TN	Springfield, IL	Youngstown, OH
28	Philadelphia, PA	Columbus, OH	Indianapolis, IN	Philadelphia, PA	San Francisco, CA	Philadelphia, PA	San Diego, CA
29	Youngstown, OH	Boston, MA	Columbus, OH	Atlanta, GA	Youngstown, OH	Chicago, IL	New York, NY
30	Chicago, IL	Philadelphia, PA	Knoxville, TN	San Diego, CA	Boston, MA	Providence, RI	Los Angeles, CA
31	San Francisco, CA	Providence, RI	Buffalo, NY	Chicago, IL	Fresno, CA	Atlanta, GA	Sacramento, CA
32	Sacramento, CA	San Jose, CA	Louisville, KY	Providence, RI	Paterson, NJ	Boston, MA	Salt Lake City, UT
33	Fresno, CA	Youngstown, OH	Philadelphia, PA	San Francisco, CA	Sacramento, CA	Paterson, NJ	Shreveport, LA
34	Los Angeles, CA	Buffalo, NY	San Francisco, CA	Sacramento, CA	San Diego, CA	Shreveport, LA	Paterson, NJ
35	Paterson, NJ	New York, NY	New York, NY	New York, NY	Springfield, MA	Bakersfield, CA	Bakersfield, CA
36	New York, NY	Chicago, IL	Los Angeles, CA	Paterson, NJ	Salt Lake City, UT	Fresno, CA	Fresno, CA

Note: See text for explanation of individual helping tests. Boxes denote ties.
Source: 1990 per capita contributions to the United Way campaigns in each city; and author's research.

The researchers conducted the experiments in downtown areas on clear summer days during primary business hours, targeting a relatively equal number of able-bodied men and women pedestrians. They conducted 379 trials of the blind-person episode; approached approximately 700 people in each of the dropped-pen, hurt-leg, and asking-for-change episodes; and left a total of 1,032 "lost" letters.

NEW YORK, NEW YORK

New York State is home to both the most and least helpful of the 36 cities. Rochester ranks first, closely followed by a group of small and medium-sized cities in the South and Midwest. New York City ranks last.

Generally speaking, the study did not find much difference from city to city. At the extremes, however, the differences are dramatic. In the dropped-pen situation, a stranger would have lost more than three times as many pens in Chicago as in Springfield, Massachusetts. Nearly 80 percent of passersby checked their pockets for change in first-place Louisville, compared with 11 percent in last-place Paterson, New Jersey. Fresno came in dead last on two measures, returning only half (53 percent) as many letters as did San Diego (100 percent). Also, Fresno's per capita contribution to United Way is less than one-tenth that of front-runner Rochester.

Why are people so much less helpful in some places than in others? Studies have shown that urban dwellers are more likely than rural people to do each other harm. Our results indicate that they are also less likely to do them good. This unwillingness to help increases with the degree of "cityness." In other words, density drives strangers apart.

"Cities give not the human senses room enough," wrote Ralph Waldo Emerson. Urban theorists have long argued that crowding brings out our worst nature, and these data support the notion. Places with lower population densities are far more likely to offer help particularly in situations that call for face-to-face, spontaneous responses such as a dropped pen, a hurt leg, or the need for change. Research shows that squeezing many people into a small space leads to feelings of alienation, anonymity, and social isolation. At the same time, feelings of guilt, shame, and social commitment tend to decline. Ultimately, people feel less responsible for their behavior toward others—especially strangers.

Population density has direct psychological effects on people. It also leads to stressful conditions that can take a toll on helping behavior. For example, people are less helpful in cities that have higher costs of living. These high costs are, in turn, related to population density, because the laws of supply and demand drive up the prices of land and other resources when they are limited.

High concentrations of people also produce stress on the environment. We compared our findings with Zero Population Growth's Environmental Stress Index, which rates the environmental quality of cities. As predicted, people were less helpful in environmentally stressed-out cities.

Stressful situations and their consequent behaviors ultimately sustain one another. Violent crime results from stress conditions but is itself a source of urban stress. Ultimately, inaction becomes the norm. Big cities see more of the worst and less of the best of human nature.

One characteristic that does not affect helping behavior is the general pace of life. In a previous study of the same cities, we looked at four indicators of the pace of life: walking speed, work speed, speaking speed, and clock and watch accuracy. Since helping people essentially demands a sacrifice of time, people who live in cities where time is at a premium would presumably be less helpful.

Yet there is no consistent relationship between a city's pace of life and its helpfulness. Some cities fit the expected pattern. New York, for example, has the third-fastest pace of life and is the least helpful place. But Rochester has the ninth-fastest pace, and its people are most helpful. Laid-back Los Angeles, the slowest city, is also one of the least helpful, ranking 34th.

Todd Martinez, who gathered data in both New York City and (pre–Rodney King situation) Los Angeles, was acutely aware of the differences between the two cities. "I hated doing L.A. People looked at me but just didn't seem to want to bother," he says "For a few trials, I was acting the hurt-leg episode on a narrow sidewalk with just enough space for a person to squeeze by. After I dropped my magazines, one man walked up very close to me, checked out the situation, and then sidestepped around me without a word.

"Los Angeles was the only city that I worked where I found myself getting frustrated and angry when people didn't help. In New York, for some reason, I never took it personally. People looked like they were too busy to help. It was as if they saw me, but didn't really notice me or anything else around them."

To real-life strangers in need, of course, thoughts are less important than actions. The bottom line is that a stranger's prospects are just as bleak in New York as in Los Angeles. People either find the time to help or they don't.

ROCHESTER'S SECOND WIN

More than 50 years ago, sociologist Robert Angell combined a series of statistics from the 1940 census to assess the 'moral integration' of 43 U.S. cities. Angell measured the degree to which citizens were willing to sacrifice their own private interests for the public good ("Welfare Effort Index") and the frequency with which people violated one another's person and property ("Crime Index"). Angell's methods are not comparable with the current study, but to our astonishment, Rochester also ranked number one on Angell's moral integration index in 1940.

Harry Reis, a psychology professor at the University of Rochester who grew up in New York City, is "not the least bit surprised" by the performance of his adopted home. "I like to describe Rochester as a nice place to live—in both the best and the mildest sense of the word," he says. "It's very traditional and not always very innovative. But it's a town where the social fabric hasn't deteriorated as much as in other places. Unlike New York City, people here don't laugh when you speak of ideals like 'family values.' They take their norms of social responsibility seriously."

Even when people do help in New York City, their altruism sometimes takes a hard edge. On the lost-letter measure, many of the envelopes we received from people had been opened.

In almost all cases, the finder had resealed the envelope or mailed the letter in a new one. Sometimes they even attached notes, usually apologizing for opening the letter. Only from New York City, however, did we receive an envelope with its entire side ripped and left open. On the back of the letter, the "helper" had scribbled, in Spanish, a very nasty accusation about the researcher's mother. Below that, he or she added in straightforward English: "F— you." It is fascinating to imagine this angry New Yorker, perhaps cursing while waking to the mailbox, yet feeling compelled by the norm of social responsibility to assist a stranger. Ironically, this rudely returned letter added to New York's helpfulness score.

While growing up in New York City, I was taught by loving, caring people to ignore the cries of strangers. I learned to walk around people stretched unconscious on sidewalks, because I was told that they just need to "sleep it off." I learned to ignore screams from fighting couples: "they don't want your help." And I was warned to disregard the ramblings of mentally disturbed street people because "you never know how they'll react." The ultimate message: "Don't get involved."

Do our data prove that urbanites are less caring people? Perhaps not. For one thing, no comparable data from small towns exist to show that people there are more helpful than are urbanites. Furthermore, city dwellers we talked with claimed over and over that they care deeply about the needs of strangers, but that the realities of city living prohibit them from reaching out. Many are simply afraid to make contact with strangers. Some are concerned that others might not want unsolicited help. They claim that the stranger might be afraid of outside contact or, in some cases, that it would be patronizing or insulting to offer them help. People speak with nostalgia about the past, when they thought nothing of picking up hitchhikers or arranging a square meal for a hungry stranger. Many express frustration—even anger—that life today deprives them of the satisfaction of feeling like good Samaritans.

To some degree, these may be the rationalizations of unwilling helpers trying to preserve a benevolent self-image. But the evidence, in fact, indicates that helping is affected less by people's inherent nature than by the environment. Studies reveal that seemingly minor changes in a situation can drastically affect helping behavior. In particular, the size of the place where one was raised has less to do with how helpful one is than does the size of one's current home. In other words, small-town natives and urbanites are both less likely to offer help in urban areas.

The future of urban helping may not be as bleak as it seems. Just as the environment can inhibit helping behavior, researchers are currently exploring ways to modify the environment to encourage it. Experiments have found that increasing the level of personal responsibility people feel in a situation increases the likelihood they will help. It also helps to make people feel guilty when they don't help others.

A little more than a century ago, John Habberton wrote: "Nowhere in the world are there more charitable hearts with plenty of money behind them than in large cities, yet nowhere else is there more suffering." The current status of helping activity in our cities is dismal. But helping, like language and other human skills, is a learned behavior. Research indicates that children who are exposed to altruistic models on television tend to follow suit. Just think how much good it could do them to see positive role models in real life.

QUESTIONS

1. List briefly the six areas the author of this article measured. Which tests required people to help a person they had never seen before?

2. Which city was found to be the most helpful? Did this city finish first in any individual categories?

3. What is the relationship between population density and helping behaviors? How does the author explain this?

4. Some researchers have suggested that people in a hurry are less likely to help others. Was this true in the current study?

5. Does this article suggest that people living in urban areas are less helpful than people in rural areas? Does it suggest that people living in the same city who grew up in an urban area will be less helpful than people who grew up in a rural area?

✛ CHAPTER 9 ✛

AGGRESSION

Reading 17: Classic

Weapons as Aggression-Eliciting Stimuli

Leonard Berkowitz and Anthony LePage

The issue of aggression is especially important in the United States, where more people are mur-dered each year than in the rest of the industrialized world combined. Because of the enormous social importance of reducing violence, the study of aggression has received considerable at-tention by psychologists in many disciplines. For example, personality psychologists have tried to identify traits that explain why some people are more aggressive than others. Surprisingly, this approach has not been very successful. Case studies of even the most violent figures often re-veal them to be very ordinary people.

By now you can probably anticipate what kinds of approaches social psychologists have taken to understand aggression. Instead of focusing on the individual, they look for factors in the social environment that can predispose any person to behave aggressively. In this next article, Leonard Berkowitz, the most prominent figure in the social psychological study of aggression, ar-gues that the mere presence of aggressive cues can cause people to behave aggressively. This empirical research report begins by reviewing previous studies and by generating specific hy-potheses to be tested in the study. Berkowitz and coauthor Anthony LePage then explain the pro-cedures they used to test the hypotheses, and they describe their results. Finally, they provide their final summary in a closing discussion, arguing that the presence of guns can have poten-tially deadly consequences.

✛

Human behavior is often goal directed, guided by strategies and influenced by ego defenses and strivings for cognitive consistency. There clearly are situations, however, in which these purposive considerations are relatively unimportant regulators of action. Habitual behavior patterns become dominant on these occasions, and the person responds relatively automati-cally to the stimuli impinging upon him. Any really complete psychological system must deal with these stimulus-elicited, impulsive reactions as well as with more complex behavior pat-terns. More than this, we should also be able to specify the conditions under which the vari-ous behavior determinants increase or decrease in importance.

The senior author has long contended that many aggressive actions are controlled by the stimulus properties of the available targets rather than by anticipations of ends that might be

Source: Berkowitz, L., & LePage, A. (1967). Weapons as aggression-eliciting stimuli. *Journal of Personality and So-cial Psychology, 7,* 202–207.

served (Berkowitz, 1962, 1964, 1965). Perhaps because strong emotion results in an increased utilization of only the central cues in the immediate situation (Easterbrook, 1959; Walters & Parke, 1964), anger arousal can lead to impulsive aggressive responses which, for a short time at least, may be relatively free of cognitively mediated inhibitions against aggression or, for that matter, purposes and strategic considerations.[1] This impulsive action is not necessarily pushed out by the anger, however. Berkowitz has suggested that appropriate cues must be present in the situation if aggressive responses are actually to occur. While there is still considerable uncertainty as to just what characteristics define aggressive cue properties, the association of a stimulus with aggression evidently can enhance the aggressive cue value of this stimulus. But whatever its exact genesis, the cue (which may be either in the external environment or represented internally) presumably elicits the aggressive response. Anger (or any other conjectured aggressive "drive") increases the person's reactivity to the cue, possibly energizes the response, and may lower the likelihood of competing reactions, but is not necessary fro the production of aggressive behavior.[2]

A variety of observations can be cited in support of this reasoning (cf. Berkowitz, 1965). Thus, the senior author has proposed that some of the effects of observed violence can readily be understood in terms of stimulus-elicited aggression. According to several Wisconsin experiments, observed aggression is particularly likely to produce strong attacks against anger instigators who are associated with the victim of the witnessed violence (Berkowitz & Geen, 1966, 1967; Geen & Berkowitz, 1966). The frustrater's association with the observed victim presumably enhances his cue for aggression, causing him to evoke stronger attacks from the person who is ready to act aggressively.

More direct evidence for the present formulation can be found in a study conducted by Loew (1965). His subjects, in being required to learn a concept, either aggressive or [neutral] words, spoke either 20 aggressive or 20 neutral words aloud. Following this "learning task," each subject was to give a peer in an adjacent room an electric shock whenever this person made a mistake in his learning problem. Allowed to vary the intensity of the shocks they administered over a 10-point continuum, the subjects who had uttered the aggressive words gave shocks of significantly greater intensity than did the subjects who had spoken the neutral words. The aggressive words had evidently evoked implicit aggressive responses from the subjects, even though they had not been angered beforehand, which then led to the stronger attacks upon the target person in the next room when he supposedly made errors.

Cultural learning shared by many members of a society can also associate external objects with aggression and thus affect the objects' aggressive cue value. Weapons are a prime example. For many men (and probably women as well) in our society, these objects are closely associated with aggression. Assuming that the weapons do not produce inhibitions that are stronger than the evoked aggressive reactions (as would be the case, e.g., if the weapons were

---

[1]Cognitive processes can play a part even in impulsive behavior, most notably by influencing the stimulus qualities (or meaning) of the objects in the situation. As only one illustration, in several experiments by the senior author (cf. Berkowitz, 1965) the name applied to the available target person affected the magnitude of the attacks directed against this individual by angered subjects.

[2]Buss (1961) has advanced a somewhat similar conception of the functioning of anger.

labeled as morally "bad"), the presence of the aggressive objects should generally lead to more intense attacks upon an available target than would occur in the presence of a neutral object.

The present experiment was design to test this latter hypothesis. At one level, of course, the findings contribute to the current debate as to the desirability of restricting sales of firearms. Many arguments have been raised for such a restriction. Thus, according to recent statistics, Texas communities having virtually no prohibitions against firearms have a much higher homicide rate than other American cities possessing stringent firearm regulations, and J. Edgar Hoover has maintained in *Time* magazine that the availability of firearms is an important factor in murders (Anonymous, 1966). The experiment reported here seeks to determine how this influence may come about. The availability of weapons obviously makes it easier for a person who wants to commit murder to do so. But, in addition, we ask whether weapons can serve as aggression-eliciting stimuli, causing an angered individual to display stronger violence than he would have shown in the absence of such weapons. Social significance aside, and at a more general theoretical level, this research also attempts to demonstrate that situational stimuli can exert "automatic" control over socially relevant human actions.

METHOD

Subjects

The subjects were 100 male undergraduates enrolled in the introductory psychology course at the University of Wisconsin who volunteered for the experiment (without knowing its nature) in order to earn points counting toward their final grade. Thirty-nine other subjects had also been run, but were discarded because they suspected the experiment's confederate (21), reported receiving fewer electric shocks than were actually given them (7), had not attended to information given them about the procedure (9), or were run while there was equipment malfunctioning (2).

Procedure

General Design. Seven experimental conditions were established, six organized in a 2×3 factorial design, with the seventh group serving essentially as a control. Of the men in the factorial design, half were made to be angry with the confederate, while the other subjects received a friendlier treatment from him. All of the subjects were then given an opportunity to administer electric shocks to the confederate, but for two-thirds of the men there were weapons lying on the table near the shock apparatus. Half of these people were informed the weapons belonged to the confederate in order to test the hypothesis that aggressive stimuli which also were associated with the anger instigator would evoke the strongest aggressive reaction from the subjects. The other people seeing the weapons were told the weapons had been left there by a previous experimenter. There was nothing on the table except the shock key when the last third of the subjects in both the angered and nonangered conditions gave the shocks. Finally, the seventh group consisted of angered men who gave shocks when there were two badminton racquets and shuttlecocks lying near the shock key. This condition sought to determine whether the presence of *any* object near the shock apparatus would reduce inhibitions against aggression, even if the object was not connected with aggressive behavior.

Experimental Manipulations. When each subject arrived in the laboratory, he was informed that two men were required for the experiment and that he would have to wait for the second subject to appear. After a 5-minute wait, the experimenter, acting annoyed, indicated that they had to begin because of his other commitments. He said he would have to look around outside to see if he could find another person who might serve as a substitute for the missing subject. In a few minutes the experimenter returned with the confederate. Depending upon the condition, this person was introduced as either a psychology student who had been about to sign up for another experiment or as a student who had been running another study.

The subject and confederate were told the experiment was a study of physiological reactions to stress. The stress would be created by mild electric shocks, and the subjects could withdraw, the experimenter said, if they objected to these shocks. (No subjects left.) Each person would have to solve a problem knowing that his performance would be evaluated by his partner. The "evaluations" would be in the form of electric shocks, with one shock signifying a very good rating and 10 shocks meaning the performance was judged as very bad. The men were then told what their problems were. The subject's task was to list ideas a publicity agent might employ in order to better a popular singer's record sales and public image. The other person (the confederate) had to think of things a used-car dealer might do in order to increase sales. The two were given 5 minutes to write their answers, and the papers were then collected by the experimenter who supposedly would exchange them.

Following this, the two were placed in separate rooms, supposedly so that they would not influence each other's galvanic skin response (GSR) reactions. The shock electrodes were placed on the subject's right forearm, and GSR electrodes were attached to fingers on his left hand, with wires trailing from the electrodes to the next room. The subject was told he would be the first to receive electric shocks as the evaluation of his problem solution. The experimenter left the subject's room saying he was going to turn on the GSR apparatus, went to the room containing the shock machine and the waiting confederate, and only then looked at the schedule indicating whether the subject was to be angered or not. He informed the confederate how many shocks the subject was to receive, and 30 seconds later the subject was given seven shocks (angered condition) or one shock (nonangered group). The experimenter then went back to the subject, while the confederate quickly arranged the table holding the shock key in the manner appropriate for the subject's condition. Upon entering the subject's room, the experimenter asked him how many shocks he had received and provided the subject with a brief questionnaire on which he was to rate his mood. As soon as this was completed, the subject was taken to the room holding the shock machine. Here the experimenter told the subject it was his turn to evaluate his partner's work. For one group in both the angered and nonangered conditions the shock key was alone on the table (no-object groups). For two other groups in each of these angered and nonangered conditions, however, a 12-gauge shotgun and a .38-caliber revolver were lying on the table near the key (aggressive-weapon conditions).

One group in both the angered and nonangered conditions was informed the weapons belonged to the subject's partner. The subjects given this treatment had been told earlier that their partner was a student who had been conducting an experiment.[3] They now were reminded of this, and the experimenter said the weapons were being used in some way by this person in his research (associated-weapons condition); the guns were to be disregarded. The other men were told simply the weapons "belong to someone else" who "must have been doing an experiment in here" (unassociated-weapons group), and they too were asked to disregard the guns. For the last treatment, one group of angered men found two badminton racquets and shuttlecocks lying on the table near the shock key, and these people were also told the equipment belonged to someone else (badminton-racquets group).

Immediately after this information was provided, the experimenter showed the subject what was supposedly his partner's answer to his assigned problem. The subject was reminded that he was to give the partner shocks as his evaluation and was informed that this was the last time shocks would be administered in the study. A second copy of the mood questionnaire was then completed by the subject after he had delivered the shocks. Following this, the subject was asked a number of oral questions about the experiment, including what, if any, suspicions he had. (No doubts were voiced about the presence of the weapons). At the conclusion of this interview the experiment was explained, and the subject was asked not to talk about the study.

Dependent Variables

As in early all the experiments conducted in the senior author's program, the number of shocks given by the subjects serves as the primary aggression measure. However, we also report here findings obtained with the total duration of each subject's shocks, recorded in thousandths of a minute. Attention is also given to each subject's rating of his mood, first immediately after receiving the partner's evaluation and again immediately after administering shocks to the partner. These ratings were made on a series of 10 13-point bipolar scales with an adjective at each end, such as "calm-tense" and "angry–not angry."

RESULTS

Effectiveness of Arousal Treatment

Analyses of variance of the responses to each of the mood scales following the receipt of the partner's evaluation indicate the prior-shock treatment succeeded in creating differences in anger arousal. The subjects getting seven shocks rated themselves as being significantly angrier than the subjects receiving only one shock ($F = 20.65$, $p < .01$). There were no reliable differences among the groups within any one arousal level. Interestingly enough, the only other mood scale to yield a significant effect was the scale "sad-happy." The aroused–seven-shocks

---

[3]This information evidently was the major source of suspicion; some of the subjects doubted that a student running an experiment would be used as a subject in another study, even if he was only an undergraduate. This information was provided only in the associated-weapons conditions, in order to connect the guns with the partner, and consequently, this ground for suspicion was not present in the unassociated-weapons groups.

TABLE 1   ANALYSIS OF VARIANCE RESULTS FOR NUMBER OF
SHOCKS GIVEN BY SUBJECTS IN FACTORIAL DESIGN

Source	df	MS	F
No. shocks received (A)	1	182.04	104.62*
Weapons association (B)	2	1.90	1.09
A × B	2	8.73	5.02*
Error	84	1.74	

$^*p < .01.$

men reported a significantly stronger felt sadness than the men getting one shock ($F = 4.63$, $p > .05$).

Aggression Toward Partner

A preliminary analysis of variance of the shock data for the six groups in the 3×2 factorial design yielded the findings shown in Table 1. As is indicated by the significant interaction, the presence of the weapons significantly affected the number of shocks given by the subject when the subject had received seven shocks. A Duncan multiple-range test was then made of the differences among the seven conditions means, using the error variance from a seven-group one-way analysis of variance in the error term. The mean number of shocks administered in each experimental condition and the Duncan test results are given in Table 2. The hypothesis guiding the present study receives good support. The strongly provoked men delivered more frequent electrical attacks upon their tormentor in the presence of a weapon than when nonaggressive objects (the badminton racquets and shuttlecocks) were present or when only the shock key was on the table. The angered subjects gave the greatest number of shocks in the presence of the weapons associated with the anger instigator, as predicted, but this group was not reliably different from the angered–unassociated-weapons conditions. Both of these groups expressing aggression in the presence of weapons were significantly more aggressive

TABLE 2   MEAN NUMBER OF SHOCKS GIVEN IN EACH
CONDITION

	SHOCKS RECEIVED	
Condition	1	7
Associated weapons	2.60_a	6.07_d
Unassociated weapons	2.20_a	5.67_{cd}
No object	3.07	4.67_{bc}
Badminton racquets	—	4.60_b

Note.—Cells having a common subscript are not significantly different at the .05 level by Duncan multiple-range test. There were 10 subjects in the seven-shocks-received–badminton-racquets group and 15 subjects in each of the other conditions.

TABLE 3   MEAN TOTAL DURATION OF SHOCKS GIVEN IN
EACH CONDITION

| | SHOCKS RECEIVED | |
Condition	1	7
Associated weapons	17.93$_c$	46.93$_a$
Unassociated weapons	17.33$_c$	39.47$_{ab}$
No object	24.47$_{bc}$	34.80$_{ab}$
Badminton racquets	—	34.90$_{ab}$

Note.—The duration scores are in thousandths of a minute. Cells having a common subscript are not significantly different at the .05 level by Duncan multiple-range test. There were 10 subjects in the seven-shocks-received--badminton-racquet group and 15 subjects in each of the other conditions.

than the angered–neutral-object condition, but only the associated-weapons condition differed significantly from the angered–no-object group.

Some support for the present reasoning is also provided by the shock-duration data summarized in Table 3. (We might note here, before beginning, that the results with duration scores—and this has been a consistent finding in the present research program—are less clear-cut than the findings with number of shocks given.) The results indicate that the presence of weapons resulted in a decreased number of attacks upon the partner, although significantly so, when the subjects had received only one shock beforehand. The condition differences are in the opposite direction, however, for the men given the stronger provocation. Consequently, even though there are no reliable differences among the groups in this angered condition, the angered men administering shocks in the presence of weapons gave significantly longer shocks than the nonangered men also giving shocks with guns lying on the table. The angered–neutral-object and angered–no-object groups, on the other hand, did not differ from the nonangered–no-object condition.

Mood Changes

Analyses of covariance were conducted on each of the mood scales, with the mood ratings made immediately after the subjects received their partners' evaluation held constant in order to determine if there were condition differences in mood changes following the giving of shocks to the partner. Duncan range tests of the adjusted condition means yielded negative results, suggesting that the attacks on the partner did not produce any systematic condition differences. In the case of the felt anger ratings, there were very high correlations between the ratings given before and after the shock administration, with the Pearson rs ranging from .89 in the angered–unassociated-weapons group to .99 in each of the three unangered conditions. The subjects could have felt constrained to repeat their initial responses.

DISCUSSION

Common sense, as well as a good deal of personality theorizing, both influenced to some extent by an egocentric view of human behavior as being caused almost exclusively by motives within the individual, generally neglect the type of weapons effect demonstrated in the present study. If a person holding a gun fires it, we are told either that he wanted to do so (consciously or unconsciously) or that he pulled the trigger "accidentally." The findings summarized suggest yet another possibility: The presence of the weapon might have elicited an intense aggressive reaction from the person with the gun, assuming his inhibitions against aggression were relatively weak at the moment. Indeed, it is altogether conceivable that many hostile acts which supposedly stem from unconscious motivation really arise because of the operation of aggressive cues. Not realizing how these situational stimuli might elicit aggressive behavior, and not detecting the presence of these cues, the observer tends to locate the source of the action in some conjectured underlying, perhaps repressed, motive. Similarly if he is a Skinnerian rather than a dynamically oriented clinician, he might also neglect the operation of aggression-eliciting stimuli by invoking the concept of operant behavior, and thus sidestep the issue altogether. The sources of the hostile action, for him, too, rest within the individual, with the behavior only steered or permitted by discriminative stimuli.

Alternative explanations must be ruled out, however, before the present thesis can be regarded as confirmed. One obvious possibility is that the subjects in the weapons condition reacted to the demand characteristics of the situation as they saw them and exhibited the kind of behavior they thought was required of them. ("These guns on the table mean I'm supposed to be aggressive, so I'll give many shocks.") Several considerations appear to negate this explanation. First, there are the subjects' own verbal reports. None of the subjects voiced any suspicions of the weapons and, furthermore, when they were queried generally denied that the weapons had any effect on them. But even those subjects who did express any doubts about the experiment typically acted like the other subjects. Thus, the eight nonangered-weapons subjects who had been rejected gave only 2.50 shocks on the average, while the 18 angered–no-object or neutral-object men who had been discarded had a mean of 4.50 shocks. The 12 angered-weapon subjects who had been rejected, by contrast, delivered an average of 5.83 shocks to their partner. These latter people were evidently also influenced by the presence of weapons.

Setting all this aside, moreover, it is not altogether certain from the notion of demand characteristics that only the angered subjects would be inclined to act in conformity with the experimenter's supposed demands. The nonangered men in the weapons group did not display a heightened number of attacks on their partner. Would this have been predicted beforehand by researchers interested in demand characteristics? The last finding raises one final observation. Recent unpublished research by Allen and Bragg indicates that awareness of the experimenter's purpose does not necessarily result in an increased display of the behavior the experimenter supposedly desires. Dealing with one kind of socially disapproved action (conformity), Allen and Bragg demonstrated that high levels of experimentally induced awareness of the experimenter's interests generally produced a decreased level of the relevant behavior. Thus, if the subjects in our study had known the experimenter was interested in observing their *aggressive* behavior, they might well have given fewer, rather than more, shocks, since giving shocks is also socially disapproved. This type of phenomenon was also not observed in the weapons conditions.

Nevertheless, any one experiment cannot possibly definitely exclude all of the alternative explanations. Scientific hypotheses are only probability statements, and further research is needed to heighten the likelihood that the present reasoning is correct.

REFERENCES

Annonymous. (1966, August 12). A gun-toting nation. *Time.*

Berkowitz, L. (1962). *Aggression: A social psychological analysis.* New York: McGraw-Hill.

Berkowitz, L. (1964). Aggressive cues in aggressive behavior and hostility catharsis. *Psychological Review, 71,* 104–122.

Berkowitz, L. (1965). The concept of aggressive drive: Some additional considerations. In L. Berkowitz (Ed.), *Advances in experimental social psychology,* (Vol. 2, pp. 301–329) New York: Academic Press.

Berkowitz, L., & Geen, R. G. (1966). Film violence and the cue properties of available targets. *Journal of Personality and Social Psychology, 3,* 525–530.

Berkowitz, L., & Geen, R. G. (1967). Stimulus qualities of the target of aggression: A further study. *Journal of Personality and Social Psychology, 5,* 364–368.

Buss, A. (1961).*The psychology of aggression.* New York: Wiley.

Easterbrook, J. A. (1959). The effect of emotion on cue utilization and the organization of behavior. *Psychological Review, 66,* 183–201.

Geen, R. G., & Berkowitz, L. (1966). Name-mediated aggressive cue properties. *Journal of Personality, 34,* 456–465.

Loew, C. A. (1965). *Acquisition of a hostile attitude and its relationship to aggressive behavior.* Unpublished doctoral dissertation, State University of Iowa.

Walters, R. H., & Parke, R. D. (1964). Social motivation, dependency, and susceptibility to social influence. In L. Berkowitz (Ed.), *Advances in experimental social psychology* (Vol. 1, pp. 231–276). New York: Academic Press.

QUESTIONS

1. Briefly describe the stimulus-elicited aggression theory as it is described at the beginning of this article. What role, if any, does anger play in this type of aggression?

2. How did the emotional reactions of the subjects who received seven shocks differ from those who received one shock? Did their different emotional reactions influence the number of shocks they later gave to the confederate?

3. Did the presence of weapons influence the number of shocks given by subjects who had received one shock? Did it influence the number given by subjects who had received seven shocks?

4. What relationship was found in this study among aggressive cues, anger, and aggression? Did either anger or aggressive cues always lead to aggression?

5. Does the demand characteristics alternative explanation for the results, raised at the end of the article, seem plausible to you? Can you think of a way of carrying out a similar study in which demand characteristics could be ruled out entirely?

Reading 18: Contemporary

Bullying or Peer Abuse at School: Facts and Intervention

Dan Olweus

Social psychologists distinguish between two types of consequences that the social environment can have on behavior. These are sometimes referred to as proximal effects and distal effects. Proximal effects have an immediate and direct impact on behavior. Distal effects have a delayed but pervasive impact on behavior. For example, in the previous reading, Berkowitz and LePage argued that the mere presence of a gun in a situation would increase people's aggressiveness in that situation. Because the presence of a gun has an effect immediately but only in that particular situation, it is said to be a proximal cause of aggression. On the other hand, it has been argued that children who watch large amounts of violence on television are more likely to be globally violent for the rest of their lives. If television violence does cause people to be more aggressive later in life and in many situations, then television viewing is said to be a distal cause of aggression.

In this next reading, psychologist Dan Olweus discusses the problem of aggression at school, or bullying. Olweus's main concern is understanding the early influences that may lead some children to become bullies. For example, he argues that the parents of children who bully tend to be less warm and less involved with their children. Olweus begins by arguing that bullying is a pervasive phenomenon that has not been adequately addressed. He then goes on to dispel some of the common myths about bullying, such as the myth that bullying is the result of competition for grades among children. Finally, he describes an intervention that he believes is successful in promoting peace on the school playground.

❖

"For two years, Johnny, a quiet 13-year-old, was a human plaything for some of his classmates. The teenagers badgered Johnny for money, forced him to swallow weeds and drink milk mixed with detergent, beat him up in the rest room and tied a string around his neck, leading him around as a 'pet.' When Johnny's torturers were interrogated about the bullying, they said they pursued their victim because it was fun."[1] Bullying among schoolchildren is certainly a very old and well-known phenomenon. Though many people are acquainted with the problem, it was not until fairly recently—in the early 1970s—that it became the object of systematic research.[2] For a number of years, these efforts were largely confined to Scandinavia. In the

Source: Olweus, D. (1995, December). Bullying or peer abuse at school: Facts and intervention. *Current Directions,* 4, 196–200.

[1]Newspaper clipping, quoted in D. Olweus, *Bullying at school: What we know and what we can do* (Blackwell, Cambridge, MA, and Oxford, England, 1993), p. 7.

[2]D. Olweus, *Hackkycklingar och översittare: Forskning om skolmobbnig* (Almqvist & Wicksell, Stockholm, Sweden, 1973); D. Olweus, *Aggression in the schools: Bullies and whipping boys* (Hemisphere Press, Washington, DC, 1978).

1980s and early 1990s, however, bullying among schoolchildren began to attract attention also in other countries, such as Great Britain, Japan, the Netherlands, Australia, Canada, and the United States.

In my definition, a student is being bullied or victimized when he or she is exposed, repeatedly and over time, to negative actions on the part of one or more other students. Negative actions can include physical contact, words, making faces or dirty gestures, and intentional exclusion from a group. An additional criterion of bullying is an imbalance in strength (an asymmetric power relationship): The student who is exposed to the negative actions has difficulty defending himself or herself.

SOME PREVALENCE DATA

On the basis of surveys of more than 150,000 Norwegian and Swedish students with my Bully/Victim Questionnaire, I estimated that in the autumn of 1983, some 15% of the students in Grade 1 through 9 (roughly corresponding to ages 7 through 16) in Scandinavia were involved in a bully-victim problems with some regularity[3] Approximately 9% of the students surveyed were victims, and 7% bullied other students. Very likely, these figures underestimate the number of students involved in these problems during a whole year.

Bullying is thus a considerable problem in Scandinavian schools, a problem that affects a very large number of students. Recent data (in large measure collected with my Bully/Victim Questionnaire) from a number of other countries, including the United States,[4] indicate that this problem certainly exists also outside Scandinavia and with similar or even higher prevalence rates.[5] Applying the Scandinavian percentages to the school population in the United States would yield a estimate (conservatively) that some 5 million students in Grades 1 through 9 are involved in bully-victim problems during a school year.

There are many more boys than girls who bully other students, and boys are also somewhat more often victims of bullying. However, there occurs a good deal of bullying among girls as well, but girls typically use more subtle and indirect ways of bullying. Also, boys often bully girls, and older students often bully younger ones. There is a good deal of evidence to indicate that the behavior patterns involved in bully-victim problems are fairly stable over time.[6] Being a bully or a victim is something that is likely to continue for substantial periods of time unless systematic efforts are made to change the situation.

---

[3]Olweus, note 1.

[4]D. G. Perry, S. J. Kusel, and L. C. Perry, Victims of peer aggression, *Developmental Psychology, 24,* 807–814 (1988); D. Schwartz, K. Dodge, and J. Coie, The emergence of chronic peer victimization in boys' play groups, *Child Development, 64,* 1755–1772 (1993).

[5]For references, see D. Olweus, Annotation: Bullying at school: Basic facts and effects of a school based intervention program, *Journal of Child Psychology and Psychiatry, 35,* 1171–1190 (1994); D. Farrington, Understanding and preventing bullying, in *Crime and justice: A review of research,* Vol. 17, M. Tonry, Ed. (University of Chicago Press, Chicago, 1993).

[6]D. Olweus, Stability of aggressive reaction patterns in males: A review, *Psychological Bulletin, 86,* 852–875 (1979); D. Olweus, Aggression and peer acceptance in adolescent boys: Two short-term longitudinal studies of ratings, *Child Development, 48,* 1301–1313 (1977); Olweus (1978), note 2.

THREE COMMON MYTHS ABOUT BULLYING

Several common assumptions about the causes of bullying have received no support from empirical data. They include the hypotheses that bullying is a consequence of (a) large class or school size, (b) competition for grades and failure in school, and (c) differences in appearance (e.g., it is believed that students who are fat, are red haired, use glasses, or speak with an unusual dialect are particularly likely to become victims of bullying).

Because the empirical data do not support these hypotheses, one must look for other factors to find the origins of bully-victim problems. The research evidence collected so far suggests clearly that personality characteristics (i.e., typical reaction patterns, discussed in the next section), in combination with physical strength or weakness in the case of boys, are very important in the development of these problems in individual students. At the same time, other factors, such as teachers' attitudes, behavior, and routines, play a major role in determining the extent to which the problems will manifest themselves in a classroom or a school.

CHARACTERISTICS OF TYPICAL VICTIMS AND BULLIES

Briefly, the typical victims are more anxious and insecure than students in general. They are often cautious, sensitive, and quiet. Victims suffer from low self-esteem; they have a negative view of themselves and their situation. If they are boys they are likely to be physically weaker than boys in general. I have labeled this type of victim the *passive or submissive victim,* as opposed to the far less common provocative victim.[23] It seems that the behavior and attitude of passive victims are a signal that they are insecure and worthless individuals who will not retaliate if they are attacked or insulted. In a nutshell, the typical victims are characterized by an anxious and submissive reaction pattern combined (in the case of boys) with physical weakness.

In a follow-up study, I found that the former victims of bullying at school tended to be more depressed and had lower self-esteem at age 23 than their nonvictimized peers.[7] The results also clearly suggested that this was a consequence of the earlier, persistent victimization, which thus had left its scars on their minds.

A distinctive characteristic of the typical bullies is their aggression toward peers, implied in the definition of a bully. But bullies tend to be aggressive also toward adults, both teachers and parents. They are often characterized by impulsivity and strong needs to dominate other people. They have little empathy with victims of bullying. If they are boys, they are likely to be physically stronger than boys in general, and the victims in particular.

In several studies, and using various methods, I have tested the common assumption that bullies are basically insecure individuals under a tough surface. The empirical results did not support this hypothesis and pointed in fact in the opposite direction: The bullies had unusually little anxiety and insecurity, or were roughly average on such dimensions.

[7]D. Olweus, Victimization by peers: Antecedents and long-term outcomes, in *Social withdrawal, inhibition, and shyness in childhood,* K. H. Rubin and J. B. Asendorf, Eds. (Erlbaum, Hillsdale, NJ, 1993).

In summary, the typical bullies can be described as having an aggressive reaction pattern combined (in the case of boys) with physical strength. I have identified four child-rearing factors that are likely to be particularly important for the development of such a reaction pattern (in boys):[8] the basic emotional attitude of the primary caretaker(s) toward the child during early years (i.e., indifference, lack of warmth and involvement); permissiveness for aggressive behavior by the child (inadequate limit setting); use of power-assertive disciplinary techniques, such as physical punishment; and the temperament of the child (active, hotheaded).

As regards the possible psychological sources underlying bullying behavior, the pattern of empirical findings suggests at least three, partly interrelated motives (in particular in boys, who have been studied more extensively than girls). First, the bullies have strong needs for power and dominance; they seem to enjoy being in control and subduing other people. Second, in light of the family conditions under which many of them have been reared,[8] it is natural to assume that they have developed a certain degree of hostility toward the environment; as a result of such feelings and impulses, they may derive satisfaction from inflicting injury and suffering upon other individuals. Finally, there is clearly an instrumental component to their behavior. Bullies often coerce their victims to provide them with money, cigarettes, beer, and other things of value. In addition, it is obvious that bullying behavior is in many situations rewarded with prestige.

Bullying can also be viewed as a component of a more generally antisocial and rule-breaking (conduct-disordered) behavior pattern. In my follow-up studies, I have found strong support for this view. Approximately 35% to 40% of boys who were characterized as bullies in Grades 6 through 9 had been convicted of at least three officially registered crimes by the age of 24. In contrast, this was true of only 10% of the boys not classified as bullies. Thus, as young adults, the former school bullies had a fourfold increase in relatively serious, recidivist criminality.

EFFECTS OF A SCHOOL-BASED INTERVENTION PROGRAM

Against this background, it is appropriate to describe briefly the effects of the intervention program that I developed and evaluated in connection with a nationwide campaign against bully-victim problems in Norwegian schools.

Evaluation of the effects of the intervention program was based on data from approximately 2,500 students originally belonging to 112 classes in Grades 4 through 7 (modal ages: 11–14) in 42 primary and secondary/junior high schools in Bergen, Norway. The subjects of the study were followed over a period of 2.5 years. Because it was not possible to use a strictly experi-

---

[8]D. Olweus, Familial and temperamental determinants of aggressive behavior in adolescent boys: A causal analysis, *Developmental Psychology, 16,* 644–660 (1980); see also R. Loeber and M. Stouthamer-Loeber, Family factors as correlates and predictors of conduct problems and juvenile delinquency, in *Crime and justice: A review of research,* Vol. 7, M. Tonry and N. Morris, Eds. (University of Chicago Press, Chicago, 1986).

mental setup, a quasi-experimental design (usually called a selection cohorts design) was chosen, contrasting age-equivalent groups who had or had not been exposed to the intervention program.[9] The main findings of the analyses can be summarized as follows:[3,9]

- There were marked reductions—by 50% or more—in bully-victim problems for the periods studied, with 8 and 20 months of intervention, respectively. By and large, the results applied to both boys and girls, and to students from all grades studied.
- There were also clear reductions in general antisocial behavior, such as vandalism, fighting, pilfering, drunkenness, and truancy.
- Various aspects of the social climate of the classroom registered marked improvement: improved order and discipline, more positive social relationships, and a more positive attitude to schoolwork and the school. At the same time, there was an increase in student satisfaction with school life.
- The intervention program not only affected already existing victimization problems; it also had a primary preventive effect in that it reduced considerably the number (and percentage) of new victims.

After a detailed analysis of the quality of the data and possible alternative interpretations of the findings, I concluded that it was very difficult to explain the results obtained as a consequence of (a) underreporting by the students, (b) gradual changes in the students' attitudes to bully-victim problems, (c) repeated measurement, or (d) concomitant changes in other factors, including general time trends. All in all, the changes in bully-victim problems and related behavior patterns were likely to be mainly a consequence of the intervention program and not of some other irrelevant factor. Self-reports, which were used in most of these analyses, are probably the best data source for the purposes of such studies.[10] At the same time, largely parallel results were obtained for two peer-rating variables and for teacher ratings of bully-victim problems at the class level; for the teacher data, however, the effects were somewhat weaker.

The reported effects of the intervention program must be considered quite positive, in particular because many previous attempts to systematically reduce aggressive and antisocial behavior in preadolescents and adolescents have been relatively unsuccessful. The importance of the results is accentuated by the fact that the prevalence of violence and other antisocial behavior in most industrialized societies has increased disturbingly in recent decades. In the Scandinavian countries, for instance, various forms of officially registered criminality, including criminal violence, have increased by 300% to 600% since the 1950s or 1960s. Similar changes have occurred in most Western, industrialized societies, including the United States.

---

[9]For methodological details, see D. Olweus, Bully/victim problems among schoolchildren: Basic facts and effects of a school based intervention program, in *The development and treatment of childhood aggression*, D. Pepler and K. H. Rubin, Eds. (Erlbaum, Hillsdale, NJ, 1991); D. Olweus and F. D. Alsaker, Assessing change in a cohort longitudinal study with hierarchical data, in *Problems and methods in longitudinal research*, D. Magnusson, L. R. Bergman, G. Rudinger, and B. Törestad, Eds. (Cambridge University Press, New York, 1991).

[10]For a brief discussion of the validity of such self-report data, see Olweus, note 5, p. 1174, footnote.

BASIC PRINCIPLES

The intervention program is built on a limited set of key principles derived chiefly from research on the development and modification of the implicated problem behaviors, in particular, aggressive behavior. It is thus important to try to create a school (and, ideally, also a home) environment characterized by warmth, positive interest, and involvement from adults, on one hand, and firm limits to unacceptable behavior, on the other. Also, when limits and rules are violated, nonhostile, nonphysical sanctions should be applied consistently. Implied in the latter two principles is also a certain degree of monitoring and surveillance of the students' activities in and out of school.[11] Finally, adults both at school and at home should act as authorities, at least in some respects.

These principles have been translated into a number of specific measures to be implemented at the school, class, and individual levels. Table 1 lists the core components that are considered, on the basis of statistical analyses and experience with the program, to be particularly important.[12] With regard to implementation and execution, the program is mainly based on utilization of the existing social environment: teachers and other school personnel, students, and parents. Non-mental health professionals thus play a major role in the desired restructuring of the social environment. Experts such as school psychologists, counselors, and social workers serve important functions planning and coordinating, counseling teachers and parents (groups), and handling relatively serious cases.

Possible reasons for the effectiveness of this nontraditional intervention approach have been discussed in some detail.[13] They include changes in the opportunity and reward structures for bullying behavior (resulting in fewer opportunities and rewards for bullying). Also, bully-victim problems can be an excellent entry point for dealing with a variety of problems that plague today's schools. Furthermore, one can view the program from the perspective of planned organizational change (with quite specific goals) and in this way link it with the current lively work on school effectiveness and school improvement.

This antibullying program is now in use or in the process of being implemented in a considerable number of schools in Europe and North America. Though there have so far been few research-based attempts to evaluate the effects of the program, unsystematic information and reports indicate that the general approach is well received by the adults in the school society and that the program (with or without cultural adaptations or additions of culture-specific components) works well under varying conditions, including ethnic diversity. In addition to the study in Bergen, there has been a recent large-scale evaluation of an implementation containing most of the core elements of the program.[14] This evaluation based on 23 schools (with

[11]G. R. Patterson, Performance models for antisocial boys, *American Psychologist, 41,* 432–444 (1986).

[12]The package constituting the intervention program consists of the Bully/Victim Questionnaire (can be ordered from the author; will be published by Blackwell in 1996), a 20-min video cassette showing scenes from the everyday lives of two bullied children (with English subtitles; can be ordered from the author), and the book *Bullying at school: What we know and what we can do,* note 1.

[13]D. Olweus, Bullying among schoolchildren: Intervention and prevention, in *Aggression and violence throughout the life span,* R. D. Peters, R. J. McMahon, and V. L. Quincy, Eds. (Sage, Newbury Park, CA, 1992).

[14]P. K. Smith and S. Sharp, *School bullying: insights and perspectives* (Routledge, London, 1994).

TABLE 1. OVERVIEW OF THE CORE INTERVENTION PROGRAM

General prerequisites
+ +   Awareness and involvement on the part of adults
Measures at the school level
+ +   Questionnaire survey
+ +   School conference day
+ +   Better supervision during recess and lunch time
 +   Formation of coordinating group
 +   Meeting between staff and parents (PTA meeting)
Measures at the class level
+ +   Class rules against bullying
+ +   Regular class meetings with students
Measures at the individual level
+ +   Serious talks with bullies and victims
+ +   Serious talks with parents of involved students
 +   Teacher and parent use of imagination

Note: + + indicates a core component; + indicates a highly desirable component.

a good deal of ethnic diversity) in Sheffield, United Kingdom, used a research design similar to that of the Bergen study and likewise showed results that were quite positive (though fewer behavioral aspects were studied). It can be argued that the success and possible generalizability of the program across the cultures is not really surprising, because the existing evidence seems to indicate that the factors and principles affecting the development and modification of aggressive, antisocial behavior are fairly similar across cultural contexts, at least within the Western, industrialized part of the world.

FINAL WORDS

The basic message of these findings is quite clear: With a suitable intervention program, it is definitely possible to reduce dramatically bully-victim problems in school as well as related problem behaviors. This antibullying program can be implemented with relatively simple means and without major costs; it is primarily a question of changing attitudes, behavior, and routines in school life. Introduction of the program is likely to have a number of other positive effects as well.

QUESTIONS

1. According to Olweus's data, what percentage of grade-school students bully others? What percentage are the victims of bullying? Considering his research methods, are these numbers likely to be overestimations, underestimations, or accurate?

2. Is there any truth to the notion that overweight children who wear glasses are the most likely to be the victims of bullying? What physical attributes are characteristics of victims?

3. Compare the self-esteem and insecurity of bullies and nonbullies. What parenting styles increase the likelihood that a child will bully others?

4. What does Olweus believe to be the appropriate form of punishment for bullying? What evidence suggests that combating bullying in school may have important benefits for the entire society?

5. Do you believe that problems with bullying should be dealt with by parents or by the schools? Defend your answer with evidence cited in this reading.

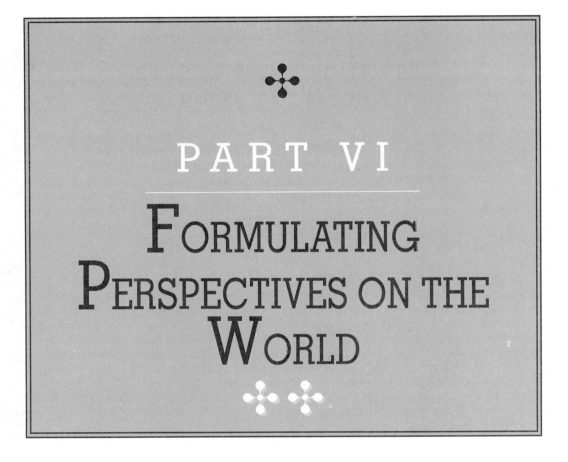

PART VI

FORMULATING PERSPECTIVES ON THE WORLD

❖ CHAPTER 10 ❖

ATTITUDES: APPRAISING OUR SOCIAL WORLD

Reading 19: Classic

Attitudes vs. Actions

Richard T. LaPiere

For social psychologists interested in attitudes, one of the central questions to be addressed is the nature of the relationship between attitudes and behavior. Theoretically, we might expect that an attitude, which is typically thought to encompass a behavioral predisposition to behave in a particular way, would be very strongly related to actual behavior. However, getting a fix on how well people's attitudes relate to their behavior has not proven simple, as this reading demonstrates.

In this article, Richard LaPiere reports a classic study regarding attitudes of hotel and restaurant personnel and their behavior. He traveled with a Chinese couple across America, and the trio was served in 66 hotels and 184 restaurants. Months later in a follow-up, he wrote to these 250 establishments. Of the 128 that answered, only one reported that it would serve Chinese guests if asked to.

❖

By definition, a social attitude is a behavior pattern, anticipatory set or tendency, predisposition to specific adjustment to designated social situations, or, more simply, a conditioned response to social stimuli.[1] Terminological usage differs, but students who have concerned themselves with attitudes apparently agree that they are acquired out of social experience and provide the individual organism with some degree of preparation to adjust, in a well-defined way, to certain types of social situations if and when these situations arise. It would seem, therefore, that the totality of the social attitudes of a single individual would include all his socially acquired personality which is involved in the making of adjustments to other human beings.

But by derivation social attitudes are seldom more than a verbal response to a symbolic situation. For the conventional method of measuring social attitudes is to ask questions (usually in writing) which demand a verbal adjustment to an entirely symbolic situation. Because it is easy, cheap, and mechanical, the attitudinal questionnaire is rapidly becoming a major method of sociological and socio-psychological investigation. The technique is simple. Thus from a

Source: LaPiere, R. T. (1934). Attitudes vs. actions. *Social Forces*, 230–237.

[1]See Daniel D. Droba, "Topical Summaries of Current Literature," *The American Journal of Sociology,* 1934, p. 513.

hundred or a thousand responses to the question "Would you get up to give an Armenian woman your seat in a streetcar?" the investigator derives the "attitude" of non-Armenian males towards Armenian females. Now the question may be constructed with elaborate skill and hidden with consummate cunning in a maze of supplementary or even irrelevant questions, yet all that has been obtained is a symbolic response to a symbolic situation. The words "Armenian woman" do not constitute an Armenian woman of flesh and blood, who might be tall or squat, fat or thin, old or young, well or poorly dressed—who might, in fact, be a goddess or just another old and dirty hag. And the questionnaire response, whether it be "yes" or "no," is but a verbal reaction and this does not involve rising from the seat or stolidly avoiding the hurt eyes of the hypothetical woman and the derogatory stares of other streetcar occupants. Yet, ignoring these limitations, the diligent investigator will jump briskly from his factual evidence to the unwarranted conclusion that he has measured the "anticipatory behavior patterns" of non-Armenian males towards Armenian females encountered on streetcars. Usually he does not stop here, but proceeds to deduce certain general conclusions regarding the social relationships between Armenians and non-Armenians. Most of us have applied the questionnaire technique with greater caution, but not I fear with any greater certainty of success.

Some years ago I endeavored to obtain comparative data on the degree of French and English antipathy towards dark-skinned peoples.[2] The informal questionnaire technique was used, but, although the responses so obtained we exceedingly consistent, I supplemented them with what I then considered an index to overt behavior. The hypothesis as then stated seemed entirely logical. "Whatever our attitude on the validity of 'verbalization' may be, it must be recognized that any study of attitudes through direct questioning is open to serious objection, both because of the limitations of the sampling method and because in classifying attitudes the inaccuracy of human judgment is an inevitable variable. In this study, however, there is corroborating evidence on these attitudes in the policies adopted by hotel proprietors. Nothing could be used as a more accurate index of color prejudice than the admission or non-admission of colored people to hotels. For the proprietor must reflect the group attitude in his policy regardless of his own feelings in the matter. Since he determines what the group attitude is towards Negroes though the expression of the attitude in overt behavior and over a long period of actual experience, the results will be exceptionally free from those disturbing factors which inevitably affect the effort to study attitudes by direct questioning."

But at the time I overlooked the fact that what I was obtaining from the hotel proprietors was still a "verbalized" reaction to a symbolic situation. The response to a Negro's request for lodgings might have been an excellent index of the attitude of hotel patrons towards living in the same hotel as a Negro. Yet to ask the proprietor "Do you permit members of the Negro race to stay here?" does not, it appears, measure his potential response to an actual Negro.

All measurement of attitudes by the questionnaire technique proceeds on the assumption that there is a mechanical relationship between symbolic and nonsymbolic behavior. It is simple enough to prove that there is no *necessary* correlation between speech and action, between response to words and to the realities they symbolize. A parrot can be taught to swear, a child

[2] "Race Prejudice: France and England," *Social Forces,* September, 1928, pp. 102–111.

to sing "Frankie and Johnny" in the Mae West manner. The words will have no meaning to either child or parrot. But to prove that there is no *necessary* relationship does not prove that such a relationship may not exist. There need be no relationship between what the hotel proprietor says he will do and what he actually does when confronted with a colored patron. Yet there may be. Certainly we are justified in assuming that the verbal response of the hotel proprietor would be more likely to indicate what he would actually do than would the verbal response of people whose personal feelings are less subordinated to economic expediency. However, the following study indicates that the reliability of even such responses is very small indeed.

Beginning in 1930 and continuing for two years thereafter, I had the good fortune to travel rather exclusively with a young Chinese student and his wife.[3] Both were personable, charming, and quick to win the admiration and respect of those they had the opportunity to become intimate with. But they were foreign-born Chinese, a fact that could not be disguised. Knowing the general "attitude" of Americans towards the Chinese as indicated by the "social distance" studies which have been made, it was with considerable trepidation that I first approached a hotel clerk in their company. Perhaps the clerk's eyebrows lifted slightly, but he accommodated us without a show of hesitation. And this in the "best" hotel in a small town noted for its narrow and bigoted "attitude" towards Orientals. Two months later I passed that way again, phoned the hotel and asked if it would accommodate "an important Chinese gentleman." The reply was an unequivocal "No." That aroused my curiosity and led to this study.

In something like ten thousand miles of motor travel, twice across the United States, up and down the Pacific Coast, only once did we meet definite rejection from those asked to serve us. We were received at 66 hotels, auto camps, and tourist homes, refused at one. We were served in 184 restaurants and cafes scattered throughout the country and treated with what I judged to be more than ordinary consideration in 72 of them. Accurate and detailed records were kept of all these instances. An effort, necessarily subjective, was made to evaluate the overt response of hotel clerks, bellboys, elevator operators, and waitresses to the presence of my Chinese friends. The factors entering into the situations were varied as far and as often as possible. Control was not, of course, as exacting as that required by laboratory experimentation. But it was as rigid as is humanly possible in human situations. For example, I did not take the "test" subjects into my confidence, fearing that their behavior might become self-conscious and thus abnormally affect the response of others towards them. Whenever possible I let my Chinese friend negotiate for accommodations (while I concerned myself with the car or luggage) or sent them into a restaurant ahead of me. In this way I attempted to "factor" myself out. We sometimes patronized high-class establishments after a hard and dusty day on the road and stopped at inferior auto camps when in our most presentable condition.

In the end I was forced to conclude that those factors which most influenced the behavior of others towards the Chinese had nothing at all to do with race. Quality and condition of clothing, appearance of baggage (by which, it seems, hotel clerks are prone to base their quick evaluations), cleanliness and neatness were far more significant for person-to-person reaction in the situations I was studying than skin pigmentation, straight black hair, slanting eyes, and

---

[3]The results of this study have been withheld until the present time out of consideration for their feelings.

flat noses. And yet an air of self-confidence might entirely offset the "unfavorable" impression made by dusty clothes and the usual disorder to appearance consequent upon some hundred miles of motor travel. A supercilious desk clerk in a hotel of noble aspirations could not refuse his master's hospitality to people who appeared to take their request as a perfectly normal and conventional thing, though they might look like tin-can tourists and two of them belong to the racial category "Oriental." On the other hand, I became rather adept at approaching hotel clerks with that peculiar crabwise manner which is so effective in provoking a somewhat scornful disregard. And then a bland smile would serve to reverse the entire situation. Indeed, it appeared that a genial smile was the most effective password to acceptance. My Chinese friends were skillful smilers, which may account, in part, for the fact that we received but one rebuff in all our experience. Finally, I was impressed with the fact that even where some tension developed due to the strangeness of the Chinese, it would evaporate immediately when they spoke in unaccented English.

The one instance in which we were refused accommodations is worth recording here. The place was a small California town, a rather inferior auto camp into which we drove in a very dilapidated car piled with camp equipment. It was early evening, the light so dim that the proprietor found it somewhat difficult to decide the genus voyageur to which we belonged. I left the car and spoke to him. He hesitated, wavered, said he was not sure that he had two cabins, meanwhile edging towards our car. The realization that the two occupants were Orientals turned the balance or, more likely, gave him the excuse he was looking for. "No," he said, "I don't take Japs!" In a more pretentious establishment we secured accommodations, and with an extra flourish of hospitality.

To offset this one flat refusal were the many instances in which the physical peculiarities of the Chinese served to heighten curiosity. With few exceptions this curiosity was considerably hidden behind an exceptional interest in serving us. Of course, outside of the Pacific Coast region, New York, and Chicago, the Chinese physiognomy attracts attention. It is different, hence noticeable. But the principal effect this curiosity has upon the behavior of those who cater to the traveler's needs is to make them more attentive, more responsive, more reliable. A Chinese companion is to be recommended to the white traveling in his native land. Strange features when combined with "human" speech and action seem, at times, to heighten sympathetic response, perhaps on the same principle that makes us uncommonly sympathetic towards the dog that has a "human" expression on his face.

What I am trying to say is that in only one our of 251 instances in which we purchased goods or services necessitating intimate human relationships did the fact that my companions were Chinese adversely affect us. Factors entirely unassociated with race were, in the main, the determinant of significant variations in our reception. It would appear reasonable to conclude that the "attitude" of the American people, as reflected in the behavior of those who are for pecuniary reasons presumably most sensitive to the antipathies of their white clientele, is anything but negative towards the Chinese. In terms of "social distance" we might conclude that native Caucasians are not averse to residing in the same hotels, auto camps, and adjoining table in restaurant or cafe. It does not follow that there is revealed a distinctly "positive" attitude toward Chinese, that whites prefer the Chinese to other whites.

But the facts as gathered certainly preclude the conclusion that there is an intense prejudice towards the Chinese.

Yet the existence of this prejudice, very intense, is proven by a conventional "attitude" study. To provide a comparison of symbolic reaction to symbolic social situations with actual reaction to real social situations, I "questionnaired" the establishments which we patronized during the two-year period. Six months were permitted to lapse between the time I obtained the overt reaction and the symbolic. It was hoped that the effects of the actual experience with Chinese guests, adverse or otherwise, would have faded during the intervening time. To the hotel or restaurant a questionnaire was mailed with an accompanying letter purporting to be a special and personal plea for response. The questionnaires all asked the same question, "Will you accept members of the Chinese race as guests in your establishment?" Two types of questionnaire were used. In one this question was inserted among similar queries concerning Germans, French, Japanese, Russians, Armenians, Jews, Negroes, Italians, and Indians. In the other the pertinent question was unencumbered. With persistence, completed replies were obtained from 128 of the establishments we had visited: 81 restaurants and cafes and 47 hotels, auto camps, and tourist homes. In response to the relevant question 92 percent of the former and 91 percent of the latter replied "No." The remainder replied "Uncertain; depend upon circumstances." From the woman proprietor of a small auto camp I received the only "Yes," accompanied by a chatty letter describing the nice visit she had had with a Chinese gentleman and his sweet wife during the previous summer.

A rather unflattering interpretation might be put upon the fact that those establishments who had provided for our needs so graciously were, some months later, verbally antagonistic towards hypothetical Chinese. To factor this experience out, responses were secured from 32 hotels and 96 restaurants located in approximately the same regions, but uninfluenced by this particular experience with Oriental clients. In this, as in the former case, both types of questionnaires were used. The results indicate that neither the type of questionnaire nor the fact of previous experience had important bearing upon the symbolic response to symbolic social situations.

It is impossible to make direct comparison between the reactions secured through questionnaires and from actual experience. On the basis of the above data it would appear foolhardy for a Chinese person to attempt to travel in the United States. And yet, as I have shown, actual experience indicates that the American people, as represented by the personnel of hotels, restaurants, etc., are not at all averse to fraternizing with Chinese people within the limitations which apply to social relationships between Americans themselves. The evaluations which follow are undoubtedly subject to the criticism which any human judgment must withstand. But the fact is that, although they began their travels in this country with considerable trepidation, my Chinese friends soon lost all fear that they might receive a rebuff. At first somewhat timid and considerably dependent upon me for guidance and support, they came in time to feel fully self-reliant and would approach new social situations without the slight hesitation. . . .

No doubt a considerable part of the data which the social scientists deals with can be obtained by the questionnaire method. The census reports are based upon verbal questionnaires

TABLE 1.   DISTRIBUTION OF RESULTS FROM QUESTIONNAIRE STUDY OF ESTABLISHMENT "POLICY"
REGARDING ACCEPTANCE OF CHINESE AS GUESTS

	Hotels, Etc., Visited		Hotels, Etc., Not Visited		Restaurants, Etc., Visited		Restaurants, Etc., Not visited	
Total	47		32		81		96	
	1*	2*	1	2	1	2	1	2
Number replying	22	25	20	12	43	38	51	45
No	20	23	19	11	40	35	37	41
Undecided: depend upon circumstances	1	2	1	1	3	3	4	3
Yes	1	0	0	0	0	0	0	1

*Replies are to the question: "Will you accept members of the Chinese race as guests in your establishment?"

†Column (1) indicates in each case those responses to questionnaires which concerned Chinese only. The figures in columns (2) are from the questionnaires in which the above was inserted among questions regarding Germans, French, Japanese, etc.

and I do not doubt their basic integrity. If we wish to know how many children a man has, his income, the size of his home, his age, and the condition of his parents, we can reasonably ask him. These things he has frequently and conventionally converted into verbal responses. He is competent to report upon them, and will do so accurately, unless indeed he wishes to do otherwise. A careful investigator could no doubt even find out by verbal means whether the man fights with his wife (frequently, infrequently, or not at all), though the neighbors would be a more reliable source. But we should not expect to obtain by the questionnaire method his "anticipatory set or tendency" to action should his wife pack up and go home to Mother, should Elder Son get into trouble with the neighbor's daughter, the President assume the status of a dictator, the Japanese take over the rest of China, or a Chinese gentleman come to pay a social call.

Only a verbal reaction to an entirely symbolic situation can be secured by questionnaire. It may indicate what the responder would actually do when confronted with the situation symbolized in the question, but there is no assurance that it will. And so to call the response a reflection of a "social attitude" is to entirely disregard the definition commonly given for the phrase "attitude." If social attitudes are to be conceptualized as partially integrated habit sets which will become operative under specific circumstances and lead to a particular pattern of adjustment they must, in the main, be derived from a study of humans behaving in actual social situations. They must not be imputed on the basis of questionnaire data.

The questionnaire is cheap, easy, and mechanical. The study of human behavior is time-consuming, intellectually fatiguing, and dependent for its success upon the ability of the investigator. The former method gives quantitative results, the latter mainly qualitative. Quantitative measurements are quantitatively accurate; qualitative evaluations are always subject to the errors of human judgment. Yet it would seem far more worthwhile to make a shrewd guess regarding that which is essential than to accurately measure that which is likely to prove quite irrelevant.

QUESTIONS

1. How does LaPiere define attitudes? Which of the three components does this definitions stress: affective (emotional), behavioral, or cognitive?

2. What does LaPiere see as the main difficulty in interpreting attitudes from questionnaires?

3. How does LaPiere describe the one time that he and his guests were refused lodgings? Was the refusal based only on the race of his Chinese guests?

4. What sorts of questions can people answer reliably? When can verbalizations of attitudes be most trusted?

5. What are the difficulties of conducting our studies of social attitudes in the manner suggested by LaPiere? What are the difficulties of interpreting the results of such studies?

Reading 20: Contemporary

Saddam Hussein: The Hitler We "Know"

Anthony R. Pratkanis and Elliot Aronson

Near the end of 1990, Saddam Hussein made headlines around the world when his country, Iraq, invaded Kuwait. Before this event, few Americans had ever heard the name "Saddam Hussein," and even fewer had any strong attitudes about him. Having no strong opinions about the people and countries (Iraq and Kuwait) involved in the conflict, many Americans were initially reluctant to support a large military effort in the Persian Gulf. The country's experiences in Vietnam had made them weary of fighting another war on foreign soil. In order to overcome this reluctance, proponents of the war worked hard to change Americans' attitudes toward Saddam.

In this next reading, social psychologists A. R. Pratkanis and Elliot Aronson discuss how people's attitudes toward Hussein were effectively changed through the technique of classical conditioning. By equating Hussein with Adolf Hitler in superficial, surface analogies, proponents of the war effort were able to transfer to Hussein Americans' preexisting negative attitudes toward Hitler.

❖

Before the Persian Gulf war of 1991, the U.S. Congress debated the positive and negative consequences of going to war. Those who supported the war described Saddam Hussein as the new Hitler: They emphasized the parallels between Saddam's gassing of the Kurds and Hitler's gassing of the Jews, Iraq's invasion of Kuwait and Germany's invasion of Czechoslovakia and Poland, and Saddam and Hitler's buildup of armaments. Those who opposed the war saw the situation in Iraq as paralleling that of Vietnam: They saw both incidents as civil wars—a fight between various Arab factions and between North and South Vietnam; worried about the U.S. military's ability to fight in difficult foreign terrain consisting of deserts and swamps; they characterized the war effort as being in support of "big business" and "big oil."

The debate over war with Iraq was really a debate over whose definition of ambiguous events was "correct." And with good reason: once it is decided how an event or person should be categorized, it becomes clear what course of action should be taken. If Saddam was truly a new Hitler, then a policy of appeasement and letting him have Kuwait would only bring additional threats to peace and ultimately a much worse war. If Iraq was another Vietnam, then U.S. intervention would lead to a long and divisive war and the country would become stuck in a quagmire with no clear victors and losers.

Source: Pratkanis, A. R., & Aronson, E. (1991). Saddam Hussein: The Hitler we "know." In *Age of propaganda* (pp. 56–60). New York: Freeman.

We "debate" how to define persons and events thousands of times a day and, although we usually do not go to war over the results, the consequences of how we interpret and define events can be quite significant. For example, we may see a political candidate as "presidential" simply because he or she shares some irrelevant mannerisms with one of our favorite politicians from the past; a college athlete may be viewed as "pro" material because he fits the mold of past successes—he's a Lynn Swann type or he reminds us of the old-style Steeler linebackers of the past; we like the new car we purchased because it is similar in style to a high-priced sporty model that we cannot afford.

Ten years before the Persian Gulf war, Thomas Gilovich published a set of experiments looking at how irrelevant associations to the past can influence decision making.[1] In one of his studies, majoring in a political science were asked to resolve a hypothetical international crisis. In this crisis, a small democratic country was being threatened by an aggressive, totalitarian neighbor that was conducting subversive activities against the democratic regime as well as massing troops along a shared border. Embedded in the information about the crisis were irrelevant phrases designed to highlight the similarities in the hypothetical crises to either the war against Nazi Germany or that against North Vietnam. For example, the political science majors were either told that minorities were fleeing the democratic country via boxcars on freight trains or via small boats; the impending invasion was referred to as a Blitzkrieg or a Quickstrike; the current U.S. president was from the state of New York (as was FDR) or from Texas (as was LBJ); the briefing concerning the crisis was held in Winston Churchill Hall or Dean Rusk Hall. Did these irrelevant "similarities" influence judgments about what should be done about the crisis? Amazingly, they did. Gilovich found that the students who were "primed" to see the crisis as like the one involving Nazi Germany were more likely to recommend U.S. military intervention than were those who saw it as another Vietnam.

In the end, debates on a course of action must come down to which definition of the situation is perceived to be correct—Is Saddam more like Hitler or is Iraq more like Vietnam? Of course, we should entertain the hypotheses that both analogies are true, that neither is true, or that perhaps other analogies also fit the situation. For example, the historian Paul Kennedy sees the U.S. military involvement in the Persian Gulf as reminiscent of Spain's foreign wars of the 1630s and 1640s.[2] One argument given by supporters of U.S. participation in the war was that the success of the war would help restore American self-confidence and break the mood of self-doubt and defeatism that had purportedly prevailed in the country since the 1960s—in other words, overcome the "Vietnam syndrome." The great Spanish minister, the Count-Duke de Olivares, made a similar argument in favor of Spain's intervention on the side of the Hapsburgs in the Thirty Years' War. Upon hearing of Spain's first battlefield success, Olivares declared it to be "the greatest victory of our times"—one that proved Spain's domestic and foreign detractors wrong; because of military prowess, Spain was still number one on the international scene. Domestically, however, Spain's industries lacked competitiveness, its

[1]Gilovich, T. (1981). Seeing the past in the present: The effects of associations to familiar events on judgments and decisions. *Journal of Personality and Social Psychology, 40*, 797–808.

[2]Kennedy, P. (1991, January 24). A declining empire goes to war. *Wall Street Journal.*

streets were filled with the unemployed and the homeless, and the nation's debts were increasing at a rapid clip. A generation later, Spain was no longer a world power.

Classical theories of rhetoric look with disdain upon analogy as a form of persuasion; any given analogy is vulnerable to the attack that it is based on faulty comparisons—that the points of similarity presented in the analogy are irrelevant and inconsequential. According to classical theory, analogies should be evaluated using two rules:

1. The similarities between two things must concern pertinent, significant aspects of the two things.
2. The analogy must not ignore pertinent dissimilarities between the two things being compared.[3]

Notice what happens if we use these two classical rules to evaluate any of the three proposed perspectives on the Persian Gulf war. We immediately desire more information and facts about the present and the past: What are the economic and social conditions of the nations involved? What happened to the Hapsburg Empire, Germany, and Vietnam after each respective war was over? What were the economic and social costs of each war? In answering such questions, we can develop a more complete understanding of the situation at hand—an analysis that can inform such important decisions as whether or not to go to war.

There is another way to evaluate the validity of a communicator's definition of the situation—by the sincerity of the communicator. In other words, does the advocate of a given view of the world really believe that is the way things are, or has he or she merely adopted this viewpoint for expedient, propaganda purposes?

For example, shortly before the onset of the Persian Gulf war on October 15, 1990, President Bush stated:

> Every day now, new word filters out [of Kuwait] about the ghastly atrocities perpetrated by Saddam's forces. . . . of a systematic assault on the soul of a nation, summary executions, routine torture. . . . newborn babies thrown out of incubators. . . . dialysis patients ripped from their machines. . . . Hitler revisited. But remember, when Hitler's war ended there were the Nuremberg trials.[4]

Was he serious? Perhaps so. But given the fact that, just a short time earlier, our government was staunchly supporting Saddam in his war against Iran, it is at least conceivable that Bush was exaggerating.

If the president was engaging in hyperbole, some people believe that it is forgivable. After all, he was intent on mobilizing the nation for what might have been a long and costly war and on gaining the approval of his fellow citizens for putting hundreds of thousands of young American men and women in harm's way in order to come to the aid of a nondemocratic nation. And

---

[3]Corbett, E. P. J. (1990). *Classical rhetoric for the modern student.* New York: Oxford University Press, p. 105.
[4]*U.S. News & World Report,* May 6, 1991, p. 19.

it worked; support for the war soared and George Bush's popularity soon reached an all-time high. During and immediately after the war, Bush's approval rating hovered around 90%.

But the use of such propaganda devices carries a price—for the communicator as well as the audience. In this case, once the American people recovered from their euphoria after the war came to a quick and (in terms of U.S. casualties) relatively bloodless end, a great many Americans began to wonder why, after having achieved total military dominance, we had allowed Saddam to remain in power with a large part of his military force intact—a force that he promptly began to use with impunity against this own civilian population.[5] Indeed, even the commander of the United Nations forces in the Persian Gulf, General Norman Schwartzkopf, was bold enough to wonder about this out loud on network television. Can you imagine the president of the United States in 1945, having won a smashing victory over Adolf Hitler, allowing Hitler to continue to govern the German people? Can you imagine the Allied forces stopping just inside the border of Germany and then turning back? Utterly impossible. If Hitler had survived he would certainly have been tried, convicted, and executed as a war criminal. Why, then, did George Bush allow Saddam Hussein free rein in Iraq? It was confusing. In a *Newsweek* poll taken on May, 1, 1991, 55% of those questioned did not view the Persian Gulf war as a victory because Saddam was still in power. President Bush's popularity began to fade— but not by much. In a sense, he got away with it.

But in a deeper sense, he did not. For, in our judgment, there was a more serious price to pay. We feel that a good case can be made that George Bush never really believed that Saddam Hussein was another Hitler. His use of the analogy was a cynical attempt to strike fear and loathing into the hearts of the American people. Saddam Hussein is certainly an unsavory villain. But an unsavory villain capable of achieving stability in Iraq—a stability that President Bush and his advisors obviously considered worth the price of allowing him to remain in office. An unsavory villain that he could live with comfortably—one we had lived with and supported in the past and not unlike a great many other unsavory villains around the world whom the United States continues to support.

The cynicism evinced by Mr. Bush is more than merely unfortunate. As citizens of a democracy, we have the right to look closely at the facts so that we might arrive at our own rational conclusions about whether or not we should go to war and whether or not it is appropriate to bring Saddam to trial as a war criminal—based not on the hyperbole of a president, but on the facts of the matter. We have a right to be angry at being manipulated by a president if he depicts our enemy as another Hitler one month and as a difficult but stabilizing force the next.

It is not our intention to single out Mr. Bush for special criticism. Unfortunately, pulling the wool over the eyes of the people has been a common practice in the White House; from Lyndon Johnson's false statements of optimism during the Vietnam war ("there is light at the end of the tunnel") to Richard Nixon's stonewalling of the Watergate affair ("I am not a crook") to Ronald Reagan's statements about the Iran/Contra scandal ("I think I don't remember"),

---

[5]What did Bush win? *Newsweek*, May 13, 1991, p. 27.

American presidents have been denying citizens the information necessary to properly analyze a situation and to act rationally. The truly unfortunate aspect of this is that most Americans have rather cynically come to take it for granted that they will be misled.

QUESTIONS

1. Why did people argue over whether the situation in Iraq in 1991 was more similar to Europe in the 1940s or Vietnam in the 1960s? Why is this a relevant question for most people?

2. Can the complexities of international relations be adequately reflected in only two analogous situations? According to classical theory, when should analogies be taken seriously?

3. Using the two classical criteria, do either of the analogies presented at the beginning of the article qualify as logically relevant?

4. Apart from the quality of an argument, what do the authors suggest as an important consideration when listening to a persuasive message?

5. What evidence suggests that Bush did not believe his own comparisons between Adolf Hitler and Saddam Hussein? Is this type of presidential propaganda common in the United States?

✛ CHAPTER 11 ✛

PERSUASION: CHANGING ATTITUDES

Reading 21: Classic

Communication and Persuasion

Carl Hovland, Irving Janis, and Harold Kelly

One of the most successful research programs in the social psychological study of attitudes and persuasion was carried out by a group at Yale University led by Carl Hovland. The researchers took an elementalist approach, reasoning that the amount of persuasion was a function of the sum of certain parts. To understand the likelihood that a message will be accepted, they divided the path of communication into five steps: attention, perception, interpretation, learning, and acceptance. Affecting persuasion at each of these stages were aspects of the communication source, of the message itself, and of the perceiver.

In their research, Hovland and his colleagues discovered that the credibility of the source of a message influenced whether people were persuaded by the message. Specifically, they found that people were more likely to follow the recommendations of a message if the source of the message was seen as knowledgeable and trustworthy. This was as expected.

What was not expected was that the effects of source credibility on persuasion appeared to be relatively short-lived. In several experiments, message acceptance differed among people who had heard low- versus high-credibility sources deliver an identical message. However, 2 or 3 weeks later, the attitudes of both groups of people became more similar, and the source effect disappeared. This became known as the "sleeper effect."

The next reading is an excerpt from the seminal work on persuasion by the Hovland group. In it they discuss the influence of source credibility and speculate about the sleeper effect.

✛

BASES OF DIFFERENTIAL EFFECTS

The fact that identical communications are evaluated differently by subjects exposed to sources of different credibility is subject to several interpretations. Judgments about content and style are often merely specific symptoms of general approach or avoidance reactions to the entire communication situation. On the basis of psychological studies of the manner in which expectations influence perceptions and of the phenomenon of "halo effect" in judg-

Source: Hovland, C., Janis, I., & Kelly, H. H. (1953). *Communication and persuasion*. New Haven, CT: Yale University Press.

mental behavior, these broad effects of different labeling of the communicator come as no surprise. They do, however, raise some questions as to the processes which mediate or make possible the differential opinion changes. For example, do persons initially negative toward the source listen less closely to the communication? Or do they, perhaps, distort the meaning of what is said, and hence judge it to have been less well presented? The more general problem here is essentially this: At what point in the process of attending to, perceiving, interpreting, learning, and believing the content of the communication do attitudes toward the source have their effect?

In accounting for the different amounts of opinion change produced by communicators of high versus low credibility, one obvious possibility would be that people tend not to expose themselves to communications from sources toward whom they have negative attitudes. However, the present experiments all involve captive audiences, typically college classes, whose members could hardly avoid being exposed to the communication. Under these conditions there remain two different explanations for the lesser effectiveness of unfavorable (e.g., low credibility) communicators in bringing about opinion change:

1. Because of their unfavorable attitudes, members of the audience do not pay close attention to the content and/or do not attempt to comprehend the exact meaning of what is said. The former could result from thinking about the communicator, while the latter might result from "reading into" the content various implications that correspond to the assumed intent of the communicator. As a result, they learn the material less well than when it is presented by a favorable source and, failing to learn it, are unable to adhere to the recommended conclusions.
2. Because of their unfavorable attitudes, members of the audience are not motivated to accept or believe what the communicator says and recommends.

With respect to choosing between these two explanations, the foregoing studies present recall data which indicate the extent to which the materials presented by the various communicators were learned. In the study of high- versus low-credibility sources, on a variety of topics, Hovland and Weiss found no significant difference in the number of fact quiz items answered correctly immediately after the communication. In the study of suspect versus non-suspect sources, Hovland and Mandell administered a fact quiz on the economics of devaluation immediately after the communication. There was no difference between the two source versions in the number of items answered correctly.

In the Kelman and Hovland study, recall for items on the communication was determined at the delayed after-test. Here again there was no significant difference between the positive and negative sources. An interesting incidental finding was that recall was significantly better when the communication was given by the neutral source than by either the positive or negative source. The authors suggest that affective responses may adversely influence the amount of material learned and recalled, and that both the positive and negative communicators were responded to with greater affect than the neutral one. An emotional reaction to the communicator may focus attention upon him to the detriment of attending to his conclusions and learning his arguments.[1] This result indicates, as we would expect, that there are some instances in which the communicator affects the degree to which the content is acquired.

In summary, the present studies of various sources in general reveal little difference between the most and least credible sources in the degree to which the content of their communications is learned. In most instances, the differences were certainly not large enough to account for the differential opinion changes produced by high- and low-credibility communicators. Thus, persons exposed to a low-credibility communicator evidently learned as much of what was said as did persons exposed to a high-credibility source, but the former accepted the recommendations much less than did the latter. These findings, together with those from Weiss's investigation, indicate that some recipients learned what was said without believing the communicator or modifying their attitudes accordingly. Change of opinion obviously requires not only learning what the new point of view is but also becoming motivated to accept it.

In some instances where there is strong resistance to the content and an opportunity to avoid exposure to it, the recipient may, of course, neither learn the content nor accept it. Not only were the captive audiences of the present experiments in classroom situations where they are generally set to pay close attention, but the communications were generally highly structured and permitted relatively little misinterpretation. Although under these conditions subjects apparently are motivated to learn and remember most of the assertions in the communications, there are large differences among experimental treatments in the degree to which the arguments are accepted and incorporated as changes in opinions. This strongly suggests that a critical aspect of opinion change is the degree to which recipients become motivated to accept the assertions contained in the communication. The evidence is quite clear that acceptance or rejection depends in part upon attitudinal reactions toward the source of the communication.

Why is acceptance likely to be heightened by increasing the credibility of the communicator? Our principal assumption is that the individual is motivated to accept conclusions and recommendations which he anticipates will be substantiated by further experiences or will lead to reward, social approval, and avoidance of punishment. These anticipations are increased when a recommendation is presented by a person who is believed to be informed,

---

[1]Kelman's and Hovland's explanation of their result is reminiscent of earlier discussions of the importance in prestige-suggestion of an emotional relation between the influencer and influencee. Murphy, Murphy, and Newcomb refer to contradictory ideas and habits which ordinarily inhibit the individual's conformity to verbal suggestions. They go on to say: "The fixation of attention upon the experimenter whom one respects (or perhaps sometimes fears) seems sufficient to block these ordinarily available counter-suggestions" (p. 178). A major difference lies in the fact that whereas these authors use emotional constriction of attention as an explanation of heightened susceptibility to influence, Kelman and Hovland suggest that it may interfere with learning what the communicator says. It seems probable that an emotional reaction to the communicator may have a double-barreled effect. On the one hand, it may have a facilitating effect where it serves to focus attention on what he says and to exclude irrelevant influences in the environment. On the other hand, when the focusing is upon the communicator per se—upon his person, dress, style of speaking, mannerisms, and so on—an emotional reaction may interfere with the acquisition of his content and hence with his effectiveness as a communicator.

insightful, and willing to express his true beliefs and knowledge, and are decreased when cues of low credibility are present. Thus the motives of the audience to accept recommendations are higher the more credible the person making them. It should also be noted that the strength of these motives probably depends upon the situation in which the recipient of the communication finds himself and upon his corresponding dependence upon others for information and advice. The motivation to seek and accept advice from credible sources seems to be increased considerably when the person is in a situation which requires finer discriminations than he is capable of or which demands specialized information not at his disposal.

ARE THE EFFECTS OF HIGH-CREDIBILITY SOURCES ENDURING?

We have noted that in terms of immediate opinion change high-credibility sources tend to be somewhat more effective than low-crediblity sources. However, delayed after-tests in the experiments by Hovland and Weiss and Kelman and Hovland indicated that this differential effectiveness had disappeared after an interval of about three weeks. . . . In both studies there was a highly significant difference between high and low communicators on the immediate after-test, but in both instances this difference had virtually disappeared several weeks later.

These results raise important questions about the long-term significance of the credibility of the communicator. Unfortunately, little other evidence is available on the degree to which communicator effects are sustained.[2] The main implication of the present results is that the credibility of the communicator may, under certain circumstances mentioned earlier, be important only with respect to the amount of *immediate* opinion change produced. Under circumstances where there is a very close association between the source and content of a communication, however, the effect of the communicator may be more enduring. The immediate effects reported here many have considerable practical significance if the purpose of the communication is to elicit some type of immediate action and if subsequent behavior is of little concern. Furthermore, if the immediate action involves some type of formal or informal commitment, lasting effects may be obtained. . . .

---

[2]Results from Kulp are often cited as indicating the persistence of the effects of prestigeful sources over a considerable period (eight weeks). Unfortunately the absence of a control group at the time of the delayed after-test leaves some uncertainty as to whether the results do indicate genuine retention of the original effects. Assuming they do, a possible explanation for the greater permanency of prestige effects in Kulp's study is his method of introducing prestige. Subjects were asked to indicate their agreement or disagreement with opinion items, using test blanks that were already marked with responses attributed to certain prestige groups. This procedure may create a condition where the "source" becomes closely associated with the test items themselves, so that on subsequent occasions they "reinstate" the prestigeful source. Note should also be taken of another important difference between Kulp's procedure and that generally used in the present studies on source credibility: the latter not merely involve the "conclusion" or opinion of the source but also include arguments and evidence in support of the conclusion. This type of supporting content may be retained in a different manner than conclusions alone; for example, arguments and evidence may be dissociated from the source more readily.

IMPLICATIONS FOR FURTHER RESEARCH

The findings in the preceding section indicated that the delivery of a communication by a communicator of high credibility increases the amount of opinion change measured immediately after exposure, and that a communicator of low credibility may bring about a decrease in opinion change. What are the limiting conditions under which such effects are obtained?

Let us begin with cases of the type where the source has been found to augment acceptance. Typically a source of high credibility delivers a communication containing arguments and assertions which, because of their lack of compellingness, their inadequate substantiation, or incompatibility with preexisting opinions, the recipient has little tendency to accept. There are certain variations from this situation in which it is fairly obvious that the credibility of the source will have little or no effect on opinion change. For example, if the message is fully accepted on its own merits, the highly credible source can have no added effect on acceptance; if the credibility of the source is negligible (e.g., the source is trustworthy but completely uninformed), the message may be accepted to no greater degree than if it were reacted to in terms of its intrinsic qualities. In general, it appears that source credibility has maximal effects on acceptance when the source and content are such that there would be considerable discrepancy between the attitudinal responses to each of them alone—in this particular case, when the communicator would produce a considerable tendency to accept whatever he says and the communication, in and of itself, would produce little or no tendency toward acceptance.

There are important variations of the typical case which would seem on theoretical grounds to represent limiting conditions for the generalization that positive communicators increase acceptance for their messages. The first to be considered consists of a highly reliable communicator giving a communication which, on its own merits, would be strongly rejected.

With respect to this first situation, the following hypothesis is suggested: Under conditions where positive attitudes toward the source are very strong (e.g., he is considered as highly credible) and where the tendency to reject the conclusions and arguments in the communication is very strong, *there is a tendency to dissociate the source and the content.* We may also speculate as to the various forms this dissociation may take. At the time of exposure, it may consist either in denying the source's responsibility for the communication or in reinterpreting the content and conclusion of the message. In effect, the individual can conclude either that "someone else gave this communication" or that "this communicator meant something else when he gave it." Dissociation may also occur in the form of not recalling who said what, as is suggested by the retention data described in the preceding section. In any event, the importance of dissociation for the effectiveness of persuasive communications is that it reduces or eliminates the direct influence of the source on acceptance of the content. To the extent that the recipient is able to dissociate source and message, the acceptance of the message will be independent of the source.

Phenomena which appear to be related to these dissociation effects have been noted in the literature and in the present research. In several reports, it appears that where a communication was highly incompatible with the audience's preconception of the alleged source, denial was made that the suggested source was really responsible for the assertion. For example,

Lewis had college students judge political slogans as to their social significance, compelling-ness to action, intelligence of their authors, etc. Subsequently, some of the subjects (those who were in sympathy with the Communist party) were given evaluations of the slogans allegedly made by Earl Browder, at that time leader of the party in the United States. The purpose was to see whether this communication, which was in considerable disagreement with the subjects' previous judgments, would affect their evaluations of the slogans. Several of the subjects suspected a hoax and refused to believe that the evaluations had been made by Browder. Another subject suggested that Broder had been misquoted by newspapermen. A similar phenomenon was observed in Birch's study. Another phenomenon of this type consists in attributing special motives to the communicator or assuming that his delivery of the communication can be discounted because of unusual circumstances. This defines the communication as a special act not to be taken at face value. For instance, confronted with contradictory evaluations supposedly coming from Franklin Roosevelt, one of Lewis' subjects, who respected Roosevelt, stated: "Roosevelt's ranking seems to me to be slightly off. Perhaps it was before he became social-conscious" (p. 246). Other subjects felt Roosevelt was trying to be objective or was deliberately using special criteria in making his judgments. Asch (pp. 427–428) provides other examples in which an incongruity between source and content is resolved by making highly specific interpretations of the source's motives for communication.

The reinterpretation of the message is related to a phenomenon which has been emphasized by Asch. It has frequently been assumed, at least implicitly, that communication-induced changes in opinion indicate reevaluation of the same objects or statements judged initially. Asch has challenged this assumption and argued strongly that these processes involve "*a change in the object of judgment, rather than in the judgment of the object*" (Asch, 1952, p. 458; italics his). The example most often cited to illustrated change in the object of judgment appears in Asch's study [1940] of college students' judgments of professions as influenced by evaluations allegedly made by 500 other students. When told that the other students had judged the profession of politics highest with respect to intelligence, social usefulness, etc., the subjects markedly raised their valuation of politicians. In subsequent interviews they reported having shifted their conception of politics from that of local ward politics to that of national politics and statesmanship. Thus, they apparently reinterpreted what it was that the 500 students were evaluating. Similar examples found in studies by Lewis (1941) and Luchins (1944) also indicate that the type of change emphasized by Asch may occur at least under some conditions.

The effects noted by these investigators suggest what happens when subjects dissociate the original source and content: they are likely to deny that the source actually was responsible for the communication or to reinterpret the "real" meaning they believe the message to have. For example, if the message given by a highly respected source is repugnant to the audience's values, the source may be thought to be someone else capable of originating such ideas, or the message will be interpreted so as to be congruent with the actual respected source. These specific tendencies, as well as some of the other effects discussed here, can be derived from Heider's logical analysis of "attitudes and cognitive organization." He suggests that we tend to maintain the same attitude toward persons as toward their possessions and actions. As applied to the problem of source credibility, the implications would be as follows: When we attribute high credibility to a person but dislike what he communicates, our attitudes related to him are in an "unbalanced" state. This tends to be resolved in any of three ways: 1) change in attitudes toward the communication (which would include either accepting it or reinterpreting it), 2) change in attitudes toward the communicator, and 3) change in perception of the communicator's role in originating the communication. These changes tend to be of such a nature as to restore a state of balance or congruence among the various attitudes related to the communicator and his actions.

Dissociation of source and content may also occur following exposure to the communication and may take the form of forgetting that the particular communicator gave the specific content. Some of the results on retention from the experiment by Hovland and Weiss bear on this hypothesis. High-credibility sources initially produced greater acceptance of the conclusion than low-credibility ones. With the passage of time, this difference disappeared. However, the subjects were able, when asked, to recall both the original source and content. The authors suggest that with the passage of time there is a decrease in tendency to "associate spontaneously" the content with the source. Some results from Kelman and Hovland on reinstatement of source suggest that subjects can be made to reestablish the association of source and content, with a resulting reappearance of the original differences in the degree to which the communications of high- and low-credibility sources are accepted. The results are generally consistent with the hypotheses that dissociation between source and content can occur following the communication and that to the degree that dissociation does occur the effect of the source on acceptance is attenuated. . . .

REFERENCES

ALLPORT, G. W., & POSTMAN, L. (1947). *The psychology of rumor.* New York: Holt.

ASCH, S. E. (1940). Studies in the principles of judgments and attitudes: II. Determination of judgments by group and ego standards. *Journal of Abnormal and Social Psychology, 12,* 433–465.

ASCH, S. E. (1952). *Social psychology.* New York: Prentice Hall.

BIRCH, H. G. (1945). The effect of socially disapproved labeling upon a well-structured attitude. *Journal of Abnormal and Social Psychology, 40,* 301–310.

BROWN, J. S. (1942). The generalization of approach responses as a function of stimulus intensity and strength of motivation. *Journal of Comparative Psychology, 33,* 209–226.

CANTRIL, H. (1941). *The psychology of social movements.* New York: Wiley.

COFFIN, T. E. (1941). Some conditions of suggestion and suggestibility. *Psychological Monographs, 53,* No. 4.

HEIDER, F. (1946). Attitudes and cognitive organization. *The Journal of Psychology, 21,* 107–112.

HOVLAND, C. I., & WEISS, W. (1951). The influence of source credibility on communication effectiveness. *The Public Opinion Quarterly, 15,* 635–650.

HULL, C. L. (1943). *Principles of behavior.* New York: Appleton-Century.

KELMAN, H. C., & HOVLAND, C. I. (1953). "Reinstatement" of the communicator in delayed measurement of opinion change. *Journal of Abnormal and Social Psychology, 48,* 327–335.

KULP, D. H., II. (1934). Prestige, as measured by single-experience changes and their permanency. *Journal of Educational Research, 27*, 663–672.

LEWIS, HELEN B. (1941). Studies in the principles of judgments and attitudes: IV. The operation of "prestige suggestion." *Journal of Social Psychology, 14*, 229–256.

LUCHINS, A. S. (1944). On agreement with another's judgments. *Journal of Abnormal and Social Psychology, 39*, 97–111.

LUCHINS, A. S. (1945). Social influences on perception of complex drawings. *Journal of Social Psychology, 21*, 257–273.

MURPHY, G., MURPHY, LOIS B., & NEWCOMB, T. M. (1937). *Experimental social psychology* (rev. ed.). New York: Harper.

ROSENBAUM, G. (1951). Temporal gradients of response strength with two levels of motivations. *Journal of Experimental Psychology, 41*, 261–267.

ROSENBAUM, G. (1953). Stimulus generalization as function of level of experimentally induced anxiety. *Journal of Experimental Psychology, 45*, 35–43.

SHERIF, M., and CANTRIL, H. (1947). *The psychology of ego-involvements.* New York: Wiley.

QUESTIONS

1. One possibility for why low-credibility sources fail to persuade is that people do not pay them any attention. Why do the authors reject this as a sufficient explanation?

2. Does message comprehension differ between conditions of low and high communicator credibility? At what stage of the attending-learning-accepting process does communicator credibility appear to have its effect?

3. How enduring are the effects of communicator credibility? Does this suggest that attempts to persuade others should not be concerned with credibility?

4. When will high credibility have the most impact on persuasion? How do people reconcile the conflict of hearing a highly credible source deliver a low-credibility message?

5. What should be the consequence of hearing a low-credibility source deliver a high-credibility message? Would hearing such a message lead to immediate attitude change? Would it lead to more distal attitude change? What name has this been given?

Reading 22: Contemporary

The Language of Persuasion

David Kipnis and Stuart Schmidt

In the next reading, psychologists David Kipnis and Stuart Schmidt discuss an approach that takes into account the social context in which a persuasive message is delivered. They begin by analyzing people's reports of the different means of persuasion they have used, and determine that the strategies can be divided into three tactics: hard, soft, and rational. While hard tactics are forceful and demanding, soft tactics rely on ingratiation, and rational tactics are used to strike deals and compromises.

As discussed in this article, people do not select their persuasion strategy randomly. Usually some attempt is made to evaluate the situation and select a strategy that is appropriate in a given situation. Of course, people are not always so careful and often choose a strategy on the basis of habit or personality. But perhaps, the authors suggest, this is a mistake. By examining our own past conflicts, we may notice a tendency to use the wrong tactics in certain situations, a tendency we would be well advised to change.

✤

"I had all the facts and figures ready before I made my suggestions to my boss." (Manager)
"I kept insisting that we do it my way. She finally caved in." (Husband)
"I think it's about time that you stop thinking these negative things about yourself." (Psychotherapist)
"Send out more horses, skirr the country round. Hang those that talk of fear. Give me mine armour."
(Macbeth, Act 5)

These diverse statements—rational insistent, emotional—have one thing in common. They all show people trying to persuade others, a skill we all treasure. Books about power and influence are read by young executives eager for promotion, by politicians anxious to sway the constituents, by lonely people looking to win and hold a mate and by harried parents trying to make their children see the light.

Despite this interest in persuasion, most people are not really aware of how they go about it. They spend more time choosing their clothes than they do their influence styles. Even fewer are aware of how their styles affect others or themselves. Although shouts and demands may make people dance to our tune, we will probably lose their goodwill. Beyond that, our opinion of others may change for the worse when we use hard or abusive tactics.

Popular books on influencing others give contradictory advice. Some advocate assertiveness, others stealth and still others reason and logic. Could they all be right? We decided to

Source: Kipnis, D., & Schmidt, S. (1985, April). The language of persuasion. *Psychology Today, 40–46.*

see for ourselves what kinds of influence people actually use in personal and work situations and why they choose the tactics they do.

We conducted studies of dating couples and business managers in which the couples described how they attempted to influence their partners and the managers told how they attempted to influence their subordinates, peers and superiors at work. We then used these descriptions as the basis for separate questionnaires in which we asked other couples and managers how frequently they employed each tactic. Using factor analysis and other statistical techniques, we found that the tactics could be classified into three basic strategies—hard, soft and rational.

These labels describe the tactics from the standpoint of the person using them. Since influencing someone is a social act, its meaning depends upon the observer's vantage point. For example, a wife might ask her husband, "I wonder what we should do about the newspapers in the garage?" The husband could consider this remark nagging to get him to clean up the garage. The wife might say her remark was simply a friendly suggestion that he consider the state of the garage. An outside observer might feel that the wife's remark was just conversation, not a real attempt to influence.

[H]ard tactics involve demanding, shouting and assertiveness. With soft tactics, people act nice and flatter others to get their way. Rational tactics involve the use of logic and bargaining to demonstrate why compliance or compromise is the best solution.

Why do people shout and demand in one instance, flatter in a second and offer to compromise in a third? One common explanation is that the choice of tactics is based upon what "feels right" in each case. A more pragmatic answer is that the choice of tactics is based strictly on what works.

Our studies show that the reasons are more complex. When we examine how people actually use influence, we find that they use many different strategies, depending on the situation and the person being influenced. We gathered information from 195 dating and married couples, and from 360 first- and second-line managers in the United States, Australia and Great Britain. We asked which influence tactics they used, how frequently and in what conditions.

The choice of strategies varied predictably for both managers and couples. It depends on their particular objectives, relative power position and expectations about the willingness of others to do what they want. These expectations are often based on individual traits and biases rather than facts.

OBJECTIVES

One of our grandmothers always advised sweetly, "Act nice if you want a favor." We found that people do, indeed, vary their tactics according to what they want.

At work, for instance, managers frequently rely on soft tactics—flattery, praise, acting humble—when they want something from a boss such as time off or better assignments. However, when managers want to persuade the boss to accept ideas, such as a new work procedure, they're more likely to use reason and logic. Occasionally, they will even try hard tactics, such as going over the boss's head, if he or she can't be moved any other way.

Couples also vary their choice of tactics depending upon what they want from each other. Personal benefits such as choosing a movie or restaurant for the night call for a soft, loving approach. When they want to change a spouse's unacceptable behavior, anger, threats and other hard tactics come into play.

POWER POSITIONS

People who control resources, emotions or finances valued by others clearly have the advantage in a relationship, whether it is commercial or personal. In our research with couples, we discovered which partner was dominant by asking who made the final decision about issues such as spending money, choosing friends and other family matters. We found that people who say they control the relationship ("I have the final say") often rely on hard tactics to get their way. Those who share decision power ("We decide together") bargain rationally and often compromise. Partners who admit that they have little power ("My partner has the final say") usually favor soft tactics.

We found the same patterns among managers. The more one-sided the power of relationship at work, the more likely managers are to demand, get angry and insist with people who work for them, and the more likely they are to act humble and flatter when they are persuading their bosses.

The fact that people change influence tactics depending on their power over the other person is hardly surprising. What is surprising is how universal the link is between power and tactics. Our surveys and those conducted by others have found this relationship among children trying to influence younger children or older children, and among executives dealing with executives at other companies more or less powerful than their own, as well as among spouses and business managers dealing with their own subordinates and bosses.

There seems to be an "Iron Law of Power." The greater the discrepancy in clout between the influencer and the target, the greater the likelihood that hard tactics will be used. People with power don't always use hard tactics as their first choice. At first, most simply request and explain. They turn to demands and threats (the iron fist lurking under the velvet glove of reason) only when someone seems reluctant or refuses to comply with their request.

In contrast, people with little power are likely to stop trying or immediately shift to soft tactics when they encounter resistance. They feel the costs associated with the use of hard or even rational tactics are unacceptable. They are unwilling to take the chance of angering a boss, a spouse or an older child by using anything but soft methods.

EXPECTATIONS AND BIASES

We have found that people also vary their strategies according to how successful they expect to be in influencing their targets. When they believe that someone is likely to do what is asked, they make simple requests. When they anticipate resistance and have the power, they use hard tactics.

THE SHAKESPEARE CONNECTION

The best art is life condensed, with its truths shown clearly and accurately. One of us (Kipnis) decided to test what has been learned about tactics of influence by comparing this understanding with how two of William Shakespeare's most famous characters go about persuading others. Each time King Lear and Macbeth try to influence someone in the play, successfully or not, the attempt was coded as hard, soft or rational. For example:

Hard tactic

"Kent, on thy life, no more."

(*Lear,* Act I, Scene 1)

Soft tactic

"Pray do not mock me. I am a very foolish fond old man."

(*Lear, Act IV, Scene 7*)

Rational tactic

"Think upon what hath chanced; and . . . the interim having weighted it, let us speak. . . . "

(*Macbeth,* Act I, Scene 3)

Both Macbeth and Lear consistently attempt to influence others throughout the plays, more in the last act than earlier. This finding is particularly interesting in regard to Lear, since he is thought of as an increasingly feeble, dying old man. Yet, when you analyze his words, he tries to exercise influence more frequently in the fifth act than at any other time in the play.

But the methods Lear and Macbeth use change dramatically during the five acts. As the table below indicates, Lear's tactics become increasingly soft, while Macbeth's become harder and harder.

Art, then, imitates life. Both Lear and Macbeth choose their tactics in relation to their power. Since Lear has given up his major base of power (his kingdom) in Act I, he must plead and use soft words. Macbeth, who has gained a kingdom, turns increasingly to tough tactics.

INFLUENCE TACTICS* IN *KING LEAR* AND *MACBETH*

Tactic	KING LEAR					MACBETH				
	Act I	Act II	Act III	Act IV	Act V	Act I	Act II	Act III	Act IV	Act V
Hard	64	57	13	14	0	33	36	44	75	77
Soft	16	38	25	79	100	33	36	9	19	4
Rational	20	5	63	7	0	33	27	47	6	19

*Expressed in percentages. Some columns don't add up to 100 because the figures are rounded off.

This anticipation may be realistic. Just as a robber knows that without a gun, a polite request for money is unlikely to persuade, a boss knows that a request for work on Saturday needs more than a smile to back it up. But less realistic personal and situation factors sometimes make us expect resistance where none exists. People who are low in self-esteem and self-confidence, for instance, have difficulty believing that others will comply with simple requests.

We found that lack of confidence and low self-esteem are characteristic of managers who bark orders and refuse to discuss the issues involved, of couples who constantly shout and scream at each other and of parents who rely on harsh discipline. There hard tactics result from the self-defeating assumption that others will not listen unless they are treated roughly.

Social situations and biases can also distort expectations of cooperation. Misunderstandings based on differences in attitudes, race or sex can lead to hard tactics. Our research, and that of others, shows that orders, shouts and threats are more likely to be used between blacks and whites or men and women. The simple perception that "these people are different than I am" leads to the idea that "they are not as reasonable as I am" and must be ordered about.

. . . [Of course there] are generalizations. They don't necessarily describe how a particular person will act in a particular situation. People may use influence tactics because of habit, lack of forethought or lack of social sensitivity. Most of us would be more effective persuaders if we analyzed why we act as we do. Simply writing a short description of a recent incident in which we tried to persuade someone can help us understand better our own tactics, why we use them and, perhaps, why a rational approach might be better.

People who know we have studied the matter sometimes ask, "Which tactics work best?" The answer is that they all work if they are used at the right time with the right person. But both hard and soft tactics involve costs to the user even when they succeed. Hard tactics often alienate the people being influenced and create a climate of hostility and resistance. Soft tactics—acting nice, being humble—may lessen self-respect and self-esteem. In contrast, we found that people who rely chiefly on logic, reason and compromise to get their way are the most satisfied both with their business lives and with their personal relationships.

QUESTIONS

1. What three types of factors determine which persuasion strategy a person will use?

2. When managers want time off from work, what strategy are they most likely to use? What strategy is most often used in a relationship to get a partner to quit an unacceptable behavior?

3. What is the "Iron Law of Power"? Do those in power always use hard tactics to get what they want?

4. What tactic is likely to be used by a powerful person with high self-esteem who expects little resistance? What tactic would a person with low self-esteem use in the same situation?

5. Is the likelihood of success the only important consideration when deciding which persuasive tactic to use? What are the interpersonal costs and benefits of the three tactics?

PART VII

SOCIAL INFLUENCE

✤ CHAPTER 12 ✤

CONFORMITY, COMPLIANCE, AND OBEDIENCE: FOLLOWING THE LEAD OF OTHERS

Reading 23: Classic

Behavioral Study of Obedience

Stanley Milgram

At the close of World War II, the world was stunned and horrified to learn about the systematic murder of Jews and other ethnic minorities in the Nazi death camps. People found it difficult to believe that a government could devise a scheme so cruel and inhumane. But more importantly, people wondered at a citizenry that could carry out such obviously immoral orders.

This event was the inspiration behind what is probably the most famous (and infamous) study in social psychology: Stanley Milgram's "behavioral study of obedience." The study is famous for conclusively demonstrating what Hannah Arendt called the "banality of evil." People could, indeed wanted to, believe that what happened in Nazi Germany was a unique event, that such blind obedience was due to a highly unusual mixture of social elements. It was argued that certainly something like that could never happen in an open democracy such as the United States. Milgram's studies make this belief untenable.

Milgram's study is infamous for what many believe was the unethical treatment of subjects. All subjects experienced considerable stress, and many left the study with the realization that they were capable of administering dangerous shocks to a total stranger. In his defense, Milgram points out that neither he, his students at Yale, nor his colleagues in the field expected the type of behavior that they subsequently observed. Keep this in mind as you read this account of his experiment.

✤

Obedience is as basic an element in the structure of social life as one can point to. Some system of authority is a requirement of all communal living, and it is only the man dwelling in isolation who is not forced to respond, through defiance or submission, to the commands of others. Obedience, as a determinant of behavior, is of particular relevance to our time. It has been reliably established that from 1933–45 millions of innocent persons were systematically slaughtered on command. Gas chambers were built, death camps were guarded, daily quotas of corpses were produced with the same efficiency as the manufacture of appliances. These

Source: Milgram, S. (1963). Behavioral study of obedience. *Journal of Abnormal and Social Psychology, 67,* 371–378.

inhumane policies may have originated in the mind of a single person, but they could only be carried out on a massive scale if a very large number of persons obeyed orders.

Obedience is the psychological mechanism that links individual action to political purpose. It is the dispositional cement that binds men to systems of authority. Facts of recent history and observation in daily life suggest that for many persons obedience may be a deeply ingrained behavior tendency, indeed, a prepotent impulse overriding training in ethics, sympathy, and moral conduct. C. P. Snow (1961) points to its importance when he writes:

> When you think of the long and gloomy history of man, you will find more hideous crimes have been committed in the name of obedience than have ever been committed in the name of rebellion. If you doubt that, read William Shirer's "Rise and Fall of the Third Reich." The German Officer Corps were brought up in the most rigorous code of obedience . . . in the name of obedience they were party to, and assisted in, the most wicked large scale actions in the history of the world [p. 24].

While the particular form of obedience dealt with in the present study has its antecedents in these episodes, it must not be thought all obedience entails acts of aggression against others. Obedience serves numerous productive functions. Indeed, the very life of society is predicated on its existence. Obedience may be ennobling and educative and refer to acts of charity and kindness, as well as to destruction.

General Procedure

A procedure was devised which seems useful as a tool for studying obedience (Milgram, 1961). It consists of ordering a naive subject to administer electric shock to a victim. A simulated shock generator is used, with 30 clearly marked voltage levels that range from 15 to 450 volts. The instrument bears verbal designations that range from Slight Shock to Danger: Severe Shock. The responses of the victim, who is a trained confederate of the experimenter, are standardized. The orders to administer shocks are given to the naive subject in the context of a "learning experiment" ostensibly set up to study the effects of punishment on memory. As the experiment proceeds the naive subject is commanded to administer increasingly more intense shocks to the victim, even to the point of reaching the level marked Danger: Severe Shock. Internal resistances become stronger, and at a certain point the subject refuses to go on with the experiment. Behavior prior to this rupture is considered "obedience," in that the subject complies with the commands of the experimenter. The point of rupture is the act of disobedience. A quantitative value is assigned to the subject's performance based on the maximum intensity shock he is willing to administer before he refuses to participate further. Thus for any particular subject and for any particular experimental condition the degree of obedience may be specified with a numerical value. The crux of the study is to systematically vary the factors believed to alter the degree of obedience to the experimental commands.

The technique allows important variables to be manipulated at several points in the experiment. One may vary aspects of the source of command, content and form of command, instrumentalities for its execution, target object, general social setting, etc. The problem, therefore, is not one of designing increasingly more numerous experimental conditions, but of selecting those that best illuminate the *process* of obedience from the sociopsychological standpoint.

METHOD

Subjects

The subjects were 40 males between the ages of 20 and 50, drawn from New Haven and the surrounding communities. Subjects were obtained by a newspaper advertisement and direct mail solicitation. Those who responded to the appeal believed they were to participate in a study of memory and learning at Yale University. A wide range of occupations is represented in the sample. Typical subjects were postal clerks, high school teachers, salesmen, engineers, and laborers. Subjects ranged in educational level from one who had not finished elementary school, to those who had doctoral and other professional degrees. They were paid $4.50 for their participation in the experiment. However, subjects were told that payment was simply for coming to the laboratory, and that the money was theirs no matter what happened after they arrived. Table 1 shows the proportion of age and occupational types assigned to the experimental condition.

Personnel and Locale

The experiment was conducted on the grounds of Yale University in the elegant interaction laboratory. (This detail is relevant to the perceived legitimacy of the experiment. In further variations, the experiment was dissociated from the university, with consequences for performance.) The role of experimenter was played by a 31-year-old high school teacher of biology. His manner was impassive, and his appearance somewhat stern throughout the experiment. He was dressed in a gray technician's coat. The victim was played by a 47-year-old accountant, trained for the role; he was of Irish-American stock, whom most observers found mild-mannered and likable.

Procedure

One naive subject and one victim (an accomplice) performed in each experiment. A pretext had to be devised that would justify the administration of electric shock by the naive subject.

TABLE 1   DISTRIBUTION OF AGE AND OCCUPATIONAL TYPES
IN THE EXPERIMENT

Occupations	20–29 Years n	30–39 Years n	40–50 Years n	Percentage of total (Occupations)
Workers, skilled and unskilled	4	5	6	37.5
Sales, business, and white-collar	3	6	7	40.0
Professional	1	5	3	22.5
Percentage of total (Age)	20	40	40	

Note:—Total $N = 40$.

This was effectively accomplished by the cover story. After a general introduction on the presumed relation between punishment and learning, subjects were told:

> But actually, we know very little about the effect of punishment on learning, because almost no truly scientific studies have been made of it in human beings.
>
> For instance, we don't know how much punishment is best for learning—and we don't know how much difference it makes as to who is giving the punishment, whether an adult learns best from a younger or an older person than himself—or many things of that sort.
>
> So in this study we are bringing together a number of adults of different occupations and ages. And we're asking some of them to be teachers and some of them to be learners.
>
> We want to find out just what effect different people have on each other as teachers and learners, and also what effect punishment will have on learning in this situation.
>
> Therefore, I'm going to ask one of you to be the teacher here tonight and the other one to be the learner.
>
> Does either of you have a preference?

Subjects then drew slips of paper from a hat to determine who would be the teacher and who would be the learner in the experiment. The drawing was rigged so that the naive subject was always the teacher and the accomplice always the learner. (Both slips contained the word "Teacher.") Immediately after the drawing, the teacher and learner were taken to an adjacent room and the learner was strapped into an "electric chair" apparatus.

The experimenter explained that the straps were to prevent excessive movement while the learner was being shocked. The effect was to make it impossible for him to escape from the situation. An electrode was attached to the learner's wrist, and electrode paste was applied "to avoid blisters and burns." Subjects were told that the electrode was attached to the shock generator in the adjoining room.

In order to improve credibility the experimenter declared, in response to a question by the learner: "Although the shocks can be extremely painful, they cause no permanent tissue damage."

Learning Task. The lesson administered by the subject was a paired-associate learning task. The subject read a series of word pairs to the learner, and then read the first word of the pair along with four terms. The learner was to indicate which of the four terms had originally been paired with the first word. He communicated his answer by pressing one of four switches in front of him, which in turn lit up one of four numbered quadrants in an answer box located atop the shock generator.

Shock Generator. The instrument panel consists of 30 lever switches set in a horizontal line. Each switch is clearly labeled with a voltage designation that ranges from 15 to 450 volts. There is a 15-volt increment from one switch to the next going from left to right. In addition, the following verbal designations are clearly indicated for groups of four switches going from left to right: Slight Shock, Moderate Shock, Strong Shock, Very Strong Shock, Intense Shock, Extreme Intensity Shock, Danger: Severe Shock. (Two switches after this last designation are simply marked XXX.)

Upon depressing a switch: a pilot light corresponding to each switch is illuminated in bright red; an electric buzzing is heard; and electric blue light, labeled "voltage energizer," flashes; the dial on the voltage meter swings to the right; various relay clicks are sounded.

The upper left-hand corner of the generator is labeled Shock Generator, Type ZLB, Dyson Instrument Company, Waltham, Mass. Output 15 Volts–450 Volts.

Details of the instrument were carefully handled to insure an appearance of authenticity. The panel was engraved by precision industrial engravers, and all components were of high quality. No subject in the experiment suspected that the instrument was merely a simulated shock generator.

Sample Shock. Each naive subject is given a sample shock on the shock generator, prior to beginning his run as teacher. This shock is always 45 volts, and is applied by pressing the third switch of the generator. The shock is applied to the wrist of the naive subject, and has its source in a 45-volt battery wired into the generator. This further convinces the subject of the authenticity of the generator.

Shock Instructions. The subject is told to administer a shock to the learner each time he gives a wrong response. Moreover—and this is the key command—the subject is instructed to "move one level higher on the shock generator each time the learner flashes a wrong answer." He is also instructed to announce the voltage level before administering a shock. This serves to continually remind subjects of the increasing intensity of shocks administered to the learner.

Preliminary and Regular Run. Pretests revealed that the procedure of reading words and administering shocks requires some practice before it can be handled smoothly. Therefore, immediately preceding the regular run, the teacher is given a preliminary series of 10 words to read to the learner. There are 3 neutral words in the practice series (i.e., words that the learner answers correctly), so that shocks are administered for 7 of the words, with the maximum shock at 105 volts (moderate shock). Almost all subjects master the procedure by the time the preliminary run is over.

Subjects are then presented with a second list, and are told that the procedure is the same as for the first list; the experimenter adds, however:

> When you get to the bottom of the list, repeat it over again, and continue giving shocks, until the learner has learned all the pairs correctly.

The experimenter instructs the subject to,

> start from 15 volts and increase the shock level one step each time the learner gives a wrong answer.

Feedback from the Victim. In all conditions the learner gives a predetermined set of responses to the word pair test, based on a schedule of approximately three wrong answers to one correct answer. In the present experimental condition no vocal response or other sign of protest is heard from the learner until Shock Level 300 is reached. When the 300-volt shock is administered, the learner pounds on the wall of the room in which he is bound to the electric chair. The pounding can be heard by the subject. From this point on, the learner's answers no longer appear on the four-way panel.

At this juncture, subjects ordinarily turn to the experimenter for guidance. The experimenter instructs the subject to treat the absence of a response as a wrong answer, and to shock the subject according to the usual schedule. He advised the subjects to allow 5–10 seconds before considering no response as a wrong answer, and to increase the shock level one step each time the learner fails to respond correctly. The learner's pounding is repeated after the 315-volt shock is administered; afterwards he is not heard from, nor do his answers reappear on the four-way signal box.

Experimenter Feedback. At various points in the experiment the subject may turn to the experimenter for advice on whether he should continue to administer shocks. Or he may indicate that he does not wish to go on. It is important to standardize the experimenter's responses to these inquires and reactions.

If the subject indicated his unwillingness to go on the experimenter responded with a sequence of "prods," using as many as necessary to bring the subject into line.

> Prod 1: Please continue, or Please go on.
> Prod 2: The experiment requires that you continue.
> Prod 3: It is absolutely essential that you continue.
> Prod 4: You have no other choice, you must go on.

The prods were always made in sequence: Only if Prod 1 had been unsuccessful, could Prod 2 be used. If the subject refused to obey the experimenter after Prod 4, the experiment was terminated. The experimenter's tone of voice was at all times firm but not impolite. The sequence was begun anew on each occasion that the subject balked or showed reluctance to follow orders.

Special Prods. If the subject asked if the learner was liable to suffer permanent physical injury, the experimenter said:

> Although the shocks may be painful, there is no permanent tissue damage, so please go on. [Followed by Prods 2, 3, and 4 if necessary.]

If the subject said that the learner did not want to go on, the experimenter replied:

> Whether the learner likes it or not, you must go on until he has learned all the word pairs correctly. So please go on. [Followed by Prods 2, 3, and 4 if necessary.]

Dependent Measures

The primary dependent measure for any subject is the maximum shock he administers before he refuses to go any further. In principle this may vary from 0 (for a subject who refuses to administer even the first shock) to 30 (for a subject who administers the highest shock on the generator). A subject who breaks off the experiment at any point prior to administering the thirtieth shock level is termed a *defiant* subject. One who complies with experimental commands fully, and proceeds to administer all shock levels commanded, is termed an *obedient* subject.

Further Records. With few exceptions experimental sessions were recorded on magnetic tape. Occasional photographs were taken through one-way mirrors. Notes were kept on any unusual behavior occurring during the course of the experiments. On occasion, additional observers were directed to write objective descriptions of the subjects' behavior. The latency and duration of shocks were measured by accurate timing devices.

Interview and Dehoax. Following the experiment, subjects were interviewed; open-ended questions, projective measures, and attitude scales were employed. After the interview, procedures were undertaken to assure that the subject would leave the laboratory in a state of well-being. A friendly reconciliation was arranged between the subject and the victim, and an effort was made to reduce any tensions that arose as a results of the experiment.

RESULTS

Preliminary Notions

Before giving an account of the experimental results, it is instructive to consider how persons predict others will perform when commanded to administer powerful shocks to another person. Fourteen Yale seniors, all psychology majors, were provided with a detailed description of the experimental situation. They were asked to reflect carefully on it, and to predict the behavior of 100 hypothetical subjects. More specifically, they were instructed to plot the distribution of obedience of "100 Americans of diverse occupations, and ranging in age from 20 to 50 years," who were placed in the experimental situation.

There was considerable agreement among the respondents on the expected behavior of hypothetical subjects. All respondents predicted that only an insignificant minority would go through to the end of the shock series. (The estimates ranged from 0 to 3%; i.e., the most "pessimistic" member of the class predicted that of 100 persons, 3 would continue through to the most potent shock available on the shock generator–450 volts.) The class mean was 1.2%. The question was also posed informally to colleagues of the author, and the most general feeling was that few if any subjects would go beyond the designation Very Strong Shock.

Result of Experiment I

Subjects Accept Situation. With few exceptions, subjects were convinced of the reality of the experimental situation, that they were administering shocks to another person, and the most potent shocks were extremely painful. In the postexperimental interview subjects were asked: "How painful to the learner were the last few shocks that you administered to him?" Subjects were instructed to indicate their answers on a printed 14-point scale ranging from "Not at all painful" to "Extremely painful." The modal response was 14 (Extremely painful) with the mean at 13.42.

Signs of Extreme Tension. Many subjects showed signs of nervousness in the experimental situation, and especially upon administering the more powerful shocks. In a large number of cases the degree of tension reached extremes that are rarely seen in sociopsychological laboratory studies. Subjects were observed to sweat, tremble, stutter, bite their lips, groan, and dig their fingernails into their flesh. These were characteristic rather than exceptional responses to the experiment.

One sign of tension was the regular occurrence of nervous laughing fits. Fourteen of the 40 subjects showed definite signs of nervous laughter and smiling. The laughter seemed entirely out of place, even bizarre. Full-blown, uncontrollable seizures were observed for 3 subjects. On one occasion we observed a seizure so violently convulsive that it was necessary to call a halt to the experiment. The subject, a 46-year-old encyclopedia salesman, was seriously embarrassed by his untoward and uncontrollable behavior. In the postexperimental interviews subjects took pains to point out that they were not sadistic types, and that the laughter did not mean they enjoyed shocking the victim.

Distribution of Scores. It had been conjectured that persons would not, in general agree to administer shocks beyond the level designated as Very Strong Shock. The distribution of maximum shocks for this experiment is shown in Table 2. The obtained distribution of scores deviates radically from the prediction.

Upon command of the experiment, each of the 40 subjects went beyond the expected breakoff point. No subject stopped prior to administering Shock Level 20. (At this level—300 volts—the victim kicks on the wall and no longer provides answers to the teacher's multiple-choice questions.)

Of the 40 subjects, 5 refused to obey the experimental commands beyond the 300-volt level. Four more subjects administered one further shock, and then refused to go on. Two broke off at the 330-volt level, and 1 each at 345, 360, and 375 volts. Thus a total of 14 subjects defied the experimenter. It is instructive to reprint their remarks at the point of defiance, as transcribed from the tape recordings:

> [0124] I think he's trying to communicate, he's knocking. . . . Well it's not fair to shock the guy . . . these are terrific volts. I don't think this is very humane. . . . Oh, I can't go on with this; no, this isn't right. It's a hell of an experiment. The guy is suffering in there. No, I don't want to go on. This is crazy. [Subject refused to administer more shocks.]
>
> [0123] He's banging in there. I'm gonna chicken out. I'd like to continue, but I can't do that to a man. . . . I'm sorry I can't do that to a man I'll hurt his heart. You take your check. . . . No really, I couldn't do it.

These subjects were frequently in a highly agitated and even angered state. Sometimes, verbal protest was at a minimum, and the subject simply got up from his chair in front of the shock generator, and indicated that he wished to leave the laboratory.

TABLE 2   DISTRIBUTION OF BREAKOFF POINTS

Verbal Designation and Voltage Indication	Number of Subjects for Whom This Was Maximum Shock
Slight Shock	
15	0
30	0
45	0
60	0
Moderate Shock	
75	0
90	0
105	0
120	0
Strong Shock	
135	0
150	0
165	0
180	
Very Strong Shock	
195	0
210	0
225	0
240	0
Intense Shock	
255	0
270	0
285	0
300	5
Extreme Intensity Shock	
315	4
330	2
345	1
360	1
Danger: Severe Shock	
375	1
390	0
405	0
420	0
XXX	
435	0
450	26

Of the 40 subjects, 26 obeyed the orders of the experimenter to the end, proceeding to punish the victim until they reached the most potent shock available on the shock generator. At that point, the experimenter called a halt to the session. (The maximum shock is labeled 450 volts, and is two steps beyond the designation: Danger: Severe Shock.) Although obedient subjects continued to administer shocks, they often did so under extreme stress. Some expressed reluctance to administer shocks beyond the 300-volt level, and displayed fears similar to those who defied the experimenter; yet they obeyed.

After the maximum shocks had been delivered, and the experimenter called a halt to the proceedings, many obedient subjects heaved sighs of relief, mopped their brows, rubbed their fingers over their eyes, or nervously fumbled cigarettes. Some shook their heads, apparently in regret. Some subjects had remained calm throughout the experiment, and displayed only minimal signs of tension from beginning to end.

DISCUSSION

The experiment yielded two findings that were surprising. The first finding concerns the sheer strength of obedient tendencies manifested in this situation. Subjects have learned from childhood that it is a fundamental breach of moral conduct to hurt another person against his will. Yet, 26 subjects abandon this tenet in following the instructions of an authority who has no special powers to enforce his commands. To disobey would bring no material loss to the subject; no punishment would ensue. It is clear from the remarks and outward behavior of many participants that in punishing the victim they are often acting against their own values. Subjects often expressed deep disapproval of shocking a man in the face of his objections, and others denounced it as stupid and senseless. Yet the majority complied with the experimental commands. This outcome was surprising from two perspectives: first, from the standpoint of predictions made in the questionnaire described earlier. (Here, however, it is possible that the remoteness of the respondents from the actual situation, and the difficulty of conveying to them the concrete details of the experiment, could account for the serious underestimation of obedience.)

But the results were also unexpected to persons who observed the experiment in progress, through one-way mirrors. Observers often uttered expressions of disbelief upon seeing a subject administer more powerful shocks to the victim. These persons had a full acquaintance with the details of the situation, and yet systematically underestimated the amount of obedience that subjects would display.

The second unanticipated effect was the extraordinary tension generated by the procedures. One might suppose that a subject would simply break off or continue as his conscience dictated. Yet, this is very far from what happened. There were striking reactions of tension and emotional strain. One observer related:

> I observed a mature and initially poised businessman enter the laboratory smiling and confident. Within 20 minutes he was reduced to a twitching, stuttering wreck, who was rapidly approaching a point of nervous collapse. He constantly pulled on his earlobe, and twisted his hands. At one

point he pushed his fist into his forehead and muttered: "Oh God, let's stop it." And yet he continued to respond to every word of the experimenter, and obeyed to the end.

Any understanding of the phenomenon of obedience must rest on an analysis of the particular conditions in which it occurs. The following features of the experiment go some distance in explaining the high amount of obedience observed in the situation.

1. The experiment is sponsored by and takes place on the grounds of an institution of unimpeachable reputation, Yale University. It may be reasonably presumed that the personnel are competent and reputable. The importance of this background authority is now being studied by conducting a series of experiments outside of New Haven, and without any visible ties to the university.

2. The experiment is, on the face of it, designed to attain a worthy purpose—advancement of knowledge about learning and memory. Obedience occurs not as an end in itself, but as an instrumental element in a situation that the subject construes as significant, and meaningful. He may not be able to see its full significance, but he may properly assume that the experimenter does.

3. The subject perceives that the victim has voluntarily submitted to the authority system of the experimenter. He is not (at first) an unwilling captive impressed for involuntary service. He has taken the trouble to come to the laboratory presumably to aid the experimental research. That he later becomes an involuntary subject does not alter the fact that, initially, he consented to participate without qualification. Thus he has in some degree incurred an obligation toward the experimenter.

4. The subject, too, has entered the experiment voluntarily, and perceives himself under obligation to aid the experimenter. He has made a commitment, and to disrupt the experiment is a repudiation of this initial promise of aid.

5. Certain features of the procedure strengthen the subject's sense of obligation to the experimenter. For one, he has been paid for coming to the laboratory. In part this is canceled out by the experimenter's statement that:

   > Of course, as in all experiments, the money is yours simply for coming to the laboratory. From this point on, no matter that happens, the money is yours.[1]

6. From the subject's standpoint, the fact that he is the teacher and the other man the learner is purely a chance consequence (it is determined by drawing lots) and he, the subject, ran the same risk as the other man in being assigned the role of learner. Since the assignment of positions in the experiment was achieved by fair means, the learner is deprived of any basis of complaint on this count. (A similar situation obtains in Army units, in which—in the absence of volunteers—a particularly dangerous mission may be assigned by drawing lots, and the unlucky soldier is expected to bear his misfortune with sportsmanship.)

---

[1]Forty-three subjects, undergraduates at Yale University, were run in the experiment without payment. The results are very similar to those obtained with paid subjects.

7. There is, at best, ambiguity with regard to the prerogatives of a psychologist and the corresponding rights of his subject. There is a vagueness of expectation concerning what a psychologist may require of his subject and when he is overstepping acceptable limits. Moreover, the experiment occurs in a closed setting, and thus provides no opportunity for the subject to remove these ambiguities by discussion with others. There are few standards that seem directly applicable to the situation, which is a novel one for most subjects.

8. The subjects are assured that the shocks administered to the subject are "painful but not dangerous." Thus they assume that the discomfort caused the victim is momentary, while the scientific gains resulting from the experiment are enduring.

9. Through Shock Level 20 the victim continues to provide answers on the signal box. The subject may construe this as a sign that the victim is still willing to "play the game." It is only after Shock Level 20 that the victim repudiates the rules completely, refusing to answer further.

These features help to explain the high amount of obedience obtained in this experiment. Many of the arguments raised need not remain matters of speculation, but can be reduced to testable propositions to be confirmed or disproved by further experiments.[2]

The following features of the experiment concern the nature of the conflict which the subjects faces.

10. The subject is placed in a position in which he must respond to the competing demands of two persons: the experimenter and the victim. The conflict must be resolved by meeting the demands of one or the other; satisfaction of the victim and the experimenter are mutually exclusive. Moreover, the resolution must take the form of a highly visible action, that of continuing to shock the victim or breaking off the experiment. Thus the subject is forced into a public conflict that does not permit any completely satisfactory solution.

11. While the demands of the experimenter carry the weight of scientific authority; the demands of the victim spring from his personal experience of pain and suffering. The two claims need not be regarded as equally pressing and legitimate. The experimenter seeks an abstract scientific datum; the victim cries out for relief from physical suffering caused by the subject's actions.

12. The experiment gives the subject little time for reflection. The conflict comes on rapidly. It is only minutes after the subject has been seated before the shock generator that the victim begins his protests Moreover, the subject perceives that he has gone through but two-thirds of the shock levels at the time the subject's first protests are heard. Thus he understands that the conflict will have a persistent aspect to it, and may well become more intense as increasingly more powerful

<hr />

[2]A series of recently completed experiments employing the obedience paradigm is reported in Milgram (1964).

shocks are required. The rapidity with which the conflict descends on the subject, and his realization that it is predictably recurrent, may well be sources of tension to him.

13. At a more general level, the conflict stems from the oppositions: first, the disposition not to harm other people, and second, the tendency to obey those whom we perceive to be legitimate authorities.

REFERENCES

Buss, A. H. (1961). *The psychology of aggression.* New York: Wiley.
Milgram, S. (1961, January 25). *Dynamics of obedience.* Washington, DC: National Science Foundation. Mimeo.
Snow, C. P. (1961, February). Either-or. *Progressive,* 24.

QUESTIONS

1. How does Milgram view obedience? Does he believe obedience is, in general, good or bad?

2. Briefly describe the subjects in this experiment. Do you consider them to be relatively representative of people in the United States?

3. Did subjects in this experiment believe in the authenticity of the shock generator? What steps were taken to ensure their acceptance?

4. What percentage of subjects gave "very strong shocks"? What percentage gave "extreme intensity shocks"? What percentage gave the highest shocks of 450 volts?

5. If this study were conducted today on your campus, what percentage of students do you think would administer the 450-volt shock? Compare your prediction with those of Yale students at the time the experiment was conducted.

Reading 24: Contemporary

Commitment and Consistency

Robert B. Cialdini

In the previous reading, Stanley Milgram discussed when and why people obey others' orders. Yet explicit orders are only one form of social influence. For example, Milgram's research cannot explain why we go along with the request of merchandisers to buy their products. This form of persuasion is much more subtle than that studied by Milgram.

The next reading is an excerpt from social psychologist Robert Cialdini's fascinating book on social influence. In the chapter from which this reading was excerpted, Cialdini discusses what has been called "the hobgoblin of little minds": foolish consistency. A foolish consistency is the tendency to avoid rethinking decisions once they have been made, even when doing so would clearly be to one's advantage. Why do people remain committed to past decisions? And how do advertisers and manufacturers use commitment to their advantage? Cialdini answers these questions, and more.

❖

A study done by a pair of Canadian psychologists (Knox & Inkster, 1968) uncovered something fascinating about people at the racetrack: Just after placing bets they are more confident of their horses' chances of winning than they are immediately before laying down the bets. Of course, nothing about the horse's chances actually shifts; it's the same horse, on the same track, in the same field; but in the minds of those bettors, its prospects improve significantly once that ticket is purchased. Although a bit puzzling at first glance, the reason for the dramatic change has to do with a common weapon of social influence. Like the other weapons of influence, this one lies deep within us, directing our actions with quiet power. It is, quite simply, our nearly obsessive desire to be (and to appear) consistent with what we have already done. *Once we make a choice or take a stand, we will encounter personal and interpersonal pressures to behave consistently with that commitment.* Those pressures will cause us to respond in ways that justify our earlier decision. We simply convince ourselves that we have made the right choice and, no doubt, feel better about our decision.

For evidence, let's examine the story of my neighbor Sara and her live-in boyfriend, Tim. After they met, they dated for a while, even after Tim lost his job, and eventually moved in together. Things were never perfect for Sara: She wanted Tim to marry her and to stop his heavy drinking; Tim resisted both ideas. After an especially difficult period of conflict, Sara broke off the relationship and Tim moved out. At the same time, an old boyfriend of Sara's called her.

Source: Cialdini, R. B. (1993). *Influence: Science and practice.* New York: Harper Collins.

They started seeing each other socially and quickly became engaged and made wedding plans. They had gone so far as to set a date and issue invitations when Tim called. He had repented and wanted to move back in. When Sara told him her marriage plans, he begged her to change her mind; he wanted to be together with her as before. Sara refused, saying she didn't want to live like that again. Tim even offered to marry her, but she still said she preferred the other boyfriend. Finally, Tim volunteered to quit drinking if she would only relent. Feeling that under those conditions Tim had the edge, Sara decided to break her engagement, cancel the wedding, retract the invitations, and let Tim move back in with her.

Within a month, Tim informed Sara that he didn't think he needed to stop drinking after all. A month later, he decided that they should "wait and see" before getting married. Two years have since passed; Tim and Sara continue to live together exactly as before. Tim still drinks, and there are still no marriage plans, yet Sara is more devoted to him than she ever was. She says that being forced to choose taught her that Tim really is number one in her heart. So, after choosing Tim over her other boyfriend, Sara became happier, even though the conditions under which she had made her choice have never been fulfilled. Obviously, horse-race bettors are not alone in their willingness to believe in the correctness of a difficult choice once made. Indeed, we all fool ourselves from time to time in order to keep our thoughts and beliefs consistent with what we have already done or decided (Conway & Ross, 1984; Goethals & Reckman, 1973; Rosenfeld, Kennedy, & Giacalone, 1986).

WHIRRING ALONG

Psychologists have long understood the power of the consistency principle to direct human action. Prominent theorists such as Leon Festinger (1957), Fritz Heider (1946), and Theodore Newcomb (1953) have viewed the desire for consistency as a central motivator of behavior. Is this tendency to be consistent really strong enough to compel us to do what we ordinarily would not want to do? There is no question about it. The drive to be (and look) consistent constitutes a highly potent weapon of social influence, often causing us to act in ways that are clearly contrary to our own best interest.

Consider what happened when researchers staged thefts on a New York City beach to see if onlookers would risk personal harm to halt the crime. In the study, an accomplice of the researchers would put a beach blanket down five feet from the blanket of a randomly chosen individual—the experimental subject. After several minutes of relaxing on the blanket and listening to music from a portable radio, the accomplice would stand up and leave the blanket to stroll down the beach. Soon, thereafter, a researcher, pretending to be a thief, would approach, grab the radio, and try to hurry away with it. As you might guess, under normal conditions, subjects were very reluctant to put themselves in harm's way by challenging the thief—only four people did so in the 20 times that the theft was staged. But when the same procedure was tried another 20 times with a slight twist, the results were drastically different. In these incidents, before leaving the blanket, the accomplice would simply ask the subject to please "watch my things," something everyone agreed to do. Now, propelled by the rule for consistency, 19 of the 20 subjects became virtual vigilantes, running after and stopping the thief, demanding an explanation, often restraining the thief physically or snatching the radio away (Moriarty, 1975).

To understand why consistency is so powerful a motive, we should recognize that, in most circumstances, consistency is valued and adaptive. Inconsistency is commonly thought to be an undesirable personality trait (Allgeier, Byrne, Brooks, & Revnes, 1979; Asch, 1946). The person whose beliefs, words, and deeds don't match is seen as confused, two-faced, even mentally ill. On the other side, a high degree of consistency is normally associated with personal and intellectual strength. It is the heart of logic, rationality, stability, and honesty. A quote attributed to the great British chemist, Michael Faraday, suggests the extent to which being consistent is approved—sometimes more than being right. When asked after a lecture if he meant to imply that a hated academic rival was always wrong, Faraday glowered at the questioner and replied, "He's not that consistent."

Certainly, then, good personal consistency is highly valued in our culture—and well it should be. Most of the time we will be better off if our approach to things is well laced with consistency. Without it our lives would be difficult, erratic, and disjointed.

The Quick Fix

Since it is so typically in our best interests to be consistent, we fall into the habit of being automatically consistent even in situations where it is not the sensible way to be. When it occurs unthinkingly, consistency can be disastrous. Nonetheless, even blind consistency has its attractions.

First, like most other forms of automatic responding, it offers a shortcut through the complexities of modern life. Once we have made up our minds about issues, stubborn consistency allows us a very appealing luxury: We don't have to think hard about the issues anymore. We don't really have to sift through the blizzard of information we encounter every day to identify relevant facts; we don't have to expend the mental energy to weigh the pros and cons; we don't have to make any further tough decisions. Instead, all we have to do when confronted with the issues is turn on our consistency tape, *whirr,* and we know just what to believe, say, or do. We need only believe, say, or do whatever is consistent with our earlier decision.

The allure of such a luxury is not to be minimized. It allows us a convenient, relatively effortless, and efficient method for dealing with the complexities of daily life that make severe demands on our mental energies and capacities. It is not hard to understand, then, why automatic consistency is a difficult reaction to curb. It offers us a way to evade the rigors of continuing thought. With our consistency tapes operating, we can go about our business happily excused from having to think too much. As Sir Joshua Reynolds noted, "There is no expedient to which a man will not resort to avoid the real labor of thinking." . . .

If, as it appears, automatic consistency functions as a shield against thought, it should not be surprising that such consistency can also be exploited by those who would prefer that we respond to their requests without thinking. For the profiteers, whose interest will be served by an unthinking, mechanical reaction to their requests, our tendency for automatic consistency is a gold mine. So clever are they at arranging to have us play our consistency tapes when it profits them that we seldom realize that we have been taken. In fine jujitsu fashion, they structure their interactions with us so that our *own* need to be consistent leads directly to their benefit.

Certain large toy manufacturers use just such an approach to reduce a problem created by seasonal buying patterns. Of course, the boom time for toy companies occurs before and during the Christmas holiday season. Their problem is that toy sales then go into a terrible slump for the next couple of months. Their customers have already spent the amount in their toy budgets and are stiffly resistant to their children's pleas for more.

So the toy manufacturers are faced with a dilemma: how to keep sales high during the peak season and, at the same time, retain a healthy demand for toys in the immediately following months. Their difficulty certainly doesn't lie in motivating kids to want more toys after Christmas. The problem lies in motivating postholiday spent-out parents to buy another plaything for their already toy-glutted children. What could the toy companies possibly do to produce that unlikely behavior? Some have tried greatly increased advertising campaigns, others have reduced prices during the slack period, but neither of those standard sales devices has proved successful. Both tactics are costly, and have been ineffective in increasing sales to desired levels. Parents are simply not in a toy-buying mood, and the influences of advertising or reduced expense are not enough to shake that stony resistance.

Certain large toy manufacturers, however, think they have found a solution. It's an ingenious one, involving no more than a normal advertising expense and an understanding of the powerful pull of the need for consistency. My first hint of the way the toy companies' strategy worked came after I fell for it and then, in true patsy form, fell for it again.

It was January, and I was in the town's largest toy store. After purchasing all too many gifts there for my son a month before, I had sworn not to enter that place or any like it for a long, long time. Yet there I was, not only in the diabolic place but also in the process of buying my son another expensive toy—a big, electric road-race set. In front of the road-race display I happened to meet a former neighbor who was buying his son the same toy. The odd thing was that we almost never saw each other anymore. In fact, the last time had been a year earlier in the same store when we were both buying our sons an expensive post-Christmas gift—that time a robot that walked, talked, and laid waste. We laughed about our strange pattern of seeing each other only once a year at the same time, in the same place, while doing the same thing. Later that day, I mentioned the coincidence to a friend who, it turned out, had once worked in the toy business.

"No coincidence," he said knowingly.

"What do you mean, 'No coincidence'?"

"Look," he said, "let me ask you a couple of questions about the road-race set you bought this year. First, did you promise your son that he'd get one for Christmas?"

"Well, yes I did. Christopher had seen a bunch of ads for them on the Saturday morning cartoon shows and said that was what he wanted for Christmas. I saw a couple of ads myself and it looked like fun; so I said OK."

"Strike one," he announced. "Now for my second question. When you went to buy one, did you find all the stores sold out?"

"That's right, I did! The stores said they'd ordered some but didn't know when they'd get any more in. So I had to buy Christopher some other toys to make up for the road-race set. But how did you know?"

"Strike two," he said. "Just let me ask one more question. Didn't this same sort of thing happen the year before with the robot toy?"

"Wait a minute . . . you're right. That's just what happened. This is incredible. How did you know?"

"No psychic powers; I just happen to know how several of the big toy companies jack up their January and February sales. They start prior to Christmas with attractive TV ads for certain special toys. The kids, naturally, want what they see and extract Christmas promises for these items from their parents. Now here's where the genius of the companies' plan comes in: They *undersupply* the stores with the toys they've gotten the parents to promise. Most parents find those toys sold out and are forced to substitute other toys of equal value. The toy manufacturers, of course, make a point of supplying the stores with plenty of these substitutes. Then, after Christmas, the companies start running the ads again for the other, special toys. That juices up the kids to want those toys more than ever. They go running to their parents whining, 'You promised, you promised,' and the adults go trudging off to the store to live up dutifully to their words."

"Where," I said, beginning to seethe now, "they meet other parents they haven't seen for a year, falling for the same trick, right?"

"Right. Uh, where are you going?"

"I'm going to take the road-race set right back to the store." I was so angry I was nearly shouting.

"Wait. Think for a minute first. Why did you buy it this morning?"

"Because I didn't want to let Christopher down and because I wanted to teach him that promises are to be lived up to."

"Well, has any of that changed? Look, if you take his toy away now, he won't understand why. He'll just know that his father broke a promise to him. Is that what you want?"

"No," I said, sighing, "I guess not. So, you're telling me that the toy companies doubled their profits on me for the past two years, and I never knew it; and now that I do, I'm still trapped—by my own words. So, what you're really telling me is, 'Strike three.' "

He nodded, 'And you're out.'

COMMITMENT IS THE KEY

Once we realize that the power of consistency is formidable in directing human action, an important practical question immediately arises: How is that force engaged? What produces the *click* that activates the *whirr* of the powerful consistency tape? Social psychologists think they know the answer: commitment. If I can get you to make a commitment (that is, to take a stand, to go on record), I will have set the stage for your automatic and ill-considered consistency with that earlier commitment. Once a stand is taken, there is a natural tendency to behave in ways that are stubbornly consistent with the stand.

As we've already seen, social psychologists are not the only ones who understand the connection between commitment and consistency. Commitment strategies are aimed at us by compliance professionals of nearly every sort. Each of the strategies is intended to get us to take some action or make some statement that will trap us into later compliance through consistency pressures. Procedures designed to create commitment take various forms. Some are bluntly straightforward; others are among the most subtle compliance tactics we will encounter. On the blunt side, consider the approach of Jack Stanko, used-car sales manager for an Albuquerque auto dealership. While leading a session called "Used Car Merchandising" at a National Auto Dealers Association convention in San Francisco, he advised 100 sales-hungry dealers as follows: "Put 'em on paper. Get the customer's OK on paper. Get the money up front. Control 'em. Control the deal. Ask 'em if they would buy the car right now if the price is right. Pin 'em down" (Rubinstein, 1985). Obviously, Mr. Stanko—an expert in these matters—believes that the way to customer compliance is through their commitments, thereby to "control 'em" for profit.

Commitment practices involving substantially more finesse can be just as effective. For instance, suppose you wanted to increase the number of people in your area who would agree to go door-to-door collecting donations for your favorite charity. You would be wise to study the approach taken by social psychologist Steven J. Sherman. He simply called a sample of Bloomington, Indiana, residents as part of a survey he was taking and asked them to predict what they would say if asked to spend three hours collecting money for the American Cancer Society. Of course, not wanting to seem uncharitable to the survey-taker or to themselves, many of these people said that they would volunteer. The consequence of this subtle commitment procedure was a 700 percent increase in volunteers when, a few days later, a representative of the American Cancer Society did call and ask for neighborhood canvassers (Sherman, 1980). Using the same strategy, but this time asking Columbus, Ohio, residents to predict whether they would vote on Election Day, other researchers have been able to increase significantly the turnout in a U.S. presidential election among those called (Greenwald, Carnot, Beach, & Young, 1987).

Perhaps an even more crafty commitment technique has been developed by telephone solicitors for charity. Have you noticed that callers asking you to contribute to some cause or another these days seem to begin things by inquiring about your current health and well-being? "Hello, Mr./Ms. Targetperson?," they say. "How are you feeling this evening?," or "How are you doing today?" The caller's intent with this sort of introduction is not merely to seem friendly and caring. It is to get you to respond—as you normally do to such polite, superficial inquiries—with a polite, superficial comment of your own: "Just fine" or "Real good" or "I'm doing great, thanks." Once you have publicly stated that all is well, it becomes much easier for the solicitor to corner you into aiding those for whom all is not well: "I'm glad to hear that, because I'm calling to ask if you'd be willing to make a donation to help out the unfortunate victims of . . . "

The theory behind this tactic is that people who have just asserted that they are doing/feeling fine—even as a routine part of a sociable exchange—will consequently find it awkward to appear stingy in the context of their own admittedly favored circumstances. If all this sounds a bit far-fetched, consider the findings of consumer researcher Daniel Howard (1990), who put the theory to test. Residents of Dallas, Texas, were called on the phone and asked if they would agree to allow a representative of the Hunger Relief Committee to come to their homes to sell them cookies, the proceeds from which would be used to supply meals for the needy. When tried alone, that request (labeled the standard solicitation approach) produced only 18 percent agreement. However, if the caller initially asked, "How are you feeling this evening?" and waited for a reply before proceeding with the standard approach, several noteworthy things happened. First, of the 120 individuals called, most (108) gave the customary favorable reply ("Good," "Fine," "Real well," etc.) Second, 32 percent of the people who got the How-are-you-feeling-tonight question agreed to receive the cookie seller at their homes, nearly twice the success rate of the standard solicitation approach. Third, true to the consistency principle, almost everyone (89 percent) who agreed to such a visit did in fact make a cookie purchase when contacted at home.

To make sure that this tactic doesn't generate its successes simply because a solicitor who uses it seems more concerned and courteous than one who doesn't, Howard conducted another study. This time callers began either with the question, "How are you feeling this evening?" (and waited for a response before proceeding) or with the statement "I hope you are feeling well this evening" and then proceeded to the standard solicitation approach. Despite the fact that the caller started each type of interaction with a warm and friendly comment, the How-are-you-feeling technique was by far superior to its rival (33 percent versus 15 percent compliance), because only it drew an exploitable public commitment from its targets. Note that the commitment was able to get twice as much compliance from these targets even though at the time it occurred it must seemed to them an altogether inconsequential reply to an altogether superficial question—yet another fine example of social jujitsu at work.

REFERENCES

ALLGEIER, A. R., BYRNE, D., BROOKS, B., & REVNES, D. (1979). The waffle phenomenon: Negative evaluations of those who shift attitudinally. *Journal of Applied Social Psychology, 9,* 170–182.

ASCH, S. (1946). Forming impressions of personality. *Journal of Abnormal and Social Psychology, 41,* 259–290.

CONWAY M., & ROSS, M. (1984). Getting what you want by revising what you had. *Journal of Personality and Social Psychology, 47,* 738–748.

FESTINGER, L. (1957). *A theory of cognitive dissonance.* Stanford: Stanford University Press.

GOETHALS, G. R., & RECKMAN, R. F. (1973). The perception of consistency in attitudes. *Journal of Experimental Social Psychology, 9,* 491–501.

GREENWALD, A. F., CARNOT, C. G., BEACH, R., & YOUNG, B. (1987). Increasing voting behavior by asking people if they expect to vote. *Journal of Applied Psychology, 72,* 315–318.

HEIDER, F. (1946). Attitudes and cognitive organization. *Journal of Psychology 21,* 107–112.

HOWARD, D. J. (1990). The influence of verbal responses to common greetings on compliance behavior: The foot-in-the-mouth effect. *Journal of Applied Social Psychology, 20,* 1185–1196.

KNOX, R. E., & INKSTER, J. A. (1968). Postdecisional dissonance at post time. *Journal of Personality and Social Psychology, 8,* 319–323.

MORIARTY, T. (1975). Crime, commitment, and the responsive bystander. *Journal of Personality and Social Psychology, 31,* 370–376.

NEWCOMB, T. (1953). An approach to the study of communicative acts. *Psychological Review, 60,* 393–404.

ROSENFELD, P., KENNEDY, J. G., & GIACALONE, R. A. (1986). Decision-making: A demonstration of the post-decision dissonance effect. *Journal of Social Psychology, 126,* 663–665.

RUBINSTEIN, S. (1985, January 30). What they teach used car salesmen. *San Francisco Chronicle.*

SHERMAN, S. J. (1980). On the self-erasing nature of errors of prediction. *Journal of Personality and Social Psychology, 39,* 211–221.

QUESTIONS

1. What does gamblers' increased confidence after placing a bet have to do with Sara's forgiving her boyfriend Tim?

2. Do you think Sara's commitment to Tim is the result of wanting to appear consistent to others? Do you think her commitment is caused by mental laziness?

3. What are the two main benefits of consistency? What is the difference between a foolish consistency and an intelligent consistency?

4. What kind of consistency forced Cialdini not to return the race-car set even after he discovered that he had been tricked? What advice would you give parents to help them avoid buying twice as many toys as they would like?

5. Do you agree that it is somewhat illogical for people to chase after someone who appears to be stealing goods that they had promised to watch? Why or why not?

CHAPTER 13

LAW AND ORDER: THE LEGAL SYSTEM AND POLITICS

Reading 25: Classic

The Basic Psychology of Rumor

Gordon W. Allport and Leo J. Postman

During World War II, the entire country rallied around the war effort. The war required a shift in the economy, and many manufacturers cut back production on nonmilitary products, devoting more resources to goods that were needed for the war. For example, factories that had produced cars before the war began producing tanks. Similarly, social scientists gave up their existing research projects in order to produce work more relevant to the war effort.

Social psychologists quickly realized that their field could contribute to the war effort in many different ways, including analyzing propaganda, surveying public opinion, and increasing national harmony by reducing prejudice. Gordon Allport, one of the leading figures in the field, contributed to the war effort by studying the process of rumors.

Especially during the early days of the war, rumors that the war was going badly for the United States swept across the country, lowering national morale. The problem was severe enough that the FBI and other government agencies used considerable resources for the express purpose of fighting rumors. Unfortunately, they had very little scientific evidence to help them in their fight.

In the following excerpt, from an address delivered to the New York Academy of Sciences, Allport describes a series of studies conducted during the war to understand rumors. The usefulness of this research extends beyond the psychology of rumors during the 1940s, into such current concerns as the accuracy of eyewitness testimony and influences of prejudice.

✣

RUMORS IN WARTIME

During the year 1942, rumor became a national problem of considerable urgency. Its first dangerous manifestation was felt soon after the initial shock of Pearl Harbor. This traumatic event dislocated our normal channels of communication by bringing into existence an unfamiliar and unwelcome, if at the same time a relatively mild, censorship of news, and it simultaneously dislocated the lives of millions of citizens whose futures abruptly became hostages to fortune.

Source: Allport, G. W., & Postman, L. J. (1945). The basic psychology of rumor. *Transactions of the New York Academy of Sciences, 8* (Series III), 61–81.

This combination of circumstances created the most fertile of all possible soils for the prop-agation of rumor. We now know that *rumors concerning a given subject-matter will circulate within a group in proportion to the importance and the ambiguity of this subject-matter in the lives of individual members of the group.*

The affair of Pearl Harbor was fraught with both importance and ambiguity to nearly every citizen. The affair was important because of the potential danger it represented to all of us, and because its aftermath of mobilization affected every life. It was ambiguous because no one seemed quite certain of the extent of, reasons for, or consequences of the attack. Since the two conditions of rumor—importance and ambiguity—were at a maximum, we had an unprece-dent flood of what became known as "Pearl Harbor rumors." It was said that our fleet was "wiped out," that Washington didn't dare to tell the extent of the damage, that Hawaii was in the hands of the Japanese. So widespread and so demoralizing were these tales that, on Feb-ruary 22, 1942, President Roosevelt broadcast a speech devoted entirely to denying the harm-ful rumors and to reiterating the official report on the losses.

Did the solemn assurance of the Commander-in-Chief restore the confidence of the people and eliminate the tales of suspicion and fear? It so happens that a bit of objective evidence on this question became available to us almost by accident. On the twenty-first of February, the day before the President's speech, we had asked approximately two hundred college students whether they thought our losses at Pearl Harbor were "greater," "much greater," or "no greater" than the official Knox report had stated. Among these students, 68 per cent had believed the de-moralizing rumors in preference to the official report, and insisted that the losses were "greater" or "much greater" than Washington admitted. Then came the President's speech. The next day, an equivalent group of college students were asked the same question. Among those who had not heard or read the speech the proportion of rumor-believers was still about two-thirds. But among those who were acquainted with President's speech, the number of rumor-believers fell by 24 per cent. It is important to note that, in spite of the utmost efforts of the highest author-ity to allay anxiety, approximately 44 per cent of the college population studied were too pro-foundly affected by the event and by the resulting rumors to accept the reassurance.

The year 1942 was characterized by floods of similar fear-inspired tales. Shipping losses were fantastically exaggerated. Knapp records one instance where a collier was sunk through accident near the Cape Cod Canal. So great was the anxiety of the New England public that this incident became a fantastic tale of an American ship being torpedoed with the loss of thou-sands of nurses who were aboard her. . . .

That rumors were harmful to national morale was quickly recognized both by federal au-thorities and by civilian leaders of opinion. The efforts of the FBI to trace subversive rumors constitute a story yet to be told; the preventive campaign conducted by OWI and other federal agencies marks another chapter in the story; the establishment of "Rumor Clinics" in at least 40 newspapers in the United States and Canada is yet another. Lectures, pamphlets, movies, posters, and "rumor-wardens" all formed part of the campaign. This activity was at its peak during 1942–43. As victory became assured, the emotional insistency of anxiety and hate sub-sided, news services became more widely believed, rumor lessened, and the immediate crisis passed.

Though it was the darker days of the war that focused our attention upon rumor as a grave social problem, still the mischief of rumor and gossip is something we always have with us. At the present time, there is reason to suppose that we may be headed for another critical period of rumor-mongering, since we anticipate sharp clashes between minority groups of Americans and majority groups during the coming years of social readjustment. Records of the bitter race conflicts in Los Angeles, Beaumont, Harlem, Philadelphia, and Detroit have taught us what a close association exists between rumors and riot. The tie is so intimate that one of the best barometers we have of social strain lies in the analysis of rumors circulating in a tense community.[1]

EXPERIMENTAL APPROACH

Leaving now the broader social setting of the problem, we ask ourselves what processes in the human mind account for the spectacular distortions and exaggerations that enter into the rumor-process, and lead to so much damage to the public intelligence and public conscience.

Since it is very difficult to trace in detail the course of a rumor in everyday life, we have endeavored by an experimental technique to study as many of the basic phenomena as possible under relatively well controlled laboratory conditions.

Our method is simple. A slide is thrown upon a screen. Ordinarily, a semi-dramatic picture is used containing a large number of related details. Six or seven subjects, who have not see the picture, wait in an adjacent room. One of them enters and takes a position where he cannot see the screen. Someone in the audience (or the experimenter) describes the picture, giving about twenty details in the account. A second subject enters the room and stands beside the first subject, who proceeds to tell him all he can about the picture. (All subjects are under instruction to report as "accurately as possible what you have heard.") The first subject then takes his seat, and a third enters to hear the story from the second subject. Each succeeding subject hears and repeats the story in the same way. Thus, the audience is able to watch the deterioration of the rumor by comparing the successive versions with the stimulus-picture which remains on the screen throughout the experiment.

This procedure has been used with over forty groups of subjects, including college undergraduates, Army trainees in ASTP, members of community forums patients in an Army hospital, members of a Teachers' Round Table, and police officials in a training course. In addition to these adult subjects, children in a private school were used, in grades from the fourth through the ninth. In some experiments, Negro subjects took part along with whites, a fact which, as we shall see, had important consequences when the test-pictures depicted scenes with a "racial angle."

All of these experiments took place before an audience (20–300 spectators). By using volunteer subjects, one eliminates the danger of stagefright. There was, however, a social influence

[1]For an account of the relation of rumors to riots see A. McC. Lee & N. D. Humphrey Internat. Race Riot. Dryden Press. New York. 1943; and J. E. Weckler & T. H. Hall, The Police and Minority Groups. Internat. City Managers Association. Chicago. 1944.

FIGURE 13–1
A sample of pictorial material employed in the experiments.
When the experiment was conducted at the New York Academy of
Sciences, the terminal (sixth) report ran as follows: "A subway
scene on the IRT, between Van Cortlandt Park and Dyckman Street.
Four people are standing, two are seated. There is a colored man
and a white man. One of them has a razor." (In the ante-terminal
report, it was said that the Negro held the razor.)

in all the audience situations. The magnitude of this influence was studied in a control group of experiments where no one was present in the room except the subject and the experimenter.

At the outset, it is necessary to admit that in five respects this experimental situation fails to reproduce accurately the conditions of rumor-spreading in everyday life. (1) The effect of an audience is considerable, tending to create caution and to shorten the report. Without an audience subjects gave on the average twice as many details as with an audience. (2) The effect of the instructions is to maximize accuracy and induce caution. In ordinary rumor-spreading, there is no critical experimenter on had to see whether the tale is rightly repeated. (3) There is no opportunity for subjects to ask questions of his informer. In ordinary rumor-spreading, the listener can chat with his informer and, if he wishes, cross-examine him. (4) The lapse of time between hearing and telling in the experimental situation is very slight. In ordinary rumor spreading, it is much greater. (5) Most important of all, the conditions of motivation are quite different. In the experiment, the subject is striving for *accuracy*. His own fears, hates, wishes are not likely to be aroused under the experimental conditions. In short, he is not the spontaneous rumor-agent that he is in ordinary life. His stake in spreading the experimental rumor is neither personal nor deeply motivated.

It should be noted that all of these conditions, excepting the third, may be expected to enhance the accuracy of the report in the experimental situation, and to yield far less distortion and projection than in real-life rumor-spreading.

In spite of the fact that our experiment does not completely reproduce the normal conditions for rumor, still we believe that all essential changes and distortions are represented in our results. "Indoor" rumors may not be as lively, as emotionally toned, or as extreme as "outdoor" rumors, and yet the same phenomena are demonstrable in both.

What happens in both real-life and laboratory rumors is a complex course of distortion in which three interrelated tendencies are clearly distinguishable.

LEVELING

As rumor travels, it tends to grow shorter, more concise, more easily grasped and told. In successive versions, fewer words are used and fewer details are mentioned.

The number of details *retained* declines most sharply at the beginning of the series of reproductions. The number continues to decline, more slowly, throughout the experiment. Figure 13–2 shows the percentage of the details initially given which are retained in each successive reproduction.

The number of items enumerated in the description from the scene constitutes the 100 per cent level, and all subsequent percentages are calculated from that base. The curve, based on 11 experiments, shows that about 70 per cent of the details are eliminated in the course of five or six mouth-to-mouth transmissions, even when virtually no time lapse intervenes.

The curve is like the famous Ebbinghaus curve for decline in individual retention, though in his experiments the interval between initial learning and successive reproductions was not as short as under the conditions of our experiment. Comparing the present curve with Ebbinghaus's, we conclude that *social memory accomplishes as much leveling within a few minutes as individual memory accomplishes in weeks of time.*

SHARPENING

We may define sharpening as the selective perception, retention, and reporting of a limited number of details from a larger context. . . . Sharpening is inevitably the reciprocal of leveling. The one cannot exist without the other, for what little remains to a rumor after leveling has taken place is by contrast unavoidably featured.

Although sharpening occurs in every protocol, the same items are not always emphasized. Sometimes, a trifling detail such as subway advertising card becomes the focus of attention and report. Around it the whole rumor becomes structured. But, in most experiments, this same detail drops out promptly, and is never heard of after the first reproduction.

One way in which sharpening seems to be determined is through the retention of odd or attention-getting words which, having appeared early in the series, catch the attention of each successive listener and are often passed on in preference to other details intrinsically more important to the story. An instance of this effect is seen in a series of protocols where the statement, "there is a boy stealing and a man remonstrating with him" is transmitted throughout

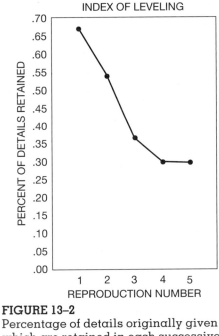

FIGURE 13–2
Percentage of details originally given which are retained in each successive reproduction.

the entire series. The unusual word "remonstrate" somehow caught the attention of each successive listener and was passed on without change.

Sharpening may also take a numerical turn, as in the experiments where emphasized items become reduplicated in the telling. For example, in reports of a picture containing the figure of a Negro, whose size and unusual appearance invite emphasis, we find that the number of Negroes reported in the picture jumps from one to "four" or "several."

ASSIMILATION

It is apparent that both leveling and sharpening are selective processes. But what is it that leads to the obliteration of some details and the pointing-up of others; and what accounts for all transpositions, importations, and other falsifications that mark the course of rumor? The answer is to be found in the process of assimilation, which has to do with the powerful attractive force exerted upon rumor by habits, interests, and sentiments existing in the listener's mind.

Assimilation to Principal Theme. It generally happens that items become sharpened or leveled to fit the leading motif of the story, and they become consistent with this motif in such a way as to make the resulting story more coherent, plausible, and well rounded. Thus, in a study conducted using a picture of a war scene, the war theme is preserved and emphasized in all reports. In some experiments using the same picture, a chaplain is introduced, or people (in the plural) are reported as being killed; the ambulance become a Red Cross station; demolished buildings are multiplied in the telling; the extent of devastation is exaggerated. All these reports false though they are, fit the principal theme—a battle incident. If the reported details were actually present in the picture, they would make a "better" *Gestalt*. Objects wholly extraneous to the theme are never introduced—no apple pies, no ballet dancers, no baseball players.

Besides importations, we find other falsifications in the interest of supporting the principal theme. The original picture shows that the Red Cross truck is loaded with explosives, but it is ordinarily reported as carrying medical supplies which is, of course, the way it "ought" to be.

The Negro in this same picture is nearly always described as a soldier, although his clothes might indicate that he is a civilian partisan. It is a "better" configuration to have a soldier in action on the battlefield than to have a civilian among regular soldiers.

Good Continuation. Other falsifications results from the attempt to complete incompleted pictures or to fill in gaps which exist in the stimulus field. The effort is again to make the resulting whole coherent, and meaningful. Thus, the sign, "Loew's Pa . . . ," over a moving picture theater is invariably read and reproduced as "Loew's Palace" and Gene *Antry* becomes Gene *Autry*. "Lucky Rakes" are reported as "Lucky Strikes."

All these, and many instances like them, are examples of what has been called, in *Gestalt* terms, "closures." Falsifications of perception and memory they are, but they occur in the interests of bringing about a more coherent, consistent mental configuration. Every detail is assimilated to the principal theme, and "good continuation" is sought, in order to round our meaning where it is lacking or incomplete.

Assimilation by Condensation. It sometimes seems as though memory tries to burden itself as little as possible. For instance, instead of remembering two items, it is more economical to fuse them into one. Instead of a series of subway cars, each of which has its own identity, reports sometimes refer only to "a billboard," or perhaps to a "lot of advertising" (Figure 13–1). In another picture, it is more convenient to refer to "all kinds of fruit," rather than to enumerate all the different items on the vendor's cart. Again, the occupants of the car come to be described by some such summary phrase as "several people sitting and standing in the car." Their individuality is lost.

Assimilation to Expectation. Just as details are changed or imported to bear out the simplified theme that the listener has in mind, so too many items take a form that supports the agent's habits of thought. Things are perceived and remembered the way they *usually* are. Thus, a drugstore in one stimulus-picture is situated in the middle of a block; but, in the telling, it moves up the corner of the two streets and becomes the familiar "corner drugstore." A Red Cross ambulance is said to carry medical supplies rather than explosives, because it "ought" to be carrying medical supplies. The kilometers on the signposts are changed into miles, since Americans are accustomed to having distances indicated in miles.

The most spectacular of all our assimilative distortions is the finding that, in more than half of our experiments, a razor moves (in the telling) from a white man's hand to a Negro's hand (Figure 13–1). This result is a clear instance of assimilation to stereotyped expectancy. Black men are "supposed" to carry razors, white men not.

Assimilation to Linguistic Habits. Expectancy is often merely a matter of fitting perceived and remembered material to preexisting verbal clichés. An odd example is found in the case of a clock tower on a chapel. In the telling, the chapel becomes a "chaplain" and the clock, having no place to go, lands on a fictitious mantelpiece.

> *Sixth Reproduction:* This is a picture of a battlefield. There is a chapel with a clock which says ten minutes to two. A sign down below gives the direction to Paris and Paris is 50 miles and Cherbourg 21 miles away. People are being killed on the battlefield.
> *Seventh Reproduction:* This is a picture of a battlefield. There is a chaplain, and a clock on the mantelpiece says ten minutes to two. There is a sign, so many miles to Cherbourg.

The powerful effect that words have in arousing images in the listener and fixing for him the categories in which he must think of the event is, of course, a major step in the conventionalization of rumor. A "zoot-suit sharpie" arouses a much more compelling image (capable of assimilating all details to itself) than more objective words, such as "a colored man with pegged trousers, wide brimmed hat, etc." (Figure 13–1). Rumors are commonly told in terms of verbal stereotypes. Over and over again, they include prejudicial judgment, such as "draft dodger," "Japanese spy," "brass-hat," "dumb Swede," "long-haired professor," and the like.

MORE HIGHLY MOTIVATED ASSIMILATION

Although the conditions of our experiment do not give full play to emotional tendencies underlying gossip, rumor, and scandal, such tendencies are so insistent that they express themselves even under laboratory conditions.

Assimilation to Interest. It sometimes happens that a picture containing women's dresses, as a trifling detail in the original scene, becomes, in the telling, a story exclusively about dresses. This sharpening occurs when the rumor is told by groups of women, but never when told by men.

Assimilation to Prejudice. Hard as it is in an experimental situation to obtain distortions that arise from hatred, yet we have in our material a certain opportunity to trace the hostile complex of racial attitudes.

We have spoken of the picture which contained a white man holding a razor while arguing with a Negro. In over half of the experiments with this picture, the final report indicated that the Negro (instead of the white man) held the razor in his hand, and several times he was reported as "brandishing it wildly" or as "threatening" the white man with it (Figure 13–1).

Whether this ominous distortion reflects hatred and fear of Negroes we cannot definitely say. In some cases, these deeper emotions may be the assimilative factor at work. And yet the distortion may occur even in subjects who have no anti-Negro bias. It is an unthinking cultural stereotype that the Negro is hot-tempered and addicted to the use of razors as weapons. The rumor, though mischievous, may reflect chiefly an assimilation of the story to verbal-clichés and conventional expectation. Distortion in this case may not mean assimilation to hostility. Much so-called prejudice is, of course, a mere matter of conforming to current folk-ways by accepting prevalent beliefs about an out-group.

Whether or not this razor-shift reflects deep hatred and fear on the part of white subjects, it is certain that the reports of our Negro subjects betray a motivated type of distortion. Because it was to their interest as members of the race to de-emphasize the racial caricature, Negro subjects almost invariably avoided mention of color. One of them hearing a rumor containing the phrase, "a Negro zoot-suiter," reported "There is a man wearing a zoot suit, *possibly* a Negro."

For one picture, a Negro reporter said that the colored man in the center of the picture "is being maltreated." Though this interpretation may be correct, it is likewise possible that he is a rioter about to be arrested by the police officer. White and Negro subjects are very likely to perceive, remember, and interpret this particular situation in quite opposite ways.

Thus, even under laboratory conditions, we find assimilation in terms of deep-lying emotional predispositions. Our rumors, like those of everyday life, tend to fit into, and support, the occupational interests, class or racial memberships, or personal prejudices of the reporter.

CONCLUSION: THE EMBEDDING PROCESS

Leveling, sharpening, and assimilation are not independent mechanisms. They function simultaneously, and reflect a singular subjectifying process that results in the autism and falsification which are so characteristic of rumor. If we were to attempt to summarize what happens in a few words we might say:

Whenever a stimulus field is of potential importance to an individual, but at the same time unclear, or susceptible of divergent interpretations, a subjective structuring process is started. Although the process is complex (involving, as it does, leveling, sharpening, and assimilation), its essential nature can be characterized as an effort to reduce the stimulus to a simple and meaningful structure that has adaptive significance for the individual in terms of his own interests and experience. The process begins at the moment the ambiguous situation is perceived, but the effects are greatest if memory intervenes. The longer the time that elapses after the stimulus is perceived the greater the three-fold change is likely to be. Also, the more people involved in a serial report, the greater the change is likely to be, until the rumor has reached an aphoristic brevity, and is repeated by rote. . . .

QUESTIONS

1. What two circumstances made rumors so prevalent in the days following the attack on Pearl Harbor? Was a presidential address to calm these fears successful?

2. What aspects of the conditions under which these studies were conducted may have decreased the accuracy of rumors? What aspects enhanced accuracy?

3. As a rumor is passed on to more and more people, does it tend to get more complex and take on new dimensions, or does it become less complex?

4. Explain the concept of "sharpening" in the spreading of rumors. What explains which items are sharpened and which are leveled?

5. Is assimilation the result of motivated processes, cognitive processes, or both? Can a rumor become fixed, or will it continue to change with each telling?

Reading 26: Contemporary

Eyewitness Suggestibility

D. Stephen Lindsay

During a trial, the second most powerful evidence that a prosecuting attorney could introduce to convince a jury of a defendant's guilt is the testimony of an eyewitness (admission of guilt by the defendant is the most powerful evidence). As illustrated in recent trials such as that of O.J. Simpson, it can be difficult to convince a jury of a defendant's guilt without an eyewitness. But is it wise for jurors to place so much emphasis on the testimony (or lack of testimony) of eyewitnesses? How reliable are they?

Most people assume that anyone willing to testify as an eyewitness must surely have a reasonably clear memory of the events in question. Yet a great deal of recent research on memory suggests that it is far more fallible than previously believed. One aspect of this fallibility is particularly relevant for evaluating the memory of eyewitnesses: postevent information.

As psychologist Stephen Lindsay discusses in the following reading, postevent information can sometimes distort people's memory of the original event. For example, if a police officer suggests to eyewitnesses a detail that they, in fact, did not notice (e.g., that the perpetrator was 6'2"), it is sometimes possible that the witnesses will later "remember" seeing that detail. In other words, police may sometimes implant new memories where they did not previously exist. After reviewing recent evidence, Lindsay concludes that postevent information can distort memory, although this bias may not be as common as some believe it to be.

❖

The attorney faces the witness with a somber and resolute gaze and asks, "Please describe for the court the events of the afternoon of Wednesday, June 3, 1992." Like many everyday tasks, providing a detailed and accurate answer to this question demands bewilderingly complex cognitive processes and skills. One of the many sources of difficulty is that during the lengthy interval between seeing an event and testifying about it in court, witnesses are often exposed to many different sources of information about the event: information implied in questions posed by police and lawyers, media reports, and statements made by other witnesses, among other sources. Some of this information may be inaccurate. What effect does such misleading postevent information (MPI) have on eyewitnesses' ability to provide accurate testimony?

We owe the modern renaissance of this line of inquiry to work by Loftus and colleagues.[1] Loftus's basic procedure consists of three phases: In Phase 1, subjects view an event; in Phase

Source: Lindsay. D. S. (1993, June). Eyewitness suggestibility. *Current Directions*, 2, 86–89.

[1]For a historical review, see S. J. Ceci and M. Bruck, The suggestibility of the child witness: A historical review and synthesis, *Psychological Bulletin* (in press). For a review of Loftus's work, see E. F. Loftus, When a lie becomes

2, they receive verbal information about the event (with or without misleading suggestions about certain "critical" details); and in Phase 3, they take a memory test that includes questions about the critical details. For example, subjects in one study watched a slide show that depicted an automobile accident; some subjects were later given a misleading suggestion concerning what kind of traffic sign had marked a particular intersection (e.g., some subjects saw a stop sign at this intersection but were later misinformed that it was a yield sign). At test, subjects were given a two-alternative, forced-choice recognition test, with instructions to indicate which item in each pair they had seen in the initial slide show. Most of the test items consisted of an event detail paired with a new distractor, but the critical test items consisted of an event detail paired with the corresponding suggested detail (e.g., stop sign vs. yield sign). On the critical test items, subjects who had received MPI were dramatically less accurate than control subjects.

This *misinformation effect* is very robust and has been replicated using a variety of procedures (including naturalistic staged crimes) in labs around the world.[4] It is also often a large effect: Differences of 20% to 30% between performance on misled and control items are not unusual. And it is a very famous effect: Most introductory psychology textbooks include a brief (and uncritical) summary of Loftus's major findings, and most cast them in Loftus's theoretical terms.

According to Loftus's "overwriting" hypothesis (aka "destructive updating" or "mental-morphosis"), when the MPI is presented, it may be added to the preexisting memory record of witnessing the event in such a way that the new information destroys and replaces memory representations with which it conflicts. This theoretical account of the misinformation effect has two important implications. First, it holds that MPI can irreparably destroy the memory trace of event details. Second, it implies that the MPI becomes an integral part of the memory of witnessing the event itself, such that when subjects later remember what was suggested to them, they will experience it as remembering witnessing that thing in the event. Both of these claims have been challenged.

MEMORY IMPAIRMENT

In 1985, McCloskey and Zaragoza published a powerful critique of purported demonstrations of memory impairment in the misinformation effect.[2] Previous theorists had already argued against Loftus's overwriting hypothesis and in favor of a *coexistence* hypothesis, according to which memory for the MPI does not destroy memory for the original event detail but instead impairs people's ability to retrieve the original memory.[3] McCloskey and Zaragoza went beyond this position and argued that the methods used could not even address the question of

memory's truth: Memory distortion after exposure to misinformation, *Current Directions in Psychological Science, 1,* 121–123 (1992).

[2] M. McCloskey and M. Zaragoza, Misleading postevent information and memory for events: Arguments and evidence against memory impairment hypotheses, *Journal of Experimental Psychology: General, 114,* 1–16 (1985).

[3] See, e.g., D. A. Bekerian and J. M. Bowers, Eyewitness testimony: Were we misled? *Journal of Experimental Psychology: Learning, Memory, and Cognition, 9,* 139–145 (1983).

whether MPI impairs ability to remember event details, because a variety of demand charac-teristics and response biases could lead subjects to perform more poorly on misled items than on control items even if there were no memory impairment effect. For example, subjects who remember the event detail might nonetheless base their test responses on the suggested detail in order to play along with the perceived desires of the experimenter.

In addition to critiquing previous studies, McCloskey and Zaragoza reported new studies that used a modified test to eliminate demand characteristics and response biases. On the crit-ical test items in the modified test, subjects choose between the event detail (e.g., stop sign) and a new item not presented in either the event or the MPI (e.g., caution sign). McCloskey and Zaragoza argued that if MPI impairs memory for the event detail, then MPI should lower performance on the modified test. In six experiments, MPI had no effect on subjects' ability to discriminate between the event detail and a new distractor.

McCloskey and Zaragoza's arguments and evidence suggested that what had long been viewed as a dramatic memory phenomenon with important practical implications was merely an artifact of demand characteristics and inappropriate testing methods. This critique had a galvanizing effect on applied memory researchers, producing a flood of new studies. Although a number of researchers have recently reported support for the hypothesis that MPI impairs ability to remember event details, the issue has remained controversial.[4]

SOURCE-MONITORING CONFUSIONS

Whereas most of the controversy in this area has revolved around the memory impairment is-sue (i.e., whether MPI impairs ability to remember what was witnessed), Marcia Johnson and I have focused on the question of whether misled subjects sometimes genuinely believe they remember seeing suggested details in the event itself.[5] From a forensic point of view, the pos-sibility that witnesses can come to believe they had witnessed things that were merely sug-gested to them may be more ominous than the possibility that suggestions can impair memory for what was witnessed.

Do misled subjects ever "remember" seeing something that was only verbally suggested to them? Johnson and I argued that subjects do sometimes experience such *source-monitoring* confusions. Every autobiographical memory has a source, defined by the conditions under which that memory was acquired (where and when the event occurred, in what media and through what modalities it was apprehended, etc.). We argued that memories do not have ab-stract "tags" or "labels" that specify their sources. Rather, memories include various kinds of information, such as records of the perceptual qualities of an experience, and the sources of

---

[4]For evidence of memory impairment among adults tested with the modified test, as well as a review of the memory impairment debate, see R. F. Belli, P. D. Windshitl, T. T. McCarthy, and S. E. Winfrey, Detecting memory im-pairment with a modified test procedure: Manipulating retention interval with centrally presented event items, *Jour-nal of Experimental Psychology: Learning, Memory, and Cognition, 18,* 356–367 (1992).

[5]For a review of the relationship between source monitoring and eyewitness testimony, see D. S. Lindsay, Mem-ory source monitoring and eyewitness testimony, in *Adult Eyewitness Testimony,* D. F. Ross, J. D. Read, and M. P. Toglia, Eds. (Cambridge University Press, New York, in press).

event memories are identified via decision-making processes performed when the events are recollected. People sometimes struggle consciously to identify the source of a recollection, but more often make such attributions without conscious awareness of any decision making.

A source-monitoring error occurs when a memory derived from one source is misattributed to another source (e.g., you recall something you heard Kathy say, and mistakenly remember the speaker as Liz). The likelihood of source misattributions varies with the amount and nature of the source-specific information in the memory record, the discriminability of the potential sources, and the stringency of the decision processes and criteria used during remembering. Thus, for example, you are more likely to mistakenly remember Liz saying something you actually heard from Kathy if the memory record is vague than if it is clear, if the two people are similar to one another than if they are dissimilar, or if the source attribution is made quickly and automatically than if it is made with careful deliberation.

One implication of these ideas is that eyewitnesses may misidentify memories of information presented before the event as memories of things they saw in the event itself, just as they may misidentify memories of postevent suggestions as memories of the event. We have demonstrated that this is indeed the case in a study in which verbal misinformation was presented before subjects viewed the scene about which they were later questioned.[6] At test, subjects often claimed to have seen things in the event that were in fact merely suggested in the information before the visual scene.

Consistent with the idea that the stringency of source-monitoring criteria plays an important role in eyewitness suggestibility, in other experiments we found that a suggestibility effect obtained among subjects tested with a recognition test was eliminated among subjects tested with a source-monitoring test that required them to identify the sources of their memories of each test item. The two tests consisted of the same list of items: Subjects given the recognition test were to respond "yes" to items they remembered seeing in the visual event and "no" to all other items, whereas subjects given the source-monitoring test were to indicate, for each item, whether they remembered seeing that item only in the event, only in the postevent information, in both sources, or in neither. As is typically found, subjects tested with the recognition test often claimed to have seen suggested items in the event. In contrast, subjects tested with the source-monitoring test correctly attributed their memories of suggested details to the postevent information. We viewed these findings as evidence that subjects tested with recognition tests sometimes misidentify memories of MPI as memories of the event because they are using lax or inappropriate source-monitoring criteria. The source-monitoring instructions led subjects to use more stringent criteria and thereby correctly attribute memories of suggested details to the postevent information.[7]

---

[6]D. S. Lindsay and M. K. Johnson, The reversed suggestibility effect, *Bulletin of the Psychonomic Society, 27,* 111–113 (1989).

[7]Zaragoza and Koshmider interpreted very similar results from independent research as a demonstration of the role of demand characteristics (i.e., they argued that the source-monitoring test reduced demands to report having seen suggested details). See M. S. Zaragoza and J. W. Koshmider, III, Misled subjects may know more than their performance implies, *Journal of Experimental Psychology: Learning, Memory, and Cognition, 15,* 246–255 (1989).

More recent research demonstrates that even subjects tested with source-monitoring tests sometimes claim to have seen suggested details in the event, provided conditions make it difficult to discriminate between memories of the event and memories of the MPI.[8] For example, Zaragoza and colleagues have shown that illusory memories of eyewitnessing are more likely to be obtained on a source-monitoring test if subjects are instructed to form visual images of the postevent information when it is presented.

Unfortunately, source-monitoring tests do not altogether eliminate the possibility that demand characteristics might contribute to apparent source-monitoring confusions. Subjects are led to believe that everything in the postevent information was also in the event, and they may wish to show that they paid attention to both the event and the postevent information. This may motivate subjects to claim that they remember things from both sources even if they are aware that they remember them only from the postevent information. Consistent with this account, subjects in these studies very rarely claimed that suggested details had been seen only in the event; rather, when they erred, they claimed that suggested details had been in both the event and the postevent information.

More compelling evidence that subjects sometimes mistake memories of postevent suggestions as memories of the event itself comes from a study using Jacoby's *opposition* procedure.[8] In this experiment, conditions were set up that the effect of knowingly using memories of the postevent information would be opposite to the effect of genuine memory source confusions. To do this, we correctly informed subjects at test that the postevent information did not include any correct answers to the test questions. Acquisition conditions were manipulated such that remembering the suggestions and their source would be very easy for some subjects and relatively difficult for other subjects. In the easy condition, subjects received the MPI 2 days after viewing the event, minutes before taking the test, and under conditions that differed from those in which they viewed the event. Thus, at test, it would be easy for these subjects to remember the MPI and its source. Subjects in the difficult condition, in contrast, received the MPI minutes after viewing the event, under very similar conditions, 2 days before taking the test. Thus, at the time of the test, it would be relatively difficult for these subjects to differentiate between memories of the event and memories of the postevent narrative.

Subjects were given a cued-recall test with six questions: Three concerned details about which MPI had been given, and three were control questions. Before taking the test, subjects were explicitly and emphatically told not to report anything they remembered from the postevent information. Subjects in the easy condition showed no tendency to report suggested details, indicating that subjects tried to avoid reporting information from the postevent information. Nonetheless, subjects in the difficult condition quite often reported the suggested

[8]D. S. Lindsay, Misleading suggestions can impair eyewitnesses' ability to remember event details, *Journal of Experimental Psychology: Learning, Memory, and Cognition, 16,* 1077–1083 (1990). For a review of Jacoby's development of the opposition procedure, see L. L. Jacoby and C. M. Kelley, A process-dissociation framework for investigating unconscious influences: Freudian slips, projective tests, subliminal perception, and signal detection theory, *Current Directions in Psychological Science, 1,* 174–179 (1992).

details as things they recalled seeing in the event. Even though subjects were specifically trying to avoid reporting memories of the MPI, they frequently did so.

MEMORY IMPAIRMENT REDUX

The opposition study described above also provided important evidence that MPI can impair subjects' ability to remember event details. Although subjects in the easy condition were able to identify the source of their memories of suggested details (and so did not erroneously report seeing them in the event), the misleading suggestions nonetheless hampered these subjects' ability to report the event details: Correct recall of event details was significantly lower on misled items than on control items. Correct recall of event details was significantly impaired by MPI even among those subjects in the easy condition who never reported any suggested details. Neither differential rates of guessing nor differential response criteria can account for the lower level of recall of event details on misled than control items in the easy condition. This is powerful evidence that misleading suggestions can impair eyewitnesses' ability to remember event details.

SUMMARY AND CONCLUSIONS

Recent research indicates that much of the large and dramatic misinformation effect typically obtained with Loftus's standard procedure is due to aware uses of memory for the postevent information. For example, some subjects may fail to notice the critical detail in the event but remember the MPI; because the postevent information is presented as a reliable source of information, such subjects would quite reasonably rely upon it when tested.

Yet it is clear that subjects do sometimes experience memories of things they read or heard about after the event as recollections of seeing those things in the event. Such source confusions are more likely when the event and the MPI give rise to high similar memory records and when source-monitoring criteria are lax. However, compelling illusory memories of eyewitnessing sometimes occur even when criteria are very stringent—even when subjects are trying to avoid making such errors.

There is also growing evidence that misleading suggestions can impair subjects' ability to remember event details. Current evidence indicates that memory impairment effects are likely to be small and nonreliable when memory is tested with appropriate recognition probes (as in McCloskey and Zaragoza's modified test) but may be considerably larger and more robust when appropriate recall measures are used (as in the opposition test). Debate about the mechanisms that underlie memory impairment effects (e.g., whether MPI degrades memory traces of event details or merely interferes with retrieval) is likely to continue for some time. At present, we can conclude that under some conditions MPI can impair people's ability to remember what they witnessed and can lead them to believe that they witnessed things they did not, but that neither of these effects is as large or robust as earlier research suggested.

QUESTIONS

1. Explain the process by which Loftus believes MPIs distort memory. Why does Lindsay disagree with Loftus's position?

2. What does Lindsay mean by "source-monitoring"? Is this a bias in storing information or recalling information?

3. In what three ways did the easy and difficult conditions differ in Lindsay's test using Jacoby's opposition procedure? Can we tell from this test which of the three differences had the greatest impact of memory?

4. Police normally try to question eyewitnesses immediately after a crime has occurred. What are the pros and cons of this strategy for eyewitness accuracy?

5. In addition to questioning eyewitnesses immediately after an event, police sometimes question them again days later. How might this strategy affect eyewitness accuracy?

PART VIII

THE SOCIAL CONTEXT OF SOCIETY

CHAPTER 14

GROUPS: JOINING WITH OTHERS

Reading 27: Classic

The Dynamogenic Factors in Pacemaking and Competition

Norman Triplett

Norman Triplett's study of "dynamogenic" factors in competition is widely considered to be the first ever social psychological study. Reviewing speed records in three different types of bicycle races, Triplett noticed that cyclists went much faster when racing with other cyclists than when racing alone. This fact was well known among cyclists, who believed that racing with another increased speeds, on average, by 20 to 30 seconds per mile.

A host of explanations, both mechanical and psychological, had been proposed to explain the observed faster times in competition and "paced" races, some of which we know today to be perfectly accurate. But Triplett believed that another set of factors was operating in addition to those that had already been proposed. His dynamogenic theory held that the physical presence of other riders increased a rider's level of arousal, which released additional energy.

To test this theory, Triplett designed a study similar to cycling but in which the mechanical and psychological factors other than dynamogenic would not be present. If competition increased performance in this experimental situation, it could only be due to the physical presence of the other competitor.

In this article, Triplett describes the various theories that can account for the benefits of paced races, the apparatus he built to test the dynamogenic theory, and the results he obtained. As expected, the majority of subjects exhibited faster times when competing with another than when performing alone.

✤

PART I: THEORIES ACCOUNTING FOR THE FASTER TIME OF PACED AND COMPETITION RACES

Of the seven or eight not wholly distinct theories which have been advanced to account for the faster time made in paced as compared with unpaced competitive races and paced races against time as against unpaced races against time, a number need only be stated very briefly. They are grouped according to their nature and first are given two mechanical theories.

Source: Triplett, N. (1897). The dynamogenic factors in pacemaking and competition. *American Journal of Psychology, 9,* 507–533.

Suction Theory

Those holding to this as the explanation assert that the vacuum left behind the pacing machine draws the rider following, along with it. Anderson's ride of a mile a minute at Roodhouse, Ill., with the locomotive as pacemaker, is the strongest argument in its favor. Those maintaining this theory believe that the racer paced by a tandem is at a disadvantage as compared with the racer paced by a quod or a larger machine, as the suction exerted is not so powerful.

The Shelter Theory

This is closely related to the foregoing. Dr. Turner accepts it as a partial explanation of the aid to be gained from a pace, holding that the pacemaker or the leading competitor serves as a shelter from the wind, and that "a much greater amount of exertion, purely muscular, is required from a man to drive a machine when he is leading than when he is following on account of the resistance of the air, and the greater the amount of wind blowing the greater the exertion, and conversely, the greater the shelter obtained the less the exertion."

This is the theory held, in general, by racers themselves. One of the champion riders of the country recently expressed this common view in a letter, as follows: "It is true that some very strong unpaced riders do not have any sort of success in paced racing. The only reason I can give for this is just simply that they have not studied the way to follow pace so as to be shielded from the wind. No matter which way it blows there is always a place where the man following pace can be out of the wind."

Encouragement Theory

The presence of a friend on the pacing machine to encourage and keep up the spirits of the rider is claimed to be of great help. The mental disposition has been long known to be of importance in racing as in other cases where energy is expended. It is still as true as in Virgil's time that the winners "can because they think they can."

The Brain Worry Theory

This theory shows why it is difficult for the leader in an unpaced competition race to win. For "a much greater amount of brain worry is incurred by making the pace than by waiting" (following). The man leading "is in a fidget the whole time whether he is going fast enough to exhaust his adversary; he is full of worry as to when that adversary means to commence his spurt; his nervous system is generally strung up, and at concert pitch, and his muscular and nervous efforts act and react on each other, producing an ever-increasing exhaustion, which both dulls the impulse-giving power of the brain and the impulse-receiving or contractile power of the muscles."

Theory of Hypnotic Suggestions

A curious theory, lately advanced, suggests the possibility that the strained attention given to the revolving wheel of the pacing machine in front produces a sort of hypnotism and that the accompanying muscular exaltation is the secret of the endurance shown by some long-distance riders in paced races. Notice that Michael was able to make the last mile of his great 30 mile competition race the fastest of all and one of the fastest ever ridden.

The Automatic Theory

This is also a factor which favors the waiting rider, and gives him a marked advantage. The leader, as has been noted, must use his brain to direct every movement of his muscles. As he becomes more distressed it requires a more intense exertion of will power to force his machine through the resisting air. On the other hand, the "waiter" rides automatically. He has nothing to do but hang on. "His brain having inaugurated the movement leaves it to the spinal cord to continue it and only resumes its functions when a change of direction or speed is necessary."— (Lagrange.) When he comes to the final spurt, his brain, assuming control again, imparts to the muscles a winning stimulus, while the continued brain work of the leader has brought great fatigue.

These facts seem to have large foundation in truth. The lesser amount of fatigue incurred in paced trials is a matter of general knowledge. It is a common experience with wheelmen, and within that of the writer, that when following a lead on a long ride the feeling of automatic action becomes very pronounced, giving the sensation of a strong force pushing from behind. Of course the greater the distance ridden the more apparent becomes the saving in energy from automatic riding, as time is required to establish the movement. It may be remembered, in this connection, that while the average gain of the paced over the unpaced record is −34.4 seconds, the difference between them for the first mile is only 23.8 seconds.

As between the pacer and the paced, every advantage seems to rest with the latter. The two mechanical factors of suction and shelter, so far as they are involved, assist the rider who follows. So the psychological theories, the stimulation from encouragement, the peculiar power induced by hypnotism, and the staying qualities of automatic action, if of help at all, directly benefit the paced rider. The element of disadvantage induced by brain action, on the contrary, belongs more especially to the rider who leads.

The Dynamogenic Factors

The remaining factors to be discussed are those which the experiments on competition, detailed in the second part hereof, attempt to explain. No effort is made to weaken the force of the foregoing factors in accounting for the better time of paced races in comparison with unpaced races of the same type, but the facts of this study are given to throw whatever additional light they may.

This theory of competition holds that the bodily presence of another rider is a stimulus to the racer in arousing the competitive instinct; that another can thus be the means of releasing or freeing nervous energy for him that he cannot of himself release; and, further, that the sight of movement in that other by perhaps suggesting a higher rate of speed, is also an inspiration to greater effort. These are the factors that had their counterpart in the experimental study following; and it is along these lines that the facts determined are to find their interpretation.

PART II: THE EXPERIMENTAL STUDY

From the laboratory competitions to be described, abstraction was made of nearly all the forces above outlined. In the 40 seconds the average trial lasted, no shelter from the wind was required, nor was any suction exerted, the only brain worry incident was that of maintaining a sufficiently high rate of speed to defeat the competitors. From the shortness of the time and nature of the case, generally, it is doubtful if any automatic movements could be established. On the other hand, the effort was intensely voluntary. It may be likened to the 100 yard dash— a sprint from beginning to end.

Description of Apparatus

The apparatus for this study consisted of two fishing reels whose cranks turned in circles of one and three-fourths inches diameter. These were arranged on a Y-shaped framework clamped to the top of a heavy table, as shown in Figure 14–1. The sides of this framework were spread sufficiently far apart to permit of two persons turning side by side. Bands of twisted silk cord ran over the well lacquered axes of the reels and were supported at C and D, two meters distant, by two small pulleys. The records were taken from the course A D. The other course B C was used merely for pacing or competition purposes. The wheel on the side from which the records were taken communicated the movement made to a recorder, the stylus of which traced a curve on the drum of a kymograph. The direction of this curve corresponded to the rate of turning, as the greater the speed the shorter and straighter the resulting line.

Method of Conducting the Experiment

A subject taking the experiment was required to practice turning the reel until he had become accustomed to the machine. After a short period of rest the different trials were made with five-minute intervals between to obviate the possible effects of fatigue.

A trial consisted in turning the reel at the highest rate of speed until a small flag sewed to the silk band had made four circuits of the four-meter course. The time of the trial was taken by means of a stop-watch. The direction of the curves made on the drum likewise furnished graphic indications of the difference in time made between trials.

Statement of Results

In the course of the work the records of nearly 225 persons of all ages were taken. However, all the tables given below, and all statements made, unless otherwise specified, are based on

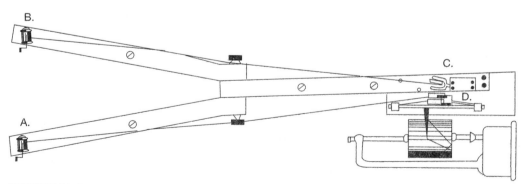

FIGURE 14–1
Competition machine.

the records of 40 children taken in the following manner: After the usual preliminaries of practice, six trials were made by each of 20 subjects in this order: first a trial alone, followed by a trial in competition, then another alone, and thus alternating through the six efforts, giving three trials alone and three in competition. Six trials were taken by 20 other children of about the same age, the order of trials in this case being the first trial alone, second alone, third a competition trial, fourth alone, fifth a competition, and sixth alone.[1] The 20 subjects given in Group A and Group B, of Table I, in nearly all cases make marked reductions in the competition trials. The averages show large gains in these trials and small gains or even losses for the succeeding trials alone. The second trial for Group A is a competition, for Group B a trial alone. The gain between the first and second trials of the first group is 5.6 seconds, between the first and second trials of the second group, 2.52 seconds. The latter represents the practice effect—always greatest in the first trials, the former the element of competition plus the practice. The third trial in Group A—a trial alone—is .72 seconds slower than the preceding race trial. The third trial in Group B—a competition—is 4.48 seconds faster than the preceding trial alone. The fourth trials in these two groups are on an equality, as regards practice, from an equal number of trials of the same kind. In the first case the gain over the preceding trial is 3.32 seconds. In the latter there is a loss of 1.58 seconds from the time of the preceding competition trial. In like manner there is an equality of conditions in regard to the sixth trial of these groups, and again the effect of competition plainly appears, the competition trial gaining 2.12 seconds, and the trial alone losing .82 seconds with respect to the preceding trial. These are decided differences. Curves No. I in Chart I is a graphical representation of them.

The 10 subjects whose records are given in Table II are of interest. With them stimulation brought a loss of control. In one or more of the competition trials of each subject in this group the time is very much slower than that made in the preceding trial alone. Most frequently this is true of the first trial in competition, but with some was characteristic of every race. In all, 14 of the 25 races run by this group were equal to or slower than the preceding trial alone. This seems to be brought about in large measure by the mental attitude of the subject: an intense desire to win, for instance, often resulting in over-stimulation. Accompanying phenomena were labored breathing, flushed faces and a stiffening or contraction of the muscles of the arm. A number of young children of from 5 to 9 years, not included in our group of 40, exhibited the phenomena most strikingly, the rigidity of the arm preventing free movement and in some cases resulting in an almost total inhibition of movement. The effort to continue turning in these cases was by a swaying of the whole body.

This seems a most interesting fact and confirmatory of the probable order of development of the muscles as given by Dr. Hall and others. In the case of those sufficiently developed to have the fast forearm movement, fatigue or over-stimulation seemed to bring a recurrence to the whole arm and shoulder movement of early childhood, and if the fatigue or excitement was sufficiently intense, to the whole body movement, while younger children easily fell into the swaying movement when affected by either of the causes named.

---

[1]In the tables, A represents a trial alone, C, a trial in competition.

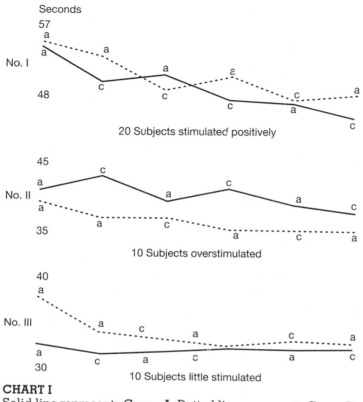

CHART I
Solid line represents Group A. Dotted line represents Group B.

It reminds one of the way in which fatigue of a small muscle used in ergographic work will cause the subject to attempt to draw on his larger muscles, or of the man who moves to the city and acquires the upright carriage and springing step of the city-bred man, who when greatly fatigued, insensible falls into the old "clodhopper" gait. This tendency to revert to earlier movements and also old manners of speech, as Höpfner has shown in his "Fatigue of School Children," is common, when, for any reason, the centers of control are interfered with. It may be said, therefore, that in the work under consideration the chief difference between this group and the large group in Table I, was a difference in control; the stimulation inhibiting the proper function of the motor centers in the one case, and reinforcing it in the other. This, at least, seemed apparent from the characteristics exhibited by the two classes. Observation of the subjects of this class under trial, and careful scrutiny of their graphic records show how decided gains were sometimes lost by the subject "going to pieces" at the critical point of the race, not being able to endure the nervous strain. Yet there exists no sharp line of division between subjects stimulated to make faster time and those affected in the opposite way. In some instances the nervous excitement acted adversely in every race trial, while in

TABLE I　SUBJECTS STIMULATED POSITIVELY

	Age	A	C	A	C	A	C
			Group A				
Violet F.	10	54.4	42.6	45.2	41.	42.	46.
Anna P.	9	67.	57.	55.4	50.4	49.	44.8
Willie H.	12	37.8	38.8	43.	39.	37.2	33.4
Bessie V.	11	46.2	41.	39.	30.2	33.6	32.4
Howard C.	11	42.	36.4	39.	41.	37.8	34.
Mary M.	11	48.	44.8	52.	44.6	43.8	40.
Lois P.	11	53.	45.6	44.	44.	40.6	35.8
Inez K.	13	37.	35.	35.8	34.	34.	32.6
Harvey L.	9	49.	42.6	39.6	37.6	36.	35.
Lora F.	11	40.4	35.	33.	35.	30.2	29.
Average	11	47.48	41.88	42.6	39.28	38.42	36.3
P. E		6.18	4.45	4.68	3.83	3.74	3.74
Gains			5.6	.72	3.32	.86	2.12

	Age	A	A	C	A	C	A
			Group B				
Stephen M.	13	51.2	50.	43.	41.8	39.8	41.2*
Mary W.	13	56.	53.	45.8	49.4	45.	43.*
Bertha A.	10	56.2	49.	48.	46.8	41.4	44.4
Clara L.	8	52.	44.	46.	45.6	44.	45.2
Helen M.	10	45.	45.6	35.8	46.2	40.	40.
Gracie W.	12	56.6	50.	42.	39.	40.2	41.4
Dona R.	15	34.	37.2	36.	41.4	37.	32.8
Pearl C.	13	43.	43.	40.	40.6	33.8	35.
Clyde G.	13	36.	35.	32.4	33.	31.	35.
Lucile W.	10	52.	50.	43.	44.	38.	40.2
Average	11.7	48.2	45.68	41.2	42.78	39.	39.82
P. E.		5.6	4.	3.42	3.17	2.89	2.84
Gains			2.52	4.48	1.58	3.78	.82

*Left-handed.

IX—35

others, a gain in control enabled the subject to make a material reduction in the last competition. A. B., one of the three adults affected adversely, is an athletic young man, a fine tennis and handball player, and known to be stimulated in contests of these kinds. It was noticed that in his competition trials time was lost because of his attempt to take advantage of the larger muscles of the arm and shoulder. After many trials and injunctions to avoid the movement, he gained sufficient control to enable him to reduce the time in the competitions.

TABLE II SUBJECTS STIMULATED ADVERSELY

	Age	A	Group A C	A	C	A	C
Jack R.	9	44.2	44.	41.8	48.	44.2	41.
Helen F.	9	44.	51.	43.8	44.	43.	41.2
Emma P.	11	38.4	42.	37.	39.6	36.6	32.
Warner J.	11	41.6	43.6	43.4	43.	40.	48.
Genevieve M.	12	36.	36.	32.6	32.8	31.2	34.8
Average	10.4	40.84	43.32	39.72	41.48	39.	37.4
P. E.		2.41	3.57	3.25	3.85	3.55	2.52

	Age	A	Group B A	C	A	C	A
Hazel M.	11	38.	35.8	38.2	37.2	35.	42.
George B.	12	39.2	36.	37.6	34.2	36.	33.8
Mary B.	11	50.	46.	43.4	42.	48.	36.8
Carlisle B.	14	37.	35.4	35.	33.4	36.4	31.4
Eddie H.	11	31.2	29.2	27.6	27.	26.8	28.8
Average	11.8	39.08	36.48	36.36	34.76	34.4	34.56
P. E.		4.61	4.07	3.89	3.71	5.33	3.45

A. V., an adult of nervous organization, went half through his race with a great gain over his trial alone, but seeing his antagonist pushing him closely, broke down and lost the most of the gain made in the first half. The time of the trial alone was 38.6 seconds, that of the competition was 37.2 seconds. A comparison of the time in which the halves of the trials were made was computed in the following way: On the ordinate of the graph is measured the distance the stylus travels across the drum during 150 turns of the reel—the number in a trial. The distance on the abscissa between the ordinates running through the ends of the curve of any trial gives the time of the trial.

Parallel abscissas were drawn at the extremities of the curves, and a third one-half way between them. Half of the turns made in a trial were thus on each side of this middle line, and the times in which these turns were made were proportional to the segments of this line made by the curve intersecting it. By this means it was found that A. V. made the first 75 turns in his competition trial in 15 seconds, the second half in 22.2 seconds. By the same means, each half of the preceding trial alone was 19.3 seconds—an exception to the rule that the last half is slower because of fatigue.

Other curves when worked out in this way gave similar results. The time record, therefore, it must be seen, is not always a true index to the amount of stimulation present. Had the trials consisted of but half as many turns, the effect of competition as it appears in the tables

TABLE III   SUBJECTS LITTLE AFFECTED BY COMPETITION

	Age	A	Group A C	A	C	A	C
Albert P.	13	29.	28.	27.	29.	27.	28.6
Milfred V.	17	36.4	29.	29.4	30.2	30.2	32.2
Harry V.	12	32.	32.	32.6	32.6	32.6	31.6
Robt. H.	12	31.4	31.4	32.2	35.4	35.	32.4
John T.	11	30.2	30.8	32.8	30.6	32.8	31.8
Average	13	31.8	30.24	30.8	31.56	31.5	31.3
P. E.		1.9	1.13	1.71	1.7	2.06	1.05

	Age	A	Group B A	C	A	C	A
Lela T.	10	45.	37.4	36.8	36.	37.2	38.
Lura L.	11	42.	39.	38.	37.	37.	38.
Mollie A.	13	38.	30.	28.	30.	30.2	29.6
Anna F.	11	35.	31.8	32.4	30.	32.	30.4
Ora R.	14	37.2	30.	29.	27.8	28.4	26.8
Average	11.8	39.44	33.64	32.84	32.16	32.96	32.16
P. E.		3.11	2.88	3.03	2.75	2.69	3.71

would have been shown much more constantly. Table II would have been a smaller group if indeed any necessity existed for retaining it.

A comparison of the time made by the different groups shows that the subjects of Table I are much slower than those of Table II, and that a still greater difference exists between this group and the subjects found in Table III. It may be said that they are slower because of greater sluggishness of disposition, and that the reductions made are largely a result of the subjects warming up. This, indeed, may be a part of the cause for it, but as the larger reductions coincide with the competition trials this cannot be held to completely account for it. A glance over the individual records discovers some facts which furnish a plausible partial explanation, when taken in connection with the following fact. The age at which children acquire control of the wrist movements, a large factor in turning the reel with speed, was found to be about 11 years in general, although a few of 9 and 10 years had this power. Now, of the 20 subjects composing Table I, 7 are 10 years of age or younger, while two others, age 13, are left-handed and being compelled to use the right hand are slow in consequence. So, here are 9 subjects, a number nearly equal to the group in Table II or Table III, who had a reason for being slow. Were these omitted from the count, the time of the initial trial would be found not to vary materially from that of Table II.

Besides the lack of muscular development of the younger subjects mentioned above, many of the subjects of Table I seemed not to have proper ideals of speed. The desire to beat, if it did nothing else, brought them to a sense of what was possible for them. The arousal of their competitive instincts and the idea of a faster movement, perhaps, in the contestant, induced greater concentration of energy.

The subjects in Table III are a small group who seemed very little affected by competition. They made very fast time, but they are older than the average; their muscular control was good, and they had the forearm movements. Practice gains while somewhat apparent at first in some cases, are, as shown by curve No. 3 of the chart, on the whole, less in amount. Their drum records show fewer fluctuations and irregularities, and less pronounced fatigue curves at the end.

There seems to be a striking analogy between these subjects and those racing men who are fast without a pace, but can do little or no better in a paced or competition race.

CONCLUDING STATEMENT

From the above facts regarding the laboratory races we infer that the bodily presence of another contestant participating simultaneously in the race serves to liberate latent energy not ordinarily available. This inference is further justified by the difference in time between the paced competition races and the paced races against time, amounting to an average of 5.15 seconds per mile up to 25 miles. The factors of shelter from the wind, encouragement, brain worry, hypnotic suggestion, and automatic movement are common to both, while the competitors participate simultaneously in person only in the first.

In the next place the sight of the movements of the pacemakers or leading competitors, and the idea of higher speed, furnished by this or some other means, are probably in themselves dynamogenic factors of some consequence.

QUESTIONS

1. What two mechanical theories are suggested to account for the effects of pacing? How does the influence of the dynamogenic factors differ from other psychological factors?

2. Which factors does Triplett say most cyclists themselves believe are responsible for the benefits of pacing? Which factors does Triplett believe are responsible?

3. Which suggested factors that influence cycle races are also present in the fishing-reel races that Triplett designed?

4. Of the 40 children whose data are discussed, what percentage show marked improvement in the competition phases? What percentage preformed equally well?

5. How does Triplett explain his findings? Can the dynamogenic process explain all three different performance patterns observed with only the dynamogenic factors?

Reading 28: Contemporary

Linking Groupthink to Unethical Behavior in Organizations

Ronald R. Sims

Many people in America today believe that our role in the war in Vietnam was plagued by over-confidence, poor judgments, and many very bad decisions. How could the combined military and civilian intellects of such a sophisticated country make so many decisions that, in retrospect, appear so obviously wrong? According to social psychologist Irving Janis, the answer lies in a phenomenon known as "groupthink."

The country was on the edge of war in Vietnam when Janis stumbled onto the concept of groupthink. Discussing the Bay of Pigs incident, Janis was struck by several dynamics of President John F. Kennedy's inner circle of advisers that may have contributed to their overlooking important evidence casting doubts on the viability of a planned invasion of Cuba. Today these same group dynamics have been linked with many of the most famous military blunders in modern times.

Does groupthink operate outside of government decisions? In the following article, Ronald Sims explains that the problems of groupthink are common in corporate America, too. Here they do not lead to failed invasions or exploding space shuttles, but they can have serious consequences. Sims argues that groupthink can lead to a culture of unethical behavior within a company. To illustrate this, he cites three recent cases of corporate scandals and suggests how groupthink might have been involved.

❖

Issues of corporate morality and business ethics are of concern to both management and their organizations (Jansen and Von Glinow, 1985; Schermerhorn et al., 1991). These issues include social responsibility, conflict of interest, payoffs, product safety, liability, and whistleblowing (Jansen and Von Glinow, 1985). On the popular front, many national newspapers and business magazines offer continuing glimpses of corporate and managerial misbehavior. Despite all the attention, such inquiries rarely and explicitly examine the link between organizational culture, and more specifically, "groupthink," and individuals who behave "unethically." It is far more common and dramatic to focus on individual culpability, a practice organizations may support out of sheer self-interest. However, greater knowledge of the role of groupthink in unethical actions may change attributions of individual culpability.

The connection between groupthink and unethical behavior could be especially helpful in understanding the role of groupthink when individuals behave unethically as well as

Source: Sims, R. R. (1992). Linking groupthink to unethical behavior in organizations. *Journal of Business Ethics, 11,* 651–662.

providing a basis for altering behavior in a more ethical direction. The purpose of this paper is to discuss the importance of groupthink in contributing to unethical behavior in organizations. The paper also will show how groupthink contributed to unethical behavior in several organizations (Beech-Nut, E. F. Hutton, and Salomon Brothers). In addition, symptoms of groupthink such as arrogance, overcommitment, and excessive cr blind loyalty to the group will be discussed along with two methods for programming conflict (devil's advocate and dialectic) into organization and group decisions (Cosier and Schwenk, 1991). Finally, the paper introduces some prescriptions for reducing the probability of groupthink. However, before discussing the relationship between groupthink and unethical behavior, a definition of groupthink and several classic examples of groupthink in action are highlighted.

GROUPTHINK DEFINED

Irving Janis (1972, 1982) laid the basis for a theory of causes and effects of groupthink, "a collective pattern of defensive avoidance" (Janis and Mann, 1977, p. 129). Janis described several shared characteristics of cohesive decision-making groups that have been responsible for some policy debacles. The following quotation from Janis and Mann (1977, p. 130) is a good example.

> Many historic fiascoes can be traced to defective policy making on the part of government leaders who receive social support from their in-group advisors. A series of historic examples by Janis (1972) suggests that the following four groups of policy advisors, like Kimmel's in-group of naval commanders, were dominated by concurrence seeking or groupthink and displayed characteristic symptoms of defensive avoidance: (1) Neville Chamberlain's inner circle, whose members supported the policy of appeasement of Hitler during 1937 and 1938, despite repeated warnings and events that it would have adverse consequences; (2) President Truman's advisory group, whose members supported the decision to escalate the war in North Korea despite firm warnings by the Chinese Communist government that U.S. entry into North Korea would be met with armed resistance from the Chinese; (3) President Kennedy's inner circle, whose members supported the decision to launch the Bay of Pigs invasion of Cuba despite the availability of information indicating that it would be an unsuccessful venture and would damage U.S. relations with other countries; (4) President Johnson's close advisors, who supported the decision to escalate the war in Vietnam despite intelligence reports and other information indicating that this course of action would not defeat the Vietcong or the North Vietnamese and would entail unfavorable political consequences within the United States. All these groupthink dominated groups were characterized by strong pressures toward uniformity, which inclined their members to avoid raising controversial issues, questioning weak arguments, or calling a halt to soft-headed thinking.

There also is evidence that groupthink was at work in the Nixon entourage, which was responsible for the Watergate cover-up, although there is some question of the cohesiveness of this group (Janis, 1982).

To add a contemporary flavor to the discussion, consider the tragedy of the Space Shuttle Challenger. This decision was the product of a flawed group decision as much as it was failure of technology. Strong pressures for uniformity also characterized the process surrounding the flawed decision of the Reagan administration to exchange arms for hostages with Iran and to continue commitment to the Nicaraguan Contras in the face of several congressional amendments limiting or banning aid.

One may be tempted to assume that groupthink is peculiar to group decision-making in government and military settings. However, evidence suggests that it frequently occurs in the business world. The design and marketing of the ill-fated Edsel automobile have been attributed to groupthink (Huseman and Driver, 1979).

GROUPTHINK: A PRECURSOR TO UNETHICAL BEHAVIOR

What guides the behavior of managers and employees as they cope with ethical dilemmas? Or keeping in line with the main focus of this paper, what results in the unethical behavior of some groups in organizations? Trevino (1986) has developed a model that suggests that individuals' (and groups') standards of right and wrong are not the sole determinant of their decisions. Instead, these beliefs interact with other individual characteristics (such as locus of control) and situational forces (such as an organization's rewards and punishments and its culture). All of these factors shape individual and group decisions and behavior that results from them. Trevino's model shows how people can choose to engage in acts they consider unethical when the culture of an organization and its prevailing reward structure overwhelm personal belief systems.

As evidenced in Trevino's (1986) work, organizational culture is a key component when looking at ethical behavior. It is the contention of this paper that the literature on "groupthink" (Janis, 1972) may help explain why some organizations develop cultures in which some individuals and groups knowingly commit unethical acts, or ignore them even though they believe the activities to be wrong. The presence or absence of ethical behavior in organizational members' actions is both influenced by the prevailing culture (ethical climate) and, in turn, partially determines the culture's view of ethical issues. The organizational culture may promote the assumption of responsibility for actions taken by individuals and groups, thereby increasing the probability that both will behave in an ethical manner. Alternatively, the culture may diffuse responsibility for the consequences of unethical behavior, thereby making such behavior more likely. In addition, there is the increased potential for groupthink, a precursor to organizational counternorms and unethical behavior.

According to Janis, groupthink is "a mode of thinking that people engage in when they are deeply involved in a cohesive in-group, when the members' striving for unanimity overrides their motivation to realistically appraise alternative courses of action" (Janis, 1972). During groupthink small groups develop shared illusions and related norms and that interfere with critical thinking and reality testing. Bales' (1950) studies of groups whose members did not previously know one another supports Janis' concept of groupthink. For the purposes of this paper, groupthink occurs when a group places a higher priority on organizational counternorms that lead to organizational benefits, thus encouraging and supporting unethical behavior. In addition, these counternorms are shaped and maintained by key organizational actors and the organization's reward system.

From this analysis of good and bad decisions made by such groups, Janis argues that antecedent conditions lead to a concurrence-seeking tendency (groupthink) in small decision-making groups (Janis and Mann, 1977).

Antecedents to groupthink are high cohesiveness, the insularity of the decision-making group, and lack of methodological procedures for searching for appraising information. It may be led in a highly directive manner, and it may operate under conditions of high stress combined with low hope for finding a better solution than the one favored by the leader or other influential people. Particularly under stress, members of the group develop a number of cognitive defenses that result in a collective pattern of avoidance. These defenses include (1) misjudging relevant warnings, (2) inventing new arguments to support a chosen policy, (3) failing to explore ominous implications of ambiguous events, (4) forgetting information that would enable a challenging event to be interpreted correctly, and (5) misperceiving signs of the onset of actual danger. . . .

Just like entering an organization, employees entering a group are provided opportunities to become schooled in and committed to the group's goals, objectives, and ways of conducting business. Such commitment is the relative strength of an individual's identification with and involvement in a particular group. It usually includes the following factors . . . : (1) group cohesiveness—a strong belief in the group's goals and values; (2) a willingness to exert considerable effort on behalf of the group; (3) a strong desire to continue as a group member; (4) excessive and almost blind loyalty to the group; (5) arrogance and overconfidence; (6) a bottom-line mentality; (7) insulation from ethical opinion and control; and (8) leader promotion of unethical solutions (that is, any behaviors that ensure that the group wins). This kind of commitment to the group then is not simply loyalty to a group. Rather, it is an ongoing process through which group members express their concern for the group and its continued success and well-being even to the extent of committing unethical actions.

A major factor contributing to the groups' defective decision making is that for each member of the cohesive group one particular incentive looms large: the approval or disapproval of his or her fellow group members and their leader. . . . The group is likely to perceive a few ethical alternatives and to ignore potential problems with the preferred alternative. The group may reject any opinion that does not support the preferred alternative, and it is unlikely to reconsider an alternative previously dismissed by the group, even in light of new evidence. Decisions made through such a process are not always unethical, but there is a higher probability of the occurrence of unethical behavior.

Groupthink can occur in decision making within almost any organization, as may have been the case at Beech-Nut, E. F. Hutton, and more recently at Salomon Brothers. The experiences provide examples of how even the most reputable of companies can suffer from an ethical breakdown through groupthink and subsequent poor judgment.

> *Beech-Nut.* The admission by Beech-Nut, the second largest baby-food producer in the United States, that it sold millions of jars of "phoney" apple juice shocked many company employees as well as industry executives. Since 1891, purity, high quality, and natural ingredients had served as the foundation of its corporate culture and had been a consistent marketing theme. What had caused Beech-Nut to stray from its heritage and reputation?

The answer to this question is complex. However, underlying the company's ethical failure were strong financial pressures. Beach-Nut was losing money and the use of the cheap, adulterated concentrate saved millions of dollars. Beech-Nut employees seemed to use two arguments to justify their actions: (1) They believed that many other companies were selling fake juice, and (2) they were convinced that their adulterated juice was perfectly safe to consume. In addition, some employees took refuge in the fact that no conclusive test existed to determine natural from artificial ingredients. Although with regard to this latter point, Beach-Nut seems to have shifted the burden of proof around. Other juicemakers have been known to cut off suppliers if the supplier cannot demonstrate that their product is genuine. At Beech-Nut, senior management apparently told R&D that *they* would have to prove that an inexpensive supplier's product was adulterated before the company would switch to another supplier. Beech-Nut compounded their problems when government investigations began by "stonewalling" rather than cooperating, apparently in order to gain time to unload a $3.5 million inventory of tainted apple juice products. Thus while at first Beech-Nut appears to have been the innocent victim of unscrupulous suppliers, the company by its later actions changed a civil matter into criminal charges (Welles, 1988).

Strong pressures also characterize the process surrounding the unethical decision of E. F. Hutton's "check kiting."

E. F. Hutton. In 1985 the E. F. Hutton Group Inc., one of the nation's largest brokerage firms, pleaded guilty to two thousand counts of wire and mail fraud, paid a fine of almost $3 million, and put over $9 million into funds to pay back defrauded banks and investors. The court case focused the nation's attention on banks' overdraft policies, but it also provided an example of how groupthink can cause trouble for even the mightiest institutions. Hutton's crime involved a form of "check kiting." A money manager at a Hutton branch office would write a check on an account in bank A for more money than Hutton had in that account. Because of the time lag in the check-collection system, these overdrafts sometimes went undetected, and Hutton could deposit funds to cover the overdraft in bank A's account on the following day. Even if the bank noticed the overdraft, it was unlikely to complain, because Hutton was such an important customer and because certain kinds of overdrafts are fairly routine.

In any case, the Hutton manager would deposit the check from bank A into an account in bank B, where the money would start earning interest immediately. In effect, the scheme allowed Hutton to earn a day's interest on bank A's account without having to pay anything for it. A day's interest may not sound like much, but Hutton was getting as much as $250 million in free loans every day, and a day's interest on such a sum is substantial (Goleman, 1988; ASA Banking Journal, 1987; Seneker, 1986).

More recently, wrongdoings by Salomon Brothers in the Treasury auction scandal provides another example of how groupthink can be linked to unethical behavior.

Everyone knows that selling jars of "phony" apple juice is unethical. In addition, everyone who has a checking account knows that bouncing checks is wrong, and you do not have to be a financial wizard to know that writing bad checks is illegal. And finally, everyone now knows that illegal bidding in Treasury auctions is wrong. So how could some of the country's most sophisticated executives and money managers become involved in such unethical behavior? The answer in all likelihood may well be groupthink, which may be fostered by what Wolfe

(1988) refers to as the *bottom-line mentality*. This line of thinking supports financial success as the only value to be considered. It promotes short-term solutions that are immediately financially sound, despite the fact that they cause problems for others within the organization or the organization as a whole. It promotes an unrealistic belief in some organizational groups that everything boils down to a monetary game. As a result, such rules on ethical conduct are merely barriers, impediments along the way to bottom-line financial success.

Beech-Nut's employees were under a lot of financial pressures and instead of cooperating with government investigators they compounded their problems by "stonewalling" rather than cooperating. Hutton's employees were under a lot of pressure to make money, and the company no doubt paid more attention to profit figures than to how those figures were achieved. The practice may even have started accidentally, but once it got going, the money managers apparently wrote unnecessary checks solely to profit from the check-kiting scheme as the money passed from bank to bank.

Company employees evidently had the necessary company loyalty and commitment to enable groupthink to come into play. Most important, once it became clear that high-level executives were not going to stop the scheme, employees became very good at ignoring any information that might lead them to conclude that the practice was illegal. An internal Hutton memo recommended that "if an office is overdrafting their ledger balance consistently, it is probably best not to request an account analysis" (Goleman, 1988). Executives at Salomon showed group characteristics found in groupthink experiences; for example, they exhibited excessive or blind loyalty, a bottom-line mentality, arrogance and overconfidence, and a promotion of unethical solutions by its leaders. In addition, like Beech-Nut and E. F. Hutton, Salomon Brothers also showed clear symptoms of groupthink and decision-making defects. . . . In each organization individuals were willing to take the approach of, "let's all close our eyes to this problem."

In a sense, individuals and groups in Beech-Nut, E. F. Hutton, and Salomon Brothers committed unethical acts because of an overabundance of characteristics that didn't allow them to operate ethically in a large, free-wheeling organization. The values of organization members in all three organizations were important. That is, groupthink and the ensuing unethical behavior may have been precipitated by arrogance. Arrogance is the illegitimate child of confidence and pride found in groups experiencing groupthink. Arrogance is the idea that not only can you never make a mistake, but no one else can ever be right.

In Beech-Nut, E. F. Hutton, and Salomon Brothers this arrogance was an insurmountable roadblock to ethical behavior. The flipside of arrogance is the ability to shine, to star, while working within the limits of ethical policies and guidelines. Another reason why groupthink may have occurred in these organizations is that they lacked the value of ethical commitment. That is, a willingness to commit to a goal that's bigger than they are—to keep acting ethically, even when there is a threat of failure, until they finally come up with the ethical business decisions.

A third reason for the unethical acts committed by Beech-Nut, E. F. Hutton, and Salomon Brothers has to do with another human value—loyalty. It's something valued in all organizations. No one wants to work with anyone who has no concern for anyone or anything else. Loyalty counts in organizations; however, it should not be an unwillingness to question the unethical behavior of a group or organization. Groupthink occurs when arrogance, over-commitment and loyalty help a group to shine above the ethical interests of an organization.

When groupthink occurs, organizations like Beech-Nut, E. F. Hutton, and Salomon Brothers are more likely to strive for unanimity, ignore the voices of dissenters and conscience, and make decisions which result in unethical behavior. But by ignoring voices of caution and conscience and working with a bottom-line mentality for short-term profit, all three companies' managers ended up severely damaging their company's reputation. To decrease the likelihood of unethical behavior, organizations must do a better job of promoting positive and ethical cultures, and reduce the probability of groupthink by programming conflict into decisions.

PROGRAMMING CONFLICT THROUGH DEVIL'S ADVOCATE AND DIALECTIC METHODS

Programmed conflict through the devil's advocate and dialectic methods can raise different opinions regardless of the personal feelings of the managers (Cosier and Schwenk, 1990) or members of groups into decisions. The usefulness of the devil's advocate technique was illustrated by Janis when discussing famous fiascoes such as Watergate and Vietnam. Janis recommends that everyone in the group assume the role of a devil's advocate and present a critique of the proposed course of action. This avoids the tendency of agreement interfering with problem solving while still serving as a precaution for the occurrence of unethical behavior. Potential unethical behaviors are identified and considered before the decision is final.

The conflict generated by the devil's advocate may cause groups to avoid false assumptions and closely adhere to guidelines for ethical analysis in decisions. The devil's advocate raises questions that force an in-depth review of the group's decision-making process. The devil's advocate is assigned to identify potential pitfalls or unethical behavior with a proposed course of action. A formal presentation to the key decision makers by the devil's advocate raises potential concerns. Evidence needed to address the critique is gathered and the final decision is made and ensuing behavior monitored. The devil's advocate decision program (Cosier and Schwenk, 1990) is summarized in Figure 14–2.

Cosier and Schwenk (1990) suggest that it is a good idea to rotate people assigned to devil's advocate roles. This avoids any one person or group being identified as the critic on all group decisions. The devil's advocate role can assist organizations like Beech-Nut, E. F. Hutton, and Salomon Brothers avoid costly mistakes by hearing viewpoints that identify pitfalls instead of foster agreement.

While the devil's advocate technique lacks what Cosier and Schwenk (1990) call an "argument" between advocates of two conflicting positions, the dialectic method can program conflict into a group's decisions while offsetting potentially unethically behavior. The dialectic method calls for structuring a debate between conflicting views regardless of members' personal feelings. The benefits of the dialectic method are in the presentation and debate of the

1. A proposed course of action is generated.

2. A devil's advocate (individual or group) is assigned to criticize the proposal.

3. The critique is presented to key decision makers.

4. Any additional information relevant to the issues is gathered.

5. The decision to adopt, modify, or discontinue the proposed course of action is taken.

6. The decision is monitored.

FIGURE 14–2

A devil's advocate decision program. Source: Cosier, R. A. and Schwenk, C. R.: 1991, 'Agreement and Thinking Alike: Ingredients for Poor Decisions,' *Academy of Management Executive* 4(1), pp. 69–74.

assumptions underlying proposed courses of action. False or misleading assumptions become apparent and can head off unethical decisions that are based on these poor assumptions. The dialectic method shown in Figure 14–3 can help promote ethical decisions and counteract groupthink.

Programming conflict into the group decision-making process allows dissent and can decrease the likelihood of groupthink and unethical behavior. Such conflict requires organizations to ensure that decisions are challenged, criticized, and alternative ideas are generated. Programmed conflict also insures that a comprehensive framework becomes a part of the group decision-making process.

1. A proposed course of action is generated.

2. Assumptions underlying the proposal are identified.

3. A conflicting counterproposal is generated based on different assumptions.

4. Advocates of each position present and debate the merits of their proposals before key decision makers.

5. The decision to adopt either position, or some other position, e.g. a compromise, is taken.

6. The decision is monitored.

FIGURE 14–3

The dialectic decision method. Source: Cosier, R. A. and Schwenk, C. R.: 1991, 'Agreement and Thinking Alike: Ingredients for Poor Decisions,' *Academy of Management Executive* 4(1),

CONCLUSION

It has not been the intent of this article to suggest that groupthink is an easy phenomenon to overcome, especially since there is some evidence that the symptoms of groupthink presented in this paper thrive in the sort of climate outlined in the following critique of corporate directors in the United States (Baum, 1986):

> Many directors simply don't rock the boat. "No one likes to be the skunk at the garden party," says (management consultant) Victor Palmieri. . . . "One does not make friends and influence people in the boardroom or elsewhere by raising hard questions that create embarrassment or discomfort for management" (p. 60).

In short, policy- and decision-making groups can become so cohesive that strong-willed executives are able to gain unanimous support for poor decisions. Still, organizations committed to ethical behavior in their organizations must work toward the reduction and prevention of groupthink. However, they must first understand what is meant by groupthink and that there is, indeed, a link between groupthink and unethical behavior. Specifically, the ultimate result of groupthink is that group members become isolated from the world around them. They read positive signs as a reaffirmation of their goals and intentions; they read negative signs as an indication that there are individuals who do not understand what they are doing and that these individuals should be ignored (and perhaps even punished). During this entire process, it is common to find the group changing to a belief that its ideals are humanitarian and based on high-minded principles. As a result, no attempt is made by the members to challenge or question the ethics of the group's behavior. A second common observation is high *esprit de corps* and amiability among the members. This often leads them to believe that those who question their approach or intentions are acting irrationally.

Quite often groupthink is only recognized after a group has made a disastrous decision. When this occurs, the members are apt to ask, "How could we have been so blind? Why didn't anyone call attention to our errors?" Unfortunately, at the time the group was making its decision(s), it is unlikely that any criticism or questioning of its actions would have been given serious consideration. Laboratory studies using college students as subjects validate portions of Janis' groupthink concept. Specifically, it has been found that:

> **Groups with a moderate amount of cohesiveness produce better decisions than low- or high-cohesive groups.
> **Highly cohesive groups victimized by groupthink make the poorest decisions, despite high confidence in those decisions (Callaway and Esser, 1984; Leana, 1985).

How can organizations like Beech-Nut, E. F. Hutton, and Salomon Brothers overcome or deal with groupthink effectively? Hodgetts suggests a number of useful rules that can be employed:

> First, the organization and its manager must encourage open airing of objections and doubts. Second, one or more outsiders should be invited into the group to challenge the views of its members. Finally, after reaching a preliminary decision, the group should hold a "second chance"

meeting at which every member expresses, as vividly as possible, all his or her doubts and the group thinks through the entire issue again before making a final decision (pp. 1, 3, 4).

Janis (1972) offers the following prescriptions for helping managers reduce the probability of groupthink:

A.   **Leader Prescriptions**

1. Assign everyone the role of critical evaluation.
2. Be impartial; do not state preferences.
3. Assign the devil's advocate role to at least one group member.
4. Use outside experts to challenge the group.

B.   **Organizational Prescriptions**

1. Do not automatically opt for a "strong" culture. Explore methods to provide for diversity and dissent, such as grievance or complaint mechanisms or other internal review procedures.
2. Set up several independent groups to study the same issue.
3. Train all employees in ethics (these programs should explain the underlying ethical, legal (Drake and Drake, 1988), groupthink-prevention techniques, and devil's advocate and dialectic methods.
4. Establish programs to clarify and communicate values.

C.   **Individual Prescriptions**

1. Be a critical thinker.
2. Discuss the group's deliberations with a trusted outsider and report back to the group.

D.   **Process Prescriptions**

1. Periodically break the group into subgroups to discuss the issues.
2. Take time to study external factors.
3. Hold second-chance meetings to rethink issues before making a commitment.
4. Periodically rotate new members into groups and old members out.

Note that all the suggestions encourage group members to evaluate alternatives critically and discourage the single-minded pursuit of unanimity, which is a key component of groupthink. By making use of the above prescriptions, organizations can give employees the confidence to be on the lookout for groupthink and act with the understanding that what they are doing is considered correct and will be supported by top management and the entire organization.

Maier (1970, 1973) suggests that organizations should realize that the actions of leaders in groups often can "make or break" the decisions made in that group. Therefore, organizations should ensure that group leaders are trained to develop the following skills:

1. Learn to state the problem or issue the group is dealing with in a nondefensive, objective manner.
2. Supply essential facts and clarify any constraints on solutions.
3. Draw out all group members. Prevent domination by one person and protect members from being attacked or severely criticized.
4. Wait out pauses. Don't make suggestions and/or ask leading questions.
5. Ask stimulating questions that move the discussion forward.
6. Summarize and clarify at several points to mark progress.

Notice that these skills are not vague attitudes, but specific behaviors. Thus, they are subject to training and practice. There is good evidence that this quality training can be accomplished through role-playing, and that it can help counteract groupthink.

Organizations must also ensure that they do not support financial success as the only value to be considered. Such an attitude will not promote a bottom-line mentality and an unrealistic belief that everything boils down to a monetary game. By not emphasizing short-term revenues above long-term consequences, organizations will create a climate in which individuals and groups understand that unethical behavior is unacceptable. In addition, organizations must be willing to take a stand when there is a financial cost to any group's decision. This stand will discourage ethical shortcuts by its members.

In order for values to provide the ethical "rules of the road" for employees, organizations must ensure that they are stated, shared, an understood by everyone in an organization. Formal programs to clarify and communicate important ethical values can help accomplish this objective in organizations and counteract groupthink. In addition, organizations should pay proper attention to employee recruitment, selection, and orientation.

The values of prospective employees should be examined and discussed, and the results used in making selection decisions. A person's first encounters with an organization and its members also "say" a lot about key beliefs and values. Every attempt should be made to teach them "the ethical way we do things here." Organizations also should develop appropriate training and development opportunities to establish and maintain skills in programmed conflict methods. In addition, values can and should be emphasized along with other important individual attributes.

Finally, organizations can make use of progressive rewards to encourage ethical behaviors by individuals and groups. Rewards in the form of monetary compensation, employee benefits, and special recognition can reinforce individual values, counteract groupthink, and maintain enthusiasm in support of ethical organizational values. Organizations can find creative ways to reward employees for displaying ethical values that are considered essential to organizational success.

In conclusion, organizations can take a number of steps to reduce the probability of groupthink. They can develop strong norms of critical appraisal. Group leaders can abstain from pushing their own views and using their influence, and instead encourage genuine debate. Groups can attempt to avoid isolation by involving more than one group in the decision-making process. Finally, an important key to counteract groupthink is to program conflict into the decision-making situation (Cosier and Schwenk, 1990; Janis, 1989). The specific impact of groupthink on the behavior of employees covered in this paper is illustrative rather than exhaustive. The paper has simply tried to familiarize the reader with some of the important aspects and with the related issues. Remember, ethical behavior foundations are first established when an organization commits itself to success that results from ethical behavior by its members.

REFERENCES

ADLER, H. J., & BIRD, F. B. (1988). International dimensions of executive integrity: Who is responsible for the world. In. S. Srivastva (Ed.), *Executive integrity: The search for human values in organization life* (pp. 243–267). San Francisco: Jossey-Bass.

ASA Banking Journal. (1987, July). A violation of business ethics or outright fraud?, pp. 30–34.

BALES, R. (1950). *Interaction process analysis* Reading, MA: Addison-Wesley.

BAUM, L. (1986, September 8). The job nobody wants. *Business Week,* p. 60.

CALLAWAY, M. R., & ESSER, J. K. (1984). Groupthink: Effects of cohesiveness and problem-solving procedures on group decision making. *Social Behavior and Personality, 12*(2), 157–164.

COSIER, R. A., & SCHWENK, C. R. (1991). Agreement and thinking alike: Ingredients for poor decisions. *Academy of Management Executive, 4*(1), 69–74.

DRAKE, B. H., & DRAKE, E. (1988, Winter). Ethical and legal aspects of managing corporate cultures. *California Management Review,* 120–121.

GOLEMAN, D. (1988, October). Following the leader. *Science, 85,* 18.

HODGETTS, R. M. (1990). *Modern human relations at work* (4th ed.). Hinsdale, IL: Dryden.

HUSEMAN, R. C., & DRIVER, R. W. (1979). Groupthink: Implications for small-group decision making in business. In R. C. Huseman & A. B. Carroll (Eds.), *Readings in organizational behavior: Dimensions of management actions.* Boston: Allyn & Bacon.

JANIS, I. L. (1972). *Victims of groupthink.* Boston: Houghton Mifflin.

JANIS, I. L. (1982). *Groupthink.* Boston: Houghton Mifflin.

JANIS, I. L. (1989). *Crucial decisions: Leadership in policy making and crisis management.* New York: Free Press.

JANIS, I. L., & MANN, L. (1977). *Decision making: A psychological analysis of conflict, choice, and commitment.* New York: Free Press.

JANSEN, E., & VON GLINOW, M. A. (1985). Ethical ambivalence and organizational reward systems. *Academy of Management Review, 10*(4), 814–822.

LEANA, C. R. (1985, Spring). A partial test of Janis's groupthink model: Effects of group cohesiveness and leader behavior on defective decision making. *Journal of Management,* 5–17.

MAIER, N. R. (1970). Male versus female discussion leaders. *Personnel Psychology, 23,* 455–461.

MAIER, N. R. (1973). Prior commitment as a deterrent to group problem solving. *Personnel Psychology, 26,* 117–126.

MOOREHEAD, G. (1982, December). Groupthink: Hypothesis in need of testing. *Group and Organization Studies,* 434.

SCHERMERHORN, JR., J. R., HUNG, J. G., & OSBORN, R. N. (1991). *Managing organizational behavior.* New York: Wiley.

SENEKER, H. (1986, January). Nice timing. *Forbes,* 102.

SICONOLFI, M., SESIT, M. M., & RITCHELL, C. (1991, August 19). Collusion and price fixing have long been rife in treasury market. *Wall Street Journal,* A1.

TREVINO, L. K. (1986). Ethical decision making in organizations: A person-situation interactionist model. *Academy of Management Review, 11*(3), 601–617.

WELLES, C. (1988, February 22). What led Beech-Nut down the road to disgrace? *Business Week*, pp. 124–128.

WOLFE, D. (1988). Is there integrity in the bottomline managing obstacles to executive integrity. In S. Srivastva (Ed.), *Executive integrity: The search for high human values in organization life* (pp. 140–171). San Francisco: Jossey-Bass.

QUESTIONS

1. Briefly describe the phenomenon of groupthink. Are all poor group decisions the result of groupthink?

2. In Janis's original conception of groupthink, did groups knowingly make bad decisions? Compare this to groupthink in businesses, as described in this article.

3. What five cognitive defenses operate in groupthink? What evidence of these defenses can be found in the Beech-Nut apple juice scandal?

4. All three of the scandals described can be explained with a very simple concept: greed. Is the additional concept, groupthink, necessary?

5. Explain the dialectic and devil's advocate methods for reducing groupthink. How do these two techniques differ?

❖ CHAPTER 15 ❖

BUSINESS, ORGANIZATIONS, AND THE ENVIRONMENT: APPLYING SOCIAL PSYCHOLOGY IN A COMPLEX WORLD

Reading 29: Classic

The Social Problems of an Industrial Civilization

Elton Mayo

The industrial revolution greatly improved the economies of many countries. The production of goods increased dramatically with the construction of larger plants employing more people. Unfortunately, the workers in these plants did not always share in the prosperity. Yet conditions in many places continued to improve, and conditions in post–World War I America were somewhat better than they had been several decades earlier. This improvement was due in part to moral and legal concerns. But beyond this, some companies began to realize that by looking out for their workers, they were helping themselves as well.

As it turned out, even for those companies whose motivated self-interest called for it, developing a content and motivated work force was not easily done. Elton Mayo, describing the situation he saw in 1923, realized that the contemporary understanding of what he called "human economics" was woefully insufficient. In the following reading, Mayo describes his first, and possibly the first, attempt by a psychologist to explain the complexities of human economics.

In 1923 Mayo was asked to investigate the problems of turnover in the mule-spinning department of a textile mill. While at first glance the working conditions seemed good enough, the workers were plagued by fatigue and low morale. Even financial incentive schemes had totally failed to improve worker morale or production. The solution that Mayo offered was small and simple; the results were anything but.

❖

Economic theory in its human aspect is woefully insufficient; indeed it is absurd. Humanity is not adequately described as a horde of individuals, each actuated by self-interest, each fighting his neighbor for the scarce material of survival. Realization that such theories completely falsify the normal human scene drives us back to study of particular human situations. *Knowledge-of-acquaintance* of the actual event, intimate understanding of the complexity of human relationships, must precede the formulation of alternatives to current economic abstractions. This is the clinical method, the necessary preliminary to laboratory

Source: Mayo, E. (1946). *The social problems of an industrial civilization* (2nd ed.). New York: Macmillan.

investigation. Only when clinically tested by successful treatment can a diagnosis be safely developed toward logical elaboration and laboratory experiment.

The first inquiry we undertook ran headlong into illustration of the insufficiency of the assumption that individual self-interest actually operates as adequate incentive. Rather more than twenty years ago we were asked to discover, if possible, the causes of a high labor turnover in the mule-spinning department of a textile mill near Philadelphia.[1] The general labor situation elsewhere in the plant seemed highly satisfactory; the employers were unusually enlightened and humane; the work was exceedingly well organized in respect of operations and the company was generally regarded as an extremely successful venture. But the president and his director of personnel were much troubled by the situation in the mule-spinning department. Whereas the general labor turnover in other departments was estimated to be approximately 5% to 6% per annum, in the spinning department the turnover was estimated at approximately 250%. That is to say, about 100 men had to be taken on every year in order to keep about 40 working. And the difficulty tended to be most acute when the factory was busily employed and most in need of men.

Several firms of efficiency engineers had been consulted; their firms had instituted altogether four financial incentive schemes. And these schemes had been a total failure; labor turnover had not dropped one point, nor had production improved: it was almost as a last resort that the firm consulted a university. Although other plants in the vicinity had apparently drifted into acceptance of low morale amongst mule spinners as inevitable, the president of this company refused to believe that the situation was beyond remedy.

On a first inspection the conditions of work in the department did not seem to differ in any general respect from conditions elsewhere in the mill. For some time Saturday work had been discontinued throughout the plant, so that the work week was of 50 hours—five days of 10 hours, two shifts of 5 hours each separated by a 45-minute lunch interval. The mule-spinner attendant was known as a piecer; his work involved walking up and down a long alley, perhaps 30 yards or more, on either side of which a machine head was operating spinning frames. These frames moved back and forth stretching yarn taken from the carding machines, twisting it, and rolling it up on cops. The number of frames operated by a machine head varied from 10 to 14. All had to be closely watched; threads constantly broke and had to be pieced together. The number of piecers in an alley, usually two or three, varied according to the kind of yarn being spun. To an observer the work looked monotonous—walking up and down an alley twisting together broken threads. The only variation in work occurred when a machine head was stopped in order to doff or to replace some spools.

Dr. S. D. Ludlum, professor of neuropsychiatry in the graduate school of medicine in the University of Pennsylvania, was of immense aid to us at this stage as later in the study. He arranged that a registered nurse, one of our group, should be able to relate her small clinic for minor troubles in the plant direct to the Polyclinic Hospital in Philadelphia. Serious cases she referred to the hospital clinicians; minor injuries, a cut or splinter, she could deal with herself.

---

[1]For a more detailed account of this inquiry, see Elton Mayo, "Revery and Industrial Fatigue," *Personnel Journal,* Vol. III, No. 8, December, 1924, pp. 273–281.

This arrangement seemed to do away with any need for further explanation. Workers gratefully accepted the services of the nurse and, in some instances, the further clinical aid of the hospital. These services were real and understandable. From the first the mule spinners formed a large part of the nurse's regular callers—and either when at work or in the clinic talked to her and to us quite freely. It was of course clearly understood that nothing said to any of us was ever repeated to anyone in the plant.

As the men began to talk to us, the picture of the situation developed quite differently from that obtained at first inspection. We discovered that almost every piecer suffered from foot trouble of one or another kind for which he apparently knew no effective remedy. Many also claimed neuritis in various localities of arms, shoulders, or legs. But above and beyond all this, the striking fact was the uniformly pessimistic nature of the preoccupations of these workers while at work. To this there seemed no exception: their own opinion of their work was low, even lower than the estimate of mule spinning held by other workers in the plant. We discovered also that the job was essentially solitary: there might be three workers in an alley, but the amount of communication between them in a day was almost nil. One might be piecing threads together here; another, 20 yards away. And the doffing process when it took place involved rapid work with a minimum of communication. Some of the men were young—in the twenties, others were in the fifties—all alike claimed that they were too fatigued to enjoy social evenings after work. Occasionally a worker would flare out into apparently unreasonable anger and incontinently leave his job.

The whole group was characterized by a species of strongly held loyalty to the company president. He had been a colonel in the regular United States Army and had seen active service both before and during the First World War. Many of the workers had been in the trenches in France under his immediate command and had the highest opinion of him; they had come with him from his regiment to the textile mill. Perhaps for this reason their pessimistic moods showed no anger against "The Colonel" or "the company." For the most part the individual seemed to be almost melancholic about himself; this mood alternated with spurts of rage against some immediate supervisor.

After some discussion the management permitted us to experiment with rest periods—two of 10 minutes' length in the morning and two again in the afternoon. We arranged these rests so that the work period should be divided thus: 2 hours' work, 10 minutes' rest; 1½ hours' work, 10 minutes' rest; and a final work period of 1 hour and 10 minutes. The actual uninterrupted work period thus diminished in morning and afternoon. In these rest periods the workers were permitted to lie down; we instructed them in the best methods of securing the maximum of muscular relaxation. We encouraged them to sleep for 10 minutes and most of them were able to do so.

We began with one team of piecers, about one-third of the total number, and the results were encouraging from the outset. The men themselves were pleased and interested; they speedily adopted the method of rest we advised. The effect was immediate—symptoms of melancholy preoccupation almost wholly disappeared, the labor turnover came to an end, production was maintained, and the morale generally improved. Such immediate effects could not be attributed to the mere elimination of physical fatigue. This was confirmed by the fact that an almost equivalent improvement showed itself in the work of the other two-thirds of the piecers. These men had discussed the experiment at lunch time with their fellows and were confident that "The Colonel" would extend the system to them if it were found satisfactory. And in the October of that year, 1923, this expectation was fulfilled; the management, pleased with the improved condition of the men and the work, decided to extend the rest period system to include the entire personnel of the spinning department. This made it possible for us to do what we could not do before—to measure the effect of the rest periods upon the productivity of the department.

Until October, 1923, the spinning department had never earned a bonus under one of the incentive systems introduced; in October and for the months recorded thereafter, with one interesting exception, the spinners consistently earned a bonus in addition to their wages. I have elsewhere described the bonus plan[2] and shall not repeat this detail here. Enough to say that, if the production of the department in any month exceeded 75% of a carefully calculated possibility, every spinner was paid an excess percentage of his flat-rate wage equivalent to the average excess percentage of production over 75%. Thus a monthly man-hour efficiency of 80% meant a 5% bonus on his monthly wage to every employee in the department. As said above, no fraction of bonus had ever been earned by the department. We were unable to get figures showing the average productivity of the department before October, 1923, when the experiment proper began; but it was generally admitted by executives and supervisors that production had never been above an approximate 70%.

The period from October, 1923, to mid-February, 1924, inclusive, showed a surprising change. The mental and physical condition of the men continued to improve, and, whereas the financial incentive of the bonus had not operated to stimulate production while they felt fatigued, they were now pleased by the fact that under conditions of work that seemed much easier they were earning bonuses as never before. The system was not, however, altogether satisfactory at this time. The immediate supervisors had never liked the sight of workers lying asleep on sacks while the mules were running; it occurred to one of them that the men should be made to "earn" their rest periods. That is to say, a task was set and, if finished within a given time, the men had their rest. For the most part, the workers had three or four rests every day and the innovation worked well enough. For example, the monthly average of productivity ran as follows:

		Efficiency	Bonus
October,	1923	79½%	4½%
November,	"	78¾	3¾
December,	"	82	7
January,	1924	78¾	3¾
February,	"	80¼	5¼

This, for workers who had never before earned a bonus, meant much.

This general condition continued until Friday, February 15, when in response to a heavy demand for goods the supervisor who had introduced the idea of earned rest periods ordered

---

[2]Elton Mayo, "Revery and Industrial Fatigue," loc. cit.

the whole system abandoned. Within five days production fell to a point lower than it had been for months. And on February 22, we found that the old pessimistic preoccupations had returned in full force, thus coinciding almost exactly with the drop in production. The executive officer in charge ordered the resumption of the rest period system on Monday, February 25; this was done, but the idea of earned rest periods was also reinstated even more strongly than before. At this point, the workers gave every symptom of profound discouragement; they professed a belief that the system would be discontinued before long. In spite of this, the daily record for March showed definite improvement, but the general average for the month was back at the old point, 70%.

At this point the president of the company, "The Colonel," took charge. His military service had taught him two important things—one, to care for this men, and, two, not be afraid of making decisions. He called a conference in his office to discuss the remarkable diminution from 80% to 70% in the department's productive efficiency. We were able to point out that in March there had been a recrudescence of absenteeism, an ill that had notably diminished in the October to February period. This meant that the men were taking their rest periods in the form of "missed" days, a proceeding that did not greatly remedy their condition and that produced chaos in the plant. We put it therefore that the question was not whether a certain proportion of their working time was to be given up to rest. We pointed out that they took the rest, whether it was given them or not. We were asking that a less proportion should be thus allotted, but that it should be done systematically. Furthermore, we were able to claim that the whole rest period system had never had a fair trial. In other words, it had not been possible for a worker to know as he entered the factory in the morning that he was assured of his four rests in the day.

In order to test our claim, the president ordered that during the month of April the spinning mules should be shut down for 10 minutes at a time four times a day and that all hands from the floor supervisor down should rest as they had been instructed to do. There was some difficulty in securing the requisite amount of floor space for approximately 40 men to lie down by their machines and in securing sufficient sacking to provide for their comfort. With the exception of the president himself, there were few who believed that this drastic alteration of method could result in increased production. The men themselves believed that 40 minutes lost by 40 men per day during a whole month could not be recovered. They pointed out that the machines could not be "speeded up" and that there was no other way of recovering the lost time. In spite of this general belief, the returns for April showed an improvement on March.[3] The March production-efficiency figure had been 70%, the April figure was 77½%. This, while it represented a 7½% gain in the company's rating, was actually a 10% gain. The men had had their rests, the pessimism had again disappeared; simultaneously, their morale had much improved, absenteeism had diminished, and every worker had earned a 2½% bonus on his wages. In the month of May and thereafter, the president ordered a return to the system of alternating rest periods, with this important difference that each group of three men in an alley was to determine for itself the method of alternation, the understanding being that every worker was to have four such rest periods daily and regularly. In the month of May, the

[3]Ibid.

average efficiency of men-hour production was 80¼%. In June it reached the then record high figure of 85%. During the following three months the department maintained its improved capacity: July, 82%; August, 83½%; September, 86½%.

It is interesting to observe the difference that an absolute certainty of a minimum number of rest periods made. The months from April to September differed from the preceding months in this respect and they revealed a steady progress. Mondays and Fridays were no longer the worst days in the week. The irregularity reported in May was due to the fact that the spinning mules were constantly "running away from the cards," that is, outdistancing the carding machines which supplied them with spooled yarn. By June, the company had put in two new carding machines, and June was as steadily above 85% as March was below 75%.

The investigation began with a question as to the causes of a very high labor turnover. In the 12 months of experiment there was no labor turnover at all. This does not mean that no worker left the factory—during a period of trade slackness, some were laid off, one at least moved his place of residence and found work elsewhere, another was found to be phthisical and sent to the country. But the former problem of a highly emotional labor turnover ceased to exist. The factory began to hold its mule spinners and no longer had difficulty in maintaining a full complement in times of rushed work. The attitude of management to the innovation was revealed in the fact that the company purchased army cots for the workers to rest upon. When these cots proved unequal to the wear and tear, management installed a bed and mattress at the end of each alley as provision for the workers' adequate rest. And the workers developed the habit of sleeping for the last three rest periods of the day, the late morning rest and both afternoon rests. Experience seemed to show that the benefit was directly proportionate to the completeness of the relaxation—hence the beds. Several years later, the president of the company said publicly that from this time the labor turnover sank to an approximate 5% or 6% per annum and stayed there until the mules were taken out and ring spinning substituted.

At the time when we completed our part in this work, we were sure that we had not wholly discovered the causes of the high labor turnover. We could not even attribute the change to the mere introduction of rest periods; inevitably many other changes had been simultaneously introduced. For example, we had listened carefully and with full attention to anything a worker wished to say, whatever the character of his comment. In addition to this, we—supported by the president—had demonstrated an interest in what was said by the introduction of experimental changes, by instruction in the best methods of relaxation. The Colonel also had demonstrated unmistakably a sincere interest in his workers' welfare; he had lived up to his Army reputation. The supervisor who instituted the earning of rest periods was swept aside by the president and the company—thereby "placing" the company's attitude in the minds of its workers.

But, in addition to this—and we did not see this clearly at the time—the president had effected another important change. He had helped to transform a horde of "solitaries" into a social group. In May, 1924, he placed the control of rest periods square in the hands of the workers in an alley with no one to say them nay. This led to consultation, not only between individuals, but between alleys throughout the group—and to a feeling of responsibility directly to the president. And the general social changes effected were astonishing—even in relationships outside the factory. One worker told us with great surprise that he had begun taking his wife to "movies" in the evenings, a thing he had not done for years. Another, equally to his surprise, gave up a habit of spending alcoholic weekends on bootleg liquor. In general the change was complex, and the difficulty of assigning the part played in it by various aspects of the experiment impossible to resolve. We should have liked to experiment further, but this desire—probably wisely in the circumstances—was disallowed. Thus the inquiry left us with many questions unanswered, but it pointed a direction for further studies, the results of which later proved helpful in reinterpreting the data of this first investigation.

But we had moved onwards. The efficiency experts had not consulted the workers; they regarded workers' statements as exaggerated or due to misconception of the facts and therefore to be ignored. Yet to ignore an important symptom—whatever its character—on supposedly moral grounds is preposterous. The "expert" assumptions of rabble hypothesis and individual self-interest as a basis for diagnosis led nowhere. On the other hand, careful and pedestrian consideration of the workers' situation taken as part of a clinical diagnosis led us to results so surprising that we could at the time only partly explain them.

QUESTIONS

1. What physical difficulties did the mule spinners initially complain of? What other difficulties did they have?

2. Mayo says that humanity is not just a "horde of individuals, each actuated by self-interest, each fighting his neighbor for . . . survival." How does this study support this supposition?

3. Did the mule spinners work harder when their rest was guaranteed or when they had to earn it? Under which system was absenteeism greater?

4. In what ways does the textile mill in this article follow the bureaucratic model? In what ways does it not?

5. Considering that Mayo introduced only one change in the mule-spinning department, why is he not sure what the improved conditions are attributable to?

Reading 30: Contemporary

Ambivalence and Stereotypes Cause Sexual Harassment: A Theory with Implications for Organizational Change

Susan T. Fiske and Peter Glick

Our final reading examines the issue of discrimination in the workplace. This form of discrimination represents a very costly problem: Some estimates suggest that discrimination in the workplace costs U.S. businesses more than $1 billion a year in lost potential earnings.

In this reading, social psychologists Susan Fiske and Peter Glick focus their attention on one form of workplace discrimination: sexual harassment. According to Fiske and Glick, gender-based discrimination is fundamentally different from other types of discrimination. Unlike most mutually antagonistic groups, men and women have many positive as well as negative attitudes about one another. This ambivalence, in conjunction with stereotypes about women and their role in the workplace, too often leads to sexual harassment.

Fiske and Glick begin by describing their theory of ambivalent sexism and explaining how it leads to harassment. Next, they examine some characteristics of the workplace that subtly encourage harassment by activating men's ambivalent stereotypes. Finally, they suggest institutional changes that could help reduce harassment by changing those aspects of office culture that normally support it.

❖

Harassment in the workplace results, we argue, from the complex interplay of ambivalent motives and gender stereotyping of women and jobs. The first section of this article describes a theoretical basis for examining men's various motives toward women, highlighting the sources of ambivalence. . . . This theory of cognitive-motivational interplay then describes the different kinds of harassment that can result. These cognitive-motivational dynamics can be encouraged by certain organizational contexts, described in the next section. Organizational remedies suggested by the theory and by social psychological research are offered in the final section of the paper.

Our purpose here is to identify the psychology of motivation and stereotyping that leads to harassment, as well as the organizational context that supports or undermines this psychology. The identified factors are not exhaustive, nor are all of them necessary in any given case of harassment, nor is any one of them a sufficient cause of harassment. But in our

Source: Fiske, S. T., & Glick, P. (1995). Ambivalence and stereotypes cause sexual harassment. A theory with implications for organizational change. *Journal of Social Issues, 51,* 97–115.

analysis, these are prominent psychological forces that underlie men's sexual harassment of women.[1]

AMBIVALENT MOTIVATIONS

Sexual harassment reflects common motivations that underlie many men's goals in many of their interactions with women. Traditionally, men's motivational orientation toward women has been deeply ambivalent, reflecting male desires for both dominance and intimacy. As a result, both positive and negative feelings coexist toward women that may lead men to experience certain feelings as subjectively positive even though they encourage behaviors that are problematic for women. Elsewhere, we have validated a scale, the Ambivalent Sexism Inventory, which distinguishes hostile and benevolent sexism (Glick & Fiske, 1994). Hostile sexism refers to sexist antipathy toward women based on an ideology of male dominance, male superiority, and a hostile form of sexuality (in which women are treated merely as sexual objects). Benevolent sexism refers to *subjectively positive,* though sexist, attitudes that include protectiveness toward women, positively valenced stereotypes of women (e.g., nurturance), and a desire for heterosexual intimacy. Both types of sexism have three components, each of which encompass a hostile and a "benevolent" aspect (see Glick & Fiske, 1994, for further evidence and references): (a) *Paternalism* is an orientation toward interacting with women as a father dealing with his children. This orientation encompasses not only attitudes of male superiority and dominance over women, but also a protectiveness toward women as "the weaker sex." (b) *Gender differentiation* is the motivation to make distinctions between the sexes. Gender identity is perhaps the first group-based component of self-identity to be learned (Maccoby, 1988). This aspect of men's identity is a source of self-esteem to the extent that women are viewed as inferior, promoting a competitive attitude toward women (particularly those who enter male domains). Traditional gender roles, however, also promote favorable attitudes toward women as mothers and homemakers (Eagly & Mladinic, 1993). (c) *Heterosexuality* makes relations between men and women uniquely different from other group relationships. Whereas ingroups and outgroups typically maintain stark social boundaries to avoid intimacy (Tajfel, 1982), our most intimate relations are more likely to be across, rather than within, gender lines (Berscheid, Snyder, & Omoto, 1989). Although men's sexual attraction can be the source of extremely positive feelings toward women and be linked to a genuine desire for intimacy, sexual desire is for men who are most likely to harass, also (or primarily) linked to hostility and a desire to dominate women (Bargh & Raymond, 1995; Pryor, Giedd, & Williams, 1995). Dominative paternalism, competitive gender differentiation, and hostile heterosexuality together compose *Hostile Sexism,* whereas protective paternalism, complementary gender differentiation, and heterosexual intimacy motives comprise *Benevolent Sexism.*

The ambivalent motives evident in these three components of sexist attitudes imply two potential core types of sexual harassment (see Table 1): an "earnest" (subjectively "benevolent")

---

[1]While we recognize that women can sexually harass men and that within-sex sexual harassment also occurs, we concentrate here on the theoretical analysis of men harassing women.

TABLE 1   TYPES OF HARASSMENT MOTIVES AND STEREOTYPES
PREDICTED BY AMBIVALENT SEXISM

Type of Harassment	Primary Motives	Reactions to Rejection	Stereotypes of Women	Stereotypes of Jobs
Earnest	Sexual intimacy	Depends on attraction and likely success	Sexy	Pink Collar
Hostile	Domination (paternalistic and competitive)	Increased harassment	Non-traditional	Blue or white collar
Ambivalent				
Paternalistic	Paternalism and sexual intimacy	Shift to hostility	Traditional and sexy	Pink collar
Competitive	Gender differentiation and sexual intimacy	Shift to hostility	Non-traditional and sexy	Blue or white collar

form motivated by a genuine desire for lasting heterosexual intimacy and a "hostile" form in which sexuality is merely another form of male domination. The earnest form is illustrated by a male pipefitter, truly named Romeo at Jacksonville Shipyard, who made repeated and unwelcome advances to a female welder, who reported that he told her "all the time that he was in love with me, wanted to go out with me" and that his penis "worked like a drill motor" (*Robinson v. Jacksonville Shipyards, Inc.*, 1989, Banks III, 72–81, 173). Here, the harassment is expressed less in ambivalence than in persistence despite clear communications to desist. One might consider it romantic although misguided, but it is harassing in its form and repetition. The hostile form is illustrated by a male shipyard worker commenting:

> Women are only fit company for something that howls. . . . There's nothing worse than having to work around women . . . [to a female co-worker:] I don't care where you go. You can go flash the sailors if you want to. (Comments by a co-worker, reported by plaintiff Robinson, I:196–202; II: 1–9; *Robinson v. Jacksonville Shipyards, Inc.*)

Upon being remonstrated by an outside observer—"Why do you treat her that way for?"—a worker replied "Well, that's the way you've got to treat them. She hasn't got virgin ears. She's heard it all before." And on another, similar occasion, he advised observers, "Don't look away and laugh [at her discomfort]. Laugh in her face" (*Robinson*, I:196–202; II:1–9). The hostility expresses a desire to dominate, whether in competition between peers over gender differentiation (removing women from men's spheres) or in dominative paternalism from a supervisor to a subordinate (dealing with uppity women).

Benevolent and hostile motives, however, are not mutually exclusive (Glick & Fiske, 1994), suggesting a third, perhaps more common, type—"ambivalent harassment." Ambivalent harassment combines elements of both hostile and benevolent sexism. Depending on which subjectively positive and hostile motivations combine, different subtypes of ambivalent harassment may occur. In one version of ambivalence, the harasser may honestly believe his motives are benevolent ("I desire her, want to love and protect her"), even though his attraction to the woman and his willingness to persist in the face of her refusals are largely the result of, for example, his superior and her subordinate position on the job. This subtype of ambivalent harassment combines overt feelings of protective paternalism and heterosexual intimacy (benevolent sexism) with (possibly covert) motivations of dominative paternalism (hostile sexism).

A second subtype of ambivalent harassment may be a mixture of "benevolent" sexual attraction and a hostile desire to "tame" an independent or competitive woman, thereby combining competitive gender differentiation (hostile sexism) with overt desires for heterosexual intimacy (benevolent sexism). This ambivalent phenomenon is often evident when a few women "invade" a previously all-male environment; for example, the "boy's club" at Jacksonville Shipyards painted "Men Only" on one of the work trailers, as well as sexually hostile graffiti in places where the women would be sure to see it; the men's harassing interactions with the women extended the hostile and exclusionary message, whereas the surface content was the expression of sexual attraction (e.g., crude sexual come-ons).

Ambivalent harassment may be particularly insidious because the man can readily justify his actions to himself as not harassment (Bargh & Raymond, 1995) but something benign (protecting the woman in the first, paternalistic, subtype; "harmless male bonding" in the second, competitive, subtype; and sexual attraction in both). Such justifications may disinhibit behavior in which a man might not otherwise engage, as may prevailing social norms that cast men as the primary initiators of heterosexual romantic relationships (Zillmann & Weaver, 1989).

The motives for harassment are likely to affect how a man reacts to a woman's refusal to accept his sexual advances. For harassment stemming from the *purely hostile* motive to dominate, a woman's refusal, disgust, or fear may simply signal to the harasser that he is achieving his goal of "putting her in her place." In contrast, for a man whose advances stem from an *earnest* desire for a lasting relationship, persistence may depend on the depth of his positive feelings for the woman and his capacity to absorb rejection. For ambivalent harassers of the *paternalistic subtype,* the man in a superordinate organizational position may maintain the illusion that even though she refuses now, eventually the woman will reciprocate his attraction. This illusion is likely to persist because many victims of harassment are reluctant directly to confront or emphatically to reject their harasser for fear of retaliation (Fitzgerald, Swan, & Fisher, 1995) and also because men in superordinate positions view their status as adding to their own sexual attractiveness (Gutek, 1985). For those with paternalistic as well as intimacy motivations, then, repeated and unambiguous refusals of their advances may destroy any benevolent feelings toward their female targets and turn their behavior from ambivalent to purely hostile. For ambivalent harassers of the *competitive subtype,* rejection signals one more arena in which they cannot compete successfully. The rejection is likely to escalate competition into overt hostility. Women who accept workplace sexual advances are in one sense reaffirming the man's sexual identify, thereby diminishing the gender competitive threat. (But these women are unlikely to be evaluated seriously as co-workers; Fiske, Goodwin, Rosen, & Rosenthal, 1994.)

In short, there is sound theoretical basis for examining men's motives toward women, highlighting the sources of ambivalence. The motives suggest different types of harassment, but these types also correspond to different cognitive images or stereotypes of women, described in the next section. . . .

The cognitive-motivational dynamics underlying harassment can be encouraged by certain organizational contexts, described in this section. The occupational groups known as pink, white, and blue collar are highly sex segregated (Gottfredson, 1981). This segregation has important effects on organizational contexts: (a) in contexts with few or no women performing a particular job, the occupational role often takes on a "masculine culture" (Gutek, 1985); (b) the few women who do break into these jobs have a "token" status (Kanter, 1977); (c) men have little history or experience of dealing with women in the job, so they react on the basis of limited information, thereby promoting stereotypes (Fiske & Neuberg, 1990); and (d) dramatic power asymmetries are created between the men and women (Fiske, 1993). All these effects together heighten the probability of sexual harassment.

Masculine Culture

The percentage of men in an occupation has a strong positive correlation to the perceived masculinity and a negative correlation to the perceived femininity of traits required to perform the job (Glick, 1991). In male-dominated jobs, the masculine sex role often "spills over" into the job, fusing masculine gender identity with the work role and culture (Gutek, 1985). For instance, even though leadership studies (Fleishman, 1967) have long emphasized the importance of the stereotypically feminine trait of "consideration" (being expressive and nurturant with subordinates), popular images of a good leader (a traditionally male work role) emphasize only masculine traits (e.g., independence, ambition). The more masculine the job culture (i.e., the stronger the association of masculine traits to the exclusion of feminine traits), the greater is the hostility likely faced by women who enter these occupations. Women in these occupations are seen as disrupting the "masculine camaraderie" that infuses the culture of the occupation.

Although a masculine culture is more the rule than the exception among male-dominated jobs, jobs with similar sex ratios do vary in this regard, with some being viewed as requiring feminine as well as masculine traits (Glick, 1991). Indeed, there may be variation among sub-specialties of the same job. Pediatric medicine, for example, is less stereotypically masculine than neurosurgery. Women seeking M.D. degrees may face less hostility if they go into the former, as opposed to the latter, specialty. Jobs that derive their "masculinity" from forms of intelligence that are viewed as uniquely masculine (e.g., engineering) or physical strength requirements (e.g., construction work) are those in which women are most likely to face hostile resistance (Gottfredson, 1981).

Solo Status

The perception of newly integrated women as disruptive comes with even the smallest inroads into these masculinized occupations, the female "token" or "solo." The presence of even a single woman can create heightened self-consciousness about gender roles and work behavior by the male majority. Certain aspects of the male job culture may normally be given no thought (e.g., in blue-collar settings, the prevalence of swearing and dirty jokes; in white-collar setting, business conducted around all-male sports). But the entrance of even more woman may force self-consciousness, and the previously easy-going atmosphere may become tense and uncomfortable for many male workers (Fiske & Ruscher, 1993). This discomfort, of course, is allegedly caused by the female solo, who may then be the target of a hostile back-lash and intimidating tests to see whether she will complain about the masculine job culture (e.g., "Let's see if she can take a ribbing like one of the guys"). Such testing often takes the form of sexual harassment.

Solo status also heightens the salience of the token woman's gender and increases the prob-ability that she will be tagged as a particular type of woman. The roles mentioned in the liter-ature (e.g., Kanter, 1977) correspond to our previously described common subtypes of women: Some solo women may be thrust into (or adopt) a traditional role that buys male pro-tection (e.g., the Mother who nurtures the boys in the group, the Mascot or Pet who functions as an admiring and sexless younger sister). Others, however, will be stereotyped as the Se-ductress, who is cast mainly as a sex object (but who may be able to buy protection from a high-status male, making her off limits to other men). Solo women who refuse to fit into a sex-typed role tend to be seen as more competent, but less agreeable and cooperative co-workers; they face hostility from the group and are often tagged as Iron Maidens (tough, threatening, and unfeminine). All three of these roles, purely traditional, purely sexual, or purely nontra-ditional, disadvantage the woman so placed. As described earlier, each of these roles elicits dif-ferent kinds of sexual harassment, unless organizations act to counteract it. . . .

ORGANIZATIONAL REMEDIES

Organizational remedies suggested by the present theory and by existing social psychological research are offered in this, the final section of the paper; these particular ideas follow from the theory, but of course many other interventions may be appropriate. The current notions are described according to the features of organizational context just noted.

Masculine Culture

To the extent that a masculine culture permeates a job and male stereotypes define it, organi-zations need to reframe people's perceptions of the job category. Job descriptions can minimize gender-associated characteristics as aspects of the job, if they are indeed superfluous. Inter-nally, inhouse recruitment notices, job titles, and stated promotion criteria all communicate whether a job is gender neutral or not. For example, the title "secretary" is more stereotypi-cally female than the title "administrative aide," but the duties could easily be similar. And of course, the actual distribution of the sexes in jobs can provide role models that convey whether "people like me" can do this job.

How people are treated once in the job can encourage or discourage stereotyping and ha-rassment. A professional environment that minimizes sexual joking, presumed intimacy, and inappropriate informality also minimizes sexual harassment (Gutek, 1985). One gender's culture is less likely to dominate, the more professional and task oriented the environment.

Certain aspects of an unprofessional work environment particularly matter to sexual harassment. There is by now ample evidence to indicate that the presence of pornography in the workplace encourages stereotyping and harassment of women (Rudman & Borgida, in press; McKenzie-Mohr & Zanna, 1990). It is not merely the sexual nature of pornography but the fact that it targets women and reduces them to their sexual characteristics that damages the workplace.

Both the company's external advertising campaigns and personnel recruitment are also relevant here. For example, the focus of the lawsuit against Stroh's Beer Company named its "Swedish bikini team" ads as contributing to a sexually harassing discriminatory work environment. And personnel ads can emphasize sexual (attractiveness) and gender-related (demeanor) traits or not. Reducing the hegemony of masculine culture, especially sexualized masculine culture, may well discourage sexual harassment.

Solo Status

The sheer numbers of men and women in a particular job category contribute to the masculine culture associated with it. Clearly, the long-term remedy is to increase the numbers of the underrepresented sex. But the applicant pool may not be immediately available or qualified; turnover may be slow, with the net effect that ratios do not change quickly. In the transition periods, some people will have solo or near-solo status.

The solution to solo structures is to achieve a critical mass of 20% or more, and not fewer than two individuals (Pettigrew & Martin, 1987). As a transitional step, the underrepresented group could be recruited department by department, with critical-mass clusters within each department, before moving on to the next department. However, this could be legally dicey, if groups are ghettoized. The ideal situation is massive and effective recruitment efforts. . . .

CONCLUSION

Our theory of ambivalent motivations and gender stereotypes proposes three core male motivations in interaction with women: paternalism, gender differentiation, and heterosexual attraction. These motives combine to produce four types of harassment: earnest (based on subjectively benevolent motives of sexual intimacy seeking), hostile (either dominative paternalism or competitive gender differentiation), paternalistic ambivalence (combining dominative and protective paternalism and sexual intimacy seeking), and competitive ambivalence (combining competitive gender differentiation and sexual intimacy seeking). Women fitting various subtypes—respectively, sexy, nontraditional, traditional and sexy, and nontraditional and sexy—seem most likely to elicit the corresponding motives and harassment.

We offer this theory in the hope of encouraging more theory-based examination of gender stereotyping and sexual harassment, as also occurs elsewhere in this issue. Theory will allow the development, testing, and application of more coherent causal analyses and less merely descriptive research on these important topics. The theory admittedly is described here without a direct empirical test. Elsewhere, we have developed and validated the Ambivalent Sexism Inventory (Glick & Fiske, 1994), which demonstrates the separate hostile and "benevolent" (i.e., subjectively positive) components of sexism, including paternalism, gender differentiation, and heterosexual attraction. These motives, the parallel stereotypes, and the corresponding harassment provide new ways to conceptualize and investigate how men and women can most constructively and happily relate to each other in the workplace.

REFERENCES

BARGH, J. A., & RAYMOND, P. (1995). The naive misuse of power: Nonconscious sources of sexual harassment. *Journal of Social Issues, 51,* 85–96.

BERSCHEID E., SNYDER, M., & OMOTO, A. (1989). The Relationship Closeness Inventory: Assessing the closeness of interpersonal relationships. *Journal of Personality and Social Psychology, 57,* 792–807.

EAGLY, A. H., & MLADINIC, A. (1993). Are people prejudiced against women? Some answers from research on attitudes, gender stereotypes, and judgments of competence. In W. Stroebe & M. Hewstone (Eds.), *European review of social psychology* (Vol. 5, pp. 1–35). New York: Wiley.

FISKE, S. T. (1993). Controlling other people: The impact of power on stereotyping. *American Psychologist, 48,* 621–628.

FISKE, S. T., GOODWIN, S. A., ROSEN, L. D., & ROSENTHAL, A. M. (1994). *Romantic outcome dependency and the (in)accuracy of impression formation: A case of clouded judgment.* Manuscript submitted for publication.

FISKE, S. T., & NEUBERG, S. L. (1990). A continuum of impression formation, from category-based to individuating processes: Influences of information and motivation on attention and interpretation. In M. P. Zanna (Ed.), *Advances in experimental social psychology* (Vol. 23, pp 1–74). New York: Academic Press.

FISKE, S. T., & RUSCHER, J. B. (1993). Negative interdependence and prejudice: Whence the affect? In D. M. Mackie & D. L. Hamilton (Eds.), *Affect, cognition, and stereotyping: Interactive processes in group perception* (pp. 239–268). New York: Academic Press.

FITZGERALD, L. F., SWAN, S., & FISCHER, K. (1995). Why didn't she just report him? The psychological and legal implications of women's responses to sexual harassment. *Journal of Social Issues, 51,* 117–138.

FLESICHMAN, E. A. (1967). Performance of assessment based on an empirically derived task taxonomy. *Human Factors, 9,* 349–366.

GLICK, P. (1991). Trait-based and sex-based discrimination in occupational prestige, occupational salary, and hiring. *Sex Roles, 25,* 351–378.

GLICK, P., FISKE, S. T. (1994). *The Ambivalent Sexism Inventory: Differentiating hostile and benevolent sexism.* Manuscript submitted for publication.

GOTTFREDSON, L. S. (1981). Circumscription and compromise: A developmental theory of occupational aspirations. *Journal of Counseling Psychology Monograph, 28,* 545–579.

GUTEK, B. A. (1985). *Sex and the workplace.* San Francisco: Jossey-Bass.

KANTER, R. M. (1977). *Men and women of the corporation.* New York: Basic Books.

MACCOBY, E. E. (1988). Gender as a social category. *Developmental Psychology, 24,* 755–765.

MCKENZIE-MOHR, D., & ZANNA, M. P. (1990). Treating women as sexual objects: Look to the (gender schematic) male who has viewed pornography. *Personality and Social Psychology Bulletin, 16,* 296–308.

PETTIGREW, T. F., & MARTIN, J. (1987). Shaping the organizational context for black American inclusion. *Journal of Social Issues, 43*(1), 41–78.

PRYOR, J. B., GIEDD, J. L., & WILLIAMS, K. B. (1995). A social psychological model for predicting sexual harassment. *Journal of Social Issues, 51,* 69–84.

Robinson v. Jacksonville Shipyards, Inc. (M.D. Fla. 1989; Case No. 86-927). Depositions by Banks, III, 72–81, 173; Robinson, I, 196–202, II, 1–9.

Rudman, L. A., & Borgida, E. (in press). The afterglow of construct accessibility: The cognitive and behavioral consequences of priming men to view women as sexual objects. *Journal of Experimental Social Psychology*.

Tajfel, H. (Ed.). (1982). *Social identity and intergroup relations*. London: Cambridge University Press.

Zillmann, D., & Weaver, J. B. (1989). Pornography and men's sexual callousness toward women. In D. Zillmann & J. Bryant (Eds.), *Pornography: Research advances and policy considerations* (pp. 95–125). Hillsdale: Erlbaum.

QUESTIONS

1. Why do Fiske and Glick believe that sexism is fundamentally different from any other form of discrimination?

2. What is "benevolent" sexism? In what sense are the attitudes of benevolent sexism positive? In what sense are they negative?

3. Why do the authors believe that ambivalent harassment may more insidious than other forms of harassment?

4. Why are women unlikely to reject directly and emphatically male colleagues' unwanted sexual advances? How might such a refusal make their situation worse?

5. What does it mean to say that a woman has "solo status"? How does this affect the likelihood that harassment will occur in the workplace? What solution do the authors suggest?

✣ CREDITS ✣